38 Basic Speech Experiences

SEVENTH REVISED EDITION

by
CLARK S. CARLILE
Emeritus Professor of Speech
Idaho State University

CLARK PUBLISHING COMPANY
c/o The Caxton Printers, Ltd.
P. O. Box 700
Caldwell, Idaho 83605
Phone (208) 459-7421

THIS BOOK IS THE PROPERTY OF:

STATE_____

COUNTY_____

PARISH_____

SCHOOL DISTRICT_____

OTHER_____

Book No._____

Enter information in one of the spaces to the left as instructed

ISSUED TO	YEAR USED	CONDITION	
		ISSUED	RETURNED

PUPILS to whom this textbook is issued must not write on any page or mark any part of it in any way; consumable textbooks excepted.

1. Teachers should see that the pupil's name is clearly written in ink in the spaces above in every book issued.

2. The following terms should be used in recording the condition of the book: New; Good; Fair; Poor; Bad.

Fifth Printing, Seventh Revised Edition

ISBN 0-931054-07-9

LITHOGRAPHED BY JOHN S. SWIFT CO., INC. ST. LOUIS · CHICAGO · CINCINNATI · CLEVELAND · MILWAUKEE
(PRINTED IN U.S.A.)

FOREWORD TO THE SEVENTH REVISED EDITION

The foreword to a previous edition (see below) continues to represent my philosophy of a speech text. In this seventh revised edition I have updated bibliographies and included numerous new sample speeches by new authors. Previous outstanding speeches have been retained. Others are my own. New suggested speech topics have been added as has a complete set of questions and answer key for written examinations, and minor changes made elsewhere, but otherwise this revision remains very close to the previous edition except that new easier-to-read type and new format have been used throughout the text. I urge all students to prepare their speeches carefully and strive for their finest work. Why be content with less?

CLARK S. CARLILE

FOREWORD

THIS BOOK WAS WRITTEN FOR STUDENTS AND TEACHERS who want to teach and learn speech by the simple process of giving speeches.

To those teachers who are plagued by the everlasting question of "What shall I assign my students for their next speeches?" this text provides thirty-eight completely worked-out projects. These speech projects are of the kind a student will be asked to continue in real life situations when he no longer is enrolled in a speech course. They are practical because they meet the needs of students who will be tomorrow's business and social leaders. The teacher may assign any one of the speaking experiences and know that the student will have all the information he needs in the assignment in order to prepare and present a dedication speech, a eulogy, a sales talk, an after dinner speech, a panel, a debate, a speech to inform, or any one of dozens of others.

The text is adaptable and flexible. Any sequence of assignments a teacher desires may be scheduled. Any specific assignment may be modified as an instructor wishes. Any basic speech text may be used as a supplement, since each speech assignment carries references to leading speech texts.

The student's job is made easy because he knows from each assignment what he must do to fulfill adequately the purpose of a specific speech. He knows because the assignment specifies clearly what he must do. The requirements, such as time limits, outlining, organizing, and reading source materials, are not easy. They are not intended to be easy. They are basic to all good speech making, and while some students may complain that it takes too much effort to time a speech properly, to make a complete sentence outline, to read two or more sources, and to rehearse aloud, yet these same students will quickly discover that as a result of such preparation they can present excellent speeches. They will see their grades go up; they will experience new thrills of self-confidence, and they will speak capably, largely because they will have learned that good speaking is carefully prepared speaking.

A speech course, well taught, and earnestly applied by the student, does more than train a person for public speaking. With this training comes the feeling of self-adequacy so necessary to mature personality. Also developed is greater ease in expressing one's thoughts and feelings effectively and understandably, which permits a relationship with people that can erase much confusion in ordinary business and social communication. An awareness of the need for honest and reliable talk should be one of the goals every thoughtful speech student strives to achieve, for without it democracies fall and demagogues flourish.

No person can afford to be satisfied with mediocrity in speech - or anything else.

CLARK S. CARLILE

TABLE OF CONTENTS

DEMOCRACY EXISTS —

only where freedom of speech exists.

SUGGESTIONS FOR THE SPEECH TEACHER

1. Most speech assignments in this text may be altered and thus repeated numerous times without creating a sense of monotony in students' minds. No teacher should accept a student's complaint that he had just done a certain speech and therefore should not do another speech like it. Great speakers do not reach this state of mind. Students seldom rise above mediocrity unless they are willing to continually strive for improvement by repeated practice and experience. Stress this point to them.

2. Variety in assignments may be achieved as follows:

   (a) Require the use of visual aids, i.e., charts, graphs, pictures, or similar illustrations which are prepared on cardboard sheets or easels. (b) Require blackboard use in assignments. (c) Have the speaker use a student assistant during a speech. (d) The use of quotations, one or more, may be stipulated. (e) Use one or more anecdotes within a speech. (f) Use two or more jokes, socially acceptable for mixed groups, that apply to points within the speech. (g) Hold a three-to-five-minute question period following the speech. (h) Permit questions from the listeners at any time throughout the speech. Appoint a student chairman to moderate as needed, permitting questions only, not heckling. (i) Designate certain speeches that require suits and ties for the boys and heels and hose for the girls, to be worn by all participants. (j) Designate combinations of the above suggestions that must be used within a given speech.

3. To teach sentence outlining and organization, prepare dittoed copies of scrambled outlines which students are assigned to unscramble. Symbols may be scrambled, sentences may be scrambled, or both may be. It's fun. Correct them in class. Students may wish to prepare scrambled outlines which they trade with each other to be unscrambled.

4. Assign different students to evaluate each speech that is presented. Immediately following a speech the student evaluator will go to the front of the room and, using notes, make a three-minute critique of the speech just completed. Grade the evaluator. This may, for variety, be a written evaluation due the next day. The speech appraisal in the back of this text may be used as a guide.

5. Appoint a different student chairman one day in advance of each class period whose duties are to collect speech outlines, arrange them according to the order of speakers, make a list of speakers and topics from the outlines, and hand the outlines in proper arrangement to the instructor to be graded during student speeches. The chairman then introduces each speaker and his topic. Following the last speech he comments briefly about the day's assignment and speeches, after which he turns the class back to the instructor. The chairman should sit on the front row, step before the class to make each introduction, be orderly, businesslike, and clever. The instructor may grade his work as chairman.

6. Appoint a timekeeper whose duty is to raise his hand briefly to signal the minimum time and to raise his hand again at the maximum time limit, keeping it up until the speaker concludes. Or require each speaker to be his own timekeeper.

7. Members of the class may be graded on their listening behavior. Communication is a two-way proposition - it must have an audience and a speaker. The audience should observe closely and thus not repeat errors they note in other speakers. The more attention a listener gives, the more he will get from a speaker.

8. Occasionally the class may select, by secret ballot, the person presenting the outstanding speech and designate him "Speaker of the Day."

9. For special training and interest, assign students to interview local officials to learn how a court case is conducted. Or have the class visit a court and observe it. Require students to know exactly what procedures are followed then set up a mock crime situation within the class. Hold a jury trial. This might require several weeks to complete.

10. Using the sales talk as a basis, conduct a sales contest in which the student actually sells an article to the class. Local businessmen will often provide sales articles. The public may be invited to an evening sales contest in which local businessmen will act as judges.

11. Examinations (written) — All or portions of any quiz may be reproduced and combined with portions of other quizzes to obtain questions covering a particular group of chapters. See Appendix I for the Answer Key to all questions.

    All quizzes may be torn from this text and distributed to students at examination time or they may be assigned for homework and open book testing. The Answer Key may be torn out or left intact depending on how an instructor wishes to administer the tests and grade them - or have students grade themselves or each other.

12. BOOKS ON SPEECH TEACHING FOR TEACHERS' REFERENCE:

    Eimas, Peter D. and Miller, J. L., eds., Perspectives on the Study of Speech, Erlbaum Associates, 1980.
    Mowrer, Donald E., A Program to Establish Speech Fluency, Merrill, 1979.
    Nadeau, Ray E. and Muchmore, J. M., Speech Communication: A Career Education Approach, Addison-Wesley, 1979.
    Sarbaugh, Larry E., Teaching Speech Communication, Merrill, 1979.

13. BOOKS ON SPEECH PATHOLOGY WHICH MAY BE OF HELP TO TEACHERS:

    Bernthal, John E. and Bankson, N. W., Articulation Disorders, Prentice-Hall, 1981.
    Bloodstein, Oliver, Speech Pathology: An Introduction, Houghton Mifflin, 1979.
    Emerick, Lon L., A Casebook of Diagnosis and Evaluation in Speech Pathology, Prentice-Hall, 1981.
    Filter, Maynard D., Speech-Language Clinician's Handbook, C. C. Thomas, 1979.
    Garbutt, Cameron W. and Anderson, John O., Effective Methods for Correcting Articulatory Defects, Interstate, 1980.
    Haag, Diana B. and Wrasman, M. W., Lessons for the Language Disabled, Interstate, 1980.
    Heasley, Bernice E. and Grosklos, J. R., Programmed Language and Speech Correction Through Perceptual Activities, C. C. Thomas, 1980.
    Holloway, Gordon F. and Berkey, Gordon, Elementary Physics of Sound for Speech Pathology and Audiology, Green, 1980.
    Hutchinson, Barbara and Others, Diagnostic Handbook of Speech Pathology, Williams & Wilkins, 1979.
    Jones, Morris V., Speech and Language Problems: An Overview, C. C. Thomas, 1979.
    Keith, Robert L., Speech and Language Rehabilitation: A Workbook . . . , Interstate, 2d ed., 1980.
    Lattman, Michelle and Seandel, Antoinette, Better Speech for Your Child, Wideview Books, 1979.
    Mysak, Edward D., Neurospeech Therapy for Cerebral Palsied, Teachers College Press, Columbia Univ., 1980.
    Peterson, H. and Marquardt, J., Appraisal and Diagnosis of Speech and Language Disorders, Prentice-Hall, 1981.
    Schaeffer, Benson and Others, Total Communication: A Signed Speech Program for Nonverbal Children, Research Press, 1980.
    Shames, George H. and Florance, C. L., Stutter-Free Speech: A Goal for Therapy, Merrill, 1980.
    Van Hattum, Rolland J., Communication Disorders, Macmillan, 1980.
    Weiss, Curtis E. and Lillywhite, Gordon, Clinical Management of Articulation Disorders, Mosby, 1980.
    Wilson, D. Kenneth, Voice Problems of Children, Williams & Wilkins, 1979.
    Yules, Richard B. and Others, Speech-Hearing Pathology and Surgery, Cliffs, 1980.

SUGGESTED ORDER OF ASSIGNMENTS

Note: From this point on the instructor should assign from the remaining chapters or repeat Chapters 8 and 9 using special requirements as suggested under point "2" in "Suggestions For The Speech Teacher."

HINTS ON OUTLINING, ASSIGNING, GRADING, AND CRITICISM

Using the above "Suggested Order of Assignments" as a guide you will note that students begin the course by presenting their first speech, Chapter 1, on the second or third day class meets, thus quickly becoming acquainted with the speaking act and their reactions to it. It is followed by Chapter 2, "Recording A Speech". This gives them activity first which they want, and secondly gives the teacher an idea of his students' abilities and needs. These two experiences provide a common ground for the entire class and show them they can profit by further study and practice.

Outlining should be taught early, perhaps shortly after the second performance, Chapter 2, "Recording A Speech". Students should study pp. xi - xii, then do scrambled outlines as noted under Suggestions For The Speech Teacher, point 3 - page vii. Whether they like it or not, students must learn to determine their purpose then to organize their ideas by outlining them in complete sentences which demand complete thoughts. This forces students to formulate definite ideas (not vague ones) and to arrange them in logical sequence. Admittedly it is not easy but to be understood by an audience it is necessary. Otherwise a rambling, disconnected, meaningless speech usually results.

It is advisable to give students a speaking assignment in writing one week in advance and to set specific dates when the speech is due. Consider it as an oral examination. Students failing to meet the assignment on time (except for extreme emergency or illness) should forfeit their opportunity to speak and receive an "F" grade. If this policy is not established overdue speeches will become the daily routine, lesson plans will be useless, and chaos will follow because a few lazy and uncaring students will seek favoritism. This alone can cause any course, speech or otherwise, to lose interest and value.

Grading speeches may be based on the outline (including neatness and spelling), and on the presentation including choice of topic and depth of ideas. Glibness, careless last minute preparation, habitual easy-personal-experience-type topics, and inadequate language use should be penalized since they contribute little or nothing to the class or the speaker. This policy should be clarified early in the course so students will know what is required.

Both oral and written evaluations may be offered by the instructor and students. By first mentioning "what you liked about the speech" followed by "suggestions for improvement", the evaluations do not tend to destroy confidence. Favorable comments may be offered on the initial speeches to build feelings of acceptance within speakers; however, ideas relative to improvement may be introduced on general bases to the entire class, say at the end of the hour following the first speech. Once the class has established a feeling of unity and purpose, after one or two speeches, comments concerning individual improvement are in order. When students have presented four or five speeches they may be assigned to prepare evaluation charts which they will suggest to the class in oral presentations, using the blackboard to illustrate.

A speech class should be enjoyable for students and teacher but not a place to play or party. Learning is fun and satisfying for all when a feeling of accomplishment is involved. A well taught speech class provides such a feeling of accomplishment besides a mastery of ideas and knowledge.

WHERE TO GO TO FIND SOURCES AND MATERIALS

One of the biggest problems confronting students in speech courses is that of finding materials on subjects which interest them. Actually this problem is easy to solve if the student is willing to "look around a bit" to find sources of information and to read what he finds. In preparing a speech, no student should say he cannot find enough material unless he has actually checked all of the possible sources.

The question which occurs most often concerning source materials is: "Where do I go to find these materials?" Aside from one's personal experience and interviews with business men, teachers, parents, and friends, there is one great source, the greatest and most valuable of all, namely, the Library. Here a person can find just about anything he wants, provided he is willing to look for it. It may well be admitted that whatever a person is hunting for will not be "growing on trees." It will be in books, magazines, newspapers, and pamphlets – often filed away on unfrequented shelves in the library but it will be there. To find these forgotten sources or others, there is one sure method – ask the librarian to help locate materials for a speech on (subject). In most cases, a librarian will provide more materials in ten minutes than the student can digest in several hours.

Besides going to the librarian for assistance, there are many sources which an individual can check for himself. A person should learn what these sources are and how to use them if he wishes to learn how to find speech materials quickly. A representative group of these research tools is listed below:

1. THE CARD CATALOGUE: check here for title and/or author of materials kept in the library.

2. ENCYCLOPEDIAS:
   A. General:
      (1) Encyclopedia Britannica: general information.
      (2) Encyclopedia Americana: general information.
      (3) New International Encyclopedia: general information.
   B. Special:
      (1) Encyclopedia of the Social Sciences: relates to social sciences.
      (2) McLaughlin. Cyclopedia of American Government.
      (3) Monroe. Cyclopedia of Education: concerns the history and philosophy of education.
      (4) Hastings. Encyclopedia of Religion and Ethics: contains articles concerning all the religions of the world.
      (5) Mythology of All Races: just what the title implies.

3. YEARBOOKS:
   A. Americana Annual: a source of current events.
   B. Britannica Book of the Year: a record of events from 1937 to date.
   C. New International Yearbook: a condensation of the world's progress from the year 1907-
   D. World Almanac and Book of Facts, from 1868- : crammed full of information, largely statistical on hundreds of subjects.
   E. Stateman's Yearbook: statistical and historical information of the states of the world.
   F. The American Yearbook: a compilation of events and progress of the U.S.

4. HANDBOOKS:
   A. Ploetz's Manual of Universal History: a history of the world in chronological outline.
   B. Political Handbook of the World: concerns party programs, world leaders, and the press.

5. INDEXES:
   A. Poole's Index to Periodical Literature: covers years up to 1906; useful for finding old material on hundreds of topics.
   B. Reader's Guide to Periodical Literature: covers years since 1900; lists sources of information in practically every field.

C. New York Times Index: lists information which is to be found in copies of the New York Times.
D. Industrial Arts Index: an index to articles on engineering, business and commerce.
E. Agricultural Index: index to articles in periodicals and bulletins pertaining to agriculture.
F. Education Index: index to articles in periodicals and bulletins pertaining to education.

6. BIOGRAPHICAL DICTIONARIES:
   A. Dictionary of National Biography: an encyclopedia of English biography of deceased persons. Kept up to date with supplements. Alphabetically arranged.
   B. Dictionary of American Biography: an encyclopedia of American biography of deceased persons. Kept up to date with supplements. Alphabetically arranged.
   C. Who's Who: principally English biographies and a few internationally famous names.
   D. Who's Who in America (biennial): brief biographies of notable living persons of the United States.
   E. National Cyclopedia of American Biography: the most complete list of American living and dead famous persons available in any one source.
   F. Webster's Biographical Dictionary: contains brief biographies of ancient and modern persons of international fame.
   G. Current Biography: short biographies of living people who are in the news today.

7. SPECIAL DICTIONARIES:
   A. Weseen. Dictionary of American Slang.
   B. Mawson. Dictionary of Foreign Terms.
   C. Keller's Dictionary of Dates: a record of early history by countries.

8. QUOTATIONS FROM LITERATURE:
   A. Stevenson. The Home Book of Quotations: approx. 50,000; arranged alphabetically by subject.
   B. Hoyt. New Cyclopedia of Practical Quotations: taken from the speech and writings of all nations. (Includes Concordance.)
   C. Bartlett's Familiar Quotations: traces quotations to their sources in ancient and modern literature.

9. GOVERNMENT PUBLICATIONS: these materials cover almost unlimited fields. Ask the librarian about them.

10. THERE ARE MANY OTHER SOURCES available on the above subjects and subjects not included here. Ask the librarian for assistance in locating them.

MAKING AN OUTLINE OF YOUR SPEECH

Below is a sample complete sentence outline. If you will study it carefully, you will note that every statement is a complete sentence. There are no incomplete sentences. There are no compound sentences. The outline is logically organized and divided into three parts – the introduction, body, and conclusion.

There are numerous ways to develop an outline and numerous sections into which it can be divided. The method followed by any one person is a matter of choice. If your instructor prefers a particular method of outlining, he will tell you what it is. The important point to remember when constructing an outline (which is the skeleton of a speech) is that it must make sense – logical sense, which is easily followed.

It takes time and effort to construct a complete sentence outline; yet the time and energy one spends in building a good outline will pay big dividends in improved speaking. The student must do his best.

Type of speech: _____Informative_____   Name: _____Your Name_____

Number of words in outline: _____134_____   Date: _____November 15, 1986_____

Purpose of this speech: (What do you want your audience to learn, to think, to believe, to feel, or do because of this speech?)

_____I want my audience to have a better understanding of body language._____

Title: BODY LANGUAGE

Introduction:
    I. Your physical movements talk for you.
        A. They tell secrets about you.
        B. They tell what kind of person you are.
            1. I will discuss the behavior we call body language.

Body:
    I. Everyone uses movements with spoken words.
        A. They are part of natural behavior.
            1. People are unaware of their movements.
                a. Posture reflects inner thoughts.
                b. Eyes, hands and feet talk eloquently.

    II. Body language can be helpful.
        A. It can make a person attractive.
            1. Movements can reflect honesty.
            2. Appearance can bring favorable responses.
            3. Behavior patterns can make friends.
        B. Employers observe body language.
            1. They make judgments from what they see.
            2. They hire or reject an applicant by watching his movements.

    III. Body language can be improved.
        A. A person can enhance personal appearance.
        B. Anyone can strive for better posture and walking habits.

Conclusion:
    I. People are born with body language.
        A. It influences life.
            1. It speaks louder than words.

Sources of Information:
    Bradley, Bert E., Fundamentals of Speech Communication: The Credibility of Ideas, Wm. C. Brown,
        3d ed., 1981.
    Stewart, John and D'Angelo, Gary, Together Communicating Interpersonally, Addison-Wesley, 2d ed.,
        1980.
    Tubbs, Stewart L. and Moss, Sylvia, Human Communication-An Interpersonal Perspective, Random
        House, 3d ed., 1980.

SAMPLE COPY OF SPEAKER'S NOTES

Below is a sample copy of notes a speaker might use in presenting a five to six minute speech on body language. Observe that each word stands for an idea, that each word is large enough to be easily seen at a glance, and that the size of the paper on which the notes are written is about equal to that of a postal card. Speaking notes should serve only as a guide, not as a crutch. The actual speech should be in the mind of the speaker, not in a mass of notes.

Hold your card of notes by the lower right hand corner between your thumb and forefinger.

```
        BODY LANGUAGE

    1. MOVEMENTS TALK
    2. EVERYONE USES
    3. HELPFUL
    4. CAN IMPROVE
    5. BORN WITH
```

HOW TO PREPARE A GOOD SPEECH

The first law of good speaking is adequate preparation.

Preparing a good speech is like preparing to run a four-forty yard dash in a track meet. Each requires many trial runs before the event actually starts. To attempt a speech without preparation is just as foolhardy as to attempt a quarter-mile run without practice. The well-trained and conditioned racer makes it look easy, just as does the well-prepared speaker. To an uninformed person, both the speaker and the racer may appear to be performing effortlessly and impromptu, yet in most cases nothing could be farther from the truth. Only many hours of intense preparation make it possible for the good speaker and the good athlete to display great ability. If there is any doubt about this point in the mind of any reader he should <u>ask the man who makes speeches or who runs races.</u>

There are several initial requisites which should be considered at this time in order to explain adequate speech preparation. Here they are:

I. YOUR SUBJECT - Consider it.

A. You should <u>be sure you can find sufficient material</u> on your subject, otherwise your speech may be too short, devoid of quantity as well as quality.

B. You should <u>be sure the subject you plan to discuss is appropriate</u> to you, your audience and the occasion. Any subject not adjusted to these three factors simply is inadequate. If you are in doubt, consult your instructor.

C. You should <u>be certain that your subject can be adequately discussed in the time allotted</u> for your speech. Preliminary investigation, narrowing the subject, and a few "trial runs" will clear up doubts about this phase of preparation.

D. Since it takes time for ideas to grow and develop, <u>you should weigh carefully the time you allow yourself for preparation</u>, otherwise your speech may not be past the infant stage when you present it, and frankly an audience dislikes seeing a baby when it comes to see a full-grown man.

E. The importance of selecting a suitable subject need not be stressed since it is so obvious, however, <u>you should decide whether your topic is too technical, trivial, trite or broad.</u> If it falls in any one of these categories then it must be altered accordingly or a new topic be chosen.

F. The <u>title of your speech should be provocative, brief, relative to your subject, and interesting.</u> It is one of the first things your audience will read about in the papers or hear before you speak. A good title can add immeasurably to the initial interest in your speech.

II. THINK OF YOUR AUDIENCE

A. To best adapt your material to your audience, you must understand the people in it. It is your obligation to find out what kind of people will likely come to hear you. How old will they be? What will their occupations be? What is their social standing? Their education? Their religion? Their prejudices and beliefs? Their wealth? <u>What do they want from you?</u> So long as you are taking the time of ten or fifteen persons, perhaps several hundred, you will be wise to give them a speech which is <u>worth their time.</u> You can be much surer you will do this if you analyze your audience. This isn't something to be done on a moment's notice. Rather it will require a definite investigation from you, but it will be well worth your efforts, provided you adapt your remarks to what you find out.

III. THE MECHANICS OF SPEECH PREPARATION

Now that you have considered your subject and analyzed your audience, you are ready to begin the mechanical preparation of your speech. Here are the steps to follow:

A. Decide on the purpose of your speech, that is, what do you want to accomplish with your speech? What reaction do you want from the people who hear you? Do you want them to understand an idea better? To appreciate something more? To be thankful? To feel honored? To change their minds? To become stirred up and aroused about something? To perform an act, such as to vote for or against a candidate or contribute to a fund or join an organization? In your own mind it is absolutely essential that you know definitely what you want your speech to do to your listeners. If you don't have this point settled, then you really don't know why you are giving your speech or why you organized it the way you did or why you are telling your audience "thus and so." In reality you don't know what you want and nobody else does. You cannot expect your audience to get anything from your speech if you yourself don't know what you want them to get. One of the most pronounced causes of poor speaking lies in the elementary fact that the speaker has nothing in mind that he wants to accomplish with his speech. This need not happen to you if you decide on a purpose and direct all your efforts toward achieving it.

B. Your next step is to gather material for your speech. Consult the chapter in this text entitled "Where To Go To Find Sources and Materials." Having located various materials, you should take comprehensive notes on what you decide to use. Be sure to indicate your sources exactly and completely. This includes the specific names of the magazines or books the material was taken from, titles of articles, authors' full names, dates of publication, and chapters or pages where the material was found. If a source is a person, identify him completely by title, position, occupation, etc. These data, telling exactly where you got your material, will prove most beneficial when someone later asks you where you found your material. The validity of your remarks will be no greater than the sources you use.

C. Your third step is to organize the material in an orderly and logical sequence. This means that all examples, analogies, facts, quotations, and other evidence which you use to support main ideas must be in their proper place where they will do the most good. The best way to achieve organization that is progressive and unified is to prepare a complete sentence outline of your speech. For a fuller understanding of a complete sentence outline, study the example elsewhere in this text under the chapter heading "Making An Outline of Your Speech." A complete sentence outline will assist you in formulating and crystallizing complete thoughts prior to presenting the speech. Without this procedure you will discover it is exceedingly difficult to prepare and present a quality speech.

D. Step number four is wording your speech. Here you must decide what words you will use when you expand your complete sentence outline into a full speech. To get in mind the words you want to use, you should employ the method best suited to you, however, two recommended methods follow. (Complete word–for–word memorization is not recommended.) One method for wording your speech is to write it out in full, then read your manuscript aloud several times to master the general ideas and the necessary details. After doing this, you should construct a set of very brief notes containing only the main ideas of your speech and rehearse aloud from them until you master the general wording and the order of the main points. Do not rehearse by mumbling in a monotone or by "thinking about" your wording. It is permissible and usually advisable to memorize the introduction and conclusion, but not the body of your speech.

A second method for wording your speech is to <u>rehearse aloud</u> from your complete sentence outline or other outline until you have attained a definite mastery of the words you plan to use. Here again it will be wise to memorize the introduction and conclusion although you should not memorize the rest of your speech word for word. You should, of course, memorize the sequence of your main points irrespective of how you practice. The number of times needed for oral rehearsal will depend solely on you, but probably it will be at least four to six times and quite possibly even more, regardless of what method you use. In any case, if you plan to use notes while speaking, be sure to use the final copy of your speaking notes during your last few rehearsals.

One of the best ways to rehearse a speech is to stand before a mirror so that you may observe your posture and other body language. Some students object to using a mirror saying that it bothers them to observe themselves. This is a flimsy excuse since those same students know they must speak before their classmates who will be forced, through courtesy, to observe them while they stumble through actions, gestures and various postures which they themselves couldn't bear to see reflected in a mirror. A few "trial runs" before a mirror will vastly improve most speeches and speakers. Of course, it will be helpful to rehearse by using a wire or tape recorder in order to check your speech by listening to play-backs. A video tape (with audio) is unexcelled.

E. Step number five involves the <u>development of a mental attitude of the speaker</u> towards himself and the entire speaking situation. He will be wise to expect nervousness and stage fright during his first few speeches. He should realize quite clearly that although his stage fright will largely disappear after a reasonably short while, his nervousness just before speaking probably will not. He should look upon it as a form of energy that will keep his speaking on a more vigorous plane than would otherwise be possible were he entirely devoid of nervous feelings. His attitude should tell him he will gain self-confidence and poise as he makes more speeches, but not to expect a miracle. The mental attitude should be one in which the student recognizes his own weaknesses, but is not morbidly disturbed because he isn't a great success on his first attempts. He should be willing to seek advice from his instructor, to make honest efforts toward a more adequate preparation of his speeches since this is the greatest guarantee for good speaking, and gradually as he progresses he should take pride in his own personal improvement and feelings of self-confidence. Every beginning speaker should look forward to a feeling of adequacy and personal satisfaction, for if he does, and if he possesses a healthy mental attitude, he is sure to attain these goals - and good speech.

BIBLIOGRAPHY FOR HOW TO PREPARE A GOOD SPEECH

Campbell, John A., <u>An Overview of Speech Preparation</u>, Science Research Associates, 1980.
Ross, Raymond S., <u>Speech Communication</u>, Prentice-Hall, 5th ed., 1980.
Schiff, Roselyn L. and Others, <u>Communication Strategy: A Guide to Speech Preparation</u>, Scott Foresman, 1981.
Tacey, William S., <u>Business and Professional Speaking</u>, Wm. C. Brown, 3d ed., 1980.
Verderber, Rudolph F. and Verderber, K. S., <u>Inter-Act: Using Interpersonal Communication Skills</u>, Wadsworth, 2d ed., 1980.

HOW TO BEGIN A SPEECH

Note: Students may be assigned to prepare and present sample introductions.

The Introduction

An introduction to a speech is what a man's trousers are to full dress when he goes out to dinner, they are a necessity. Without them he is undressed and he shocks many people. A speech without an introduction is undressed, it shocks many people. It can be said that with few exceptions every speech demands a pair of trousers, i.e., an introduction. It has also been said that every speaker has the audience's attention when he rises to speak and that if he loses the attention, it is after he begins to speak, hence the importance of the introduction becomes apparent.

There are several purposes a speaker normally wishes to achieve by means of his introductory remarks in order to be most effective. These purposes may be listed as follows:

I. One purpose of the introduction may be to <u>gain attention, arouse the interest and excite the curiosity</u> of listeners. This may be effected in numerous ways.

   A. The speaker may refer to the occasion and purpose of the meeting with a few brief remarks explaining and commenting on why the audience have gathered on this occasion. He may refer to special interests of the audience and show how his subject is connected with these interests. In no way should he apologize for his speech.

   B. The speaker may <u>pay the audience a genuine compliment</u> relative to their hospitality, their interest in the subject to be discussed, their concern over bettering their community, their progressive educational program, the outstanding leadership of the group sponsoring the speech. The sincerity of the speaker should be genuine since the audience's judgment of his speech will be strongly influenced by his opening phrases.

   C. The speaker <u>may open by telling a story</u> (human interest, humorous, exciting, etc.) that catches interest and arouses curiosity. He should of course link the story to his subject. If the story is not related to the subject, it should not be told.

   D. The speaker <u>may refer to a recent incident that the audience is acquainted with</u>.

   Example:
> "Three persons were burned to death a week ago because of a schoolhouse which had improper fire escape exits."

   This paves the way for his discourse, the need for a new schoolhouse.

   E. The speaker <u>may use a quotation to open his remarks</u> and set the stage for the introduction of his ideas. The quotation should be relevant to what he plans to say and be tied to his thoughts with a few brief explanations. He should not prolong this type of introduction too much.

   F. The speaker <u>may use a novel idea or a striking statement</u> to arouse curiosity and interest or to gain attention. This should not be overdone. If it is sensationalism it will lose its punch because the remainder of the speech cannot be so shocking.

   Example of an introduction to a speech on atomic power is:
> "It is hard to imagine fifty thousand persons destroyed in a few seconds – it is hard to imagine a ship driven around the world on a glass of water, or a rocket shot to the moon on a pound of metal, yet the day may not be far off when atomic power will make these possibilities either horrible or helpful realities."

   G. The speaker <u>may refer to a preceding speaker</u> and his thoughts in order to secure interest and attention, however, too much elaboration should not occur.

   Example:
> "Ladies and Gentlemen: The preceding speaker, Mr. McIntosh, has given you a peculiarly striking and graphic picture of what we may expect within the next ten years in the development of atomic power. I would like to expand his ideas further by telling you how this power may be harnessed so that it will wash your dishes and heat your houses."

H. The speaker may put pertinent and challenging questions to the audience to arouse their curiosity. "Did you know that . . . ? Do you want such to happen to you?" etc. These questions should have a bearing on the material which is to follow, otherwise they will be just so much noise.

I. Various combinations of the above suggestions may provide an effective introduction. The combinations which should be used will depend on the audience, occasion, speaker, speech and environment.

II. A second purpose of the introduction may be to prepare and open the minds of the hearers for the thoughts which are to come. This is particularly necessary if the audience is hostile. It may be accomplished by giving background and historical information so that the audience can and will understand the subject. This purpose may be further achieved if the speaker establishes his right to speak by recounting the research he has done on his subject, by naming prominent persons associated with him in his endeavor, and by modestly telling of certain honors, offices and awards he has received as a result of his accomplishments in fields closely related to his topic.

III. A speaker's third objective of an introduction may be to indicate the direction and purpose of his speech and the end it will reach. This may be achieved by stating generally his subject and by announcing and explaining the thesis of his talk. To give only a naked statement of the topic is not enough. It is uninteresting and in most cases dull. An appropriate and interesting exposition of any general statement of the subject should be made in reference to the topic. In other words, to announce only the title of a speech and to consider this an adequate introduction is a grave mistake.

Example:
"Ladies and Gentlemen: I have chosen to speak with you today on the subject of crime, which is costing our nation untold billions of dollars annually. It is my desire to explain to you the causes of crime as well as the preventions. It is only when crime is understood that people are enabled to combat it and decrease its scope."

There are a few points to remember when preparing and delivering an introduction. Dullness and triteness, undue length of opening remarks, false leads that are not followed up, stories which are suggestive or risque used only to fill time, or a mere announcement of the topic should all be avoided. Any apologies or remarks which might be construed to be apologies for the speech should definitely be omitted. There is nothing so invigorating, so appreciated, so likely to secure good will as an introduction which provides an original, fresh and sparkling meeting between the audience and the speaker and his subject. Work for it.

Generally speaking, an introduction is prepared last. This is practical because a speaker needs to have the body of his talk outlined and his ideas developed and ripe before he can best determine how they should be introduced. The length of an introduction may vary considerably; however, it should not comprise more than one-fourth of the entire speech. It may comprise much less.

One more important aspect of the beginning of a speech is the speaker's behavior before he takes the platform and after he gets there. If he is sitting on stage in full view of his audience he should remain comfortably and calmly alert, yet politely seated. People are carefully appraising him while he waits. Feminine speakers while seated should be careful not to cross their knees. Crossing the ankles is permissible, although it is safer to keep both feet on the floor with the knees together. When the speaker is introduced, he should rise easily without delay or noise and move to his place on the platform. After arriving there, a few seconds should elapse while he deliberately surveys the scene before him. Then after addressing the chairman, if he has not already done so, he is ready to begin his introductory remarks.

BIBLIOGRAPHY FOR THE INTRODUCTION OF A SPEECH

Fettig, Art, How to Hold an Audience in the Hollow of Your Hand: Seven Techniques for Starting Your Speech, Eleven Techniques for Keeping It Rolling, Fell, Frederick, 1979.

Mudd, Charles S. and Sillars, M. O., Speech: Content and Communication, Harper & Row, 4th ed., 1979.

Ross, Raymond S., Speech Communication: Fundamentals and Practice, Prentice-Hall, 5th ed., 1980.

Tacey, William S., Business and Professional Speaking, Wm. C. Brown, 3rd ed., 1980.

HOW TO END A SPEECH

Note: Students may be assigned to prepare and present sample conclusions.

The Conclusion

A day is never ended without a sunset of some kind. If the sunset is captivating the entire day is often long remembered because of its impressive ending. A speech is much the same. It must have an ending and to be most successful the ending should be impressive.

The conclusion brings together all the thoughts, emotions, discussions, arguments, and feelings which the speaker has tried to communicate to his audience. The closing words should make a powerful emotional impression on the listeners, since in most cases logic alone is insufficient to move an audience to act or believe as the speaker suggests. Not only this but the conclusion is the last opportunity to emphasize the point of the speech. It should be a natural culmination of all that has been spoken. It should not be weak, insipid remarks which are begun or ended just as the speaker starts a hesitating but very obvious journey towards his chair.

The conclusion should be, without exception, one of the most carefully prepared parts of a speech. Just when it should be prepared is largely a matter of opinion. Some authorities advise preparing it first because such a practice enables a speaker to point his talk toward a predetermined end. Other speakers suggest preparing the conclusion last because this procedure allows a person to draw his final words from the full draft of his speech. Regardless of when a conclusion is prepared, there is one point on which all authorities agree and it is that the conclusion must be carefully worded, carefully organized, carefully rehearsed and in most cases committed to memory or nearly so. The conclusion should be brief, generally not more than one-eighth to one-tenth of the entire speech, perhaps less, depending on the speech, the speaker, the audience, the occasion and the environment in which the speech is delivered. A conclusion should never bring in new material, since such an action requires a discussion of the new material which in turn unnecessarily prolongs the speech. Also the introduction of new material brings about an undesirable anticlimax and frequently irritates an audience because a speaker runs past a perfect place to stop.

When a speaker moves into his conclusion, it should be obvious that he is closing his remarks. His intentions should be so clear that he should not have to tell the audience what he is doing by saying, "In conclusion . . . "

The importance of the delivery of a conclusion cannot be overemphasized. The total organism, mind, body and soul, must be harmoniously at work. The eye contact should be direct, the gestures and actions appropriate, the posture alert, and the voice sincere, distinct and well articulated. The speaker's effort in delivering the conclusion may be likened to a foot racer who culminates an entire race in one great, last surge of power as he lunges toward the tape – and victory.

Now that you have been told what should be contained within a conclusion, there remains one major question which is, "How do you actually go about attaining these ends, i.e., what methods should be used?"

There are numerous ways to develop a conclusion. Some of the better known are listed as follows:

1. Summary is a method often utilized in closing a speech. It is sometimes expressed by restatement of the speech title, of the purpose, of some specific phrase that has been used several times in the speech, by an apt quotation, either prose or poetry, which adroitly says what the speaker wishes to be said, or by any other means which tends to bring the main point of the speech into final focus for the audience. An example of a very brief summary is contained in the following words which were once used by a speaker to summarize a speech against Russia's aggression in Czechoslovakia:

   Example:
   "Czechoslovakia will live again! The hordes of Russia, the Bears of Europe, the intrigue of Moscow shall not swallow up this mighty and prideful people. They shall rise up and fight their horrible aggressor. Yes, Czechoslovakia will live again!"

2. <u>Recapitulation</u> may be used in longer formal speeches when it is necessary to restate points in a <u>one, two, three order</u>. The danger of this method is that it may become monotonous and uninteresting. Short speeches do not require this type of conclusion, since the points are easily remembered. A short speech may close with the last main point if it is a strong point. Usually, however, more is needed to close a speech, even a short one.

Example of recapitulation in a speech favoring world federation:
"To be sure that we all understand my reasons for believing as I do let me restate my main points. First, world federation is the only type of government which will save the world from destroying itself. Second, world federation is the only type of government which is acceptable to the several nations, and third, world federation is the most democratic type of world government yet conceived by man. It is for these reasons that I favor the establishment of a world government."

3. A striking <u>anecdote</u>, an <u>analogy</u>, or a <u>simile</u> may be employed as closing remarks, or any one of them or a suitable combination of them may be interwoven with the summary or recapitulation type of conclusion. One conclusion which utilizes the analogy for a speech concerning old cars is:

Example:
"These old cars of ours are like the wonderful one horse shay. Let us hope that they, too, do not suddenly fall apart, scattering nuts and bolts across our neighbor's lawn."

4. <u>An emotionalized or idealized statement of the thesis</u> may serve as a useful conclusion. If the thesis were "American Honesty," one conclusion of the above type could be:

Example:
"Honesty is and always has been the moral fibre of our country. Honesty is the heritage of over two hundred million Americans. To this criterion of national manliness the world pays respect and offers admiration. It reveres American honesty as a true indication of Christian living. Let us not blot out this bright star which outshines all the myriads of lesser lights. Let us continue to deserve the right to be known as the world's most honest nation."

5. <u>There may be a powerful restatement of the thesis.</u> If the subject were "America's Might," the final words could be:

Example:
"America will live forever, strong, defiant to aggression, relentless in attack, mighty in defense, humble before God."

6. <u>A vivid illustration of the central idea</u> may fittingly conclude a speech. If it were on the Navy's might, the following words could be used:

Example:
"The famous words of John Paul Jones, who said he had not yet begun to fight, are emblazoned again across the world's horizon, for tonight the American Navy launched ten new battle ships!"

7. <u>A call for action from the audience</u> may clinch a speech. It must of course pertain to the ideas of the speaker. This is an excellent type of conclusion, particularly when the purpose has been to stimulate or to get action from the audience. If a speech were on "Building Good Government," a conclusion could be:

Example:
"Let us no longer sit here doing nothing while the crooked politicians corrupt our government and steal our money. Let's go out one by one, by two's and three's or by the hundreds and vote for clean government and honest officials. Let's do it tomorrow – it's election day and our only hope!"

One final word of warning is this: When the speech is done the speaker should hold the floor for a second or two (this cannot be stressed enough), then return to his chair, seat himself politely and remain seated until the chairman adjourns the audience. Display or frivolity of any kind on the part of the speaker after the speech may sharply alter many good impressions which he has made while on the platform. A person should not let his actions portray how well or how poorly he thinks he has done on his speech. The audience will decide this point.

BIBLIOGRAPHY FOR THE CONCLUSION OF A SPEECH

Ross, Raymond S., Speech Communication: Fundamentals and Practice, Prentice-Hall, 5th ed., 1980.
Tacey, William S., Business and Professional Speaking, Wm. C. Brown, 3d ed., 1980.

COMMUNICATION – A FEW IDEAS ABOUT IT

Communication may not be what you think so let's first agree on what it is. Basically whenever you do anything (intentionally or not) that causes people to see, smell, hear, taste or feel you, they receive messages from you. Most people think communication occurs only when someone speaks, yet you know how people gesture with their hands, nod their heads, move their legs or shoulders, smile or frown, raise eyebrows or wiggle their noses all the while they talk. These physical movements which you see tell more sometimes than what is said with the speaker's words. Actually what a person does is express his feelings and ideas two ways simultaneously, one way with words and another with bodily movements. It is almost impossible to talk without accompanying physical movements, thus a person often sends out messages he does not intend to send because of these movements. An example would be an individual who tells you he is unafraid with words but you know he is scared to death by observing his movements. An embarrassed or frightened person often communicates how he feels by his actions.

The point is, communication occurs anytime someone else sees and/or hears you, and what you communicate may be what you intended or it may not be. However, words are one of your most powerful communication devices.

As a small child learning to talk, every word you learned had a special meaning to you because of your association with it. The word "puppy" meant only your puppy because to you there was no other. And so it was with all your words, each had your own special meaning and everytime you spoke, your words referred to the meaning you gave them. This remained true as you grew from childhood and will remain true all your life. Your words now carry broader meanings because you have learned there are many kinds of puppies but you still attach your meaning to your words. The trouble in trying to convey (symbolize) your ideas to someone else is that for every word you speak the listener interprets it with his special meaning which is different from yours. When this happens he does not fully understand you. It means that you communicated something but not exactly what you intended.

The process of putting words together in phrases and sentences to represent your feelings and ideas is called encoding. A listener has to interpret your words by sorting out ideas they create in his mind, which is called decoding, somewhat like figuring out a message sent in secret code.

Still another way you communicate when talking is how loud, how fast, how high or low your voice is — all reflect meanings about things for which you have no specific words. People hearing you usually can tell by your vocal variety whether you are happy, sad, tired or angry. A good example would be the way a friend greets you when he says, "Good morning." You know instantly something is bothering him because he communicated this feeling by his voice quality, perhaps he muttered his words, possibly by a frown on his face or the way he walked, but he communicated this feeling whether he intended to or not. Because people don't have words to completely express all their thoughts and feelings they use vocal variety and thousands of muscular movements in addition to their words. The latter we call body language.

Since words have different meanings to the speaker and listener the question rises, "How does one talk so he can be understood more precisely?" Perhaps the best way is to use accurate and specific words. For example do not say, "It was bright colored." Instead say, "It was red and orange." Instead of, "He was a big man," say, "He was six feet three inches tall and weighed 225 pounds." Omit words such as pretty, nice, beautiful, bad, good, great, very, most, much, fast, slow and similar terms with generalized meanings. In other words say specifically what you mean, use correct grammar, articulate clearly, and pronounce distinctly. And finally, say it in as few words as possible. Don't make a listener decode fifty words to get your message when you can say the same thing using twenty-five.

You also tell people all about yourself by your appearance. Neatly pressed <u>clean clothes</u>, carefully groomed hair, no offensive odors, clean hands, face, and body, all communicate by sight and smell what you are. The person who ignores these fundamental facts about his appearance communicates as plainly as if he carried a large sign reading, "I'M DIRTY AND SMELL BAD. STAY AWAY FROM ME." And people will. (He won't get a job either.)

Everyone also communicates by taste and touch. Kiss a tiny baby and it actually <u>tastes</u>; it <u>feels</u> so delicate and fragile you instinctively protect it. The baby has communicated. Shaking hands with friends in greeting, holding hands with the opposite sex and kissing, all communicate by taste, touch, smell, sight, and sound. Think about these ideas a minute and I believe you will agree.

Now in a broader sense you hear much about business, social, political, economic, and educational communication. It's popular to say, "He didn't communicate," to explain misunderstandings, however, it would be more appropriate to say, "<u>He wasn't specific</u>," or "<u>He wasn't definite</u>," or "<u>He wasn't accurate</u>," or "<u>He used technical language</u>," or "<u>He wasn't complete</u>." You could say in many instances, "He didn't speak plainly," or "He wrote sloppily and misspelled words," or "He did not signal (communicate) his message when he was supposed to." (Too early or too late.)

On the other side it can be said that some people don't listen to understand but instead to argue and talk about their own thoughts. They don't read carefully, or they hear and read only a part of what is said and pretend they heard and read everything. Thus they only partially decode messages they receive and foolishly wonder why they don't understand.

We can summarize these remarks when we say communication can be improved by being definite, specific, accurate and complete in speaking and writing. When receiving messages we must listen, observe, and read carefully and completely. It's that simple. Add to these communication principles, attentiveness, appropriate bodily movements and gestures, a clean and neat personal appearance and an earnest desire to understand or to be understood.

Here's an interesting device. Next time you argue with someone try to restate his point of view so he will say, "That's exactly what I mean." Have him restate your views likewise. Do this on every point of disagreement then each will know what the other is talking about. Continue your discussion only if you both can do this.

BIBLIOGRAPHY FOR COMMUNICATION

Barker, Larry L., <u>Communication</u>, Prentice-Hall, 2d ed., 1981.

Meyers, Gail and Myers, Michele, <u>The Dynamics of Human Communication</u>, McGraw, 1980.

Mudd, Charles S. and Sillars, M. O., <u>Speech: Content and Communication</u>, Harper & Row, 4th ed., 1979.

Patton, Bobby R. and Giffin, Kim, <u>Interpersonal Communication in Action: Basic Text & Readings</u>, Harper & Row, 3d ed., 1980.

Taylor, Anita and Others, <u>Communicating</u>, Prentice-Hall, 1980.

Zimmerman, Gordon and Others, <u>Speech Communication: A Contemporary Introduction</u>, West, 2d ed., 1980.

QUIZ NO. 1 — QUESTIONS NUMBERED 1 THROUGH 20 COVER PAGES X THROUGH XXI, THERE-
AFTER A CHAPTER NUMBER APPEARS BY EACH QUESTION SO ITS SOURCE CAN
BE READILY LOCATED. <u>CIRCLE CORRECT ANSWERS.</u> THESE QUESTIONS MAY
BE REPRODUCED FOR CLASSROOM USE.

NAME _____ DATE _____

(P.XI)   1. How many of the following are considered a good place to find sources and materials?

            (a) encyclopedias   (b) yearbooks   (c) special dictionaries   (d) government publications

(P.XI)   2. The sample speech outline in your text has how many parts besides the introduction?

            (a) one   (b) two   (c) three   (d) four

(P.XI)   3. The sample complete sentence outline in your text is constructed with which of the fol-
                lowing? (mark best answer)

            (a) phrases   (b) clauses   (c) one phrase and four complete sentences

            (d) complete sentences only

(P.XIII)   4. In speech preparation, whether or not you can find sufficient material on your subject is:
                (two answers)

            (a) not very important   (b) quite important   (c) a matter of opinion

            (d) could cause your speech to be short

(P.XIII)   5. In speech preparation thinking about your audience:

            (a) has little to do with it   (b) should be of no concern

            (c) is the last thing a speaker does   (d) none of the above answers

(P.XIV)   6. The first step in speech preparation is:

            (a) deciding on your purpose   (b) gathering material   (c) wording your speech

            (d) organizing your material

(P.XII)   7. Although a speaker's notes are usually permissible the actual speech should be:

            (a) in the mind of the speaker   (b) in well constructed notes   (c) carefully memorized

(P.XIII)   8. In speech preparation how many of the following are true regarding your subject?

            (a) decide whether your topic is too technical

            (b) your title should be provocative and brief

            (c) your subject should be appropriate to you

            (d) the time required to prepare your speech is not to be considered

(P.XVI)   9   One purpose of the_____ may be to gain attention and excite the curiosity
                of listeners: (select one answer)

            (a) subject   (b) outline   (c) wording   (d) introduction

(P.XVI) 10. If you pay the audience a compliment and refer to the purpose of the meeting and occasion which part of the speech are you likely to be in?

(a) introduction   (b) body   (c) conclusion

(P.XVII) 11. If you try "to prepare and open the minds of the hearers for the thoughts which are to come" you are likely in which part of your speech:

(a) introduction   (b) body   (c) conclusion

(P.XVIII) 12. That part of a speech which brings together thoughts, emotions, discussions, arguments, and a speaker's feelings is called the:

(a) introduction   (b) body   (c) conclusion   (d) strategy

(P.XVIII) 13. Summary is a method often used:

(a) to conclude a speech   (b) to begin a speech   (c) to organize the body effectively

(P.XIX) 14. A call for action by the speaker usually occurs in the:

(a) introduction   (b) body   (c) conclusion

(P.XX) 15. Whenever people see, smell, taste, touch, or hear you they receive some kind of communication.

(a) partially true   (b) true   (c) false   (d) partially false

(P.XX) 16. The process of putting words together in phrases and sentences to represent your feelings is called:

(a) imagination   (b) analysis   (c) encoding   (d) structure

(P.XX) 17. A listener who interprets your words by sorting out ideas they create in his mind does what is called:

(a) deciding   (b) decoding   (c) ciphering   (d) faulting

(P.XXI) 18. "You tell people about yourself by your appearance."

(a) partially true   (b) true   (c) partially false   (d) false

(P.XXI) 19. Communication can be improved by being definite, specific, accurate, and complete in speaking and writing.

(a) partially true   (b) true   (c) partially false   (d) false

(P.XX) 20. Two people together who are alternately encoding and decoding are likely:

(a) silent   (b) thinking silently   (c) angry   (d) conversing

Chapter 1

YOUR FIRST SPEECH

Question: *Does one ever overcome nervous tension before giving a speech?*

Answer: *Probably not entirely. He should not since this would likely mean a lifeless speech.*

This speech is due:
Time limits: None.
Speaking notes: Tear off those at the end of this chapter.

PURPOSE OF YOUR FIRST SPEECH

This speech is your first to be presented in this course. Your first speech gives you a chance to stand before your classmates and to tell them something about yourself. You are not expected to give a long biographical account of your life; that is not what is wanted. By answering the questions at the end of this assignment, you introduce yourself to your audience (classmates) and you make your first speech. You will get the feel of standing on your feet and talking before a group of persons. Since you must start somewhere, this experience will provide a good beginning.

HOW TO PREPARE FOR YOUR FIRST TALK

One reason for making your first talk is to tell your audience enough concerning yourself that they will know something about you. In other words, they will get acquainted. Another purpose of this experience is to give you an opportunity to learn what it is like to see many persons sitting before you waiting to hear what you have to say. Some students get a thrill from it; others get a scare. Actually the scare is only a feeling that comes to a speaker because certain glands in his body are functioning more than they usually do in a speech situation. Because people dislike the feeling caused by their glandular functions, they say they are scared. Instead of being scared of speaking, they are scared of a normal physical action taking place within themselves. They associate this feeling with speechmaking and, tying the two together, say, "speaking scares them."

To be scared is normal. To be nervous is normal. To be tense is normal. You must experience these feelings; otherwise you would be as lifeless as an old shirt. These feelings are present in football players before and during a game. Great actors have them. Great speakers have them. Nervousness is the high octane gas which provides these persons the drive to give life to their performances. They want a normal amount of it because they use it. You see, they control their nervousness (energy) and that is all

you need to do. Do not try to rid yourself of nervousness entirely; you will gain control of this power. As you give more speeches throughout this course, you will discover your control growing stronger – and that is what you want.

Study the questions at the end of this assignment. Decide generally how you will answer them. It will help you to practice aloud several times by standing in front of a mirror while you speak. Do not memorize your answers word for word, since this would make your remarks sound like a recitation.

HOW TO PRESENT YOUR FIRST SPEECH

Tear the questions along the perforated line so that you may take them with you to be used as notes. Do this before your instructor asks you to speak.

When your name is called walk quietly to the front of the room. Avoid "stomping" your feet, clicking your heels on the floor or calling unnecessary attention to yourself. When you get there, stand politely on both feet. Do not place one foot forward, throw out a hip and rest your weight on your rear foot, assuming a bashful boy slouch. Keep your weight on both feet or on your slightly forward foot. An attitude of a soldier at attention or any similar stance is undesirable. Be alert and polite, and you may be sure that you look all right.

Let your hands hang loosely at your sides unless you care to bring the one holding your notes up in front of you. It is certainly permissible to place a hand in your pocket, on a table top, or a chair back, if you do not call attention to the act. Grasp your notes lightly between the thumb and index finger. Do not palm them, roll, crumple, twist or disfigure them in any way by continuous handling. When you refer to your notes, raise them high enough that you do not need to lower your head to glance at them.

If you feel like moving around a few paces, do so naturally, without shuffling or scraping your feet. When you are not changing positions, stand still and keep your feet quiet.

When you begin your speech, talk with your normal voice just as you would if you were telling about yourself to a group of good friends. Good speaking is good conversation. Make an introductory statement for a beginning. Show some interest in your remarks. Be sure that everyone can hear you. Look your audience directly in the eyes; however, avoid a shifty, flitting type of gaze that never really stops anywhere. You may look at certain persons in different parts of the group, since you cannot very well look at everybody during the short time you are speaking.

When you are ready to close your remarks, conclude with a brief summarizing statement. Pause at least two seconds after your final words; then go easily and politely to your chair. Do not rush or hurry or crumple your notes into a wad and shove them in your pocket. Upon reaching your chair, avoid slouching down in it, sprawling out, heaving a big sigh and in general going through a pantomime which says in effect, "Boy I'm glad that's over!" You may feel that way; however, this is one time that advertising does not pay. Sit comfortably in your chair and remember that you are still giving impressions of yourself. If you have done your best, no one will complain.

IMPROVE YOUR VOCABULARY

Gambol – (găm'bol) n. or v. – Play, rollick, frolic, romp, frisk, to leap and skip about. Example: The neighbor's child would gambol about like a young colt.

Look – Do you use this word too much? If so, you can improve your vocabulary and conversation by giving look a rest. Synonyms are: gage, inspect, observe, regard, survey, scan, discern, contemplate, glance, etc.

BIBLIOGRAPHY FOR YOUR FIRST SPEECH

Mudd, Charles S. and Sillars, M. O., Speech: Content and Communication, Harper & Row, 4th ed., 1979.
Ross, Raymond S., Speech Communication: Fundamentals and Practice, Prentice-Hall, 5th ed., 1980.

- -

Copy the notes below. Use them while giving the information they request.

1. My name is (what shall we call you?)
2. Where and how did you spend your childhood? Explain.
3. Tell about your home town.
4. What is your hobby? Explain.
5. Who is your favorite movie actor and actress? Why?
6. What is your favorite sport? Why?
7. Conclude with a summarizing statement about your school plans.

Chapter 2

RECORDING A SPEECH

Question: *Is speaking over the radio the same as speaking in person?*

Answer: *No. Radio speech depends on voice alone, is usually read, and has no body language for the listener to see.*

This speech is due:
Time limits: See your instructor for the exact time.
Speaking notes: Ten or fifteen words should be enough.

PURPOSE OF RECORDING A SPEECH

This assignment is proposed in order that you may hear and judge your own speaking. It calls for a speech that you will record and keep for yourself as a record of how you talked when this course started. At a later date near the end of the course, you may wish to make another recording to compare with your first recording, thus noting your progress.

EXPLANATION OF A RECORDED SPEECH

A recorded speech may be any kind for any occasion. It simply is a speech which is recorded and played back at will. In other words, it becomes a record in voice rather than a record in writing. These are its chief purposes: rebroadcasting from a radio station, private use, or classroom study. Its special feature is the time limit placed on the speaker. Its time has to be observed within a matter of seconds. Any person who is not willing to adhere to the time limit pays for disc space he does not use because his speech is short. If he has too much speech and runs out of time, he either makes an awkward conclusion or is cut off in the middle of a sentence or summary.

Occasions for recording a speech occur any time a speech needs to be preserved for later use. Occasions may arise in the home, school, church, club, business, politics, government, theatre, radio station, and the like. (All the preceding applies to television and video tape.)

SUGGESTED TOPICS FOR RECORDING

If you are recording a speech during the first part of the school year with the thought in mind that you will make a later recording for purposes of comparison, it might be wise to use the first speech experience suggested in this book, the one in which you introduced yourself to the class. If you do not care to do this, check through the many possibilities listed under "Suggested Topics" in each of the other speech experiences. Be sure your selection meets the time limit which you will be required to observe. Consult your instructor for further information.

If this is your first recording or you are inexperienced, do not try to be profound in your remarks. Rather, select a topic which will best represent you at your present stage of development as a speaker. On the other hand, if you merely wish to make a recording of a speech, your topic will have little to do with it.

HOW TO PREPARE A SPEECH FOR RECORDING

For this particular speech your purpose is to secure a record of your speaking ability. Decide according to the first assignment notes what you are going to say; then practice aloud until you have your thoughts well in mind, but not memorized. Know the general outline of your ideas.

If you choose to speak on some other topic, simply prepare it as you would any speech by observing good speech preparation practices. In all cases observe your time limits within ten seconds if possible.

Should you choose to read your speech (with your instructor's consent), organize it as you would any speech. Keep it right on the nose as to time.

HOW TO PRESENT A SPEECH FOR RECORDING

You should begin your speech by saying, "This is (George Jones) speaking on (date) . . . " After your first sentence, go ahead with your talk. Speak in your natural voice as you normally would. Be careful not to vary the distance from the microphone by moving your head a great deal or your recording may be loud at first and then weak. Also avoid coughing, clearing your throat, sneezing, or shouting, into the "mike." Ask your instructor how close to stand to the microphone; however, ten inches is considered a good distance.

While speaking, watch your progress so that you may be sure to finish before your time runs out.

If you use notes, avoid rustling them near the microphone. Any sound they make will be picked up and exaggerated. When one piece of paper is finished, let it quietly drop from your hands to the floor or speaker's stand.

SPECIAL NOTES

If discs are used for recordings, the following may apply. When a group of recordings is concluded, the instructor may play them back to the class; then members of the class may discuss the individual speakers. Points to listen for are the whistled "s", nasality, harshness, resonance, pitch, force, articulation, pronunciation . . . .

The instructor, at his discretion, may keep the records on file until the end of the course when a final recording may be made for comparative purposes. The student may then receive the record with a speech on each side for his own use and analysis.

Blank discs may be procured from a local music store or if the instructor wishes, he may write to various record-making companies for them. He should ask for educational discounts, regardless of where he gets them. Each student should be prepared to pay for the disc used in making his recording unless the school provides for this expense.

If a wire or tape recorder is used, there will be no expense attached unless the spool is retained for future reference. Should this be done, another spool will be needed to replace it. Even in this case, the used spool may be filed until near the end of the term at which time it can be reused without cost.

If a video tape machine is available it will afford an effective means for students to see and hear how they look and sound while speaking. Also it provides opportunity to those students wishing to use it for rehearsal. Wisely used the video tape recorder can assist student speakers to become their own best teachers.

IMPROVE YOUR VOCABULARY

On the nose – This is a term used in radio to designate that the speaker or actor concluded his performance exactly on time. Learn to use it when talking about radio. Example: He finished his speech on the nose.

Hot – Use synonyms for this word. It is overworked. Examples are: burning, scorching, boiling, heated, excited, strong, raging, fiery, etc.

Chapter 3

SPEECH OF PERSONAL EXPERIENCE

Question: *How can you improve your pronunciation?*

Answer: *Keep a dictionary handy. Carry a small one with you. Read aloud fifteen minutes daily making sure of all pronunciations.*

This speech is due:
Time limits: 3-4 minutes.
Speaking notes: 10-word maximum limit.
Source of information: Use your own personal experience.
Outline of speech: Prepare a 50-100 word complete sentence outline to be handed to your instructor when you rise to speak. He may wish to write criticisms on it regarding your speech. Write the number of words in upper left hand corner of the paper. Use the form at the end of this chapter.

PURPOSE OF A SPEECH OF PERSONAL EXPERIENCE

You take a step forward in your speaking experience when you present a speech of personal experience. While this speech is essentially about yourself, it still requires a definite preparation and interesting presentation. You should learn the importance of these two requirements early in your speech training. Aside from becoming acquainted with these aspects of speechmaking, you should feel increased confidence and poise as a result of this speech experience. Your ease before the group will improve noticeably. By giving your best to this speech you will achieve a creditable improvement and desirable personal satisfaction.

EXPLANATION OF A SPEECH OF PERSONAL EXPERIENCE

A speech of personal experience may be one of any four basic types: that is, the speech may be given to (1) inform, (2) to stimulate or arouse, (3) to convince, or (4) to entertain. The specific purpose of your remarks will determine which of these types you plan to present. If you want to tell of funny or amusing personal experiences, you will plan to entertain your listeners. If you wish to tell how you trap muskrats, your purpose will be to inform your listeners. It is advisable to confine your efforts to one of these two kinds of speeches. To attempt either of the others this early would be too hazardous to recommend now. You should study the chapter elsewhere in this book that deals with the type of speech you plan to present.

All this speech requires from you is a good thorough preparation. You must know the order in which you plan to tell of your experiences. You also need to know how you will tell them, that is, the words you will use. This does not mean you are to memorize your speech. Do not memorize your speech either now or later. This point will be discussed in subsequent paragraphs under the headings: "How To Prepare a Speech of Personal Experience" and "How To Present a Speech of Personal Experience."

Unlimited occasions for a speech of personal experience occur at all kinds of meetings – such as before school assemblies, clubs, business meetings, religious gatherings, and other groups. You have probably heard such a speech from a war veteran, a war correspondent, from a missionary, a newspaper reporter, a great athlete, or from a person like yourself who tells what has happened to him.

SUGGESTED TOPICS FOR A SPEECH OF PERSONAL EXPERIENCE

1. Wrecks	*12. A trip
2. Conflagrations	13. Flying
3. Falling through ice	14. An experiment
4. Swimming	15. Sickness
5. Hunting	16. Wrestling
6. Camping	17. At a carnival
7. Hiking	18. Embarrassment
8. Climbing	19. A funny incident
9. Racing – any kind	20. Building something
10. Sports contests	21. Speaker's choice
11. Rodeos	

* Do not choose this topic unless you have more to tell than items, such as: the time you started, where you ate your meals, the hotels you stayed in, the cities you passed through, and when you returned. A speech of this kind should carry some element of special interest which makes it different from any ordinary trip.

HOW TO CHOOSE A TOPIC FOR A SPEECH OF PERSONAL EXPERIENCE

Read the foregoing list of topics carefully. They are intended to suggest ideas to you. If you have had an exciting experience similar to one of them, select it for your speech. Whatever you decide to talk about should be vivid in your memory and quite clear. As you think about it you may feel prickly chills race up your spine, you may laugh, you may feel sad. But whatever it is, the experience should be personal.

Do not begin stalling before making a choice of topic because you do not know anything interesting to talk about. This is an old, worn-out excuse which explorers used before Columbus; they could not make up their minds about what to discover. In all likelihood they did not try. The topic that you choose will not be interesting in itself. It is your responsibility to plan to tell the personal experience in an interesting way. You can do this with a little effort. Choose a topic without delay, and then read the rest of this assignment to find out how to prepare and present a speech on the topic you have chosen.

HOW TO PREPARE A SPEECH OF PERSONAL EXPERIENCE

First, decide on your purpose for giving this speech. Do you want to inform your listeners? Do you want to entertain them? It will be wise to work toward one of these ends for this speech. Having decided this point, your next step is to find out how you go about informing or entertaining. You may do this by reading the chapter in this text dealing with these types of talks.

Now let us assume that you know generally what is expected of you when you give your speech. Let us assume, too, that you have your purpose constantly before you (to entertain or to inform). Now develop your speech in the following order:

I. Outline your speech in considerable detail. This means that you must set up the order of events you want to talk about.

   A. Be sure your outline places these events in their most effective order throughout your talk. A little thought about arrangement will tell you how to place your ideas.

      1. In arranging what you will talk about, include your own personal feelings and reactions, the activities of other persons or animals, and objects that made your experience thrilling, exciting, funny, . . . This will add interest.

II. Practice your speech aloud before friends and in front of a mirror. Do this until you have memorized the sequence of events, not the words. You will quite naturally tend to memorize certain words and phrases and this is all right. But do not under any circumstances memorize the whole speech word for word. Every time you rehearse you will tell the same things, but never with exactly the same words. Each rehearsal will set the pattern of your speech more firmly in mind until after several practices (the number depends on the individual) you will be able to present your speech with full confidence and the knowledge that you know what you are going to say; that is, you know the events and feelings you are going to talk about and describe.

III. Make a final evaluation of your speech before marking it "ready for presentation". Ask yourself the following questions and be sure that your speech answers each question adequately.

   A. Does your speech merely list a series of persons, places, things, and time without telling what happened to these persons and things? (You should vitalize these persons and things by describing what happened and by pointing out unusual or exciting incidents, such as: dangers, or humorous occurrences.) Avoid unnecessary details.

   B. Is your speech about you only? If so, you can improve it by talking about the influences that were operating in your presence. For example, if you rescued a drowning person, do not be satisfied to say, "I jumped in and pulled him out." Tell what he was doing, describe his struggles, tell how deep the water was, how far he was from shore, recount your fears and other feelings as you pulled him toward shore, tell how the current almost took you under, demonstrate the way you held him by the hair, . . . Emphasize such items as your fatigue and near exhaustion as you fought to stay afloat. Here is an example of a "thriller": "We were in swimming. I guess we'd been in about an hour. John got the cramps and yelled for help. I swam over and pulled him out. He almost took me under once, but I got him out and gave him artificial respiration. I learned that when I was a kid. Boy, I sure was scared."

(Author's note: Was this an interesting story of an experience? It could have been, had it been told with vividness and description.)

C. Do you have a curiosity-arousing introduction, one that catches the attention? Check this point carefully.

D. Do you have a conclusion? A speech is never finished without one.

HOW TO PRESENT A SPEECH OF PERSONAL EXPERIENCE

Your attitude regarding yourself and your audience will exert a singular influence upon you and your listeners. You should have a sincere desire to entertain or inform. If it is information that you earnestly desire to give, then you must try to make your audience understand what you are telling. If it is entertainment you want to provide, then you must strive to give enjoyment by amusing and causing smiles and perhaps some laughter. You should not feel that what you have to say is simply not interesting and never was, which is the attitude of some students. Consider for a moment the child who runs to you eagerly, grasps your hand, and excitedly tells you about a big dog two doors down the street. His story no doubt captivates your interest; yet there is nothing inherently interesting about a big dog you have seen many times. Why then are you interested? The answer lies largely in the extreme desire of the child to tell you something. He wants you to understand him, and therein lies the basic secret of giving information to

which people will listen attentively. You must have a desire to make your audience understand you or enjoy what you are saying.

As for your body language, demonstrate those points which you can. Let your arms and hands gesture whenever you feel an impulse to do so; otherwise your hands may hang comfortably at your sides, rest easily on a table top or chair back, or be placed conveniently in a pocket. Be calm about putting your hands anywhere. Change your stage position by moving laterally a few feet. This will cause attention to be drawn to your presentation.

Use your voice normally and conversationally. Talk earnestly and loudly enough to be heard by everyone present. If you are truly interested in your audience's understanding you, your voice modulation and force will take care of themselves very well.

If you use speaking notes, observe the ten-word maximum limit. Have these written in large handwriting so that they may be easily read. Use a paper at least three by five inches in size, preferably larger. Do not fiddle with the paper or roll it into a tube. Hold the notes calmly between your thumb and forefinger in either hand. When referring to your notes, raise them to a level that permits you to glance at them without bowing your head. Do not try to hide them, nor act ashamed of using them. They are your map. Treat them as casually as you would a road map were you taking a trip.

IMPROVE YOUR VOCABULARY

Avid - (ăv'ĭd) a. To desire very much. Greedy, rapacious, eager, keen, anxious, athirst, etc. Example: He was an avid wrestling fan. Use this word three or four times daily until it is yours. It will give you a new and expressive term.

Get - Omit this word. Use a synonym to give variety to your speech. Here are examples: achieve, earn, gain, procure, secure, obtain, acquire, attain, receive, win, etc.

BIOGRAPHY FOR SPEECH OF PERSONAL EXPERIENCE

Linkletter, Art, Public Speaking For Private People, Bobbs Merrill, 1980.
Zimmerman, Gordon I., Public Speaking Today, West Publishing, 1979.

PERSONAL EXPERIENCE SPEECH

By Gail Anderson

THE EARTH TREMBLED

"And Jesus uttered a loud cry, and breathed his last. And the curtain of the temple was torn in two, from top to bottom." Mark 15:37-38. Good Friday holds a point in destiny unequaled since the dawning of all mankind. March 27, 1964, Good Friday alike, holds an eminent position in the stream of my life as the day of the Alaska earthquake.

I was thirteen at the time, living in Anchorage, Alaska. The fact was that a "Good Friday suppertime" sort of atmosphere was beginning to creep into the minds of each of the members of my family. We might even have been bored had it not been for the anticipation of the evening meal that was near completion.

The day was calm. My father was typically absorbed in the newspaper. "Kitchen-puttering" occupied my mother. My brother was both engaged and absorbed in some nonsensical whiling away of time. Snow was falling in a soft and gentle manner, combatting boredom with me. The subtle and peaceful cloaking it lent the earth, could only be viewed as ironic now, in the face of what was to come.

The snow was still falling when the hanging light fixtures began to swing and the rattle of furniture could be heard on the tile floor. At first, our reaction could only have been termed amusement. But our amusement soon became terror. As we stumbled down stairs and through doors, trying to avoid tumbling objects, we heard and felt the rumble of our earth mount. As the front door forcibly flung us into the mounds of snow in the front yard, the earth continued to roll and groan. And then sprawled on the side-walk, the ground ceased to tease us with its laughing rumbles. Now it was cracking. Around me the snow was forming rifts as great expanses of the frozen earth were separating.

The noises somehow were strangely deafening. Hysterical cries of neighbors blended with the laughing of the earth and the creaking of the houses to produce a wicked sound system matched only by the horror of its backdrop.

Our station wagon bounced as if it were a rubber ball. The picture windows of the house were distorted to the point of being diamond-shaped. Trees on high-crumbling mountains in the distance were waving like a wheatfield in a breeze.

Finally the earth became dormant once again. Now it was still. And as the curtain of night shrouded our stricken Alaska, we were left to our contemplations. The hesitancy of the only partially existent radio gave our own woes a universality. Only then did we realize the encompassing scope of this earthquake. Sitting in my rocking chair (attempting to camouflage any further shaking), I heard of this demon which had left me alive and glad with my saved family, and spared home, but had taken the lives and homes of so many others.

In Anchorage the next day we saw the effects of disaster. Homes, schools, and businesses lay in ruin, paradoxically powdered with snow. But the people were together, helping one another. The homes left standing were crowded, but a unity of cause made these conditions endurable.

Immediately work began to rebuild, to restore. Radio announcers neglected their families to keep the people informed, as televisions and newspapers were not to be lines of communication for some time. People were living without heat, water, mail service, and many other things. Essentials were the essence of a united survival.

I wish that I could have understood the agonizing pleas for survival, for salvation. But only now, as my mind becomes a victim of time, do I have any understanding of the emotional or intellectual influence a natural disaster exercises on life and the perception of it.

And so, as on the original Good Friday, man was to be a recipient of one of the most vividly educational experiences in a lifetime. As the tragedy of the crucifixion and resurrection of Jesus Christ, the tragedy of the earthquake was to bring man closer to God, more desirous of salvation, and more understanding of both his God and himself.

SPEECH OUTLINE

Construct a neat, complete sentence outline on this sheet, tear it out, and hand it to your instructor when you rise to speak. He may wish to write criticisms of the outline and speech in the margins.

Type of speech:_____ Name: _____

Number of words in outline: _____ Date: _____

Purpose of this speech: (What do you want your audience to learn, to think, to believe, to feel, or do because of this speech?) _____

_____

TITLE:

INTRODUCTION:

BODY:

CONCLUSION:

Instructor's comments may concern choice of topic, development of ideas, organization, language use, personal appearance, posture, physical activity, sources, and improvement.

(Write sources of information on back of sheet)

SOURCES FROM LITERATURE

Fill out source requirements completely.
Write "none listed" if an author's name or copyright date is not listed.

1. Author's name _____

   Title of book or magazine used _____

   Title of article in above book or magazine _____

   Chapter and/or pages read _____

   Date of above publication _____

2. Author's name _____

   Title of book or magazine used _____

   Title of article in above book or magazine _____

   Chapter and/or pages read _____

   Date of above publication _____

3. Author's name _____

   Title of book or magazine used _____

   Title of article in above book or magazine _____

   Chapter and/or pages read _____

   Date of above publication _____

INTERVIEW SOURCES

1. Person interviewed _____ Date of interview _____

   His position, occupation, and location _____

   Why is he a reliable source? Be specific _____

   _____

2. Person interviewed _____ Date of interview _____

   His position, occupation, and location _____

   Why is he a reliable source? Be specific _____

   _____

PERSONAL EXPERIENCE OF SPEAKER

1. Tell (1) when, (2) where, and (3) conditions under which you became an authority on subject matter in

   your speech _____

   _____

   _____

   _____

THE PET PEEVE OR OPINION SPEECH

Question: *Is it all right to ask questions when giving a speech?*

Answer: *Yes. Rhetorical questions are effective. Other questions should be directed to the entire audience, however, no answer is expected or required.*

This speech is due:

Time limits: None.

Speaking notes: Do as you like – you will probably be more effective without them.

Source of information: Yourself.

Outline of speech: None is required.

To the instructor: This speech usually works well after students have had two or three previous assignments.

PURPOSE OF THE PET PEEVE OR OPINION SPEECH

Thus far in your speeches you have probably felt varying degrees of nervousness and tension. As a result you may have taken stage fearfully, spoken in hushed and weak tones, used little or no bodily action, and scarcely any gestures. Perhaps you have not looked your audience in the eye (called eye contact) or you may have lacked sufficient enthusiasm. Such behavior on your part is probably caused by thinking of yourself and how you are doing.

One way to overcome tensions and nervousness is by talking of something about which you are intensely aroused. This speech is designed to give you the feeling of real, live speaking in which you cast aside all inhibitions, fears, and thoughts of yourself. See what you can do with it.

EXPLANATION OF THE PET PEEVE OR OPINION SPEECH

Your talk should be about your pet peeve. It should concern your innermost personal feelings on that peeve which causes you greater disturbance and anger or stronger feeling that anything else. It should make your blood boil just to think of it. It may be about something of recent occurrence or it may concern an event that happened some time ago. It must, however, be about an incident that is vivid in your memory. Probably it should be of recent date; otherwise, you may have cooled off too much to make a strong speech about it.

SUGGESTED TOPIC

My pet peeve - or anything else that stirs you up.

HOW TO PREPARE A SPEECH ABOUT A PET PEEVE

No particular preparation is required. All that you need do is to decide what your most annoying and irritating pet peeve is. Once you make your choice of peeve, mull over the irritating idea and make up your mind that you are going to "blow off a lot of steam" to your audience. If you wish to rehearse before presentation, so much the better. However, for this specific assignment you are not asked to practice. All that you are asked to do is to make sure that you are "red hot" about a particular subject. If you are, your preparation is sufficient for this speech.

HOW TO PRESENT YOUR SPEECH

There is just one way to deliver a speech about a pet peeve. Put your whole body and soul into it. Mean every word. Use plenty of force framed in dynamic and colorful language. Let a slow fire that has been smoldering within you suddenly explode. Pour hot verbal oil on the blaze and let it roar and burn! In other words, let yourself go as never before. Quit pussy footing around and acting like a meek little lamb that has lost its way. Be a man and do not be afraid to let the world know it. If your arms feel like waving, let them wave. If you feel like scowling in disgust - scowl. If you feel like shouting - shout. Whatever you do, just be sure you go all out. No doubt you will be surprised at your own ability - when you really "unload your pet peeve".

After your speech, the instructor and class will comment orally on your effectiveness. They should be able to tell you whether or not you really meant what you said. It will be helpful to you to find out how they reacted.

IMPROVE YOUR VOCABULARY

<u>Banal</u> – (băn'ăl, bā'năl) a. commonplace, hackneyed, trite. Example: Avoid banal language.

<u>Give</u> – Use a synonym for this very common verb. Here are a few examples: Bestow, cede, deliver, confer, communicate, donate, grant, impart, supply, present, etc.

BIBLIOGRAPHY FOR THE PET PEEVE OR OPINION SPEECH

Fletcher, Leon, <u>How to Design and Deliver a Speech</u>, Harper & Row, 1979.
Friant, Ray J., Jr., <u>Preparing Effective Presentations</u>, Pilot Books, rev ed., 1979.
Garff, Royal L., <u>You Can Learn to Speak</u>, Deseret Book, 1980.

★　★　★　★　★

PET PEEVE SPEECH

By Mike Nestor

MY KIDS ARE ADDICTED TO TV

I came home from work the other day to notice my kids watching television. I said, "Johnnie, can't you help your mother with the dinner?"

"No, I've got to watch the <u>Brady Bunch</u>."

"Well, what's so great about the <u>Brady Bunch</u>?"

"It's one of the better re-runs," he said without ungluing his eyes from the set. I went into the kitchen exasperated that I had to compete with a two-foot by two-foot tube. "What did it have that I didn't?" I thought resentfully.

But the television has made its debut into our children's lives and is now the second-important thing in their lives . . . second only to sleep. The latest figures show that our children spend six and one-half hours a day in front of the tube. Six and one-half hours! Why when I was a kid, we wouldn't think of such a thing. We had to work if we wanted to eat. Now Mommy and Daddy can do it all. While the kid sits in front of that ghastly tube! The average child now sits in front of the set from the time he gets home from school until he goes to bed with little let up.

With this much time spent watching television, it seems there should be at least something educational to watch . . . after all, TV is having a big part in shaping that youngster's life. And the shows that are on! One rare moment, I found myself watching <u>Joe Forrester</u> alone . . . a cop show which I detest. So I reached over and turned the station . . . to the <u>Rookies</u> — another cop show. Near panic, I turned again to be faced by <u>Police Woman</u>. With a sinking feeling in my stomach I slammed the TV off and picked up the paper.

Why couldn't they make shows like they used to? Whatever happened to Randolph Scott? America, you had better give us something besides <u>Police Woman</u> if you want our kids to turn out anything like we did.

Chapter 5

THE SPEECH TO DEVELOP BODY LANGUAGE

Question: *Is it all right to lean on the speaker's stand?*

Answer: *No. It makes you appear tired and uninterested in your subject.*

This speech is due:
Time limits: 4-5 minutes.
Speaking notes: 10-word maximum limit.
Sources of information: Two are required, preferably three. For each source give the specific magazine or book it was taken from, title of the article, author's full name, date of publication, and the chapter or pages telling where the material was found. If a source is a person, identify him completely by title, position, occupation, etc. List these on the outline form.
Outline your speech: Prepare a 75-150 word complete sentence outline. Designate the exact number of words in your outline. Use the form at the end of this chapter.

PURPOSE OF THE SPEECH TO DEVELOP BODY LANGUAGE

Speaking is a total bodily activity. To be really effective a person has to talk all over. He has to use his feet and legs, his hands and arms, his trunk, his head, his eyebrows – every part of him. Many beginning speakers do not realize this, despite the fact that they themselves use total bodily expression all the time in their normal conversation. One sees such speakers standing before a class very stiff and rigid making their speeches. They move only their vocal cords, their tongue and jaws. Actually, they are half speaking (communicating) because they are using only half of their communicating tools. If they would put all their communicating power into action, they would include bodily action and gestures. A speech assignment of this kind is made because it will provide an experience which will demand that the speaker use bodily actions and gestures, and thus improve his speech.

EXPLANATION OF BODY LANGUAGE IN SPEECH

A speech to illustrate body language may be any kind, since bodily actions and gestures should be used in every speech with varying degrees. The purpose of your speech need not be influenced because increased body language is required. These activities will be aids in assisting you to communicate in a manner which fulfills your purpose, regardless of what it is.

Bodily actions may be defined as the movements of the body as it changes places. Gestures may be defined as movements of individual parts of the body, such as: raising an eyebrow, shrugging the shoulders, pointing . . . . But all movements are body language.

This speech in which you will deliberately use bodily actions and gestures should be considered as an experience in which you plan to utilize your entire organism and then do it. By carrying through you will understand how much more effective you really are and thus set a pattern of speaking to be used in your future speeches.

As far as this writer knows, it is impossible to speak without some body language. Just because you may not be aware of all that goes on while you speak, in no sense means that you are not using some actions. Your very nervousness and stage fright elicit certain gestures which tell your audience you are nervous. Now, if you substitute meaningful activity, you at once improve your communication and release many nervous tensions which accompany speaking. The point to bear in mind is that all speech communication should be accompanied by appropriate and meaningful bodily actions and gestures which should not be interpreted to mean that you must employ constant bodily movements and incessant gestures. Such monotony of motion would be nerve wracking to an audience. Someone once said that moderation is good to practice in all things. This is true of total bodily expression. Keep this in mind.

SUGGESTED TOPICS FOR SPEECHES TO DEVELOP BODY LANGUAGE

1. How to saddle, bridle, and mount a horse.
2. How to take a picture.
3. How to use a golf club.
4. How to hold and pitch a baseball to make it curve.
5. How to catch and throw a football.
6. How to dribble and "shoot" a basketball.
7. How to box.

8. How to wrestle.
9. How to type properly.
10. How to operate a snow mobile.
11. How to revive a drowning person.
12. How to play a musical instrument.
13. How to cast with a fishing rod.
14. How to shoot a gun (pistol, rifle, shotgun).
15. How to fly an airplane.
16. How to hang glide.
17. How to use a lasso.
18. How to give a referee's signals for any sport.
19. How to dance (different steps should be demonstrated and explained. Also different types of dancing such as square, tap, ballet . . .).
20. How to apply facial make-up correctly.
21. How to use body language while speaking.
22. How to ice skate or roller skate.
23. How to construct something.
24. How to do card tricks (this must be a demonstration which uses bodily action and gesture - not a mere performance of a few tricks).
25. How to ski, toboggan . . .
26. Speaker's choice.

HOW TO CHOOSE A TOPIC FOR A SPEECH TO DEVELOP BODY LANGUAGE

Since the purpose of presenting this speech is to improve your use of bodily action and gesture, you should select a subject which you can demonstrate while talking about it. On the other hand, the purpose of the speech itself will be to inform your listeners. It will be wise then for you to choose a topic in which you are interested and about which you can find source materials. You must also adapt your material (your speech) to your audience; hence it must be suitable to them as well as to you.

Study the above list carefully; then make your decision. After your choice is made, stick to it even though you discover it more difficult to prepare than you had anticipated. Do not change topics just because you misjudged the amount of effort it would take for preparation.

It is important that you make your selection of a topic without delay, for this speech will require considerable planning. There is no reason to put off a decision regarding a topic. Make up your mind now; then pursue your materials until you have what you want.

HOW TO PREPARE A SPEECH TO DEVELOP BODY LANGUAGE

In the speech to develop body language, your communicative purpose will be to inform your listeners in such a way that they understand what you are talking about. You will find out all about this type of speech by reading the chapter in this text, "The Speech to Inform". You develop your speech in the manner suggested for the informative speech.

In rehearsing this talk, you will need to practice bodily actions and gestures, as these will constitute a great part of this speech. These actions should not be memorized in detail, which would result in a mechanical performance on your part. Instead, you should stand before a mirror while you practice. If possible, use a large mirror that reflects your whole body rather than just the upper half of it. However, if only a small mirror is available, do the best you can with it. A friend who will watch you and give helpful criticisms will provide an excellent means for improvement.

While you rehearse, your efforts should be exerted to create a well-organized set of spontaneous actions. As stated above, you must not memorize these actions. They must be motivated by the earnestness of your desire to make your hearers understand you. You must feel impelled to use your body and hands in expressing yourself. These actions of your body and hands need not be like those of anybody else - they are your own, the same as your walk and style of dancing are your own. All that you need to do is to observe yourself in practice in order to eliminate awkwardness, undesirable posture and foot positions, and distracting mannerisms.

The thought is that if you are willing to try and to undergo a little self-inflicted criticism, you can develop your own style of gesture and bodily action. In doing this, it is advisable that you read several references on body language. However, for your assistance you may find it helpful to know of the following general types of hand and arm gestures:

1. Pointing - use the index finger. Have some vigor in this gesture. Do not use a half-crooked finger.
2. Palm up (one or both hands) - this is seen most when giving or receiving, whether it be an idea or an object.

3. Palm down (one or both hands) – this is used in rejecting, pushing things away from you. Imagine that a pup jumped on you, putting his front paws against your body. Push him away – palms down! The same goes for ideas while speaking.
4. Palm oblique, about shoulder high – this is used in cautioning. Imagine yourself patting a friend on the shoulder while you say, "Take it easy, John, there's danger ahead."
5. The clenched fist (it must be vigorously clenched so that the muscles stand out on the forearm and shoulder) – both fists may be used if the gesture is appropriate. Usually one fist clenches sympathetically with the other if the gesture is really meant. Use this gesture for emphasis. Do not pound the table. Just almost touch it on the down stroke, that is, if a table is around.

Your posture should be one of alertness in which you stand tall. Keep your weight on the balls of your feet and on the forward foot.

Bodily action should be free, relaxed, easy. It should have tonicity, vigor and coordination, without the appearance of extreme nervous tension, which is characterized by shuffling feet and restless tiger-like pacing. In moving to the left, lead with the left foot; to the right, with the right foot. Avoid crossing your legs in order to get started. Move quietly without "clomping" heels and scraping soles. Be sure that the movement is motivated and acts as a transition between ideas, as an emphasis, as a device for releasing bodily tension and holding attention. Use bodily action deliberately until you habitually make it a desirable part of your speech, a part that communicates meanings and ideas.

Before you consider this speech completely prepared, construct the outline indicated at the beginning of this chapter.

HOW TO PRESENT A SPEECH TO DEVELOP BODY LANGUAGE

When you present this speech, approach the speaker's stand with the attitude of a person determined to win. Have no fear or shame that your gestures and actions will be wrong or inappropriate. Take pride in the fact that you are going to use your entire organism in speaking. With this attitude you cannot lose.

When you actually present your speech, concentrate on one point which will make the audience understand what you are informing them about. They have to understand you, or you will not be getting your ideas across (communicating). Now, while you are earnestly presenting your ideas, try to make them clearer by demonstrating what you have to say. Do this by acting out certain parts as you talk. If you tell the audience that it is best to mount a horse a certain way, show them how to do it. If you say a baseball should be thrown a certain way, demonstrate it with all the force and energy you would use were you actually pitching. If your demonstration is so vigorous that it makes you short of breath, so much the better; you will have been truly trying to show, as well as tell what you have to say. You may exhibit pictures, charts, diagrams, write on the blackboard . . . If you do, be sure that your equipment is ready for exhibition before you begin.

Do not be afraid to try; do your best, and you will do a good job. Plan to continue using body language in your future speeches.

IMPROVE YOUR VOCABULARY

Furtive – (fûr'tĭv) a. done stealthily – sly, secret, covert, underhand, clandestine. Example: The cat cast a furtive glance toward the approaching dog. Use this word three times daily for three days. Make it a part of your vocabulary.

Quiet – Omit this word for a week. Use a synonym to give your speech variety and to add new words to your vocabulary. Here are a few examples: calm, motionless, serene, placid, taciturn, reticent, hushed, inactive, uncommunicative, etc.

BIBLIOGRAPHY FOR THE SPEECH TO DEVELOP BODY LANGUAGE

Milham, Dick, Charis-Magic in Public Speaking: The Power to Move People, Prentice-Hall, 1980.
Rice, George P., Foundations For Conversation, Christopher Publishing, 1979.

SPEECH TO DEVELOP BODY LANGUAGE

By Joann Bopp

START CANOEING AND ENJOY YOUR WEEKENDS

Props needed for this speech are canoe paddles, an armless chair, and a small rug. You should wear lightweight sports clothes. Before you are asked to deliver your speech see that the chair is in front of the class. When you are called to speak carry the small rug and the paddles with you. Lay the paddles across the seat of the chair and spread the rug on the floor near the chair. You can now stand in front of the class or at the podium and begin your speech.

Wouldn't you like to get more fun and relaxation out of your leisure time? Those two-day weekends could be spent away from the busy, hurried city life that most of us lead. Just put a canoe on top of your car and head for water. A canoe can float on as little as four inches of water. A quiet lake or stream or pond may hold more fascination than you ever imagined. It is a delight to quietly skim over calm waters and see the natural beauty of the shoreline or catch a glimpse of wildlife going about their unhurried activities. A canoe could also bring the thrills of shooting rapids of a swift running river, but this is for the experienced boatman, or you can find much pleasure with little effort in canoeing secluded little bodies of water.

I would like to give you a few rules and demonstrations to show you how to canoe in a very short time. Number one rule is getting in and out of a craft correctly. Canoeing is often thought of as being very dangerous but the danger usually occurs when getting in or out of the canoe. To get in, you step first to the center, lengthwise, and place the other foot behind (demonstrate on rug). Then lower yourself to a kneeling position which is the correct canoeing position (demonstrate by kneeling on rug). There are braces across the canoe to lean against. Once you have established this low center of gravity the canoe has great stability. Getting out is just reverse. Keep your weight to the center as much as possible (demonstrate by getting off the rug).

These are the paddles (show paddles), they are made of fir, a soft wood which holds up well in water and is lightweight. To select the paddle measure it to your height. It should come to about your chin (demonstrate). (Sit in the chair to demonstrate paddling strokes). To hold the paddle grip the end with one hand and with the other hand grasp it a little above the blade (demonstrate). Holding in this manner you are ready to start paddling.

The basic stroke is called the "cruising stroke," or the "bow stroke." Extend the paddle in front of you (demonstrations follow), close to the canoe, and dip into the water, bringing it straight back to the hip by pushing with the top hand and pulling with the lower hand. Now bring the paddle back and repeat. The paddling is usually done by a two-man team called tandem paddling. In tandem paddling the person in front is the sternman who steers the boat. The person in the rear is the bowman and he provides the power. The bowman uses the bow stroke most of the time (demonstrations follow). The sternman uses the bow stroke also, but often makes a hook outward on the end of the stroke to keep the canoe on course. This version of the bow stroke is called the "J-Stroke." The sternman also uses the "sweep stroke" for turning. It is a wide, sweeping, arc-like stroke made close to the water surface (demonstrate). To stop or go backwards the "backwater stroke" is used. Simply place the paddle into the water at right angles to the canoe and hold it firmly to stop (demonstrate). To go backwards reverse the "bow stroke" (demonstrate).

(Rise to a standing position with paddles in hand.)

This is by no means all there is to know about canoeing, but if you can accomplish these things you will be able to have fun. So to enjoy the outdoors and take a break from a humdrum routine. I hope you will try canoeing. (Pick up rug, and with paddles and rug, resume your seat.)

SPEECH OUTLINE

Construct a neat, complete sentence outline on this sheet, tear it out, and hand it to your instructor when you rise to speak. He may wish to write criticisms of the outline and speech in the margins.

Type of speech: _____ Name: _____

Number of words in outline: _____ Date: _____

Purpose of this speech: (What do you want your audience to learn, to think, to believe, to feel, or do because of this speech?) _____

_____

TITLE:

INTRODUCTION:

BODY:

CONCLUSION:

Instructor's comments may concern choice of topic, development of ideas, organization, language use, personal appearance, posture, physical activity, sources, and improvement.

(Write sources of information on back of sheet)

SOURCES FROM LITERATURE

Fill out source requirements completely.
Write "none listed" if an author's name or copyright date is not listed.

1. Author's name _____

   Title of book or magazine used _____

   Title of article in above book or magazine _____

   Chapter and/or pages read _____

   Date of above publication _____

2. Author's name _____

   Title of book or magazine used _____

   Title of article in above book or magazine _____

   Chapter and/or pages read _____

   Date of above publication _____

3. Author's name _____

   Title of book or magazine used _____

   Title of article in above book or magazine _____

   Chapter and/or pages read _____

   Date of above publication _____

INTERVIEW SOURCES

1. Person interviewed _____ Date of interview _____

   His position, occupation, and location _____

   Why is he a reliable source? Be specific _____

   _____

2. Person interviewed _____ Date of interview _____

   His position, occupation, and location _____

   Why is he a reliable source? Be specific _____

   _____

PERSONAL EXPERIENCE OF SPEAKER

1. Tell (1) when, (2) where, and (3) conditions under which you became an authority on subject matter in

   your speech _____

   _____

   _____

   _____

Chapter 6

BODY LANGUAGE - THE PANTOMIME

Question: *What is posture?*

Answer: *It is the speaker's bodily position in any upright or sitting position.*

This pantomime is due:
Time limits: 2-3 minutes.
Source of information: Yourself.
Outline of pantomime: Prepare a 50-100 word complete sentence outline of the pantomime you intend to present. Write the number of words used in the upper right hand corner of the page. Hand it to your instructor when you rise to take stage. Use the form at the end of this chapter.

PURPOSE OF THE PANTOMIME

This experience, a pantomime, should assist you in acquiring a new freedom of bodily actions and gestures. As you perhaps have discovered by now, unhampered bodily action is highly important to effective speech. By producing a good pantomime you will emphasize all of the elements of speech except the spoken word itself. In so doing, you will bring into play the silent but yet extremely important factors that often speak what words cannot. Once you master these silent helpers you should find your speech improved. This pantomime is intended to help you to learn to use your bodily actions and gestures more freely with the result that in your next speech you will talk all over, instead of using only your voice.

EXPLANATION OF THE PANTOMIME

Pantomime is utilized as a part of drama, as an individual performance, and as a part of communicating. As you know, it involves only body language. It requires that you express ideas and thoughts, emotions and feelings by actions instead of sound (voice). The purpose of pantomime is to tell your audience with your actions what you normally would say with voice and action. If you have seen people give a stage performance called pantomime, you have seen it as one generally thinks of it. However, every time you observe someone telling someone else something without using his voice or the written word, you see pantomime. You might say that pantomime accompanies the spoken word, if we think of pantomime as actions. From this point of view, watch how your friends do pantomime while they talk. They beckon and wave and show by a thousand different motions what they are trying to tell another person. Sometimes they shrug their shoulders, kick their feet, frown, scowl, grin, smile, blink their eyes, wrinkle their foreheads, shake their heads from side to side or up and down.

They use all these motions and many, many more.

Some people actually carry on conversation and never utter a sound. They are the deaf-mutes who talk with a highly organized sign language. As for yourself, you probably have talked to many of your friends without speaking a word. Think of the times you have sent a sly wink across a room, have placed a finger to your lips as you pursed them to indicate silence, or have crooked your finger toward yourself and moved it rapidly to say in effect, "Come here." When you used these actions alone, they were pantomime. When you used them while you were speaking, they were a part of communication.

SUGGESTIONS FOR PANTOMIME

1. A robbery.
2. Building something.
3. Flying an airplane.
4. Driving a car.
5. Baking something.
6. Dressing.
7. At a party.
8. Arguing.
9. Buying.
10. Selling.
11. Singing.
12. Hitchhiking.
13. Studying.
14. Escorting a date.
15. Fishing.
16. Giving.
17. Hunting for something.
18. In a restaurant.
19. Shopping.
20. Bowling.
21. Pitching baseball.
22. Applying make-up.
23. Skating.
24. Speaker's choice.

HOW TO CHOOSE AN ACT TO PANTOMIME

Look over the suggestions. Find one you know enough about that you can act it out in full detail. Be sure you have an interest in the subject you plan to pantomime. Do not put off making a choice until just before class time. If you do you will not have time to prepare an outline or practice, the lack of which will definitely weaken your performance.

HOW TO PREPARE A PANTOMIME

Follow the methods you would normally use in preparing a speech regarding topic, audience, occasion, and rehearsal. Your purpose for this pantomime will be to work out a series of meaningful actions that tell something. It will help you to list (outline) the scenes you intend to present; then break them down into smaller and more detailed scenes until you have a complete series of well–planned actions. Your next step is rehearsal. Practice as many times as necessary to completely master your act. Ask a friend to observe you and offer helpful suggestions.

It is well to note here that you will have no reason for not utilizing the proper time limits. To prolong your act or to cut it short will be an indication of insufficient preparation. It is a rare case, indeed, in which the student has not sufficient time to prepare adequately.

HOW TO PRESENT A PANTOMIME

Before beginning your performance, make a thorough check to make certain that all the chairs or other properties you intend to use are in place. Any unusual use made of properties should be briefly explained to your audience. You may then announce your act or you may begin the performance at once and permit your audience to discover the act as it unfolds.

In presenting your pantomime, stay in character. Be watchful that you express fully what you desire to tell your audience. In most instances it is safe to "let yourself go" and not to worry about overacting. Your bodily actions, facial expressions and other gestures, if freely employed, should insure a successful portrayal. You should keep in mind that no one expects you to do a professional pantomime. The act is, in its final analysis, an experience that will help you to improve your speaking through better body language.

After concluding your performance, it will be helpful to you to remain on stage while your classmates comment on your act. They will tell you whether or not you communicated your ideas effectively. They will give you suggestions for improvement.

Helpful hints:
1. Complete any activity you start. For example, if you are dressing for a party, do not forget to put your shoes on.
2. Observe the timing of your movements so they are natural.
3. At the conclusion of your act break character only after the last detail has been finished. Walk politely to the front of the stage and bow slightly to indicate that you have ended your pantomime.

IMPROVE YOUR VOCABULARY

Facile – (făs'ĭl) a. Easily done, easily surmounted or mastered, approachable, easily persuaded, yielding, pliant, "giving in" to an idea. Example: As a person he was facile, as a speaker he was firm. Use this word four times daily for a few days and it will be yours.

Entertain – Use a synonym for this word. One of the best ways to improve your vocabulary is to use synonyms. Here are some for entertain: amuse, beguile, cheer, disport, divert, enliven, gratify, recreate, please, etc.

BIBLIOGRAPHY FOR THE PANTOMIME

Alberts, David, Handbook of Mime and Pantomime, Plays, Inc., 1980.
Enters, Angna, On Mime, Columbia Univ. Press, 1978.
Keysell, Pat, Mime Themes and Motifs, Plays, Inc., 1980.
Shepard, Richmond, Mime: The Technique of Silence, Drama Book, 1979.
Stoltzenberg, Mark, Exploring Mime, Sterling Publishing, 1979.
Tanner, Fran Averett, Basic Drama Projects, Clark Publishing, 4th ed., 1982.

SPEECH OUTLINE

Construct a neat, complete sentence outline on this sheet, tear it out, and hand it to your instructor when you rise to speak. He may wish to write criticisms of the outline and speech in the margins.

Type of speech:_____ Name: _____

Number of words in outline: _____ Date: _____

Purpose of this speech: (What do you want your audience to learn, to think, to believe, to feel, or do because of this speech?) _____

_____

TITLE:

INTRODUCTION:

BODY:

CONCLUSION:

<u>Instructor's comments</u> may concern choice of topic, development of ideas, organization, language use, personal appearance, posture, physical activity, sources, and improvement.

(Write sources of information on back of sheet)

SOURCES FROM LITERATURE

Fill out source requirements completely.
Write "none listed" if an author's name or copyright date is not listed.

1. Author's name _____

   Title of book or magazine used _____

   Title of article in above book or magazine _____

   Chapter and/or pages read _____

   Date of above publication _____

2. Author's name _____

   Title of book or magazine used _____

   Title of article in above book or magazine _____

   Chapter and/or pages read _____

   Date of above publication _____

3. Author's name _____

   Title of book or magazine used _____

   Title of article in above book or magazine _____

   Chapter and/or pages read _____

   Date of above publication _____

INTERVIEW SOURCES

1. Person interviewed _____ Date of interview _____

   His position, occupation, and location _____

   Why is he a reliable source? Be specific _____

   _____

2. Person interviewed _____ Date of interview _____

   His position, occupation, and location _____

   Why is he a reliable source? Be specific _____

   _____

PERSONAL EXPERIENCE OF SPEAKER

1. Tell (1) when, (2) where, and (3) conditions under which you became an authority on subject matter in

   your speech _____

   _____

   _____

Chapter 7

SPEECH OF SELF-DISCLOSURE AND STAGE FRIGHT

Question: *How can you speak to an older group on equal grounds?*

Answer: *Know more about your subject than they.
Older persons respect well informed students.*

This speech is due:

Time limits: None.

Speaking notes: Make a list of your "speech fears" if you wish.

Outline of speech: Prepare a list of your fears on the form at the end of this assignment. Hand the list to your instructor when you rise to tell about yourself.

PURPOSE OF THE SPEECH OF SELF-DISCLOSURE AND STAGE FRIGHT

The speech of self–disclosure and stage fright is unique. It is also important because it does a great deal for the student. By carrying it through, a person sometimes achieves a mastery over himself which before he had thought impossible. The student sees that practically all inexperienced speakers suffer similar fears and physical reactions, including apathy, speechlessness, short breath, dry mouth, weak knees, pain in the stomach, and nervous trembling. Because improvement so often is an immediate result of this speech experience, it is offered here with the thought that every student will gain much from it. As you will see, it is not a speech ever to be presented to a public audience.

EXPLANATION OF THE SPEECH OF SELF-DISCLOSURE AND STAGE FRIGHT

This speech is absolutely unrehearsed. It requires a maximum of honesty, sincerity, understanding of the other fellow, and straight-from-the-heart truth. Without complete honesty and frankness, many benefits are lost.

When your turn to speak is called or you volunteer, merely take the floor and honestly tell your audience about all the peculiar, strange, and queer feelings you have when you talk to them. If your knees are shaking, you say so and go even further - you let them shake while you show your audience, without exaggeration, how they shake. In other words, <u>tell everything</u>.

You may be amused at your fears as you recount them. Your audience may be amused with you,

but not at you. They undoubtedly have many of the same fears. After making known all your fears, the class will tell you voluntarily how they think you can overcome your various nervous tensions. After the class suggestions, it will be your turn again. You will honestly tell them how you feel at that moment. You will likely be surprised to find yourself calm, greatly relaxed, and poised. If not, you probably will not have told the group all your fears and will still be trying to hide certain feelings which you hope your audience will not recognize. If you feel "pretty good," then it is likely that you have told everything and no longer are trying to hide a great number of normal nervous reactions. Throughout this experience you will remain standing.

SUGGESTED TOPIC FOR SELF-DISCLOSURE AND STAGE FRIGHT

You need no specific topic for this speech. Just tell how you feel before speaking, when speaking, and after you finish a speech. Also tell what you think really causes your fears.

HOW TO PREPARE A SPEECH OF SELF-DISCLOSURE AND STAGE FRIGHT

You should think of all the many sensations and thoughts and insignificant reactions that have flashed into your mind during your past speeches. In order not to overlook anything, write out a list of these bothersome gremlins and study them carefully so that you may orally trade stories with other class members. If something funny has happened to you because of stage fright, plan to tell the group about it. You will enjoy a good joke on yourself and so will they. It will be good mental hygiene.

Your best preparation is to give yourself a definite "set of mind" in which you make a decision to tell all without reservation.

HOW TO PRESENT A SPEECH OF SELF-DISCLOSURE AND STAGE FRIGHT

This should be the simplest, most undramatic and sincere discussion you have made. It should come straight from the heart from start to finish – nothing more, nothing less. Your style should be you talking with a group of friends who will reciprocate. You do not need any notes unless they comprise a simple list of the fears and sensations you want to talk about.

The order of the speech should be these three steps:

1. Describe all your fears and sensations.
2. Ask your audience to tell you informally how they think you can improve yourself.
3. After the audience conclude their remarks, tell them exactly how you feel at the moment; then retire to your chair.

IMPROVE YOUR VOCABULARY

Trepidation – (trĕp'i-dā'shun) n. A vibration or trembling, especially when from fright. A state of alarm or trembling, terror, fear, dread, panic, etc. Example: The speaker refused to give up despite much trepidation. Use this word five times daily for several days until it is yours. It is a good word to know. You can use it in describing your fear when speaking.

Love – Love may be everywhere, but you can best describe its shades of meaning with useful synonyms. Here are a few examples: affection, attachment, attraction, charity, devotion, fondness, friendship, liking, regard, tenderness, affinity, etc. Use these synonyms. They will make your conversation more interesting.

BIBLIOGRAPHY FOR THE SPEECH OF SELF-DISCLOSURE AND STAGE FRIGHT

Eisenson, Jon, Voice and Diction: A Program For Improvement, Macmillan, 4th ed., 1979.
Garff, Royal L., You Can Learn to Speak, Deseret Book, 1980.
Modisett, Noah F. and Luter, J. G., Speaking Clearly: The Basics of Voice and Diction, Burgess, 1979.

- -

OUTLINE YOUR FEARS

Make no outline of your speech. Merely list here all the feelings, fears, and sensations you have before you make a speech, while you are speaking, and after you close a speech. Prepare to hand the list to your instructor when you rise to tell about yourself.

1. _____   6. _____

2. _____   7. _____

3. _____   8. _____

4. _____   9. _____

5. _____   10. _____

_____
(Signature of Student)

QUIZ NO. 2 — COVERS CHAPTERS 1-7. <u>CIRCLE CORRECT ANSWERS.</u> THESE QUESTIONS MAY BE REPRODUCED FOR CLASSROOM USE.

NAME _____ DATE _____

(Ch. 1)   21. When giving your first speech it is normal: (mark correct answers only)

        (a) to be scared   (b) to be nervous   (c) to be tense   (d) to get a thrill

(Ch. 1)   22. Synonyms for the word "gambol" are: (mark correct answers only)

        (a) frisk   (b) romp   (c) frolic   (d) hide

(Ch. 2)   23. When speaking with a microphone how many inches should you normally stand from it?

        (a) five   (b) ten   (c) fifteen   (d) twenty

(Ch. 2)   24. The term "on the nose" means:

        (a) talking too fast   (b) talking too slowly   (c) concluding a performance early

        (d) concluding a performance exactly on time

(Ch. 3)   25. A personal experience speech may be how many of the following kinds?

        (mark correct answers only)

        (a) to inform   (b) to stimulate or arouse   (c) to convince   (d) the interview

(Ch. 3)   26. "Avid" means:

        (a) exciting   (b) sober   (c) hearty   (d) eager   (e) ill

(Ch. 4)   27. (Blockbuster) "Banal" means: (two answers)

        (a) commonplace   (b) sloppy   (c) trite   (d) funny   (e) entertaining

        (f) light-hearted   (g) song-like

(Ch. 5)   28. Body language may be how many of the following?

        (a) bending a knee   (b) frowning   (c) loud voice   (d) staring at the floor

(Ch. 5)   29. Body language is all movements a person makes.

        (a) partially true   (b) true   (c) partially false   (d) false

(Ch. 5)   30. In preparing a speech to develop body language you should: (mark correct answers only)

        (a) memorize your actions in detail   (b) not memorize your movements in detail

        (c) practice before a mirror   (d) make an outline of your speech

(Ch. 5) 31. "Furtive" means:

(a) covert   (b) serene   (c) placid   (d) reticent

(Ch. 6) 32. Pantomime involves body language only.

(a) partly true   (b) true   (c) partly false   (d) false

(Ch. 6) 33. What kind of persons carry on conversation by pantomime involving mostly, hand, finger, and arm gestures?

(Write your answer here) _____

(Ch. 6) 34. When presenting a pantomime you should: (one answer only)

(a) overact   (b) be quite active   (c) never smile   (d) stay in character

(Ch. 6) 35. (Blockbuster) "Facile" means: (two answers)

(a) beguile   (b) easily done   (c) disport   (d) pliant   (e) stiff   (f) resourceful

(Ch. 7) 36. Practically all inexperienced speakers suffer similar fears such as: (two answers)

(a) apathy   (b) fluency   (c) calm   (d) short breath

(Ch. 7) 37. Talking openly and frankly to classmates about your stage fright can help you feel much more at ease and diminish stage fright.

(a) true   (b) false

(Ch. 7) 38. (Blockbuster) The words terror, fear, dread, panic, are synonyms for which one of the following words?

(a) affinity   (b) trepidation   (c) plaintive   (d) comely

Chapter 8

THE SPEECH TO INFORM

Question: *How can one easily choose interesting material?*

Answer: *There is no easy way. Interesting material is found by research and personal experience.*

This speech is due:

Time Limits: 4-5 minutes.

Speaking notes: 10-word maximum limit.

Sources of information: Two are required, preferably three. For each source give the specific magazine or book it was taken from, title of the article, author's full name, date of publication, and the chapter or pages telling where the material was found. If a source is a person, identify him completely by title, position, occupation, etc. List these on the outline form.

Outline your speech: Prepare a 75-150 word complete sentence outline. Designate the exact number of words in your outline. Use the form at the end of this chapter.

PURPOSE OF THE SPEECH TO INFORM

No one knows how many speeches are given each year. Neither does anyone know exactly what kinds of speeches are presented. We do know, however, that of the millions and millions of talks, many of them are made specifically to inform people - to tell them something they will find beneficial to include in their knowledge. While no one can foretell accurately what kind of speeches you may be called upon to present in the future, it is a safe bet that you will speak many times to inform people. Because so many speeches are informative in nature, you are offered here the opportunity to become acquainted with the informative speech.

EXPLANATION OF THE SPEECH TO INFORM

The speech to inform people provides them a clear understanding of the speaker's ideas upon a subject. It also arouses interest in the subject because the material which is presented is relevant to the lives of those who hear it. It is incumbent upon the speaker to provide this relevant material with its accompanying interest if he is to inform intelligently. To accomplish the ends of informative speaking, one is obliged to select a subject of interest to himself and his listeners. This can be done by an apt analysis of the audience - in this case your classmates. You, as the speaker, are charged further with the serious responsibility of knowing what you are talking about, knowing more about it, in fact, than anyone in your audience does. For this reason, your talk demands

that you study not one but several (no less than two) sources of information. Under no consideration should you be satisfied to glance hurriedly through an article in a popular magazine, jot down a few notes, toss the periodical aside, and rush off to a "coffee drink," content with the world and a "sloppy" job of acquiring knowledge. This kind of preparation does not even begin to prepare you to give an informative discourse.

Occasions for the informative speech are many. They occur on the lecture platform, in the pulpit, in the classroom, at business meetings; in fact wherever you find reports being made, instructions given, or other ideas being presented by means of lectures and discussions. The point to bear in mind is that any time information is disseminated, an occasion for an informative speech arises.

SUGGESTED TOPICS FOR SPEECHES TO INFORM

1. Marriage customs.
2. Peculiar customs.
3. Jet propulsion
4. Human organ transplant.
5. Sports (how to play a certain game).
6. Mining safety.
7. Living in outer space.
8. Swimming.
9. Rescuing a drowning person.
10. Musical instruments.
11. Pollution.

12. How a bill becomes a law.
13. New inventions.
14. Precious stones.
15. History of anything.
16. How to get along with people.
17. The environment.
18. How to make something.
19. Card tricks.
20. Speaker's choice.

HOW TO CHOOSE A TOPIC

Study the above list carefully. Select something that interests you and that is appropriate to the audience you are to address. Be sure that you can find information about the topic you select. Do not put off choosing a topic.

HOW TO PREPARE A SPEECH TO INFORM

To prepare for this speech, or any speech, you must know and follow certain fundamentals of preparation. These consist of the following steps: (1) choose your subject; (2) analyze the occasion; (3) diagnose the audience; (4) gather your material; (5) organize and support your main points with evidence; (6) word your speech by writing it out in full, in part, or by rehearsing it from an outline; (7) practice aloud.

If you wish to organize your thoughts logically, you should decide early what objective you hope to attain and what reaction you want from this particular audience. Next, if you wish, you may divide your discourse into three conventional parts: an introduction, the body, and the conclusion. To be more effective, some speakers break down their talks by using various combinations of the following steps: (1) gain attention; (2) make your audience want to hear your ideas; (3) present your ideas; (4) tell why this material is important to your listeners and how it affects them; (5) ask your audience to study the topic further or to take some action on it. The time required for any one division of a speech varies greatly; however, more time is given to the presentation of ideas than any other division of the speech.

The wording of your talk may be accomplished either by writing it out in full from the outline, or by considerable practice. In any event, rehearse before a mirror as many times as necessary (usually about four) to fix the proper steps and the order of their content, along with desirable stage appearance and bodily action. Do not memorize the words.

The use of notes is somewhat a matter of opinion. If you are adequately prepared, you will not need notes. You will talk extemporaneously, which is the most commanding method known. If you must refer to notes, they should be either short sentences, phrases, or single words which have a particular meaning to you. Whatever notes you hold in your hands should be brief, concise, meaningful, and entirely familiar. A glance at your notes should be sufficient for you to gather their full meaning so that you may speak fluently yet logically. The notes should be on a piece of paper the size of a postal card or larger.

One other point is important. The information you present must be accurate. For accuracy of information, acceptable sources of information written by reliable and competent authorities must be consulted. Your audience should know where you get your material. What is more, you are the person to identify these sources and authorities. You are expected to go even further in this matter of giving information: you are expected to offer your conclusions and views and evaluations of your information. All this entails the neat assimilation of all you have pulled together – that is, your entire speech.

A few hints might well be offered at this point. First, have only two or three main points to your speech. Buttress these well with examples, illustrations, analogies, and facts. Second, do not be afraid to inject humor and anecdotes into your thought to add interest. Be sure these additions are suited to your subject and audience. Third, be sure your speech moves ahead. Do not allow the speech to drag or become stalemated. And, last, bend plenty of effort toward an interesting introduction and an equally effective conclusion.

OUTLINE YOUR SPEECH

Outlining your speech is necessary if you wish to secure organization, logical order of material, coherence, and unity. Without these rhetorical qualities, your thoughts will be a jumbled mass of words with little direction or definite goal. An outline is to the speaker what a map is to a person taking a trip; it shows him where he is going and how to get there.

After neatly constructing a 75-150 word sentence outline, be prepared to hand the outline to your instructor when you rise to speak. He will undoubtedly wish to follow this while listening to your speech. He may write suggestions on it for your improvement. Remember that this outline is not to be used while you are speaking. State two or three sources of information.

Read at least two references on outlining. Ask your instructor for assistance.

HOW TO PRESENT A SPEECH TO INFORM
Use an easy, energetic presentation. Be enthusiastic and original in what you have to say. Use your hands to demonstrate how to do things. Draw pictures, exhibit charts, in fact, do whatever is necessary to make your ideas understood and interesting. Take stage properly, utilize expressive bodily action, maintain direct eye contact, observe time limits, and stop when your speech is finished. Your conclusion should be as strong and appropriate and as well prepared as your beginning remarks.

IMPROVE YOUR VOCABULARY

Empennage – (ĕm'-pĕ-nāj') n. The tail assembly of an airplane, dirigible, or flying machine. Know this word. It is important to the aircraft industry and the air age. Example: The empennage was damaged when the plane landed.

Pretty – This word is used so often it has lost much of its charm. You can improve your speech by employing synonyms in its place. Here are a few suggestions whose use depends on what you are talking about: music, for example, might be plaintive, moving, thunderous, bewitching, captivating, stirring, exquisite, magnificent, haunting, disturbing, rollicking, tantalizing. A girl may be graceful, buxom, lovely, comely, dainty, blooming. A house can be artistic, elegant, original, attractive. A dress may be becoming, rich, etc., a rug handsome or a flower delicate. It is a good idea not to label everything "pretty" indiscriminately.

BIBLIOGRAPHY FOR THE SPEECH TO INFORM

Andrews, James R., Essentials of Public Communication, Wiley, 1979.
Bennett, Millard and Corrigan, J. D., Successful Communication and Effective Speaking, Prentice-Hall, 1976.
Cohen, Edwin, Speaking the Speech, Holt, Rinehart & Winston, 1980.

★ ★ ★ ★ ★

INFORMATIVE SPEECH

By Nancy Isaacson

BEHIND THE GLAMOUR

The annual Miss America beauty pageant is truly one of the most cherished and publicized institutions in modern society. Viewers are well acquainted with the glamour of the pageant — silky evening gowns, dazzling smiles, and of course, the jubilant tears. Yet the audience is not aware of the extremely complicated problems and processes involved in the selection of Miss America.

Perhaps the greatest problem of the Miss America contest is that the audience and the judges view the contestant in entirely different lights. One of the 1975 judges, Frank DeFord, suggests a reason for this obvious problem. The audience watching the Miss America pageant falls in love with a girl seen on a huge stage or television. The judges, however, are able to interview each girl individually. They are then able to share a more personal relationship with each girl. DeFord stresses the fact that this type of problem exists each year. However, he cites one unfortunate incident in which the disagreement between the audience and the judges was quite evident. In 1973, when Rebecca King was chosen as the new Miss America, the audience immediately voiced its disapproval. Catcalls were heard throughout Convention Hall.

In order for the audience to better understand the choice of the panel of judges, it is necessary to explore the areas of judging. The pageant contestants are judged in three basic categories: 1) a lively, intelligent mind, 2) the body as displayed in a bathing suit, and 3) the talent presentation.

Of these three categories, the quest for a lively, intelligent mind is perhaps the greatest challenge. DeFord cites one example which vividly illustrates the need for such a mind. Several weeks after her election, Tawny Godin, Miss America of 1976, was cornered at a press conference by a tough TV news reporter who snapped: "A lot of people think you're just a piece of meat. What do you say to that?" Tawny immediately responded: "I don't think you'd be talking to me if you thought I were just a piece of meat." This response overwhelmed the reporter who later returned to apologize.

Although each contestant is graded in the bathing suit competition, it is interesting to note that Miss America never publicly appears in a swimsuit after she is crowned. DeFord acknowledges the notion that the women judges look at specific parts of the body, while the men observe the entire body. The women are supposed to be catty, while the men are to be desirous.

DeFord describes the talent competition as the least subjective exercise and a diversion intended to distract attention from the real issue. While the girl's personality and looks are crucial to the role of Miss America, it is talent which is awarded double points, simply because the Pageant wants to have a good show.

When the next "Miss America" is held, the viewers will certainly be aware of the obvious trademarks of the pageant — the tears, silky gowns, dazzling smiles. It is also hoped that the viewers will be able to understand the processes involved in the selection of Miss America.

SPEECH OUTLINE

Construct a neat, complete sentence outline on this sheet, tear it out, and hand it to your instructor when you rise to speak. He may wish to write criticisms of the outline and speech in the margins.

Type of speech:_____   Name: _____

Number of words in outline: _____   Date: _____

Purpose of this speech: (What do you want your audience to learn, to think, to believe, to feel, or do because of this speech?) _____

_____

TITLE:

INTRODUCTION:

BODY:

CONCLUSION:

Instructor's comments may concern choice of topic, development of ideas, organization, language use, personal appearance, posture, physical activity, sources, and improvement.

(Write sources of information on back of sheet)

SOURCES FROM LITERATURE

Fill out source requirements completely.
Write "none listed" if an author's name or copyright date is not listed.

1. Author's name _____

   Title of book or magazine used _____

   Title of article in above book or magazine _____

   Chapter and/or pages read _____

   Date of above publication _____

2. Author's name _____

   Title of book or magazine used _____

   Title of article in above book or magazine _____

   Chapter and/or pages read _____

   Date of above publication _____

3. Author's name _____

   Title of book or magazine used _____

   Title of article in above book or magazine _____

   Chapter and/or pages read _____

   Date of above publication _____

INTERVIEW SOURCES

1. Person interviewed _____ Date of interview _____

   His position, occupation, and location _____

   Why is he a reliable source? Be specific _____

   _____

2. Person interviewed _____ Date of interview _____

   His position, occupation, and location _____

   Why is he a reliable source? Be specific _____

   _____

PERSONAL EXPERIENCE OF SPEAKER

1. Tell (1) when, (2) where, and (3) conditions under which you became an authority on subject matter in

   your speech _____

   _____

   _____

   _____

Chapter 9

THE SPEECH TO STIMULATE OR AROUSE

Question: *Should a speech be long or short?*

Answer: *Speeches today seem to be growing shorter. Leave an audience wanting more rather than having had too much.*

This speech is due:
Time limits: 4–5 minutes.
Speaking notes: 10-word maximum limit. (Try speaking without them.)
Sources of information: Two are required, preferably three. For each source give the specific magazine or book it was taken from, title of the article, author's full name, date of publication, and the chapter or pages telling where the material was found. If a source is a person, identify him completely by title, position, occupation, etc. List these on the outline form.
Outline your speech: Prepare a 75-150 word complete sentence outline. Designate the exact number of words in your outline. Use the form at the end of this chapter.

PURPOSE OF THE SPEECH TO STIMULATE OR AROUSE

It is an accepted truth that people need to be stimulated or aroused if they are to be concerned about a proposition or problem that is laid before them. Often a speaker appeals to his audience to do something, to change their minds, to give consideration to an idea, but he does not stir them sufficiently to make them willing to be more than mildly interested. As a speaker it is to your advantage to learn the methods and approaches that cause audiences to be stimulated by speech. This assignment will provide an experience for the speech to arouse or stimulate so that you will be fully aware of the importance of this type of speech.

EXPLANATION OF THE SPEECH TO STIMULATE OR AROUSE

The speech to stimulate an audience is one that does just that - it stimulates. It makes people want to do something, perhaps generalized, to correct a problem, although a specific action may not be in mind. If its purpose is fulfilled, it touches the emotions and influences the intellect of the audience sufficiently that they feel impelled to adopt new attitudes and/or take action suggested by the speaker. The basic features of this speech are these: use of vivid language, obvious sincerity and enthusiasm on the part of the speaker, and appeals to basic drives that all persons possess. Much of the stimulation is achieved by utilizing

catchy slogans, concreteness, specific examples, illustrations, and facts. Contrast is stressed by playing the big against the little, the bad against the good, the money that can be earned against that which will not be earned, the sick against the well.

Best known occasions for the speech to stimulate are anniversary memorials, dedications, commencement exercises, religious gatherings, conventions, rallies, pep meetings, sales promotions, and between-halves situations in which a coach arouses his men to a high pitch of fury accompanied by a will to win.

The speech demands that the speaker himself be aroused and vigorous. It calls for enthusiasm, energy, force, power, and spirit - the quantity and quality depending upon the response sought from the audience. But most of all it requires that the speaker be sincere.

SUGGESTED TOPICS FOR A SPEECH TO STIMULATE OR AROUSE

Keep in mind that these topics are only suggested. They are intended to give you a few ideas so that you may make a selection from this group, or develop a topic of your own.

1. School anniversary
2. Memorial to a classmate
3. Dedication of a new athletic field, clubhouse, etc.

4. Any kind of commencement
5. Patriotic meeting
6. Religious gathering
7. Convention of any kind
8. Promotional meeting – sales, political sports
9. Rally of any kind
10. Any kind of campaign – Community Chest, Red Cross, Scouting, Salvation Army, election, etc.
11. Drugs – silent enemies
12. Political meeting
13. Rest homes
14. To gain a new school building or student union
15. Morals today
16. To gain support for the team
17. Inflation – our nation's enemy
18. To secure a better social program for the school
19. To end terrorism
20. To decrease crime
21. To end political corruption
22. A call for peace
23. Speaker's choice

HOW TO CHOOSE A TOPIC

Regardless of what kind of speech you present, it should always possess <u>sincerity</u>. Of all the many kinds of speeches there is none that demands sincerity from the speaker more than the speech that is intended to stimulate or arouse. Therefore, in choosing a topic from the above list or in formulating your own topic, place sincerity foremost in your thinking. Do not try to find a subject that is suitable for the national congress or for presentation over a national radio network. Find a discussion suitable for your audience, in this case, your classmates. It does not have to be something big, something startling or overwhelming. The occasion does not call for such a speech. It does call for a speech appropriate to your situation, your audience, one within the scope of your experiences, and, above all, one in which you are sincere.

HOW TO PREPARE A SPEECH TO STIMULATE OR AROUSE

Basically, you will prepare this speech according to the steps followed in preparing any speech. It is essential that you give more than passing attention to your purpose to stimulate or arouse. This purpose will be behind every statement you utter. It will be superimposed over your entire construction, hence it will receive first consideration.

Having made yourself keenly aware of your purpose, you will next set about achieving this purpose. Naturally, your attention turns to organization. We will assume that you have gathered your materials and are ready to arrange them under the various divisions of your organization. First, as always, you will think of your introduction. It may be that you will construct it or alter it after certain other parts of your speech are completed, but certainly you will give it close attention before you are ready to state that your speech is prepared. In arranging and organizing the main body of your remarks, the language will undergo no little scrutiny. Vivid phraseology, word pictures, graphic illustrations, all aptly told must be presented with words that contain acute meanings and definite associations in the minds of the listeners. You may also offer slogans and catchy phrases to make your ideas stick and remain with your hearers. You will also be concrete and specific by naming certain persons and definite places that the speech calls for. You will avoid the abstract and intangible when giving examples, illustrations, and facts. This does not mean that you are to employ needless detail, but it does mean that your ideas must be aimed to hit their mark and make a strong impact. If you do not do this, it will be like trying to drive a spike with a tack hammer. As was stated in the paragraph entitled "Explanation of the Speech to Stimulate or Arouse," you will use contrast as a means of clarifying your thoughts and pointing up their significance. And last, you will stimulate your audience because throughout your entire speech you will have appealed to the basic drives in people: security from enemies, saving or making money, keeping their homes intact, gaining recognition, enjoying social prominence, having a cleaner city or town, knowing new experiences . . . You will have touched your listeners' pride, their pocketbooks and bank accounts, their sympathies, their family and home affections – yes, even their fighting spirit. Once you have stimulated your audience, thoroughly aroused them, if the speech demands it, be sure to tell them what to do or what action to take, whether it be to think or perform. If you do not do this you will have generated power but failed to use it.

As usual, there is no better source of materials for a speech than the library. The librarian will gladly assist you in locating materials. Your instructor will advise you also in this matter. There may be persons on the faculty or friends you know who have special knowledge that you can use. Do not overlook interviews with them.

The last step in preparing this speech will be rehearsal. Be sure you rehearse enough that you know from memory the sequence of ideas, not words, that you plan to present. Practice before a mirror and/or friends until you feel competent to stand before an audience.

HOW TO PRESENT A SPEECH TO STIMULATE OR AROUSE

A forceful, dynamic, and energetic presentation should be used unless you are speaking on a solemn occasion involving reverence, devotion or deep feeling. In such cases your voice and manner should be an animated and sincere projection of your ideas, accompanied by appropriate bodily action and gestures. On other occasions, indications should show that you are alive with your subject, full of it, and eager for others to share it. Above all, you must be sincere and earnest. Remember that your audience will reflect your activity and eloquence. They will be just as lively or solemn as you stimulate them to be.

The use of appropriate diagrams, charts, and demonstrations can add much to your speech.

IMPROVE YOUR VOCABULARY

Erratic - (ĕ-răt'ĭk) a. Having no definite course, wandering, departing from an accepted course in opinion or conduct, queer, strange or odd. Example: Are you erratic when you try to be different? Use this word several times daily during the next week. Make it yours.

Job - This word does too much overtime work. As a result it is less potent and meaningful than it should be. Try using one of the following synonyms in place of job. Here they are: task, duty, business, vocation, calling, undertaking, responsibility, service, profession, craft, trade, errand, position, chore, etc.

BIBLIOGRAPHY FOR SPEECH TO STIMULATE OR AROUSE

Colburn, William and Weinberg, Sanford, An Orientation to Listening and Audience, Science Research Associates, 1980.
De Vito, Joseph, Elements of Public Speaking, Harper & Row, 1980.
Ehninger, Douglas and Others, Principles of Speech Communication, Scott Foresman, 8th ed., 1979.
Fletcher, Leon, How to Design and Deliver a Speech, Harper & Row, 1979.

★   ★   ★   ★   ★

SPEECH TO STIMULATE OR AROUSE

By LeAnne Herbert

THE POPULATION BOMB

"While you are reading these words, four people will have died from starvation. Most of them children." — Dr. Paul R. Ehrlich

There was an estimated human population in 6000 B.C. of about five million people, taking about one million years to get there from two and one-half million. The population did not reach 500 million until almost 8,000 years later - about 1650 A.D. This means it doubled roughly once every 1,000 years. It reached one billion people around 1850, doubling in some 200 years. It took only 80 years for the next doubling as the population reached two billion around 1930. We have almost reached the third big doubling of four billion people! The doubling time at present seems to be about thirty-seven years.

Let's say it continues at this rate for about 900 years. There would be <u>60 million billion</u> people on the face of the earth. This is about 100 persons for each square yard of the Earth's surface - land and sea!

A British physicist, J. H. Fremlin, guessed that such a multitude might be housed in a continuous 2,000 story building covering our entire planet. This is just enough space for the people to move around a little bit and to sleep.

At least half the world's people are undernourished. They have either too little food or are malnourished. If our population continues at the rate it is going, the United States will need all the food it produces to feed people here. What will people in India do? Each year underdeveloped countries get farther and farther behind in their food production. A minimum of three and one-half million will starve to death this year - mostly children. But this is a mere handful compared to the numbers who will be starving in a decade or so. The key to the whole situation is held by the United States. We are the most influential superpower; we are the richest nation in the world. We must set an example. The birth rate must be brought into balance with the death rate or mankind will breed itself into oblivion.

Some say science will come up with a solution - that they will find a way for us to occupy other planets. If we skip for a moment the problem of their being uninhabited or the problem of moving billions of people at the present rate we are now able, it would take only 50 years to populate Venus, Mercury, and Mars to the same population density as Earth.

The first chapter of Genesis tells man and women to replenish Earth and subdue it, but of more importance in the second chapter, it states that man should dress and keep the land. This means that man must be concerned with what happens to the land, its resources and human beings who inhabit it.

What can we do? Set an example. Conception of a child should be the result of a positive choice before God. A choice made by the parents together considering what they can offer that child and if they truly want the child. We should plan our families. We can organize groups to let people know about planned parenthood, but most of all we should let people in underdeveloped countries know about planned parenthood. The classes in schools are getting smaller, but we cannot let our guards down now. Birth control concerning overpopulation was seriously introduced in the early 1970's and it has helped. We must continue with what we have started. We must plan our families and make sure we want the child we are talking about having - <u>every</u> child!

SPEECH OUTLINE

Construct a neat, complete sentence outline on this sheet, tear it out, and hand it to your instructor when you rise to speak. He may wish to write criticisms of the outline and speech in the margins.

Type of speech:_____ Name: _____

Number of words in outline: _____ Date: _____

Purpose of this speech: (What do you want your audience to learn, to think, to believe, to feel, or do because of this speech?) _____

_____

TITLE:

INTRODUCTION:

BODY:

CONCLUSION:

Instructor's comments may concern choice of topic, development of ideas, organization, language use, personal appearance, posture, physical activity, sources, and improvement.

(Write sources of information on back of sheet)

- 37 -

SOURCES FROM LITERATURE

Fill out source requirements completely.
Write "none listed" if an author's name or copyright date is not listed.

1. Author's name _____

    Title of book or magazine used _____

    Title of article in above book or magazine _____

    Chapter and/or pages read _____

    Date of above publication _____

2. Author's name _____

    Title of book or magazine used _____

    Title of article in above book or magazine _____

    Chapter and/or pages read _____

    Date of above publication _____

3. Author's name _____

    Title of book or magazine used _____

    Title of article in above book or magazine _____

    Chapter and/or pages read _____

    Date of above publication _____

INTERVIEW SOURCES

1. Person interviewed _____ Date of interview _____

    His position, occupation, and location _____

    Why is he a reliable source? Be specific _____

    _____

2. Person interviewed _____ Date of interview _____

    His position, occupation, and location _____

    Why is he a reliable source? Be specific _____

    _____

PERSONAL EXPERIENCE OF SPEAKER

1. Tell (1) when, (2) where, and (3) conditions under which you became an authority on subject matter in

    your speech _____

    _____

    _____

Chapter 10

TO CONVINCE AN AUDIENCE

Question: *Should a speaker talk down to his audience?*

Answer: *Never. Use understandable, nontechnical language. Audiences are intelligent.*

This speech is due:

Time limits: 5-6 minutes.

Speaking notes: Try not to use any. <u>Know your material.</u>

Sources of information: Two are required, preferably three. For each source give the specific magazine or book it was taken from, title of the article, author's full name, date of publication, and the chapter or pages telling where the material was found. If a source is a person, identify him completely by title, position, occupation, etc. List these on the outline form.

Outline your speech: Prepare a 75-150 word complete sentence outline. Designate the exact number of words in your outline. Use the form at the end of this chapter.

PURPOSE OF THE SPEECH TO CONVINCE AN AUDIENCE

A speech to convince is used so widely that we are probably unaware of its frequency. Actually, very few persons do what someone else suggests unless they are convinced. The most common method used in convincing someone is a system of talking. The pattern of ideas employed is not always known to the person who uses it but, generally, the speaker uses certain techniques to gain conviction.

It is probable that you will be asked to present ideas and arguments at some future date. When this time arrives, you will find it a much easier task if you have had previous experience. This speech assignment will offer you excellent practice in the art of convincing an audience.

EXPLANATION OF THE SPEECH TO CONVINCE

The speech to convince is one which causes your audience to accept willingly your proposal through logic, evidence, and emotion. You must present sufficient logic and evidence to swing the audience to your belief on a debatable proposition. This usually means that you will also ask them to take the action which you suggest. It is usually wise and necessary to appeal to emotions that accompany attitudes and decisions which you desire from your audience. These basic emotions may be reached by certain basic appeals; such as, their wealth, love of country, self-preservation, desire for recognition, sex, desire for new adven-

ture, loyalty, political beliefs, religion, and the like. This necessitates a thorough analysis of your audience so that you may base your appeal on their beliefs and attitudes. It also means that you must present your logic and evidence in such a way that it directs their thinking through channels they readily follow.

The speech to convince is utilized on many kinds of occasions. At most popular gatherings, such as: political meetings, lecture forums, charity drives, community drives, church services, and other civic gatherings, an effort is made to convince. Business meetings involve conviction at any time differences of opinion prevail. Decisions are reached by convincing someone. Any time that a debate is in progress, even though it be a formal argument between two rival schools, within a legislative body, among three farmers, or in court proceedings – the statements of the speakers involve persuasion through logic, evidence, and emotion. (Could it be that the last time you asked your father for the car you gave a most convincing argument containing much logic, considerable evidence, and some emotion by stating why you should have it?)

SUGGESTED TOPICS FOR SPEECHES TO CONVINCE

1. Eighteen years should be the national minimum age limit for marriage.
2. Every mentally able person should be compelled legally to attend school until he is seventeen years old.

3. All state colleges and universities should be tuition free.
4. No student should be permitted to play a roll in more than two public three-act plays while he is in high school.
5. Rest homes should be government subsidized.
6. States should provide free textbooks to private and parochial schools.
7. All seniors with a four-year B average should be excused from final examinations.
8. School offices should be filled half with girls and half with boys (by school law).
9. Strikes should be prohibited by law.
10. Compulsory arbitration of all labor disputes should be established by law.
11. No president should be permitted to serve more than one term.
12. Sex education should or should not be taught in public schools.
13. Liquor should be rationed nationally.
14. Weather should not be modified by man.
15. Persons convicted of driving a car while under the influence of drugs or intoxicating beverages should pay a fine of at least one thousand dollars.
16. Population should be controlled by law.
17. Riding bicycles on sidewalks should be punishable by fine and/or jail sentence.
18. All towns, cities, should have dog laws.
19. All high schools and colleges should have courses pertaining to marriage.
20. Speaker's choice of a controversial subject.

HOW TO CHOOSE A TOPIC

Study the suggestions; then make your choice on the basis of suitability to you, your audience, and the occasion. Be sure you can secure at least two sources of information on your topic. Do not delay your choice of a topic. The sooner you make up your mind the better are your chances for preparing an excellent speech.

If you do not select one of the suggested topics, be extremely careful in the choice of a topic of your own. The points to watch are the way you word your topic and what you propose to convince your audience of. In wording your topic be sure you propose to your audience that they should adopt a certain debatable proposition. For example, if you decide to convince your listeners that "All school books should be free," notice the word "should." It implies "ought to be." So your purpose is to persuade your audience to believe this is a sound

idea and it will be beneficial if carried out. You are not asking them to carry it out by standing behind a book counter and handing out free textbooks.

A sales talk is not a speech to convince because your purpose is to make your customer reach down in his pocket, pull out his money, and give it to you. This requires him to do something. Naturally a certain amount of convincing will precede your request for his money, but your actual purpose is to cause him to hand you one hundred dollars. You do not care whether he changes his mind or not, just so you get his money. We may conclude then that a speech to convince is not a sales talk, is not primarily to stimulate or arouse, but it is one in which your purpose is to change a person's mind about something on which there is definite disagreement.

Your topic must be a proposition which is specific and which offers a debatable solution to a controversial problem. It is not adequate to propose the subject "We should all drive more carefully." We agree on this already. To talk on such a broad topic would be merely to stimulate or arouse us. (See the chapter covering the speech to stimulate or arouse.) If you wish to do something to make us more careful drivers, suggest a definite and debatable solution, such as: "The legislature should pass a law limiting speed on the highways to sixty miles per hour," or "All persons who are convicted of traffic violations should be compelled to attend a driver's school for two weeks." These are proposals about which people disagree. We can readily say yes or no to them. We can debate them, but we cannot debate the subject that "We should all drive more carefully," since we agree on it.

Examine your topic closely to be certain you have a correct topic on which to base your speech to convince. If you are in doubt, consult your instructor.

HOW TO PREPARE A SPEECH TO CONVINCE

In preparing the speech to convince remember that your purpose is to swing people over to your beliefs so that they not only will think what you want them to think but so that they will also do what you tell them to do. This is obviously not an easy task; however, it is not at all impossible. To achieve the "convincing effect," you need to look carefully into the organization of your speech. Briefly, it may be as follows:

1. Present a history of the problem. Discuss the events leading up to the present time that make the topic important. Tell why it is significant that the audience hear the discussion you are about to present. (Do not spend too much time on the history – you have other points to cover.)

2. Discuss the present day effects of the problem. Give examples, illustrations, facts, and views of authorities that clearly demonstrate the situation you are talking about. These are musts if you wish to be convincing.

3. Discuss the causes that brought about the effects you listed in point 2. Here again you must present examples, illustrations, facts, and views of authorities to prove your points. Be sure you show how the causes have and are bringing about the effects you mentioned. For example, if you say your car "upset" (effect) because of a blowout (cause) you must definitely establish this cause rather than permit your audience to believe that the car may have upset because the steering mechanism on the car suddenly broke.

4. List possible solutions to the problem. Discuss briefly the various alternatives that could be followed but show they are not effective enough to solve your problem. Give evidence for your statements; examples, illustrations, authorities' views, facts, and analogies.

5. Give your solution to the problem. Show why your solution is the best answer to the proposition you are discussing. Present your evidence and the reason for believing as you do. This must not be simply your opinions. It must be logical reasoning backed up by evidence.

6. Show how your proposal will benefit your audience. This is the real meat of your entire speech, if you have thoroughly fulfilled each preceding step up to this point. Here is that part of your speech where you must convince. You definitely have to show your listeners how they will benefit from your proposals; for example: How they will make more money, how they will be safer from an enemy, how they will live longer, how they will be happier, how they will get better roads, better schools, lower taxes, cheaper groceries, . . . In other words, your listener must see clearly and vividly that your proposal will help him.

7. What do you want your audience to do? Here is the proof of your effectiveness. You now will tell your hearers what you want them to do. If you have been convincing up to this point, they will probably go along with you; if not, you have "stumbled" somewhere in your speech. That is why it is very necessary that you develop your talk very carefully and completely. You may ask the audience to write to their congressman, to vote for or against a bill, to give money to charity, to attend a rally, to clean up their town, to declare war, to subscribe funds for a new church, . . .

If you do not care to follow the preceding organization of a speech to convince, here is one which accomplishes the same end but is described differently:

1. State your proposition in the introduction.
2. Present a history of the problem which brought up the proposal you are asking for adoption.
3. Show that your proposal is needed. Offer evidence which establishes a need for your proposal. No other proposal (solution) will do.
4. Show that your proposition is practical. Give evidence to prove that it will do what you say it will do. In other words, show that it will work.
5. Show that your proposition is desirable. This means to give evidence showing that what it will do will be beneficial rather than harmful. For example: concerning the desirability of military training people say, "Yes, military conscription will work, but it is undesirable because it will bring on a militaristic control of our government."
6. Conclude your speech with a final statement in support of your proposal.

Note: If you are opposed to a certain proposal, you may establish your point of view by offering arguments which show any one of the following to be true:

1. The proposition is not needed. (Give evidence.)
2. The proposition is not practical. (Give evidence.)
3. The proposition is not desirable. (Give evidence.)

Of course, if you can establish all three of these points, you will be more convincing than if you prove only one.

You should be warned that you will face untold difficulty from your audience if you fail to have the body of your speech properly organized and all your points supported by evidence. The best guarantee of success is careful preparation. In addition to a well-organized speech with its points supported by evidence, you must have a well-constructed introduction and a powerful conclusion. Besides these considerations in relation to the materials of the speech itself, your oral practice will determine whether or not you are actually prepared to present a convincing speech. Even though you possess volumes of evidence, clear-cut organization, and vivid language, you must deliver the speech confidently and well, without excessive use of notes, if anyone is to be very convinced that you yourself are convinced of your own proposal.

Materials for preparing your subject can be secured from your library. Encyclopedias, reader's guides, magazine and newspaper guides – all offer excellent sources. Check with your instructor and librarian for assistance.

HOW TO PRESENT A SPEECH TO CONVINCE

In general a frank, enthusiastic, and energetic presentation is desirable. A reasonable amount of emotion should be evident; however, it should not be overdone.

Your bodily action should suit the words you utter and be such an integral part of your overall presentation that no attention is directed toward it. Vigor and intensity should characterize your bodily action. You must show by your actions that you are convinced.

Your voice should reflect a sincere belief in your views, and through inflections and modulations, carry the ring of truth and personal conviction. Sufficient force should be utilized to convey sound and meaning to all who listen.

Naturally, your presentation must vary according to your audience, the occasion, the size of the room, its acoustics, and the type of meeting before which you present your speech. You would not speak to a small group of business men in the same manner that you would address a large political gathering.

If you use notes, restrict them to ten words on a paper at least three by five inches in size. Know them thoroughly. Do not try to hide them. Hold them high enough when looking at them that your head is now bowed. After the conclusion of your talk, remain standing at least two minutes to answer questions from your audience.

IMPROVE YOUR VOCABULARY

Languid – (lăn'gwĭd) a. Drooping from exhaustion, sluggish, tired, apathetic, listless, slow, weary, feeble, heavy, torpid, without energy. Example: A languid speaker is not convincing. Use this word in your everyday speech during the next week. Make it work for you.

Nice – Use a synonym for this adjective. Liven up your vocabulary with new words. Examples are: delightful, delicious, attractive, pleasant, fastidious, discriminating, hypercritical, pleasing, kind, delicate, dainty, alluring, refreshing, etc.

Note: The proper use of these synonyms for nice depends on what you are talking about such as time, place, or thing.

BIBLIOGRAPHY FOR THE SPEECH TO CONVINCE

Friant, Ray J., Jr., Preparing Effective Presentations, Pilot Books, rev. ed., 1979.
Golde, Roger A., What You Say Is What You Get, Dutton, 1979.
Jones, James E., Saying Is Believing: Developing Credential Speeches, Kendall-Hunt, 1979.
Milham, Dick, Charis-Magic in Public Speaking: The Power to Move People, Prentice-Hall, 1980.

SPEECH TO CONVINCE

By Frank L. Lundburg

IN FAVOR OF THE AFFIRMATIVE

There is an opportunity available to most high school students that is taken advantage of by comparatively few. It is sad too, for certainly if more students, particularly seniors planning to go to college, were to have some training in the fundamentals of debate, they would be better prepared for the future. The techniques and knowledge acquired from debating will help the student in almost every field of study; however, unfortunately, many students have some misconceptions about the activity.

When most people think of debate they think of the Senate or of the House of Representatives and of politicians discussing some particular piece of legislation, or perhaps they think of candidates airing their views before election day. What those people fail to realize, however, is that there is much more to debate than that. In reality most of life consists of making decisions and debating and reasoning in one form or another, and certainly, training in the basic concepts of argumentation and logic will help an individual later in life.

Now how does debating train a person to make decisions? The answer is found in looking at the goal of debate as stated by Arthur N. Kruger, Professor of English and Speech at Wilkes College. He tells us that "The paramount goal of academic debate is to train the student in the tools of argumentation, to train him how to construct logical arguments and to detect weaknesses or lapses from logical standards in the arguments of others." "But," you may say, "I don't want to spend my time arguing about some topic of which I know very little." Therein lies the point: debating will teach you not to argue, in the common sense of the word, but rather will teach you to reason, and to draw significant conclusions from that reasoning and in learning to reason, you must do research — to learn all about your topic. And in learning to do research on debate topics you get an added bonus. The abilities and techniques you acquire doing research for the debate topic will help you to gain information in many fields, and more important, to put that information to use in the form of clear concise reports and term papers.

But there is more to be gained from debate than just raw knowledge. Your method of thinking will change. You will learn to understand more about yourself and those around you, and in doing so, will mature. How is this true? First of all, debating teaches tolerance of differing points of view. By studying many sides of a question you are better able, and more likely, to want to see the position of a person whose ideas differ from yours. In presenting your particular side in a debate, too, you learn to think quickly and to have a logical answer for almost any situation. And by presenting your ideas orally in front of people you develop an awareness of your own abilities and limitations, and also an awareness of the abilities and limitations of those people around you. The rewards gained from such experience will only begin to manifest themselves in the classroom. Far more important than all the trophies or certificates is the knowledge that you, as an individual, will, later in life, still be using these abilities, that you will be able to speak and conduct yourself with assurance and confidence, that you will be able to meet new challenges head on and will have an awareness and tolerance of ideas that are new and different.

Debating has paid off for many. A recent publication of the Pi Kappa Delta Speech Honorary lists among its former members men who have indeed made good use of their training in high school and college debate. To name a few: Clinton P. Anderson, Senator from New Mexico and Chairman of the Committee on Interior and Insular Affairs; Chet Huntley, N.B.C. news broadcaster; George H. Mahon, Congressman from Texas and Chairman of the House Committee on Appropriations, one of the most powerful committees in the Congress; William L. Shirer, author of THE RISE AND FALL OF THE THIRD REICH. The list could go on and on. The point is that debate is more than just a static scholastic exercise. It is basic and dynamic.

Like the Biblical man who built his house on the rock, the high school student who acquires proficiency in debate will build a good foundation on which he can learn to communicate with his fellow-man. To debate is to consider and to understand issues and individuals, and if a person understands he will learn to think and to reason. And if a person learns to think and to reason and to impart this knowledge to others it will bring more than a small drop of order to a not so orderly world.

SPEECH OUTLINE

Construct a neat, complete sentence outline on this sheet, tear it out, and hand it to your instructor when you rise to speak. He may wish to write criticisms of the outline and speech in the margins.

Type of speech:_____ Name: _____

Number of words in outline: _____ Date: _____

Purpose of this speech: (What do you want your audience to learn, to think, to believe, to feel, or do because of this speech?) _____

_____

TITLE:

INTRODUCTION:

BODY:

CONCLUSION:

<u>Instructor's comments</u> may concern choice of topic, development of ideas, organization, language use, personal appearance, posture, physical activity, sources, and improvement.

(Write sources of information on back of sheet)

SOURCES FROM LITERATURE

Fill out source requirements completely.
Write "none listed" if an author's name or copyright date is not listed.

1. Author's name _____

   Title of book or magazine used _____

   Title of article in above book or magazine _____

   Chapter and/or pages read _____

   Date of above publication _____

2. Author's name _____

   Title of book or magazine used _____

   Title of article in above book or magazine _____

   Chapter and/or pages read _____

   Date of above publication _____

3. Author's name _____

   Title of book or magazine used _____

   Title of article in above book or magazine _____

   Chapter and/or pages read _____

   Date of above publication _____

INTERVIEW SOURCES

1. Person interviewed _____ Date of interview _____

   His position, occupation, and location _____

   Why is he a reliable source? Be specific _____

   _____

2. Person interviewed _____ Date of interview _____

   His position, occupation, and location _____

   Why is he a reliable source? Be specific _____

   _____

PERSONAL EXPERIENCE OF SPEAKER

1. Tell (1) when, (2) where, and (3) conditions under which you became an authority on subject matter in

   your speech _____

   _____

   _____

   _____

Chapter 11

THE HECKLING SPEECH

Question: *When is it correct to use sarcasm in a speech?*

Answer: *As a rule it is wiser to omit it. Some speeches to entertain employ sarcasm. Be careful.*

This speech is due:

Time limits: 5-6 minutes.

Speaking notes: 10-word maximum limit.

Sources of information: Two are required, preferably three. For each source give the specific magazine or book it was taken from, title of the article, author's full name, date of publication, and the chapter or pages telling where the material was found. If a source is a person, identify him completely by title, position, occupation, etc. List these on the outline form.

Outline your speech: Prepare a 75-150 word complete sentence outline. Designate the exact number of words in your outline. Use the form at the end of this chapter.

PURPOSE OF THE HECKLING SPEECH

A speaker never knows when he will be heckled by persons in his audience. Sometimes heckling occurs when it is least expected. At other times it does not develop when the occasion is ripe for it. But when heckling does come, a speaker should be ready to meet it whether it be mild or boisterous. This experience will provide practice in speaking while under the pressure of heckling from your audience. It should be valuable training for you.

Another reason why this assignment is given is that a student speaker often becomes aroused when under fire from his audience. He quite frequently discovers that he throws off his habitually meek speaking personality and suddenly faces his tormentors with a great surge of confidence and power – something he always possessed but did not use. This is a good feeling and inspires confidence in a speaker. However, because of the positive effect on him the student should not think that he must be stimulated always by questions and heckling in order to make a strong speech. This experience is intended primarily to make the student aware of his latent powers of expression so that he will use them in forthcoming speeches.

EXPLANATION OF A HECKLING SPEECH

The heckling speech is one that a speaker delivers while being subjected to heckling from his audience. Usually it supports or opposes a definite proposition. Normally, the speaker's purpose is to convince. A speech could inform or stimulate, but in either of these types of speeches, heckling is likely to be slight. The speaker selects one side of a contention which he will support and then does his best to justify his views. He presents argument and evidence that strengthen his stand. All the while he is doing this, the audience is free to heckle him in any way it sees fit. His problem is to control the volatile attention of his somewhat disturbing listeners, and at the same time successfully propound his ideas. It is necessary that the speaker possess positive self-control, retain his sense of humor, be fully prepared, and understand how to handle hecklers.

This type of speech is not encountered on any specific occasion. It arises somewhat unexpectedly. A speaker should be ready for it at any time.

SUGGESTED TOPICS FOR A HECKLING SPEECH

Note: Remember you are to take a side on one of these subjects, and that you are to uphold that side of the argument. You will have to work out the actual statement of your proposition.

1. Compulsory military training should or should not be established in the United States.
2. Third or fourth terms for governors should be prohibited by law.

3. National marriage laws with a minimum age limit, physical examination, and waiting period after applying for a license should be established by Congress.
4. National prohibition should be established by law.
5. National gambling should be legalized by law.
6. School dances should be free.
7. Girls should help pay the expenses of a date - they are liberated.
8. A woman should be elected President of the United States.
9. War should be declared only by a majority of the people.
10. The atomic bomb should be outlawed.
11. Hazing should be abolished on all college campuses.
12. There should be no clothing restrictions in public eating houses.
13. Married women should be prohibited from gainful employment.
14. The student newspaper should have no faculty control.
15. The student Council should try all discipline cases.
16. Athletes should receive extra help from the school.
17. Students should be free to choose their own subjects.
18. Car tags should be free.
19. Picketing should be prohibited.
20. Speaker's choice of a proposition.

HOW TO CHOOSE A SUBJECT FOR A HECKLING SPEECH

When studying the above list of propositions, visualize yourself as being for or against one of the suggested topics. For this reason, select a subject upon which you hold a definite opinion and one which will also require you to secure additional information. Make your selection without delay so that you may give your subject adequate preparation.

HOW TO PREPARE FOR A HECKLING SPEECH

The purpose of the heckling speech is to convince your audience. At least we shall consider that your purpose for this particular occasion. Because you know now that you will be heckled, your secondary purpose will be to control your audience and put your ideas across.

The organization of this speech should be modeled after that of any Speech to Convince.

Read the chapter bearing this heading for information on organization. Besides having your sequence of ideas well in mind, it will be wise for you to know this sequence so thoroughly you cannot forget it. Why? Under heckling pressure, loss of memory may be so overwhelming that you may stand blankly before your audience. If they can disturb you to this extent, they will be delighted no end. Such speechlessness need not trouble you if you are prepared for many interruptions. But you must not permit interruptions to cause you to forget the organization of your speech or to depart from it.

Prepare a complete sentence outline as indicated at the heading of this assignment.

HOW TO PRESENT A HECKLING SPEECH
Keep your head.

Your attitude should be one of firmness and good humor. Your firmness should not become officiousness or haughtiness. Your good humor should not permit you to be so sensitive to its presence that you laugh or turn to histrionics every time someone shoots a question at you or puts you on the spot. You should not be insensitive to a situation that demands a witticism or similar response from you. You should demonstrate enough flexibility in meeting your hecklers that you display the basic qualities of poise and self-confidence.

Your audience will be greatly pleased if they can disturb you or cause you to become so confused that you forget your speech or fly off into the wild blue yonder on a tangent, leaving your speech somewhere behind you. And your hecklers will try to accomplish these results. The question is: How can you avoid losing your poise? The answer can be stated in a few words. First, know your speech and know it well. Do not have a memorized talk, but have a memorized sequence of points which comprise your main ideas. Second, refuse to answer irrelevant questions that are nothing more than quips, pop-offs, or teasers. Simply state that such remarks are irrelevant, do not pertain to your speech, and hence cannot be answered. Third, whenever you are in doubt as to what your interrogator wants, ask him to repeat his question. Fourth, if you encounter a persistent heckler, you may sometimes silence him by a quick retort to some of his senseless chatter. For example, a college student was once speaking in defense of a certain race against which a strong prejudice existed. Suddenly one of his auditors yelled out, "Would you want your sister to marry a _____?" The speaker turned with a blazing eye and pointing his finger like a gun at the heckler, he thundered his reply, "I'd a thousand times she married a _____ than a guy like you!" The heckler sank in his seat and did not speak a word during the remainder of the speech. Other hecklers became more cautious; the speaker continued his talk with relatively few interruptions. Afterward, he said that he had been waiting for that question, and that when it came he gave it all he had.

No one will criticize you for staying with your speech. For this reason, you should expect all kinds of interruptions, but not be disturbed by them. If the questions are legitimate, clear them up or tell the group that you will answer a certain question later in your speech when you discuss the point that has just been brought up. Before you end your remarks, draw your thoughts together with a good conclusion.

Throughout your speech, talk clearly, forcefully, and correctly. Be sure that everyone can hear you. While you are speaking, accompany your words with effective bodily actions and gestures. Look and act the way you feel - confident.

Observe these special hints: (1) be firm but flexible, (2) retain a sense of humor but do not interpret everything as something you should handle as if you were a comedian, (3) exhibit no anger and do not be afraid to stand up and face your audience vigorously and forcefully, (4) maintain self-control, (5) take advantage of opportunities offered by events occurring while you speak, (6) stay with your speech by refusing to be "jockied" out of position, and (7) keep your head.

HOW TO HECKLE
Interrupt the speaker at will, while you are either sitting or standing. Project such questions as: How do you know? Who's your authority? Where did you read that? What do you mean? Will you please explain _____? What is your evidence? Members of the audience may argue with the speaker (if he is naive enough to fall into such a trap), talk with each other, turn their backs on him, stand and address the audience, and the like.

These practices should not be overdone; however, the audience is obliged to see that each speaker knows, when he has finished his speech, that he has been through the fire; otherwise his experience will be weakened. Generously applaud each speaker when he concludes.

IMPROVE YOUR VOCABULARY

Chicanery - (shĭ-kān'-ĕr-ĭ) n. Questionable practice, trickery, sophistry, deceit. A person should not resort to chicanery to gain his point.

Anger - Use a synonym for this word. It will add color to your vocabulary. Here are several examples: animosity, displeasure, exasperation, fretfulness, fury, impatience, indignation, ire, passion, peevishness, pettishness, vexation, wrath, resentment, etc.

BIBLIOGRAPHY FOR THE HECKLING SPEECH

Garner, Dwight L., Idea to Delivery: A Handbook of Oral Communication, Wadsworth, 3d ed., 1979.
King, Robert G., Fundamentals of Human Communication, Macmillan, 1979.
Meyers, Gail and Myers, Michele, The Dynamics of Human Communication, McGraw, 1980.

A GREAT SPEECH IN AMERICAN HISTORY
(This is a famous speech to convince)
Lincoln
THE "HOUSE DIVIDED AGAINST ITSELF" SPEECH
(1858)

If we could first know where we are, and whither we are tending, we could better judge what to do, and how to do it. We are now far into the fifth year since a policy was initiated with the avowed object, and confident promise, of putting an end to slavery agitation. Under the operation of that policy, that agitation not only has not ceased, but has constantly augmented. In my opinion, it will not cease until a crisis shall have been reached and passed. "A house divided against itself can not stand." I believe this government can not endure permanently half slave and half free. I do not expect the Union to be dissolved; I do not expect the house to fall; but I do expect that it will cease to be divided. It will become all one thing, or all the other. Either the opponents of slavery will arrest the further spread of it, and place it where the public mind shall rest in the belief that it is in the course of ultimate extinction; or its advocates will push it forward till it shall become alike lawful in all the States, old as well as new, North as well as South. Have we no tendency to the latter condition? Let any one who doubts carefully contemplate that now almost complete legal combinatipn - piece of machinery, so to speak - compounded of the Nebraska doctrine and the Dred Scott decision.

Put this and that together, and we have another nice little niche, which we may, ere long, see filled with another Supreme Court decision, declaring that the Constitution of the United States does not permit a State to exclude slavery from its limits. And this may especially be expected if the doctrine of "care not whether slavery be voted down or voted up," shall gain upon the public mind sufficiently to give promise that such a decision can be maintained when made.

Such a decision is all that slavery now lacks of being alike lawful in all the States. Welcome or unwelcome, such decision is probably coming, and will soon be upon us, unless the power of the present political dynasty shall be met and overthrown. We shall lie down pleasantly dreaming that the people of Missouri are on the verge of making their State free, and we shall awake to the reality, instead, that the Supreme Court has made Illinois a slave State. To meet and overthrow that dynasty is the work before all those who would prevent that consummation. That is what we have to do. How can we best do it?

There are those who denounce us openly to their own friends, and yet whisper to us softly that Senator Douglas is the aptest instrument there is with which to effect that object. They wish us to infer all, from the fact that he now has a little quarrel with the present head of the dynasty; and that he has regularly voted with us on a single point, upon which he and we have never differed. They remind us that he is a great man and that the largest of us are very small ones. Let this be granted. "But a living dog is better than a dead lion." Judge Douglas, if not a dead lion, for this work, is at least a caged and toothless one.

How can he oppose the advance of slavery? He does not care anything about it. His avowed mission is impressing the "public heart" to care nothing about it. A leading Douglas Democratic newspaper thinks Douglas's superior talent will be needed to resist the revival of the African slave-trade. Does Douglas believe an effort to revive that trade is approaching? He has not said so. Does he really think so? But if it is, how can he resist it? For years he has labored to prove it a sacred right of white men to take negro slaves into the new Territories. Can he possibly show that it is less a sacred right to buy them where they can be bought cheapest? And unquestionably they can be bought cheaper in Africa than in Virginia.

He has done all in his power to reduce the whole question of slavery to one of a mere right of property; and as such, how can he oppose the foreign slave-trade? How can he refuse that trade in that "property" shall be "prefectly free," unless he does it as a protection to the home production? And as the home producers will probably ask the protection, he will be wholly without a ground of opposition.

Senator Douglas holds, we know, that a man may rightfully be wiser today than he was yesterday - that he may rightfully change when he finds himself wrong. But can we, for that reason run ahead, and infer that he will make any particular change, of which he himself has given no intimation? Can we safely base our action upon any such vague inference? Now, as ever, I wish not to misrepresent Judge Douglas's position, question his motives, or do aught that can be personally offensive to him. Whenever, if ever, he and we can come together on principle, so that our cause may have assistance from his great ability, I hope to have interposed no adventitious obstacle. But, clearly, he is not now with us - he does not pretend to be, he does not promise ever to be.

Our cause, then, must be entrusted to, and conducted by, its own undoubted friends - those whose hands are free, whose hearts are in the work - who do care for the result. Two years ago the Republicans of the nation mustered over thirteen hundred thousand strong. We did this under the single impulse of resistance to a common danger. With every external circumstance against us, of strange, discordant, and even hostile elements, we gathered from the four winds, and formed and fought the battle through, under the constant hot fire of a disciplined, proud, and pampered enemy. Did we brave all then, to falter now? - now, when that same enemy is wavering, dissevered, and belligerent! The result is not doubtful. We shall not fail - if we stand firm, we shall not fail. Wise counsels may accelerate, or mistakes delay it; but, sooner or later, the victory is sure to come.

Delivered at the Illinois Republican State Convention at Springfield, on June 16, 1858, after he had been chosen the party candidate for the United States Senate, as the successor of Stephen A. Douglas.

SPEECH OUTLINE

Construct a neat, complete sentence outline on this sheet, tear it out, and hand it to your instructor when you rise to speak. He may wish to write criticisms of the outline and speech in the margins.

Type of speech:_____ Name: _____

Number of words in outline: _____ Date: _____

Purpose of this speech: (What do you want your audience to learn, to think, to believe, to feel, or do
because of this speech?) _____

_____

TITLE:

INTRODUCTION:

BODY:

CONCLUSION:

Instructor's comments may concern choice of topic, development of ideas, organization, language use, personal appearance, posture, physical activity, sources, and improvement.

(Write sources of information on back of sheet)

SOURCES FROM LITERATURE

Fill out source requirements completely.
Write "none listed" if an author's name or copyright date is not listed.

1. Author's name _____

   Title of book or magazine used _____

   Title of article in above book or magazine _____

   Chapter and/or pages read _____

   Date of above publication _____

2. Author's name _____

   Title of book or magazine used _____

   Title of article in above book or magazine _____

   Chapter and/or pages read _____

   Date of above publication _____

3. Author's name _____

   Title of book or magazine used _____

   Title of article in above book or magazine _____

   Chapter and/or pages read _____

   Date of above publication _____

INTERVIEW SOURCES

1. Person interviewed _____ Date of interview _____

   His position, occupation, and location _____

   Why is he a reliable source? Be specific _____
   _____

2. Person interviewed _____ Date of interview _____

   His position, occupation, and location _____

   Why is he a reliable source? Be specific _____
   _____

PERSONAL EXPERIENCE OF SPEAKER

1. Tell (1) when, (2) where, and (3) conditions under which you became an authority on subject matter in
   your speech _____
   _____
   _____
   _____

Chapter 12

THE SPEECH TO ENTERTAIN

Question: *Should a person learn to tell good jokes?*

Answer: *Yes. You will enjoy it and so will others.*

This speech is due:
Time limits: 5-6 minutes.
Speaking notes: None.
Sources of information: Two are required, preferably three. For each source give the specific magazine or book it was taken from, title of the article, author's full name, date of publication, and the chapter or pages telling where the material was found. If a source is a person, identify him completely by title, position, occupation, etc. List these on the outline form.
Outline your speech: Prepare a 75-150 word complete sentence outline. Designate the exact number of words in your outline. Use the form at the end of this chapter.

PURPOSE OF THE SPEECH TO ENTERTAIN

Many persons try to be entertaining when giving speeches. Some succeed and some do not. There is a common misconception about the difficulty of presenting a speech to entertain: the idea is current that the speech to entertain is a "breeze," that nothing is diffult about it, and that a series of risque stories meet the requirements for a speech to entertain. This is far from the truth: a humorous speech is one of the most difficult to present effectively. Because of this difficulty and for the reason that you may be called at a future date to deliver a humorous speech, this assignment has been prepared.

EXPLANATION OF THE SPEECH
TO ENTERTAIN

A humorous speech is one which entertains by utilization of humor. It may rely on words, anecdotes, bodily actions, gestures, voice, speech construction, special devices, demonstrations, unusual situations, pantomimes or a combination of any or all these factors.

Its purpose varies both in relation to the amount and type of humorous response the speech is planned to elicit from the audience. Some speeches make listeners laugh gaily and loudly; others produce only chuckles and snickers; and others bring forth only grins and smiles of amusement. It is important for a student to understand that a humorous speech does not need to be uproariously funny to entertain. We might be better understood if we were to call this speech a speech to amuse.

The special feature of a humorous speech is that it does not demand that a speaker do more than catch the attention and interest of an audience and then hold these by developing a trend of thought or an idea. The speaker is not required to make the audience feel that they are closely related to his subject and that they must derive a moral or new philosophy from his remarks. Nor does he have to ask them to take any action. It should be understood at this point, however, that a humorous speech may do more than simply entertain. There is nothing to prevent its being informative, stimulating, or convincing, provided none of these goals becomes the chief aim of the speaker. The chief aim of the speech is to entertain. An idea may, and it is usually advisable that it should, be the main road which the speech travels. The humor is achieved by hitting a few bumps, skidding around a bit, getting stuck in a mud hole, having a flat tire and flirting with the farmer's daughter while you journey down the main highway. Thus, when you arrive at your destination, you have traveled a straight road but you have had a pleasant time doing it.

The thought or ideas presented are the core of the speech around which humor is built. The overall effect is one in which the audience finds a definite trend of thought and philosophy presented delightfully and entertainingly.

Occasions for humorous speeches are found ordinarily at dinners, club meetings, special assemblies, parties, and gatherings at which weighty discussions are inappropriate and out of harmony with the mood of the occasion.

SUGGESTED TOPICS FOR A SPEECH
TO ENTERTAIN
1. How to be serious
2. How to be funny
3. My great embarrassment
4. School life

5. Get rich quick
6. Pockets
7. Styles
8. Learning to fly
9. Hotels
10. Hospitals
11. He played football
12. Never say "no"
13. Shopping
14. Bring up father
15. How to get what you want
16. Gold is where you find it
17. I don't want to be rich
18. Sugar is sweet
19. The horse went away but the tractor came
20. Woman's most powerful weapon
21. Men
22. Children
23. Courting
24. Husbands are men
25. Sweethearts are human
26. A senator's life
27. If I were the teacher
28. After dinner speeches
29. Flattery versus praise
30. I predict
31. I am going to write a column
32. Words don't mean what they say
33. Why I read the comic strips
34. When time goes slowly
35. Where my money goes
36. Grandpa's first car
37. Grandma was a lady
38. Why people laugh
39. Wives are women
40. Speaker's choice

HOW TO CHOOSE A TOPIC FOR A SPEECH TO ENTERTAIN

In selecting a topic for a humorous speech, keep in mind the five necessary considerations that govern the selection of any speech topic, that is, the audience, the occasion, the speaker (you), the speech itself, and the surroundings in which the speech will be given. Your choice of a topic must be keyed to controlling factors. It is important to note that you may have a mixed audience with a widespread interest or taste. You must consider the probable speaking environment. Of course, since you will be the speaker, the subject that you choose must be one which you can present acceptably. The topic should be viewed from the standpoint of the time allowed for preparation, the availability of materials from which to build the speech, your own personality, your position in the community, your ability to present certain kinds of material and ideas, and your type of presentation. You should make your choice of topic with all of these considerations in mind.

One more point is significant. Do not postpone making your choice of subject. Take five minutes or so and choose carefully; be certain that you have the required information about all of the factors in the selection of a topic mentioned in the preceding paragraph. If you do not have the information, get it at once; then make up your mind. The student who leaves his choice of topic until the last minute does not leave much to his chances for giving a successful speech.

HOW TO PREPARE A SPEECH TO ENTERTAIN

As in the preparation of any good speech, in that of a speech to entertain, particular attention must be paid to organization of points, the arrangement of materials, and the rehearsal of the speech. The purpose, to entertain, should be clearly in mind; the purpose is assisted by a thorough understanding of the methods to be used for fulfilling this purpose. This type of speech requires a considerable study of references and some consultation with your instructor. In addition to the factors of good speech preparation previously studied, ample rehearsal is positively necessary. It is difficult to imagine anything more grotesque than a speaker's attempting to present a humorous speech and constantly referring to notes, because of his inadequate preparation of his speech.

The humorous speech should not degenerate into a series of unrelated funny stories, nor should it merely consist of the telling of one story. Exaggerations or episodes used as illustrations must apply to the theme of the speech or in some way assist the speaker in making his point. Only careful preparation and rehearsal will assure one that he is using his illustrations properly.

A few methods sometimes used to achieve humor are the following:

1. Telling a joke on oneself.
2. Telling a joke on someone in the group or some well-known person.
3. Making reference to the speech situation, local, state, or national situation.
4. Making reference to the occasion or other occasions.
5. Associating a speech with past incidents.
6. "Panning" members of the group, local, state, national, or world figures.
7. Exaggeration.
8. Deliberate underestimation.
9. Sudden change of thought.
10. Surprise thoughts.
11. After-thoughts tacked to the end of an otherwise serious statement.
12. Twisting ideas (do not overdo this).
13. Misinterpreting facts or figures (be clever about this).

14. Intentionally making errors (this must be skillfully done).
15. Intentionally placing oneself in a humorous situation.
16. Misquoting someone present or a well-known authority (be discreet).
17. Restating a well-known quotation to give it a humorous twist.
18. Pantomime.
19. Gestures poorly timed or timed too late.
20. Facial grimaces.
21. Using anecdotes.
22. Giving examples that are entertaining or that make an amusing point.
23. Impersonating a character that is used as an illustration (do not make your whole speech an impersonation).
24. Demonstrating or dramatizing a point (do this for purpose of illustrating to achieve humor).
25. Clever wording (concoct new words, apply certain words to new situations or give them new meanings, join two or more words together with hyphens then apply them to your speech).
26. Be quick to adapt your opening remarks to slips of the tongue of the toastmaster or other speakers. Do not overwork this device or it will become tiresome and trite; be appropriate.
27. Persons in public life, international situations, recent happenings in the news ... all offer excellent opportunities for entertainment.

In actually setting up the speech to entertain you will follow the principles laid down for any speech; you will construct a clever and interesting introduction; you will develop your remarks point by point in logical order; you will bolster these points with examples, illustrations, facts, quotations from authorities, analogies, and conclusions, which you will draw from the material you present. Lastly you will have a conclusion to your speech which is appropriate to all you have said. It becomes evident that a speech to entertain simply does what every other speech does, and in addition, – this is important – it utilizes materials that in themselves carry and imply humor. The selection of these humorous materials, their arrangement in the speech, and the words used to present the ideas are what achieve the effect of entertainment.

Now, you ask, "How do I know my speech will be entertaining?" The answer is that you do not.

The only assurance you can get is from your preparation. Frankly this is dependent entirely on your own effort and ability. It is difficult, very difficult, to select, to organize, to word, and to rehearse a speech to entertain, but you must do these preparations, nevertheless. Your own ingenuity and your own intelligence are the only assets you can have in preparing the humorous speech for presentation. Use these inherent personal resources well and you will have little to worry about. As far as this writer knows, there simply is no quick, easy way to prepare an entertaining speech – or any other for that matter. If any student is looking for a short cut, he will be wise to end his search and to apply himself in preparation, for that is what he will have to do in the end anyway; that is, if anything more than a mediocre speech is to be prepared for presentation.

HOW TO PRESENT A SPEECH TO ENTERTAIN

The humorous speech is characterized generally by a lively presentation. The speaker may be whimsical, facetious, gay, jovial, or he may present a mixture of these moods. He should be pleasant, of course. His entire bearing and decorum should reflect visibly the feelings and tenor of his remarks.

The speech should progress with a smooth forward motion. Delays and hesitations should be avoided, excepting those employed for a special effect. If laughter is incited, the speaker should carefully refrain from resuming his talk until he can be heard. Usually, this is at that moment just before all laughter has stopped. The speaker should never laugh at his own jokes or indicate that he knows he is funny. It is necessary, however, that he enjoy his audience and himself, and that this should be obvious.

One of the greatest dangers is that the inexperienced speaker will prolong his anecdotes, his jokes, or his whole speech. This may happen either because he enjoys himself so much that he forgets to keep moving or that he has improperly prepared his remarks. Then, too, nervousness may cause memory lapses and confusion. The principal point is, however, to hit the punch lines when they are hot and then to move on to the next ones. A speech, even an excellent one, is somewhat like ice cream – it is good and tickles the palate pleasantly if you do not eat too much of it at one time.

There is one last word of caution: watch your posture; use appropriate bodily actions and gestures; speak loudly enough to be heard by everyone; articulate well; and use good English.

IMPROVE YOUR VOCABULARY

Nasality – (nā-zal'-ĭ-tĭ) n. The sound a person makes when talking through his nose. Example: The speaker's nasality was quite noticeable.

Smart – This word is often overused. You may add new enjoyment to your speech by using synonyms. Here are several: modish, trim, well-groomed, elegant, chic, fashionable, dashing, trig, etc. Give these synonyms a chance. They will do wonders for your conversation.

BIBLIOGRAPHY FOR THE SPEECH TO ENTERTAIN

Harral, Stewart, When It's Laughter You're After, Univ. of Oklahoma Press, 1969.
Ross, Raymond S., Essentials of Speech Communication, Prentice-Hall, 1979.

★   ★   ★   ★   ★

SPEECH TO ENTERTAIN

By John E. Koch

THE PLIGHT OF THE ONION

Ordinarily, Ladies and Gentlemen, I am a very peaceful individual. It requires an event of great importance to stir my peaceful nature. Lately, such an event has come to pass. I must speak out in defense of my convictions, for silence would prove me a traitor not only to my own generation, but to generations to come. I cannot display indifference when the issue demands enthusiasm.

Just what is this issue that stirs the hearts of men to take arms against that sea of troubles and by opposing, end them? I do not feel that I am unique in being affected by this onslaught on human liberty. You, Ladies and Gentlemen, have also been touched by this debasement of our customs and traditions. Like the dark of nights, this creature has crept upon us, enveloping us in its deadly grasp, extinguishing the lamp of liberty and pinning the arms of the goddess behind her. What is this menace of which I speak that poses such a threat to all that we hold so dear? Is it a green-eyed fire-spouting monster from Mars, or a creature from the moon? No, it is not. It is one of our own kind. It is referred to as a scientist.

It will suffice to mention no names since we must judge them by their works. The intrusion of these people on our liberties has caused many to sound the call to arms; for when we are enveloped by that sea of troubles, we must fight back or swim.

The scene of attack is Idaho State University. There, a group of scientists as they call themselves, have been secretly experimenting, unbelievable as it may seem, to deprive the onion of its cooking odor. In some secret cache are hidden away thousands of odorless onions, the first of a line of odor-free American vegetables.

Picture the onion without its smell. A tired husband home from a weary day's toil would no longer have his appetite quickened by that tangy aroma drifting through the air. Take away the cooking odor of onions and you deprive millions of Americans of a familiar fragrance that signaled the secrets of the coming meal. To remove its odor is to destroy all that is dear to it — its personality. The thought is enough to cause tears to come to one's eyes.

Although this be bad enough, the scientists will not stop here. They will not remain content with having removed the odor from the onion, but with their long tentacles they will reach out farther into the realm of life. What will be their next victim — the smell of cooking cabbage, the grit of spinach, the hot of peppers, and soon the removal of color and taste? Will our diet become a mass of odorless, tasteless, colorless nourishment? It might, if we do not arise and take arms to prevent this calamity. I beg you to rally defenders to the cause of the onion. Go forward to loose the bonds from the hands of liberty, with the slogan, "Keep the odor in the onion; keep the onion out of college."

As Americans, we must demand the onion with its odor, the spinach with its grit, the pepper with its hot. Let us not sit here idly any longer — Arise and carry that plea to all Americans. Keep the scientist out of the kitchen; keep the onion out of college.

SPEECH OUTLINE

Construct a neat, complete sentence outline on this sheet, tear it out, and hand it to your instructor when you rise to speak. He may wish to write criticisms of the outline and speech in the margins.

Type of speech: _____ Name: _____

Number of words in outline: _____ Date: _____

Purpose of this speech: (What do you want your audience to learn, to think, to believe, to feel, or do because of this speech?) _____

_____

TITLE:

INTRODUCTION:

BODY:

CONCLUSION:

Instructor's comments may concern choice of topic, development of ideas, organization, language use, personal appearance, posture, physical activity, sources, and improvement.

(Write sources of information on back of sheet)

SOURCES FROM LITERATURE

Fill out source requirements completely.
Write "none listed" if an author's name or copyright date is not listed.

1. Author's name _____

   Title of book or magazine used _____

   Title of article in above book or magazine _____

   Chapter and/or pages read _____

   Date of above publication _____

2. Author's name _____

   Title of book or magazine used _____

   Title of article in above book or magazine _____

   Chapter and/or pages read _____

   Date of above publication _____

3. Author's name _____

   Title of book or magazine used _____

   Title of article in above book or magazine _____

   Chapter and/or pages read _____

   Date of above publication _____

INTERVIEW SOURCES

1. Person interviewed _____ Date of interview _____

   His position, occupation, and location _____

   Why is he a reliable source? Be specific _____

   _____

2. Person interviewed _____ Date of interview _____

   His position, occupation, and location _____

   Why is he a reliable source? Be specific _____

   _____

PERSONAL EXPERIENCE OF SPEAKER

1. Tell (1) when, (2) where, and (3) conditions under which you became an authority on subject matter in

   your speech _____

   _____

   _____

   _____

Chapter 13

AFTER DINNER SPEAKING

Question: *What is the best type of speech for a beginner?*

Answer: *Generally an informative speech.*
Don't avoid other kinds.

This speech is due:

Time limits: 3 minutes – This time limit is necessary in order that each person may be permitted to speak. Longer speeches may extend the time too much.

Speaking notes: None.

Hint: Although you are not required to prepare an outline or to read source materials, it will be wise to do both for your own benefit.

PURPOSE OF AFTER DINNER SPEAKING

One of the best ways to learn anything is actually to experience it. From the experience of preparing this speech assignment, you will gain first-hand knowledge of after dinner speaking. You will see how the program is arranged, how the order of serving is coordinated with the speeches, and how the toastmaster must carry on and keep events moving. You will acquire much other valuable information concerning after dinner speaking. You will learn it because you will help build the entire program and because you will be a speaker at the dinner.

This experience is proposed so that you may broaden your knowledge of the various types of after dinner speeches and their related activities.

NOTE TO INSTRUCTOR

If it is impossible to carry out the plan which is suggested in the following pages, a first alternative may be worked out in class. This alternative may be one in which students sit in a group that is rectangular in shape to simulate positions around a table at a banquet. Toastmasters should be placed at the head of an imaginary table, with the speakers seated as they would be, had a dinner just been completed. Insofar as possible, an after-dinner-speaking atmosphere and environment should be created.

A second alternative to a real banquet is one in which the students eat a light, inexpensive lunch in a suitable room somewhere in the school building. The food should be served so as to duplicate banquet and after-dinner-speaking conditions insofar as is practicable.

It is the writer's belief that a real after-dinner-speaking situation is the most desirable atmosphere of all for practice of after dinner speaking. Full explanations follow which may be applied to any of the suggested plans for supplying a proper background for this speech experience.

EXPLANATION OF AFTER DINNER SPEAKING

After dinner speaking is giving a speech following a meal at which a group has gathered. The speech may have a serious purpose or it may be designed to give entertainment and pleasure. The type of speech which you present depends on the purpose of your talk. The type of speech is governed also by the occasion, its objective, and the reason for your remarks. After dinner speeches require that the speaker follow closely all the rules of organization previously noted, particularly those for serious talks. Entertainment, as a motive, charges you with the responsibility of altering the organization of the speech to the extent that is necessary to make your ideas fulfill the purpose of entertaining.

Occasions for the after dinner speech are many. They may be business luncheons, club dinners, committee meetings, special breakfasts, promotional gatherings, campaign inaugurations, afternoon teas, socials, celebrations, anniversaries, or any one of a dozen other occasions.

SUGGESTED TOPICS FOR AFTER DINNER SPEECHES

1. When I get married
2. Courting in an airplane
3. My first date
4. Money and women

5. Three girlfriends
6. Why men and women talk
7. If I were president
8. Now it can be told
9. Never ask why
10. Silence is not always golden
11. It happened this way
12. Parking as I see it
13. Christmas shopping
14. My first job
15. The first days are hardest
16. The fish that got away
17. How to hitchhike
18. Income taxes
19. How to win friends and their money
20. A successful moocher
21. Of all the sad words
22. I own a car but –
23. Tipping
24. Waitresses are human
25. Ten years from now
26. If I had a million
27. Tomorrow's opportunities
28. A better world for all
29. Gold is where you find it
30. Speaker's choice

Note: These topics should be suitable suggestions unless a particular theme is followed at the dinner. In this case, new topics should be chosen that are in keeping with the theme.

HOW TO CHOOSE A TOPIC FOR AFTER DINNER SPEAKING

Decide on the purpose of your speech. Be sure you can develop your topic to fulfill that purpose. Select something suitable and interesting to you, yet adapted to the occasion and audience. Do not put off deciding about a topic.

HOW TO PREPARE AN AFTER DINNER SPEECH

First of all, study this assignment carefully to learn fully the requirements of successful after dinner speaking. Follow previous information relative to speech organization, wording, and practice. Plan to use no notes. If you are a toastmaster, knowledge of and preparation for your task are the only assurances of a satisfactory performance.

The speaker's obligations: The preparation for this talk is no different from that of any other speech of the type you intend to present. Possibly your thoughts will be to entertain. If this is true, of course you will prepare a speech to entertain.

Should you not be familiar with the requirements of this kind of speech, read how it is done in the section of this book entitled "The Speech to Entertain." Follow this procedure for any type of speech you wish to deliver whether it be the speech to convince, to inform, or to stimulate.

Having ascertained your subject and the manner in which you will treat it, complete the preparation of your speech carefully. Before you consider yourself fully prepared, find out all you can about the program, when you will speak, who will precede you, and who will follow you. Then be sure that your speech is in line with the occasion.

It is not necessary and certainly not always advisable that a speaker plan to tell a joke on the toastmaster, regardless of what the toastmaster may do in the way of introduction. If the occasion calls for humor, a person should be ready to meet it. If it is doubtful what to do, play it safe. Good taste never offends. As far as risque stories go, leave them at home. If you do not have a clean story that packs a wallop, you have not tried to find one. The world has a great storehouse of humor and clean stories for all who want them and these are excellent for after dinner speeches.

To complete the preparation of your after dinner speech, practice it aloud several times before a mirror. It is a splendid idea to ask a friend or friends to hear you in rehearsal. Before you accept their advice or criticisms too literally, give some thought to their suggestions and the reliability of their advice.

The toastmaster's obligations: The toastmaster has an important task. He must see that everything is ready to go; he must open the proceedings, keep them going, and close the meeting. Let us examine these duties separately. First, to arrange everything, he should arrive at the meeting place early, at least a half hour. He will then perform the following chores: (1) He will advise the waiters in detail as to how the meal is to be served; (2) he will note the arrangement of the banquet room and suggest any changes he desires; (3) he will inquire about a checkroom or other space for wraps and make certain it is available and ready for use; (4) he will locate restrooms and be ready to direct persons to them; (5) shortly before serving time, he will personally count the plates and check place cards on the tables to be sure that the right number are available; (6) he will keep careful check on the persons as they arrive so that he will know when everyone is there; (7) he will indicate to the group when they are to go into the dining hall, that is, if they have been waiting in a lobby. If everyone has previously gathered in the dining room, he will be the first to seek his chair as a signal that the others should follow suit; (8) his general duty will be to see that guests are welcomed by himself or another designated person, that they are introduced, their wraps properly disposed of, and that they are entertained and put at ease; (9) during the banquet he will constantly remain alert to see that all goes well, and (10) he will see that the committee pays for the banquet or makes definite arrangements to settle the account later. He will also see that a tip is left for the waiters.

Of course, when there are several toastmasters, these duties may be divided among them. Everyone should know specifically what he is to do and should carry out each obligation conscientiously.

In regard to the actual work of introducing the speakers, considerable information must be gathered and set up several days early. This includes these necessary items: (1) The names of the speakers; (2) their topics; (3) data concerning speakers that will be suitable to use when introducing them; and (4) the order of the speakers. All this must be drawn together at a toastmasters' meeting and definitely agreed on by mutual consent. The act of introducing the speakers requires ingenuity and planning. A toastmaster should learn early that he is not to make speeches. This pleasure belongs to the after dinner speakers. The toastmaster merely presents each speaker by giving him a short introduction. Thirty seconds usually suffices, sometimes less, but never more than a minute or two, at the maximum. At this banquet the thirty second limit should prevail. The introduction may be a clever statement or two about the speaker, his name, and his topic. A fitting anecdote is in order if the occasion demands it. After the speaker concludes his speech, the toastmaster should get on with the show and not take time out to offer a rebuttal to some remark made by the speaker.

Throughout the evening's performances, the toastmasters should be agreed on matters such as when and whom to applaud and any other activities or procedures that should be initiated by the toastmasters.

HOW TO PRESENT AN AFTER DINNER SPEECH
Your presentation should reflect the type of speech you deliver. Generally speaking, a simple

organization, graphic word pictures, sufficient humor, lively and animated delivery, and a forward motion of ideas characterize after dinner speeches.

Voice and bodily action should be in harmony with the speech occasion and environment. The chances are that you will not need to talk loudly to be heard, nor will you be permitted much bodily action because of room accommodations and arrangement. Care should be exercised when rising to speak, or your chair may scrape noisily on the floor making you appear awkward. To prevent this, see that your chair is far enough from the table that you may rise freely without moving the chair. When the chairman, toastmaster, or president introduces you, rise and address him according to the position he holds; such as, "Mr. Toastmaster," "Mr. Chairman," and the like.

If during the program some person appearing ahead of you unknowingly steals your speech, the best thing for you to do when you speak is to refer to his remarks in support of your statements. You can go ahead then with your own thoughts and elaborate on them as is necessary and as has been planned.

Note: Keep your remarks in line with the occasion and purpose of your speech. "Ad lib" and improvise as the situation demands. Retain a sense of humor; use it if it is appropriate, and observe your time limits. Remember that the program committee allotted only a certain amount of time to you.

GROUP PLANS TO BE MADE
To make this experience real, you should by all means hold this meeting at a local hotel, cafe, or other place where the class can meet and eat without crowding. The atmosphere should be absolutely real, no make-believe.

In order to prepare successfully for this dinner, the following arrangements should be completed by separate committees:

Committee No. 1:
The reservation and menu committee. It should set a date for the luncheon and reserve a suitable place to hold it. Committee members should check carefully the size of the room and whether or not there will be extra charge for the use of the room. Serving facilities should be ascertained and assurance should be received that the group will not be disturbed by customers, if

they are in a public eating house. It is to be noted also if there is lobby space in which to gather and check wraps before going into the dining room. At least three different menus and their respective costs should be investigated and submitted to the class. One menu should be adopted and a price limit established. The time the meal will be served should be announced. It may be a noon or evening function, but preferably an evening one.

Committee No. 2:

The decorations committee. This committee decides what, if any, decorations are to be used. A fund must be established to cover any costs. Expenditures must be kept within the limits of this fund.

Committee No. 3:

The toastmaster's committee. Approximately twenty-five percent of the class will act as toastmasters. They should be elected by secret ballot. Each class member will write on a piece of paper as many names as there are to be toastmasters. If five is the number of toastmasters, then the five persons whose names are written the greatest number of times will be declared elected. They in turn, will meet as a committee to decide the order in which they will preside and the order of those they will introduce. They will learn in advance the topic of each speaker, thus preventing overlapping talks. Each toastmaster should plan to introduce a series of speakers, after which he will present the next toastmaster who will continue in the same manner. The first toastmaster will open the meeting and introduce guests. This may be done just before starting to eat, or it may be done at the first part of the program following the dinner. The last toastmaster, after introducing his speakers, should make appropriate closing remarks and adjourn the meeting. It is often embarrassing to everyone present if the last toastmaster does not make it absolutely clear that the banquet is concluded.

This use of several toastmasters may be somewhat unconventional but this arrangement gives more persons the experience as toastmaster. It adds variety to the program, provides opportunity for originality, and generally enhances the experience. It also suggests a basis for comparison of ideas as to what makes a good toastmaster.

Committee No. 4:

The collection committee. It is the responsibility of this committee to collect in advance the proper amount from each class member.

They will divide and deliver this money to each committee chairman whose group has incurred a debt which must be paid immediately following the dinner. Persons who have a plate reserved at the dinner but who do not come should expect to forfeit the price of the meal. Most hotels will charge for the places set.

SUMMARY:

Needless to say, all of the above committees must coordinate their efforts and work as a unit. Each reports its activities so all may know what progress has been made. It is likely your instructor will act as coordinator. It will be wise to seek his advice, besides reading numerous references pertaining to banquet procedure.

The group may or may not wish to invite guests. It is highly desirable that parents, friends, teachers, or dates be invited. This makes the affair a real banquet. While it is advisable to bring guests, those who do so should remember that they will be expected to pay for the guests' dinners.

Here are several points to investigate:

1. How early should you arrive? (A minimum of five minutes early.)
2. What clothes should you wear? (Hint - better make this dinner informal.)
3. What is the proper etiquette? (Good manners and willingness to make conversation - do not "freeze up.")
4. When and whom should you applaud? (Follow the toastmaster's lead.)
5. What are the toastmasters' duties? (To set the pace throughout the banquet.)
6. When should the food be served? Between speeches? Just how? (Hint - better settle this point definitely and be sure your waiters are correctly informed. It is desirable that speeches come after dessert has been finished.)
7. What should you do if you make a blunder? (The answer is, do nothing; go on.)
8. Supposing someone is late; what then? (Wait a few minutes then start the banquet.)
9. What if you should forget your speech? (Hint - do not ever memorize it. Have your main points in mind. Rehearse.)
10. How and when should you seat youself? Where? (If there are no place cards, find your own seat.)
11. What should you do when the toastmaster dismisses the group? Linger? Just what? (Go home, unless other arrangements have been made.)

IMPROVE YOUR VOCABULARY

Facetious - (fȧ-sē'-shŭs) a. Given to wittiness or characterized by pleasantry; witty. Example: An after dinner speaker frequently makes facetious remarks.

O.K. - Use a synonym for this word. It is tired from too much use. Here are a few examples: agreeable, satisfactory, splendid, excellent, elegant, admirable, choice, exquisite, etc. Employ these synonyms wisely. They don't have the same application.

BIBLIOGRAPHY FOR AFTER DINNER SPEAKING

Prochnow, Herbert V. and Prochnow, H. V., Jr., The Toastmaster's Treasure Chest, Harper & Row, 1979.
Weeks, Thelma E., Born to Talk, Newbury House, 1979.

★   ★   ★   ★   ★

AFTER DINNER SPEECH

By Lloyd Guderjohn

THE TERRIBLE MENACE

Ladies and Gentlemen: I would like to advise you of a terrible danger that threatens America today. Yes, a menace that threatens the welfare of every man, woman, and child. I refer not to an attack by a foreign power, I am speaking not of subversive Communists. No, I am talking of a deadly device found within our own homes and which is, I might add, an instrument of our own making.

Perhaps I frighten you with talk of a creature about to turn on its own maker like Frankenstein's monster or the hydrogen bomb; however, these creatures are mere playthings compared with the destructive possibilities of this horror. There is a vast number of these infernal devices. They are possessed by a highly developed organization and they are very definitely plotting the destruction of mankind. They present a threefold menace. They threaten our lives, our health and our safety. Who or what are these unspeakable horrors? How do they threaten our lives, our health and safety? What can we do to avoid this approaching doom?

Ladies and Gentlemen, this menace is none other than the common doorknob. You may find this shocking fact hard to believe. Yes, the doorknob constitutes a deadly menace. Firstly, they menace our lives. Have you ever noticed the position of the doorknob upon the door? Do you realize that it is located in such a position that if the door were to open suddenly, anyone who happened to be looking thru the keyhole would be struck a terrible blow? Yes! The doorknob threatens our very lives.

Secondly, a doorknob endangers our health. As you all know, when a person wants to enter a washroom to wash his hands he must first open the door. He grasps the knob and thereby rubs all the dirt off his hand and onto the knob. When he returns he picks up the dirt and germs again. So as you can see, washing does no good.

Thirdly, doorknobs threaten our safety. Can you imagine the confusion if the doorknobs should go on strike for shorter hours, or for whatever they should want to strike? Do you know that if they should go on strike, half of us would be locked out? Do you also realize that the other half would be locked in? The danger seems incredible and one can hardly believe that such a danger confronts us.

The doorknobs are very numerous. There are two on every door. Every room has at least two doors. This would make twenty in the average five-room house. If five people were living there they would be outnumbered four to one. In addition to this, doorknobs may be found where we work, in schools, and in hospitals. In addition, they are very highly organized. They always work in pairs.

As I have shown you, doorknobs are indeed a menace. To circumvent disaster there is only one thing we can do. We must gather every doorknob and destroy them all. Of course we would have to learn to get along without them and this would indeed be difficult. But the inconvenience suffered would be well worth the sacrifice.

Chapter 14

IMPROMPTU SPEAKING

Question: *Are impromptu (unprepared) or extemporaneous (prepared) speeches more effective?*

Answer: *The extemporaneous speech (well prepared but not memorized) is the most effective known.*

This speech is due:

Time limits: 2-3-4 and 5 minutes. (Start with two minutes. Increase the length of speeches until a student can talk five minutes.)

Speaking notes: During the first two experiences you may use notes which designate a "method." After this, memorize your method and apply it as you speak.

PURPOSE OF THE IMPROMPTU SPEECH

This speech experience is for the purpose of further enlarging your speech knowledge. It is to expose you to impromptu speaking and to provide you with a rudimentary acquaintance with the difficulties and nature of unprepared discourse. Many students assume that impromptu speaking is easy. Nothing could be further from the truth. In reality impromptu speaking is extremely difficult. It is used effectively only by experienced speakers. There are methods, however, which if properly used, will enable a person to perform acceptably on the spur of the moment. This assignment will assist you in learning these methods.

EXPLANATION OF IMPROMPT SPEAKING

Impromptu speaking is giving an unprepared talk. A person simply takes the floor, selects a subject, and begins. Various methods are used to conduct impromptu expression. A common procedure is one in which the speaker takes the floor after being asked to talk on a certain subject which he may or may not know much about. This is another method: one topic is suggested by each of several persons in the audience; a few seconds are permitted the speaker to choose from the list of topics the topic on which he feels himself best suited to expound; then he begins his conversation. Differences in the manner of selecting a topic are many; however, in any case, one fundamental principle is that the ideas voiced are unrehearsed and unprepared.

The purpose of presenting the speech is the same as that for any other type of speaking. The distinctive feature is the unprepared delivery and the suddenness with which a person is confronted with a speech situation. Impromptu speaking is often required at those times when a person is called upon without warning "to say a few words" at a luncheon, special meeting, social gathering, or other occasion.

SUGGESTED TOPICS FOR IMPROMPTU SPEECHES

Write three suggestions in the spaces below. They should be suitable to those who will be asked to use them as subjects. Avoid those such as: "What Did You Do Last Night?", "A Trip to Yellowstone Park,"... Your instructor will ask you to supply a topic from time to time as needed during the class. Examples of suitable topics for impromptu speaking are: dancing, movies, what is your opinion about (1) labor, (2) prohibition, (3) gambling, (4) free school books, (5) traffic laws, (6) radio programs, (7) . . .

1. _____

2. _____

3. _____

HOW TO CHOOSE A TOPIC FOR IMPROMPTU SPEAKING

There is one general rule to follow in selecting your topic; that is, if you have a choice. This rule is: choose the one on which you are best fitted to speak. Consider your audience and the occasion when you are making a choice of topic.

HOW TO PREPARE FOR AN IMPROMPTU SPEECH

Naturally you cannot prepare for an unknown topic, but you can prepare a method of attack on surprise offerings from your audience. One system of doing this is to have in mind various orders by which to develop your ideas.

One order might be the time sequence in which events occur by the hour, day, month, or year, moving forward or backward from a certain time. This example will illustrate the principle involved: Topic - Houses: (1) Give the history of houses from a definite date; (2) Tell which part of the country houses were first built in and their subsequent westward movement with time; (3) Describe how with time the styles of houses change, 1620-1700-1775-1800, and the like.

A space order would take you from east to west, top to bottom, front to rear . . . ; for example: take the topic, Houses. Then develop the speech in space order, giving the items in this way: (1) Specify the location of houses and their types, starting in California and traveling east; (2) Locate various classes of houses found in a city, starting at a slum area and moving to the wealthy outlying districts, (3) Describe houses according to locations in various parts of the world.

Using causal order, you might discuss certain forces and then point out the results which follow. Use this example: Topic - Houses: (1) Eskimos live in igloos. Why? Give reasons (causes). Or you might mention that South Pacific tribes dwell in grass and mud huts. Why? Give reasons (causes). (2) Prefabricated houses are now being built. Why? Give the causes that led to their development. (3) There are many hundreds of styles of houses of different architecture. Why? Give causes for this great diversification.

A special order is one of your own devising. For example take the same topic - Houses: (1) Tell how to build a house or different kind of houses. (2) Give the legal aspects of house construction - such as, wiring, sewage disposal plants, plumbing, type of dwelling in restricted areas, distance from street, . . . (3) How to contract for house construction, . . .

Another method which your writer has found effective is given below. It should be borne in mind that any method a speaker elects to use is not self-propelled. The person who applies the method will need to keep his wits about him and utilize only those portions of the device which are adapted to his particular speech, the occasion, his audience, and his own background and knowledge. He will find it necessary to literally memorize the points which follow. If he does this and then develops his topic in the order of the various headings, he will make a logical discussion.

I. Why is this topic important to your audience? To you?

II. Give a history of important events which will show the background and development of your subject.

III. What are the overall effects of your topic (such as, gambling) on your audience, the state, the nation, the world?
   A. What are the effects geographically?
   B. What are the effects politically?
   C. What are the effects economically?
   D. What are the effects socially?
   E. What are the effects religiously?
   F. What are the effects educationally?
   G. What are the effects morally?
   H. What are the effects agriculturally?
   I. . . . .

IV. What caused these effects? (Give as many causes as you can which will explain the effects you have enumerated. You may do this by discussing an effect and then by giving the cause of it immediately after.)

V. What are the different solutions to the problems? (You have told what is happening (effects) and you have told what brought them about (causes). Naturally, you must tell now what you propose to do about the problem or problems. Thus, you will have offered several different solutions.)

VI. Discuss the advantages and disadvantages of each solution you propose.

VII. Select one or two solutions which you think are best. Tell why they are best.

VIII. How do you propose to take action on these solutions? How may you and your audience go about putting your solutions into practice? Mention one or more ways to do this.

IX. Conclude your speech.
   A. You may summarize.
   B. You may appeal to your audience.
   C. You may ask your audience to do a specific act. Example:
      (1) Write to your congressman,
      (2) vote against _____ ,
      (3) and others, according to your own desire.

HOW TO PRESENT AN IMPROMPTU SPEECH

In presenting an impromptu speech your attitude is a deciding factor in determining your effectiveness. First of all, you must maintain poise. It does not matter how surprised you are, how difficult your topic is. It does not make any difference what happens when you receive your subject or while you are speaking or after you have concluded your speech, you still must maintain poise. It is impossible to over-emphasize the importance of poise. Now you ask, how do you maintain poise? Here are a number of suggestions and answers. (1) Do not fidget around at your seat before you speak, just because you know you will soon be "on the spot." (2) When you are called on to speak, rise calmly and take your place before your audience. (3) If you know your topic when you take the platform, begin your remarks calmly, without hurrying (have some vigor and force), and be sure that you have a plan in mind by which you will develop your thoughts. Do not apologize to your audience in any way, by word or action. (4) If you do not know your topic when you rise to speak but are offered several choices after obtaining the floor, simply stand calmly before the group and listen carefully to the suggestions which are made. You should ask that a topic be repeated if you do not understand it. After you have received all of the proposed subjects, either stand calmly or walk calmly back and forth a few seconds while you decide which offering you will talk about. Ten seconds should be the maximum time taken to decide. Once your selection is made, decide immediately what method or plan you will use in developing it. This plan should have been committed to memory before you ever attended class or placed yourself in a position where you might be asked to give an impromptu speech. After you have chosen your method of development, you will make your introductory remarks by telling why the subject is important to your listeners. When you begin to speak, do not make any apology of any sort whatsoever. Get on with your speech.

In actually delivering an impromptu talk, it is wise not to start too fast but rather to pick up speed and power as you go along. Aside from this, you should observe bodily actions and gestures which are in keeping with the speech situation. Your voice should be filled with meaning and easily heard by all. Naturally, your articulation, pronunciation, and grammar will be of high standard.

There is little to fear from impromptu speaking if you follow a preconceived method of attack on your subject. The way to do this is to refuse to allow yourself to become panicky, to recognize that some nervousness is a good sign of readiness, and to realize that your audience will expect nothing extraordinary from you because they, too, will know you are speaking impromptu. Actually, they will be "pulling for you." So you see, if you go about your task with poise and determination, your chances of success are exceedingly good. We might add here that a well-rounded knowledge attained from a strong reading program will assist you immeasurably.

IMPROVE YOUR VOCABULARY

Indolent – (ĭn'dō-lĕnt) a. A liking for ease or idleness, avoidance of exertion, idle, lazy, slothful, languid. Example: Indolent persons dislike preparing interesting speeches.

Huh – Omit this. It is a vulgarism which enjoys an unwarranted usage. Use a more desirable synonym. Examples are: What? I didn't understand? Please? Pardon? Sir? Madam? Yes? etc.

BIBLIOGRAPHY FOR IMPROMPTU SPEAKING

Carlile, Clark S., Project Text for Public Speaking, Harper & Row, 4th ed., 1981.
Ross, Raymond S., Speech Communication: Fundamentals and Practice, Prentice-Hall, 5th ed., 1980.

A GREAT SPEECH IN AMERICAN HISTORY
(The example below is for student appreciation and is not intended for any particular assignment in this text.)

Patrick Henry

THE "GIVE ME LIBERTY OR GIVE ME DEATH" SPEECH
(1775)

No man thinks more highly than I do of the patriotism, as well as abilities, of the very worthy gentlemen who have just addressed the House. But different men often see the same subject in different lights; and, therefore, I hope it will not be thought disrespectful to those gentlemen, if, entertaining as I do opinions of a character very opposite to theirs, I shall speak forth my sentiments freely and without reserve. This is no time for ceremony.

The question before the House is one of awful moment to this country. For my own part, I consider it as nothing less than a question of freedom or slavery; and in proportion to the magnitude of the subject ought to be the freedom of the debate. It is only in this way that we can hope to arrive at truth, and fulfill the great responsibility which we hold to God and our Country. Should I keep back my opinions at such a time, through fear of giving offense, I should consider myself as guilty of treason toward my country, and of an act of disloyalty toward the Majesty of Heaven, which I revere above all earthly kings.

Mr. President, it is natural to man to indulge in the illusions of hope. We are apt to shut our eyes against a painful truth, and listen to the song of that siren, till she transforms us into beasts. Is this the part of wise men, engaged in a great and arduous struggle for liberty? Are we disposed to be of the number of those, who, having eyes, see not, and having ears, hear not, the things which so nearly concern their temporal salvation? For my part, whatever anguish of spirit it may cost, I am willing to know the whole truth; to know the worst, and to provide for it.

I have but one lamp by which my feet are guided, and that is the lamp of experience. I know of no way of judging of the future but by the past. And judging by the past, I wish to know what there has been in the conduct of the British ministry for the last ten years to justify those hopes with which gentlemen have been pleased to solace themselves and the House. Is it that insidious smile with which our petition has been lately received? Trust it not, sir; it will prove a snare to your feet. Suffer not yourselves to be betrayed with a kiss. Ask yourselves how this gracious reception of our petition comports with those warlike preparations which cover our water and darken our land. Are fleets and armies necessary to a work of love and reconciliation? Have we shown ourselves so unwilling to be reconciled that force must be called in to win back our love? Let us not deceive ourselves, sir. These are the implements of war and subjugation; the last arguments to which kings resort.

I ask gentlemen, sir, what means this martial array, if its purpose be not to force us to submission? Can gentlemen assign any other possible motive for it? Has Great Britain any enemy in this quarter of the world to call for all this accumulation of navies and armies? No, sir, she has none. They are meant for us: they can be meant for no other. They are sent over to bind and rivet upon us those chains which the British ministry have been so long forging. And what have we to oppose to them? Shall we try argument? Sir, we have been trying that for the last ten years. Have we anything new to offer upon the subject? Nothing. We have held the subject up in every light of which it is capable; but it has been all in vain.

Shall we resort to entreaty and humble supplication? What terms shall we find which have not been already exhausted? Let us not, I beseech you, sir, deceive ourselves longer. Sir, we have done everything that could be done, to avert the storm which is now coming on. We have petitioned; we have remonstrated; we have supplicated; we have prostrated ourselves before the throne, and have implored its interposition to arrest the tyrannical hands of the ministry and Parliament. Our petitions have been slighted; our remonstrances have produced additional violence and insult; our supplications have been disregarded, and we have been spurned, with contempt, from the foot of the throne!

In vain, after these things, may we indulge the fond hope of peace and reconciliation. There is no longer any room for hope. If we wish to be free – if we mean to preserve inviolate those inestimable privileges for which we have been so long contending – if we mean not basely to abandon the noble struggle in which we have been so long engaged, and which we have pledged ourselves never to abandon, until the glorious object of our contest shall be obtained – we must fight! I repeat it, sir, we must fight! An appeal to arms and to the God of Hosts is all that is left us!

They tell us, sir, that we are weak – unable to cope with so formidable an adversary. But when shall we be stronger? Will it be the next week, or the next year? Will it be when we are totally disarmed, and when a British guard shall be stationed in every house? Shall we gather strength by irresolution and inaction? Shall we acquire the means of effectual resistance by lying supinely on our backs and hugging the delusive phantom of hope, until our enemies shall have bound us hand and foot?

Sir, we are not weak if we make a proper use of those means which the God of nature has placed in our power. Three millions of people armed in the holy cause of liberty, and in such a country as that which we possess, are invincible by any force which our enemy can send against us. Besides, sir, we shall not fight our battles alone. There is a just God who presides over the destinies of nations, and who will raise up friends to fight our battles for us. The battle, sir, is not to the strong alone; it is to the vigilant, the active, the brave. Besides, sir, we have no election. If we were base enough to desire it, it is now too late to retire from the contest. There is no retreat but in submission and slavery! Our chains are forged! Their clanking may be heard on the plains of Boston! The war is inevitable – and let it come! I repeat it, sir, let it come!

It is in vain, sir, to extenuate the matter. Gentlemen may cry, Peace, Peace – but there is no peace. The war is actually begun! The next gale that sweeps from the north will bring to our ears the clash of resounding arms! Our brethren are already in the field! Why stand we here idle? What is it that gentlemen wish? What would they have? Is life so dear, or peace so sweet, as to be purchased at the price of chains and slavery? Forbid it, Almighty God! I know not what course others may take, but as for me, give me liberty or give me death!

Delivered on March 23, 1775, before the Second Revolutionary Convention of Virginia, in the old church in Richmond.

NAME _____ DATE _____

(Ch. 8) 39. The speech to inform does which one of the following?

(a) provides listeners a clear understanding of the speaker's ideas upon a subject

(b) causes listeners to get excited and stirred up

(c) attempts to cause listeners to agree with the speaker on a debatable subject

(d) tries to get listeners to take a specific action such as voting, etc.

(Ch. 8) 40. The speech to inform requires a speaker to: (two answers)

(a) select a subject of interest to himself and his listeners

(b) know more about his subject than his listeners

(c) memorize his speech carefully

(d) cut his conclusion to a few words only

(Ch. 8) 41. Which one of the following subjects would be used for an informative speech?

(a) terrorists should be given life imprisonment   (b) terrorists are murderers

(c) write your congressman about terrorists   (d) facts about terrorists

(Ch. 8) 42. The number of informative speeches given in a year's time is:

(a) very few   (b) limited to television and radio   (c) probably in the millions

(d) none because they are illegal

(Ch. 8) 43. Information presented in an informative speech:

(a) can be based on hearsay   (b) may be secured from sources not necessarily reliable

(c) need not be entirely accurate, but almost   (d) must be accurate

(Ch. 8) 44. The words bewitching, exquisite, lovely, attractive, are synonymous with which one of the following?

(a) character   (b) inherent   (c) facial   (d) pretty   (e) posture   (f) trivial

(Ch. 8) 45. (Blockbuster) Which part of your body could be referred to as your empennage?

(a) head   (b) shoulders   (c) hips   (d) heels   (e) ears   (f) stomach

(g) elbows   (h) ankles   (i) knees

(Ch. 8) 46. In presenting an informative speech it is advisable to: (one answer)

(a) draw pictures and use charts if needed   (b) talk no faster than 100 words per minute

(c) limit your subject to females only   (d) use unusual body language for conviction

(Ch. 9) 47. A speech to stimulate and arouse would be considered successful if:

(a) it caused the listeners to go forth and take a very specific action

(b) it touched the listeners' emotions and intellects sufficiently that they felt impelled to adopt new attitudes and/or take actions discussed by the speaker

(c) it gave the audience a lot of new information so they understood the subject

(d) it caused certain listeners to become angry and walk out

(Ch. 9) 48. Basic features of a speech to stimulate are: (one answer)

(a) calm and slow presentation by the speaker   (b) fast talk by the speaker and loud

(c) vivid language, obvious sincerity and enthusiasm by the speaker

(d) much body language and witty humor to amuse the listeners

(Ch. 9) 49. How many of the following would be likely occasions for a speech to stimulate?

(a) pep meeting   (b) political rally   (c) sales promotion

(d) classroom lecture on chemistry

(Ch. 9) 50. One most effective way to stimulate an audience is to build your speech around:

(a) basic drives in people – security, recognition, pleasure, self preservation, etc.

(b) the desire to laugh   (c) the use of important sounding words, some which are foreign

(d) the use of loud noises and explosions on a hidden tape recorder

(Ch. 9) 51. (Blockbuster) If you said you saw an erratic driver you probably saw: (one answer)

(a) a person driving straight down the road   (b) a boy with his date

(c) a woman applying makeup while she drove

(d) a person's car wandering over the road as he drove

(Ch. 9) 52. The words business, vocation, task, profession, are synonyms for:

(a) economy   (b) money-making   (c) job   (d) office

(Ch. 10) 53. A speech to convince is one:

(a) which attempts to make listeners agree with your point of view

(b) which stirs people up

(c) which gives facts, examples, opinions, etc., so listeners will understand your subject

(d) which entertains listeners so they want you to continue

(Ch. 10) 54. Which one of the following topics would be suitable for a speech to convince?

(a) the history of kidnapping   (b) all kidnappers have big noses

(c) kidnappers – our greatest threat to children

(d) kidnappers, when convicted, should be given the death sentence

(Ch. 10) 55. Two persons arguing for and against a solution to a problem are: (two answers)

(a) giving speeches to stimulate   (b) giving speeches to convince

(c) having an informal debate   (d) giving speeches to inform

(Ch. 10) 56. If you give a speech in which you argue "we should all drive more carefully," it is not a speech to convince: (two answers)

(a) because we already agree on it   (b) because it is informative only

(c) because it is not a solution to a debatable proposition

(d) because there is no information available about it.

(Ch. 10) 57. Usually the first point you discuss in a speech to convince is:

(a) give your solution to the problem   (b) present a history of the problem

(c) discuss causes that brought on bad effects

(d) discuss how your solution will benefit the listeners

(Ch. 10) 58. If you want to argue against any proposition, you may show: (three answers)

(a) it is not needed   (b) it is not practical   (c) it is not desirable

(d) it is not suitable for discussion

(Ch. 10) 59. Besides having your speech to convince well organized and containing much evidence another part of preparation is:

(a) getting eight hours sleep the final night

(b) doing oral practice until you are capable of presenting your material without excessive use of notes   (c) memorizing your speech word for word

(d) eating a good meal before speaking

(Ch. 10) 60. When presenting a speech to convince: (two answers)

(a) your voice should reflect a sincere belief in your views

(b) all show of emotion and strong feeling should be avoided

(c) an energetic presentation is desirable

(d) you should try to be a bit funny to liven up your speech

(Ch. 10) 61. (Blockbuster) How many of the following words are synonyms of "languid"?

(a) apathetic   (b) listless   (c) torpid   (d) animosity   (e) heavy   (f) energetic

(g) voiceless   (h) whispering

(Ch. 10) 62. Synonyms for "nice" are: (two answers)

(a) pretty   (b) delightful   (c) slender   (d) pleasant

(Ch. 11) 63. The best way to keep your poise under heckling is: (two answers)

(a) know your speech and know it well but don't have it memorized

(b) have a memorized speech   (c) refuse to answer irrelevant questions

(d) look quite stern

(Ch. 11) 64. Several hints for handling hecklers are: (three answers)

(a) be firm but flexible   (b) retain a sense of humor but don't become a comedian

(c) stay with your speech

(d) depart from your speech to surprise and confuse your hecklers

(Ch. 11) 65. (Blockbuster) Chicanery means: (two answers)

(a) indignation   (b) sophistry   (c) animosity   (d) deceit   (e) anger   (f) vengeful

(g) harrowing   (h) situational

(Ch. 11) 66. Synonyms for "anger" are: (mark all correct answers)

(a) ire   (b) trickery   (c) animosity   (d) vexation

(Ch. 12) 67. The speech to entertain is: (one answer)

(a) easy   (b) a series of risque stories   (c) nothing difficult

(d) difficult to present effectively

(Ch. 12) 68. A humorous speech may rely in part on: (mark the most appropriate answers)

(a) anecdotes   (b) body language   (c) special devices   (d) risque jokes

(e) memorized speech

(Ch. 12) 69. The speech to entertain may: (mark correct answers)

(a) make listeners laugh loudly   (b) produce only chuckles and grins

(c) bring forth only smiles of amusement

(d) not need to be uproariously funny to entertain

(Ch. 12) 70. A humorous speech may only catch the attention and interest of an audience.

(a) true   (b) false

(Ch. 12) 71. The chief aim of a speech to entertain is humor, however, it may be informative in places.

(a) partially true   (b) true   (c) partially false   (d) false

(Ch. 12) 72. Preparing a speech to entertain: (mark wrong answers)

(a) is easier than most speeches   (b) requires very little organization

(c) does not require much rehearsal   (d) should have many notes

(Ch. 12) 73. A good humorous speech: (mark correct answers)

(a) may be a series of unrelated funny stories   (b) may use exaggerations

(c) may use effective illustrations   (d) may involve sudden changes of thought

(Ch. 12) 74. The humorous speech: (mark correct answers)

(a) normally does not have a lively presentation

(b) probably will not have a smooth forward motion

(c) should have a smooth forward motion

(d) will have a speaker who may be facetious, jovial, and whimsical

(Ch. 12) 75. If laughter is incited during a humorous speech: (two answers)

(a) the speaker should slow down

(b) the speaker should resume his talk when he can be heard

(c) the speaker usually resumes his talk just before all laughter has stopped

(d) the speaker should indicate that he knows he is funny

(Ch. 12) 76. (Blockbuster) If a speaker has "nasality" he:

(a) has his mouth too nearly closed

(b) is not using his tongue, teeth, and lips to articulate

(c) is using too much breath   (d) is talking through his nose

(e) none of the other answers

(Ch. 12) 77. Synonyms for "smart" are:

(a) trite   (b) trig   (c) trim   (d) chic   (e) arrogant   (f) angry   (g) industrious

(h) funny   (i) beautiful

(Ch. 13) 78. An after dinner speech may be how many of the following?

(a) to stimulate   (b) to convince   (c) to entertain   (d) to inform

(Ch. 13) 79. The toastmaster at a banquet: (mark correct answers)

(a) should arrive at least 30 minutes early

(b) will advise waiters in detail how the meal is to be served

(c) will locate restrooms and be ready to direct persons to them

(d) will note the arrangement of the banquet room and suggest needed changes

(Ch. 13) 80. To effectively introduce speakers at a banquet the toastmaster should gather how many of the following items of information several days early?

(a) names of the speakers   (b) names of the speakers' dates if any

(c) speakers' topics   (d) data concerning the speakers to be used when introducing them

(e) who the first speaker is, second speaker, third speaker and so on

(Ch. 13) 81. The toastmaster's introduction of a speaker should be: (one answer)

(a) fairly long   (b) medium long   (c) around two minutes   (d) about 30 seconds

(Ch. 13) 82. After a speaker finishes, the toastmaster should: (one answer)

(a) offer rebuttal to some remark made by the speaker

(b) tell a joke about the speaker who just finished

(c) wait a minute or two then introduce the next speaker

(d) get on with the show at once

(Ch. 13) 83. If during the program some person appearing ahead of you unknowingly steals your speech you should:

(a) apologize and sit down   (b) act like it had not happened and proceed

(c) refer to his remarks in support of your statements and proceed

(d) give an entirely new impromptu speech

(Ch. 13)   84. How early should you arrive at a banquet?

        (a) at the exact time it starts   (b) two minutes late is in order

        (c) one minute before it starts   (d) a minimum of five minutes early

(Ch. 13)   85. (Blockbuster) If you made a "facetious" remark it would be: (one answer)

        (a) sarcastic   (b) loud   (c) witty   (d) insulting   (e) reliable   (f) true

(Ch. 13)   86. According to your text synonyms for the word "O.K." are: (mark correct answers)

        (a) splendid   (b) reciprocal   (c) ratteen   (d) elegant

(Ch. 14)   87. Impromptu speaking means:

        (a) giving an unprepared talk   (b) using a few notes, not over ten words, when speaking

        (c) a partly memorized speech   (d) a fully memorized speech

(Ch. 14)   88. If called upon to give an impromptu speech a person should: (one answer)

        (a) say a prayer and hope it is answered

        (b) begin speaking and say anything he can think of   (c) refuse to speak

        (d) use a plan or plans he has memorized and apply one or more to his topic

(Ch. 14)   89. A "space order" used to develop an impromptu speech means:

        (a) discuss causes then talk about their effects

        (b) discuss the hour, day, month, or year moving forward or backward from a certain time

        (c) discuss past, present, future

        (d) discuss east to west, top to bottom, front to rear, inside to outside, etc.

(Ch. 14)   90. After you know you must speak impromptu and take the platform you should: (mark correct answers)

        (a) wait five to ten seconds before starting

        (b) begin calmly without hurry but with some vigor.

        (c) make a brief apology about being unprepared

        (d) keep your poise – no panic

(Ch. 14)   91. (Blockbuster) An "indolent" speaker is:

        (a) lively   (b) lazy   (c) vulgar   (d) unprepared   (e) active   (f) forgetful

        (g) scared

(Ch. 14)   92. Mark the synonym for "indolent" that is <u>not</u> correct:

        (a) slothful   (b) languid   (c) idle   (d) violable

Chapter 15

A SPEECH TO GAIN GOODWILL

Question: *How long does it take to prepare a good five-minute speech?*

Answer: *Three to five hours would not be too much. Short speeches require proportionately more preparation time than long speeches.*

This speech is due:

Time limits: 6-7 minutes. Observe your time limits!

Speaking notes: Do not use them – your speech should be in you, not on paper.

Sources of information: Two are required, preferably three. For each source give the specific magazine or book it was taken from, title of the article, author's full name, date of publication, and the chapter or pages telling where the material was found. If a source is a person, identify him completely by title, position, occupation, etc. List these on the outline form.

Outline your speech: Prepare a 75-150 word complete sentence outline. Designate the exact number of words in your outline. Use the form at the end of this chapter.

PURPOSE OF A SPEECH TO GAIN GOODWILL

One type of speech being utilized many thousands of times each year is the kind that secures goodwill from an audience. The popularity and usefulness of goodwill speeches are not likely to decline, but rather to grow. Your place in society may at any time demand that you join the parade of those who present speeches designed to secure goodwill. Because this type of speech occurs so often, you should, by all means, have experience with it. This assignment provides such an opportunity for you.

EXPLANATION OF THE SPEECH TO GAIN GOODWILL

A speech to gain goodwill is one in which the purpose is to secure a favorable attitude toward the speaker and for the group which he represents. Normally this speech is presented to a friendly audience, which necessitates the presentation of what might easily be called a speech to inform. This will be the apparent purpose, as far as the audience is concerned. However, the thought behind the presentation of information is this: by causing listeners to understand and appreciate the group he represents, the speaker will secure goodwill from them.

Occasions for goodwill speeches occur at luncheons, club meetings, special demonstrations, school meetings, religious gatherings, conventions, business meetings, ... Any group that convenes to hear a speaker give them information, whether it be a straight informative talk, an illustrated lecture, the showing of a film, or the demonstration of a new product, likely will be the recipient of a goodwill speech. One might classify a goodwill speech as a very subtle or indirect sales talk.

SUGGESTED TOPICS AND AUDIENCES

Construct a goodwill speech in which you represent a certain group on a definite occasion.

1. Represent a mining company to a civic club.
2. Represent an aircraft manufacturing corporation to a chamber of commerce.
3. Represent a car manufacturing company to a Lions Club.
4. Tell how your company makes ladies' hats – to a sorority.
5. Represent a washing machine company – to a group of women.
6. Represent an insurance company to a group of students.
7. Represent a college to a high school.
8. Represent a "baby food company" to a group of young mothers.
9. Represent a correspondence school – to industrial workers.
10. Represent a foreign country – to a college assembly.
11. Represent the United States – to a foreign country.
12. Represent a publisher – at a teachers' meeting.
13. Represent an implement company – at a rural gathering.
14. Represent a "salesmanship school" – to a group of business men.
15. Represent the Navy, Army, or Air Corps – to a student body.
16. Represent a city at another city.
17. Represent a church – before a civic group.
18. Represent a "sports club" at a college assembly.
19. Represent a farmer's organization – before a group of business men.
20. Speaker's choice.

HOW TO CHOOSE A TOPIC

As always, choose a topic that has a compelling interest for you. Choose one you know something about; one about which you can get more information. Make your selection without too much delay. Putting off a decision that can be made now will not improve your speech.

HOW TO PREPARE A SPEECH TO GAIN GOODWILL

First of all, remember that your purpose is to secure goodwill. Keep this in mind. Second, do not forget that your remarks will be necessarily of an informative nature. We will assume that you you have analyzed your audience and selected your topic.

Naturally, as soon as you have done this, you should gather your materials. Practically all large companies and corporations will gladly send you information if you will write for it. Many local business houses and Chambers of Commerce will provide pamphlets and brochures. Encyclopedias and Readers' Guides are excellent sources. If you are willing to show a reasonable amount of initiative, you will have no difficulty in locating materials to supplement your own knowledge. If you reach an impasse, ask your instructor for assistance.

After you have gathered your material, you will need to organize it logically so that it can be easily followed. You must decide on the order, the arrangement, the illustrations and examples, an effective introduction, and a strong conclusion. In other words, the entire pattern of your speech must be worked out carefully.

There are several characteristics of the goodwill speech which you should note. First, be sure you have interesting facts, new material – the novel or out of the ordinary subject–matter that the listeners have not heard before. Another point is that you should show a definite relationship between your corporation, institution, a profession and the lives of your listeners. They should be made to see that their happiness and prosperity are tied in with your activities or those which you represent. In making this point do not be so bold that you ask their approval or request their approbation. You should take it for granted that they already approve. And last, be sure you offer them a definite service. It may be in the form of souvenirs, samples, or an invitation to visit your plant, city, or institution. It could be special favors or accommodations to members of the audience, or merely the answering of questions they cared to raise at the conclusion of your remarks. Above all, remember that you are willing to help your audience - you are at their service. (Do not forget to practice this speech aloud before you present it to your audience.)

HOW TO PRESENT A SPEECH TO GAIN GOODWILL

This is a speech in which friendliness, good humor, and modesty count to a high degree. You will be talking about yourself and your organization. Bragging will have no place – bragging is out. The information that you present will have to be strong and interesting enough to do its own talking. You must be tolerant of your competitors and gracious in your appraisal of them. You must be careful about forcing your material on your audience. If you possess the necessary good feeling and friendliness for your auditors, they will reciprocate these attitudes.

Dress yourself for the occasion, give attention to your posture, be alert and eager to communicate. Talk to be heard and understood. Avoid unnecessary formality. Bodily action and gesture will be in order, as always, if they are used appropriately. Avoid being suave and bland; just be friendly and sincere.

IMPROVE YOUR VOCABULARY

Use the following word in your speech today and five times each day during the next week.

Laconic - (lá-kŏn'ĭk) a. Expressing a great deal in few words; concise, terse. Example: He used a laconic manner of expression, in fact he was almost curt.

Funny - Omit this word. Do not use it for ten days. It is completely "fagged." Use a synonym to brighten your speech. Examples: laughable, absurd, comical, ludicrous, humorous, waggish, droll, whimsical, burlesque, etc. - or, odd, strange, singular, unique, weird, eccentric, irregular, quaint, grotesque, freakish, etc.

BIBLIOGRAPHY FOR THE SPEECH TO GAIN GOODWILL

Gronbeck, Bruce E., The Articulate Person: A Guide to Everyday Public Speaking, Scott Foresman,
1979.
Huen, Richard and Huen, Linda, Public Speaking: A New Speech Book, West Publishing Co., 1979.
Jeffrey, Robert C. and Peterson, Owen, Speech: A Text With Adapted Readings, Harper & Row, 3rd ed.,
1980.
Myers, Gail E., and Myers, M. T., Communicating When We Speak, McGraw-Hill Book Company, 1975.

★ ★ ★ ★ ★

GOODWILL SPEECH

By Steven Rigby

SO, YOU WOULD LIKE TO BE A DOCTOR

Many of you will be graduating from high school this May, and enrolling in premedical courses in colleges and universities next September. If I were to ask a few of you just why you think you want to be doctors, I would get many different answers in reply — some good answers, some bad ones. But each of you, for one reason or another, feels that your goal should be medicine. You think that medicine has something to offer you and that you have something to offer medicine. On your list of priorities, medicine is number one.

Many of you see the years of study that lie ahead of you as a mysterious blur. You know, of course, that you will go to college for three to four years. You know that you will then go on to medical school — if you're accepted — for another four years, taking courses in anatomy, physiology and many other courses with long names. And then you will intern in a hospital for a year. You may even decide to specialize and go to school for a few more years. You realize that you have to invest a long period of time and a frightening amount of money, in order to complete your goal of becoming a medical doctor.

But just remember the practice of medicine has always meant something more than just another way to make a living, and that an education in medicine implies something more than the completion of certain science courses and the reading of certain textbooks.

A modern physician can look forward to various rewards for his contribution to medicine. Most doctors make a good living from their work. I am not going to list average incomes of doctors in their respective specialties as they are listed today because they probably will be quite different by the time you become a doctor. But, by and large, I think you would have to look for quite a while to find a doctor who is starving to death.

Certainly, a physician has a high degree of security. A doctor will never have to worry about finding a job; there has always been a shortage of doctors. He can expect to have a home of his own and a new model automobile. He will be able to provide a good education for his children.

On the other hand, it would be a mistake to have medicine as your goal because of the tangible rewards that are offered. There are many other occupations in which you can make much more money with much less effort, if that is your major concern.

Aside from income, there is a multitude of rewards that face the physician. A doctor most always enjoys respect in his community. There is no other profession which is held in as high esteem as the profession of medicine. A doctor is respected for merely being a doctor. He is often regarded as public property and is expected to take part in community progress. He may be consulted for completely non-medical community affairs.

Most important, the physician derives immense satisfaction from doing work that is worthwhile, work which is needed and received with much gratitude. He takes pride in doing work which few others can do, and doing it well. He finds satisfaction every day from the positive benefit that comes from his work.

But at the same time he must assume certain unusual responsibilities. Very often patients forget that doctors are people, as well as being doctors. A doctor must be available when he is needed. Even if that happens to be at two in the morning, he is still expected to accept the call. Most all physicians work hours that would astonish the average person. And they accept this as a way of life.

A doctor's home life is often a very trying situation, especially when he is establishing his practice. He may not see his wife and children regularly. It has been said that any woman who marries a doctor is either an idiot or a fool; if this is the truth, I know quite a few very charming idiots and fools who are willing to share their husbands with the numerous duties of a medical profession, duties which take the doctor away from home usually half the night and always at meal times.

This demand on a doctor's time is accepted by the profession as part of the game. This is the way a doctor lives, and that's all there is to it. If you don't think you would like this kind of life, you shouldn't be a doctor. There is no one the profession scorns more than the physician who shirks his duties, that is, puts his personal life above the life he must dedicate to his profession. The rest of the profession accepts this life — why shouldn't he?

It is true that many doctors form group practices where they take turns being on call. This does eliminate some of the interruptions a doctor may encounter, but the responsibility still exists.

Who knows, by the time many of you become doctors the single practitioner working twenty hours a day may well be a thing of the past although I think the responsibilities will always be there. True, I think it takes a very special type of person to become a doctor, because the incentive must be there. The opportunities and rewards always outweigh the disappointments. If you have made up your mind to become a doctor, I want to congratulate you and wish you success, because I don't think you will ever regret your decision.

SPEECH OUTLINE

Construct a neat, complete sentence outline on this sheet, tear it out, and hand it to your instructor when you rise to speak. He may wish to write criticisms of the outline and speech in the margins.

Type of speech:_____ Name: _____

Number of words in outline: _____ Date: _____

Purpose of this speech: (What do you want your audience to learn, to think, to believe, to feel, or do because of this speech?) _____

_____

TITLE:

INTRODUCTION:

BODY:

CONCLUSION:

Instructor's comments may concern choice of topic, development of ideas, organization, language use, personal appearance, posture, physical activity, sources, and improvement.

(Write sources of information on back of sheet)

SOURCES FROM LITERATURE

Fill out source requirements completely.
Write "none listed" if an author's name or copyright date is not listed.

1. Author's name _____

   Title of book or magazine used _____

   Title of article in above book or magazine _____

   Chapter and/or pages read _____

   Date of above publication _____

2. Author's name _____

   Title of book or magazine used _____

   Title of article in above book or magazine _____

   Chapter and/or pages read _____

   Date of above publication _____

3. Author's name _____

   Title of book or magazine used _____

   Title of article in above book or magazine _____

   Chapter and/or pages read _____

   Date of above publication _____

INTERVIEW SOURCES

1. Person interviewed _____ Date of interview _____

   His position, occupation, and location _____

   Why is he a reliable source? Be specific _____

   _____

2. Person interviewed _____ Date of interview _____

   His position, occupation, and location _____

   Why is he a reliable source? Be specific _____

   _____

PERSONAL EXPERIENCE OF SPEAKER

1. Tell (1) when, (2) where, and (3) conditions under which you became an authority on subject matter in your speech _____

   _____

   _____

   _____

Chapter 16

THE INTRODUCTION SPEECH

Question: *When I pick a topic do I have to know everything about it?*

Answer: *No. you should research it thoroughly so you may speak with authority and possess a basis for your views.*

This speech is due:

Time limits: 1-2 minutes.

Speaking notes: None.

Sources of information: They may be fictitious or real.

Outline your speech: Prepare a 50-100 word complete sentence outline. Designate the exact number of words in your outline. Use the form at the end of this chapter.

PURPOSE OF THE INTRODUCTION SPEECH

Many untrained speakers are asked to give introduction speeches. Some of the introductions are well done; far too many are haphazard and embarrassing, because the person making the introduction is untrained. This brings criticism upon the person who must present a speaker and it also weakens programs that feature lecturers. Of all the types of speeches you may make in the future, it is probable that one of them will be the introduction of a featured speaker. This assignment will provide an introduction speech experience.

EXPLANATION OF THE INTRODUCTION SPEECH

An introduction speech is one in which a chairman or other person introduces a speaker to an audience. The purpose is to bring an audience and speaker together in the proper spirit. Several of the requirements are that: the speech should be short; it should make the audience and speaker feel comfortably acquainted; it should interest the audience in the speaker and his subject; it should put the speaker at ease, announce his subject, and give his name.

The introducer should avoid attempts at being funny. He should never embarrass the speaker either by heaping too much praise upon him or by belittling him. The person introducing a speaker should not call attention to himself nor say or do anything to detract from what the speaker plans to say. The person who once said, "Get up, speak up, shut up," probably was thinking of the individual who makes introduction speeches; and the introducer can hardly go wrong if he follows this advice.

Occasions for the introduction speech arise every time a speaker is introduced. They probably number in the millions annually.

SUGGESTED INTRODUCTION SPEECHES

1. Your college president to a high school audience.
2. The student body president to the freshman class.
3. A lecturer to the student body.
4. A lecturer to your class.
5. The mayor to a public gathering.
6. A famous explorer visits your school.
7. A missionary at a religious meeting.
8. A war hero speaks. Introduce him/her.
9. A noted aviator speaks.
10. A great inventor speaks.
11. A famous scientist will lecture.
12. The governor visits your city and school.
13. A high government official is the speaker.
14. A commencement speaker.
15. A baccalaureate speaker.
16. The valedictorian to an audience.
17. Any lecturer to a civic organization.
18. A Hollywood celebrity to your school.
19. A foreign speaker.
20. Speaker's choice.

HOW TO CHOOSE AN INTRODUCTION SPEECH

Look over the list of suggestions above. If you like one of the ideas, select it at once. If not, you may have some other topic which you prefer. In this case, make up your mind without delay and start thinking about your speech. You will have to decide for yourself as to the type of imaginary audience and occasion you will use. You will also find it necessary to arrive at some decision concerning the specific person you plan to introduce. Be sure that your speaker is a suitable one for the occasion. Above all do not attempt to be different by improvising a speech built around a classmate whom you place in an impossible or ludicrous position. This will defeat you as a speaker and will not meet the assignment.

HOW TO PREPARE AN INTRODUCTION SPEECH

In preparing this speech you may draw your information from four sources: the speaker, his subject, the audience, or the occasion. Not all of these may be necessary in every speech; however, they are all often suitable if not required sources. You will not need much material, but that which you have must be accurate and pertinent. As for the speaker, get his name and be absolutely certain you have it right. Know how to pronounce it correctly. Discover any background the speaker has that should be known by the audience. This may concern his education, special training, travel experience, special honors, membership in organizations, important positions he has held, books he has written, or any other notable achievements. Of course, if he is a famous and well-known person, little need be said, possibly nothing. An example of the latter is the introduction often heard: "Ladies and Gentlemen, the President." However, almost all speakers require more to be said than do the President of the United States, a governor or other high state official. You should know the title of the speaker's subject. As with his name, you must have it right. But you should say nothing about the speech that will tend to "steal the thunder" of his remarks. You should inquire thoroughly into the personnel of your audience so that you may adjust your remarks to them. The occasion of the address should be well-known to you. From the four sources just mentioned and a fifth, yourself, you will construct your introduction speech. Short though this speech is to be, what you say must really "count." Thus, you must organize and arrange it carefully, selecting those bits of information that are most important.

Before you set your ideas, you should confer with the person you are going to introduce and, in conference, arrive at a definite understanding regarding what you plan to say in your introduction speech. After this point is decided, then rehearse aloud until you are confident that you are thoroughly prepared.

HOW TO PRESENT AN INTRODUCTION SPEECH

When the moment arrives for you to introduce the speaker of the evening, rise calmly, take your place on the platform, pause until the assembly grows quiet, and then deliberately address the audience in your normal voice, yet speak loudly enough for all to hear. Avoid straining or using greater force than is needed. You may say, "Ladies and Gentlemen," or use some other salutation or form of introduction appropriate to the audience and the occasion.

Your bodily action and gesture will be limited. There will likely be no necessity for using either more than moderately. Your voice should be well modulated, the words spoken clearly, and your pronunciation correct - especially that of the speaker's name.

Keep in mind your part of the occasion. People did not come to hear you or see you. You are only a convenient but necessary cog in the events surrounding the speaker. Your poise and confidence and appropriate but brief remarks are all that are expected or wanted from you. You may greet the audience and mention the occasion, extend felicitations, and note the fact that there is an exceptionally good audience (if there is). If there is a poor audience, do not remark about it and do not make any apologies.

At the moment you present the speaker, announce his name and subject somewhat as follows: "I am happy to present Mr. A, who will address you (or speak to you) on _____ (mention the subject)." Then turn to the speaker with the words, "Mr. A." You may bow slightly or nod and take your chair when he rises and approaches the front of the platform.

If you are chairman of the assembly, it will be appropriate for you to express publicly the appreciation of the audience to the speaker at the conclusion of his address.

IMPROVE YOUR VOCABULARY

Ephemeral - (ē-fĕm'ẽr-ăl) a. Beginning and ending in a short period of time, say one day, existing or continuing for a short time only, transient, passing, fleeting, evanescent, momentary. Example: The book had only an ephemeral utility. Use ephemeral in this speech and five times a day for the next week. Make it work for you.

Good - Omit this word. Good is a bad word to overwork. Add color to your vocabulary by using synonyms. Examples: palatable, delicious, tempting, delectable, luscious, excellent, commendable, delightful, stimulating, well-made, exquisite, superior, creditable, valuable, meritorious, etc.

BIBLIOGRAPHY FOR THE INTRODUCTION SPEECH

Baird, John E., Jr., Speaking For Results: Communication by Objectives, Harper & Row, 1980.
Cole, Ronald A., ed., Perception and Production of Fluent Speech, Erlbaum Associates, 1980.
Logue, Cal and Others, Speaking: Back to Fundamentals, Allyn & Bacon, 2d ed., 1979.

★ ★ ★ ★ ★

INTRODUCTION SPEECH

(Introducing Coach Bob Dunkin to a High School Lettermen's Banquet)

By Brent Peterson

Principal Norton, coaches and lettermen of Valley High School. Meeting this evening as a group of athletes we all recall during many basketball games a most unforgettable shot, the "dunk." The gigantic pivot-men made it look simple, nevertheless the excitement came in watching the little fellow leap and stuff the ball through the hoop. It is a privilege to have with us such a man who thrilled many spectators. A little six-foot guard through hard work perfected the thrilling shot and became known as "Dunker" to match his own name, Bob Dunkin.

Bob, a three-year basketball letterman at Northside High in Kennington, attended banquets similar to this one. Upon receiving the free throw trophy after making seventy-six percent of his free throws, at the banquet his junior year Bob announced, "Next year I'll shoot over ninety percent." The following year persistent Bob made ninety-two percent of his free throws due to his consistent practice during the summer. Coach Dunkin remembers well his high school experiences and conducts summer basketball camps to develop the abilities of young ball players because he is interested in them.

A competitive college athlete said, "You must always give one hundred percent effort; if you don't, someone, somewhere will and he will beat you." "Dunker" Dunkin made that statement and has always gone the extra mile in all his life's endeavors and has rarely been beaten. At State U, "Dunker" was all-conference twice, led the conference in free-throw shooting and his team to a berth in the NCAA post season tournament. As Northside High coach his team lost only five times in three years and was rated number one in the state for two years. He has continued as an outstanding coach motivating athletes to their best performance. His teams have won 131 and lost 21 games during his five years at Southern State College. He's a winner.

Bob Dunkin's life is the story of persistence, hard work and success. It has been said, "No chance, no destiny, no fate can circumvent or hinder or control the firm resolve of a determined soul." Athletes, I want you to meet and hear this determined man who will speak to you concerning the value of reaching your own potential. Coach Dunkin.

SPEECH OUTLINE

Construct a neat, complete sentence outline on this sheet, tear it out, and hand it to your instructor when you rise to speak. He may wish to write criticisms of the outline and speech in the margins.

Type of speech:_____ Name: _____

Number of words in outline: _____ Date: _____

Purpose of this speech: (What do you want your audience to learn, to think, to believe, to feel, or do because of this speech?) _____

_____

TITLE:

INTRODUCTION:

BODY:

CONCLUSION:

Instructor's comments may concern choice of topic, development of ideas, organization, language use, personal appearance, posture, physical activity, sources, and improvement.

(Write sources of information on back of sheet)

SOURCES FROM LITERATURE

Fill out source requirements completely.
Write "none listed" if an author's name or copyright date is not listed.

1. Author's name _____

   Title of book or magazine used _____

   Title of article in above book or magazine _____

   Chapter and/or pages read _____

   Date of above publication _____

2. Author's name _____

   Title of book or magazine used _____

   Title of article in above book or magazine _____

   Chapter and/or pages read _____

   Date of above publication _____

3. Author's name _____

   Title of book or magazine used _____

   Title of article in above book or magazine _____

   Chapter and/or pages read _____

   Date of above publication _____

INTERVIEW SOURCES

1. Person interviewed _____ Date of interview _____

   His position, occupation, and location _____

   Why is he a reliable source? Be specific _____

   _____

2. Person interviewed _____ Date of interview _____

   His position, occupation, and location _____

   Why is he a reliable source? Be specific _____

   _____

PERSONAL EXPERIENCE OF SPEAKER

1. Tell (1) when, (2) where, and (3) conditions under which you became an authority on subject matter in

   your speech _____

   _____

   _____

Chapter 17

THE SPEECH OF WELCOME

Question: *What is meant by "adjusting to the situation"?*

Answer: *You should make your speech fit the assignment, the audience, the environment, your own abilities and the occasion.*

This speech is due:

Time limits: 2-3 minutes.

Speaking notes: Do not use them. Be prepared.

Sources of information: None required. They may be real or fictitious.

Outline your speech: Prepare a 50-100 word complete sentence outline. Designate the exact number of words in your outline. Use the form at the end of this chapter.

To the teacher: It is a good practice to assign welcome speeches and speeches in response to a welcome to pairs of students because the latter speech is dependent upon the former.

PURPOSE OF THE SPEECH OF WELCOME

A speech of welcome is of sufficient importance that you should know how it is organized and what it should do. It occupies a high place in speechmaking, upon its effectiveness hinges much of the success of your public relations among groups that convene daily throughout the land. You may be asked to give a speech of welcome in your own community at any time. It is not enough that you pass the request off lightly or refuse to assist in promoting goodwill because you do not know how to present a speech of welcome. This assignment will provide the experience that will show you how to prepare and present a good speech of welcome. Study it carefully.

EXPLANATION OF THE SPEECH OF WELCOME

A speech of welcome is one made to a single individual or to a group of individuals with the purpose of extending greetings and promoting friendship. The person being welcomed should be made to feel that he is sincerely wanted and that his hosts are delighted to have him among them. The warmest kind of hospitality should be expressed in the welcoming speech. Its genuineness should be so marked that the hearer enjoys a spirit of gladness because he is the guest of a gracious host. The speech is characterized by brevity, simplicity, geniality, and sincerity.

The occasions for the speech of welcome may be extremely varied. The occasion may be a reception for a distinguished visitor, for a native son returning, or for a total stranger. It may welcome home a citizen from foreign travel, missionary work, diplomatic service, or business enterprise. It could welcome a school official, the new minister, or a county officer. If the occasion is to honor an organization,

the welcome may be for a delegation – such as an advertisers' club, a chamber of commerce, a booster club, or a group of county, city, school, or community representatives. In some cases, the welcome may be a special gesture to a conference or convention. But, whatever the occasion, the speech of welcome plays a prominent part.

SUGGESTED SPEECHES OF WELCOME

Study the occasions listed below to discover which one interests you most.

1. Welcome a distinguished visitor.
2. A native son returns home.
3. A stranger visits a local civic organization.
4. A prominent citizen returns from foreign travel.
5. A successful diplomat pays your city a visit.
6. A missionary returns from foreign service.
7. A new minister comes to town.
8. A newly elected school superintendent arrives in your city.
9. A banquet is held for the new teachers.
10. A state official visits your community.
11. The governor stops over a few days on state business.
12. A neighboring city sends a friendly delegation.
13. A booster club visits your city.
14. An advertisers' club comes to your community.
15. A neighboring chamber of commerce is your guest.
16. A nearby city sends a delegation to study your community's excellent school system, water works, fire department . . .
17. An organization holds a convention in your city.

18. An important conference meets in your city.
19. Candidate for governor stops in your community.
20. Speaker's choice.

HOW TO CHOOSE A SPEECH OF WELCOME
Select the occasion that interests you most. Decide definitely the organization you will represent and what position you will hold in the organization. Select one that you know something about or one about which you can secure information. Do not procrastinate in making your decision. Study the list and make your choice or else set up your own occasion if none of the above suggestions suits you. The important point is do not put off your choice of occasion until the day before your speech is due.

HOW TO PREPARE A SPEECH OF WELCOME
First, fix your purpose in mind: you are to make your guests glad to be there. They should admire your hospitality. Next, get your information and set up your speech. Some suggestions follow. You may need to explain the organization which you represent. If so, mention its character, the work it is doing, and points of interest about it, including future plans. Pay a tribute to your guests for their work and tell of advantages gained by their visiting you. Note who the guests are, where they are from, and whom they represent. Explain briefly what their coming means and comment on the common interests your organization holds with them. You should speak of the occasion - its present enjoyment and its future importance. Express anticipated pleasant associations and mutual benefits which are to be derived from the meeting. Invite your guests to feel at home and participate fully in your community. Speak for those whom you represent.

Keep in mind the fact that not all of the above material is always needed in a speech of welcome. You will use only that which is appropriate and you will also adjust it to meet the occasion, whether it be for an individual or for a group of individuals.

Do not say too much or too little. There are plenty of the right thoughts to be expressed in a speech of welcome. Plan to make your remarks brief and to include the appropriate material. Considerable thought and organization will be required. Practice aloud until you have thoroughly mastered your material. Do not memorize the speech word for word.

HOW TO PRESENT A SPEECH OF WELCOME
Let the occasion govern your presentation. If it is formal act and speak appropriately. If it is informal, adjust yourself and your remarks accordingly. In either case be sincere and genuine. Feel what you say. Give your guests a degree of hospitality and warmth of welcome which they will remember; however, do not overdo it and spoil the effectiveness of the speech. Portray the same gentility and friendliness that is present when you open the door of your home to a friend and invite him in.

Speak loudly enough to be heard. Use your normal voice. Speak clearly, pronounce all names distinctly and correctly, and smile pleasantly as is fitting.

Let your body language be appropriate to the occasion, the mood, and your remarks.

Your spoken language should be simple, vivid, appropriate, and devoid of slang and redundancy.

Be brief in time used but complete in your welcome.

IMPROVE YOUR VOCABULARY

Succinct - (sŭk-sinkt') a. Succinct speech is compressed and frequently carries the impression of crispness. Concise, terse, short, brief, summary, laconic. Example: The speaker used rather succinct remarks when he became aroused. Use succinct in this speech and five times a day for the next week. Put it to work for you.

Hunch - Omit this word for a week or two. Use a synonym that enjoys more color and power. Example: Premonition, intuition, presentiment, forewarning, omen, prevision, hallucination, etc.

BIBLIOGRAPHY FOR THE SPEECH OF WELCOME

Cragan, John and Wright, David, Introduction to Speech Communication, Waveland Press, 1980.
Easley, Wayne and Creech, Kenneth, Communication: A Configurative Approach, Kendall-Hunt, 1979.
Jabusch, David M. and Littlejohn, Stephen, Elements of Speech Communication, Houghton Mifflin, 1981.

SPEECH OF WELCOME

By Setits Raclile

Principal Rogers and delegates to the Seventh Regional School Government Conference. It is my pleasure as senior class president to welcome you to our school where we hope you will learn a lot of new information and have a good time doing it. This is the first time you have honored Western America High School by selecting us as your host and I'm glad to tell you we are both proud and happy to have you here today.

Our achievements and our problems are no doubt similar to yours and they make us either joyous or perplexed, depending on whether we are doing something notable or having trouble. I do believe however, every achievement by schools represented here today should be shared so we all may benefit from each other's successes. And I believe just as strongly we should discuss those problems we all face every year. By doing this we can learn from each other how to improve our individual governments and thus improve our schools in this region.

I told you Western America High is pleased to have you as our guests and to show you we really mean it, our school governing council has arranged free bus tours over Exhibition Scenic Drive during our afternoon recess. Just climb on a bus in the parking lot and you'll get the ride of your life with more hairpin curves and thrilling views than you ever dreamed of. Then tonight at 8 o'clock in this building, there will be a delegates' free dance with an outstanding band, which our students will attend to help make your evening more enjoyable.

Once again I want to tell you how glad we are that you are here. We will do our best to help you have a successful conference and a pleasant visit, thus we will all profit greatly from this wonderful experience. When you leave tomorrow we want you to take our friendship and best wishes with you, but until then have a good time and thank you for joining us on this happy occasion.

A GREAT SPEECH IN WORLD HISTORY

**(The example below is for student appreciation and is not
intended for any particular assignment in this text.)**

THEIR FINEST HOUR

By Winston Churchill

The Battle of France is over. I expect that the Battle of Britain is about to begin. Upon this battle depends the survival of Christian civilization. Upon it depends our own British life, and the long continuity of our institutions and our Empire. The whole fury and might of the enemy must very soon be turned on us. Hitler knows that he will have to break us in this Island or lose the war. If we can stand up to him, all Europe may be free and the life of the world may move forward into broad, sunlit uplands. But if we fail, then the whole world, including the United States, including all that we have known and cared for, will sink into the abyss of a new Dark Age made more sinister, and perhaps more protracted, by the lights of perverted science. Let us therefore brace ourselves to our duties, and so bear ourselves that, if the British Empire and its Commonwealth last for a thousand years, men will still say, "This was their finest hour."

(The above paragraph contains the conclusion only. The speech was delivered to the House of Commons,
London, England, then broadcast June 18, 1940, in the early stages of World War II.)

SPEECH OUTLINE

Construct a neat, complete sentence outline on this sheet, tear it out, and hand it to your instructor when you rise to speak. He may wish to write criticisms of the outline and speech in the margins.

Type of speech:_____ Name: _____

Number of words in outline: _____ Date: _____

Purpose of this speech: (What do you want your audience to learn, to think, to believe, to feel, or do because of this speech?) _____

_____

TITLE:

INTRODUCTION:

BODY:

CONCLUSION:

Instructor's comments may concern choice of topic, development of ideas, organization, language use, personal appearance, posture, physical activity, sources, and improvement.

(Write sources of information on back of sheet)

SOURCES FROM LITERATURE
Fill out source requirements completely.
Write "none listed" if an author's name or copyright date is not listed.

1. Author's name _____

   Title of book or magazine used _____

   Title of article in above book or magazine _____

   Chapter and/or pages read _____

   Date of above publication _____

2. Author's name _____

   Title of book or magazine used _____

   Title of article in above book or magazine _____

   Chapter and/or pages read _____

   Date of above publication _____

3. Author's name _____

   Title of book or magazine used _____

   Title of article in above book or magazine _____

   Chapter and/or pages read _____

   Date of above publication _____

INTERVIEW SOURCES

1. Person interviewed _____ Date of interview _____

   His position, occupation, and location _____

   Why is he a reliable source? Be specific _____

   _____

2. Person interviewed _____ Date of interview _____

   His position, occupation, and location _____

   Why is he a reliable source? Be specific _____

   _____

PERSONAL EXPERIENCE OF SPEAKER

1. Tell (1) when, (2) where, and (3) conditions under which you became an authority on subject matter in

   your speech _____

   _____

   _____

   _____

Chapter 18

THE RESPONSE TO A SPEECH OF WELCOME

Question: *How does one overcome talking fast?*

Answer: *Give individual words and phrases greater emphasis. Utilize more pauses. Articulate words distinctly. Make a conscious effort to speak slower.*

This speech is due:

Time limits: 1-2 minutes.

Speaking notes: None. This will be impromptu on many occasions. When it is prepared it is so brief that no notes are needed.

Sources of information: None required. They may be real or fictitious.

Outline your speech: If this is a prepared response, construct a 40-75 word complete sentence outline. Designate the exact number of words in your outline. Use the form at the end of this chapter.

To the teacher: It is helpful to assign students in pairs to give speeches of welcome and response since the latter is dependent on the former. It is a good technique to assign impromptu as well as prepared response speeches. This can be accomplished by a mixed assignment or two separate assignments.

PURPOSE OF THE RESPONSE TO A SPEECH OF WELCOME

Throughout the land many organizations meet on various occasions when visitors are in attendance. Sometimes they just drop in as members of a national fraternal group. At other times they come, representing a similar organization, or they are guests at a convention at which a certain society may be host. On such occasions the visitors are welcomed by a speech. It is of course natural that a response to the welcome be made. Because you may at some time be asked to respond to a welcome speech, it is wise to study a speech of response. The purpose of this assignment is to acquaint you with this type of speech.

EXPLANATION OF THE RESPONSE TO A WELCOME

The speech in response to a welcome is simply a reply to the felicitations expressed by a host. Its purpose is to cement goodwill and friendship, and express these mutual feelings that exist between the groups. It is short, brief, courteous, and friendly. Often, the response is impromptu in nature - which places a burden of doing fast thinking and uttering logical thoughts on the person who presents it. It also demands sincerity and cordiality of manner from the speaker. Naturally, this implies ability and art in the speaking process.

Occasions for this speech occur any time a welcome is given, although a response speech is not always necessary. These occasions may be at conventions, meetings of civic, religious, educational, fraternal, and business organizations, and the like.

SUGGESTED SPEECHES OF RESPONSE

1. Respond to a Rotary Club welcome.
2. Respond to a Lions Club welcome or any other civic organization.
3. You are with a booster group; respond to your welcome.
4. You are a mayor visiting another city. Respond.
5. You are chief of police new to a city. Respond to your welcome.
6. You are a visiting student. Respond to a student council welcome.
7. You are a government official. Respond to a Farm Bureau welcome.
8. You are a student at a religious convention. Respond for your school.
9. You visit a neighboring school athletic council. Respond.
10. You are a teacher visiting another school. Respond to the principal's welcome.
11. You are a debater at a tournament. Respond for your squad.

12. Visit a new chapter of your organization. Respond to the president.
13. Visit a business similar to your own. Respond to the board of directors.
14. You are a new church member. Respond to a welcome at a dinner.
15. You are a new citizen. Respond to a welcome for newcomers at a dinner.
16. You join a new organization. Respond to their welcome.
17. You are a Hi-Y representative at a convention. Respond to a welcome for all representatives.
18. Visit a foreign country. Respond to a welcome at one of their schools.
19. You are a 4-H club member visiting a similar club. Respond to their welcome.
20. Speaker's choice.

HOW TO CHOOSE A TOPIC FOR A RESPONSE SPEECH

If you have been in a situation similar to one of those mentioned above, why not select it for your response? If not, choose a response situation that you believe you would enjoy. Your choice should hold an interest for you. Regardless of how apathetic you may be at the moment choose a topic for your response. Do not put off your choice of a topic, thinking it will be easier later on. As the time approaches for your speech, you may become panicky because you do not know what you will talk about. Such feelings of insecurity are to be expected if you have not selected your response-speech situation early enough.

HOW TO PREPARE A SPEECH OF RESPONSE

First, keep in mind the purpose of your talk, namely, to express your appreciation of the hospitality extended you and to strengthen mutual feelings of friendship. Second, follow an organization that permits use of good speech construction. Include an introduction and conclusion. Make your entire speech brief.

In general you will make the occasion of the welcome overshadow your own personality. Compliments proffered you may be adroitly yet easily directed to the occasion. More specifically, your remarks may be developed in the following manner. Address the host and those associated with him; acknowledge his greeting of welcome and the hospitality of the organization; and express sincere thanks for their courtesies. Extend greetings from your organization and show how the occasion is mutually advantageous to the host and your group. Explain briefly what your organization is, what it stands for. Mention the benefits to be derived from the attitude of mutual helpfulness and enjoyment which are prevalent at this meeting. Predict future pleasant associations with the host organ-

ization, showing this acquaintance to be only a beginning of a long-lasting cooperation of friendship. Mention in conclusion that you have been made to feel most welcome and at home. Thank your hosts again for their hospitality, extend best wishes, and then be seated.

This speech may have to be impromptu. Because of the frequent possibility of impromptu speeches of response, you should set up a basic sequence of ideas which you can use in replying to any speech of welcome. Of course, if you are designated ahead of time to present the speech, you should carefully organize and rehearse your speech until you have it well in mind. Under either circumstance, you can be prepared if you give attention to the points presented in the preceding paragraphs.

HOW TO PRESENT A RESPONSE SPEECH

Your attitude and demeanor must be a happy combination of appreciation and friendliness. Your remarks must have the qualities of sincerity and gratitude. The only way to reach these ends is to demonstrate them through appropriate bodily actions and a simple understandable language. There is no call for ostentation, sarcasm, bragging, or for any attempt to show off your personal qualities.

When you are presented by your host, rise politely, smile pleasantly, and begin your response. Avoid scraping your chair if you are at a table, or playing with the dinnerware if it lies before you. Maintain your poise by observing an alert posture. Make yourself heard by all but do not shout or speak overly loud. Adhere to the policy of brevity but do not give the appearance of having nothing to say. When you have finished the speech, sit down. Remember that you are still under observation.

Here are a few additional suggestions:

- Be sure that your speech is appropriate to the audience and the occasion. If the occasion is formal, conduct yourself accordingly; if it is not formal, adjust yourself to this situation.

- Have a few serious thoughts in your speech, even though gaiety fills the air. Do not resort to telling nothing more than a series of stories or anecdotes.

- Do not apologize or attempt the trite pose of your being surprised. You should know that as a guest you are subject to being called on at any time. Accept your responsibility and meet it as a mature person by having something worthwhile to say.

IMPROVE YOUR VOCABULARY

Invidious - (ĭn-vĭd'ĭ-ŭs) a. Tending to cause ill will or envy, likely to offend, disagreeable, unjustly and irritatingly discriminating, hateful. Example: The invidious distinctions between classes in America is a national problem.

Mighty - Try not to use mighty for several days. You probably rely on it too much. Liven up your speech with synonyms. Examples are: extremely, overwhelmingly, highly, inordinately, immoderately, exasperatingly, preposterously, excessively, enormously, remarkably, notably, signally, incredibly, stupendously, etc.

BIBLIOGRAPHY FOR THE RESPONSE TO A SPEECH OF WELCOME

Ochs, Donovan J. and Winkler, A. C., A Brief Introduction to Speech, Harcourt Brace Jovanovich, 1979.
Samovar, Larry and Mills, Jack, Communication: Message and Response, Wm. C. Brown, 1980.
Zimmerman, Gordon and Others, Speech Communication: A Contemporary Introduction, West, 2d ed., 1980.

★　★　★　★　★

RESPONSE TO A SPEECH OF WELCOME

By Yenan Noscaasi

Fellow delegates and Principal Rogers. I want to thank Mr. Raclile for his most friendly remarks and tell him we do feel the sincere welcome he speaks of. Already there seems to be present among us a spirit of cooperation and strong desire to exchange information helpful to every school represented at this conference. I truly believe that if each of us can gain only one new idea from our various group meetings and the guest speakers we will all return home with the satisfaction of having attained something worthwhile.

We all trust that our presence here will in a sense express the esteem we hold for Western America High School. It's a privilege to come here to share our experiences and thoughts with Western's students and delegates in their outstanding facilities. We can all see how much preparation they have made for us and also see they are doing everything possible to make this conference a success.

As representative-at-large from all schools present I want to thank Western America High for arranging our housing and meals; also for the bus tour coming up this afternoon and the big dance tonight. I'm sure everyone will enjoy these events. By having a good time together and exchanging ideas we will have a conference second to none. So to our hosts I want to say on behalf of all of us "thanks for everything".

SPEECH OUTLINE

Construct a neat, complete sentence outline on this sheet, tear it out, and hand it to your instructor when you rise to speak. He may wish to write criticisms of the outline and speech in the margins.

Type of speech:_____ Name: _____

Number of words in outline: _____ Date: _____

Purpose of this speech: (What do you want your audience to learn, to think, to believe, to feel, or do because of this speech?) _____

_____

TITLE:

INTRODUCTION:

BODY:

CONCLUSION:

Instructor's comments may concern choice of topic, development of ideas, organization, language use, personal appearance, posture, physical activity, sources, and improvement.

(Write sources of information on back of sheet)

SOURCES FROM LITERATURE

Fill out source requirements completely.
Write "none listed" if an author's name or copyright date is not listed.

1. Author's name _____

    Title of book or magazine used _____

    Title of article in above book or magazine _____

    Chapter and/or pages read _____

    Date of above publication _____

2. Author's name _____

    Title of book or magazine used _____

    Title of article in above book or magazine _____

    Chapter and/or pages read _____

    Date of above publication _____

3. Author's name _____

    Title of book or magazine used _____

    Title of article in above book or magazine _____

    Chapter and/or pages read _____

    Date of above publication _____

INTERVIEW SOURCES

1. Person interviewed _____ Date of interview _____

    His position, occupation, and location _____

    Why is he a reliable source? Be specific _____

    _____

2. Person interviewed _____ Date of interview _____

    His position, occupation, and location _____

    Why is he a reliable source? Be specific _____

    _____

PERSONAL EXPERIENCE OF SPEAKER

1. Tell (1) when, (2) where, and (3) conditions under which you became an authority on subject matter in

    your speech _____

    _____

    _____

    _____

Chapter 19

PRESENTING A GIFT OR AWARD

Question: *How can you lower the tone of your voice?*

Answer: *This should be undertaken only with the advice and supervision of a trained speech pathologist. Consult such a person.*

This speech is due:
Time limits: 1-3 minutes.
Speaking notes: None.
Sources of information: None required. They may be real or fictitious.
Outline your speech: Prepare a 50-75 word complete sentence outline. Designate the exact number of words in your outline. Use the form at the end of the chapter.

PURPOSE OF THE SPEECH EXPERIENCE OF PRESENTING A GIFT OR AWARD

Many centuries ago, ancient peoples presented gifts and awards. The practice continues today without abatement. Every time the occasion of presenting a gift or award occurs, someone must make the presentation speech. It is not easy to make a public presentation graciously, to handle the situation with ease, and to utter thoughts that symbolize the spirit of the event. Yet, at any time you may be designated to perform this task. When this necessity does arise, you should know something about making a presentation speech. This assignment will tell what to do and say on such an occasion.

To the teacher: It might be wise to assign students in pairs, one to present an award, the other to receive it. This provides an excellent experience. See the following chapter.

EXPLANATION OF THE PRESENTATION SPEECH

A presentation speech is one made in conjunction with the presentation of an award or gift. It is short, sincere, and commendatory of the recipient. It requires tact and good taste because of divided attitudes towards the recipient of the award. Too much nor too little should be said about the recipient, because others, no doubt, are just as worthy of the award or gift as he is. Intense rivalry may have been present in seeking the award. Feelings and emotions may have been high. To understand the tenor of the audience, to avoid embarrassing the winner, and to use a language appreciated by all or even a majority requires a simple yet artistic quality of speech.

Occasions for this type of speech vary. One of these occurs when a prize is won in a contest. Here the prize is known beforehand; for this reason there is no surprise relative to what it will be. There will be partisan desire, expectancy, uncertainty, and even divided opinion among the judges regarding the winner. This poses a delicate problem for the speaker who makes the presentation – which may be formal. Emphasis will be placed upon interest, the careful consideration of the judges, and their delicate position.

Another occasion is one in which an object is given to an organization, such as a school, church, city, society, or other group. It is likely that the whole atmosphere will be formal. The procedures, plans, and persons who participate will be known long before the actual donation takes place. There will be no surprise. The speech will be pointed to emphasize the symbolism or utility of the gift.

A third occasion involves awarding a medal or other recognition for service. The surprise element may or may not be present. Depending on the occasion and the type of recognition, much emotion may be present. The ceremony and speech should not make it difficult for the recipient. The deed will obscure the gift, although tribute will be paid the one who is honored. During times of national crisis or emergency, this is a frequent occasion for presentations.

A fourth kind of award is one made in appreciation of service. Surprise is often present. There is no rivalry, but rather good fellowship and possibly a little sadness. Examples of this kind of award are the retirement of a president or other official from a society, a school or civic organization, the leave taking of a pastor, or the departure of any prominent citizen from community or group service. Here, emphasis is placed on the happy side of joyful fellowship. Some regret for the departure is expressed, but hope for the future is given a prominent place.

SUGGESTED TYPES OF PRESENTATION SPEECHES

Construct a short speech around one of the following occasions:

1. Present a scholarship.
2. Present a cash prize to an essay contest winner.
3. Present a cup to a beauty contest winner.
4. Present a cup to the winner of a tournament.
5. Present a cash prize to the winner of a sales contest.
6. Present an organ to a church.
7. Present a set of books to a library.
8. Present a swimming pool to a city.
9. Present $5000 to the college to apply on a new building.
10. Present a safe-driving award.
11. Present a medal for good conduct.
12. Present a medal for meritorious service during a fire.
13. Present a medal for outstanding leadership in the community.
14. Present an award for making a new scientific discovery.
15. Present an award to a retiring school official.
16. Present an award to the oldest employee in a business.
17. Present an award to an employee with the longest tenure.
18. Present an award to a minister who is leaving.
19. Present an award to the head of a business firm.
20. Speaker's choice.

HOW TO CHOOSE A TOPIC

Study the above list carefully. The suggestions represent different occasions for gifts or awards. Choose one that you would like to present by visualizing the occasion and ceremony. Make your choice without long delay so that you may adequately prepare your speech.

HOW TO PREPARE A PRESENTATION SPEECH

In preparing this speech, make certain that you are fully aware of the occasion and any particular requirements governing it or the presentation. Keep in mind that it is an honor to present a gift or award, that it is not an opportunity to make a speech on your pet subject. By all means observe proper speech construction.

In preparing your talk, there are several predominating thoughts to bear in mind. First, do not overpraise the individual. Overpraise will do more harm than good. Second, it is desirable to pay deserving tribute to the recipient, if wise restraint is exercised. Third, be careful not to over-emphasize the gift or its value. Stress instead the work or merit which the award signifies. Let glory abide in achievement, not in the material object.

Briefly, your specific organization of ideas may fall into the following sequence: Make appropriate remarks to the audience; let these remarks refer to the occasion that brought them together. Relate a short history of the event that is now being fittingly culminated. Give the immediate reasons for the award and show that, regardless of its value, the award is only a token of the real appreciation for the service rendered or the esteem felt for the recipient of the award.

As for the recipient, recount his personal worth and tell how this worth was recognized or discovered. If you personally know him, mention the fact that you are intimately aware of his service or merit.

Next, explain the character and purpose of the gift or award. Should the object be a picture or statue, the custom is to have it veiled until the speech is concluded or nearly concluded; then at the proper moment withdraw the veil. If the gift or award is to be presented to an organization, the ceremony will go more smoothly if someone is informed ahead of time that he is to represent his group in receiving the gift.

Prepare your ideas by rehearsing aloud until you have them thoroughly in mind. Do not memorize your speech but be sure to know what you are going to say.

HOW TO PRESENT A PRESENTATION SPEECH

Your attitude and manner must convey the sincerity behind the entire occasion. There must be no ostentation, show, or flamboyancy in your speech or actions.

Be sure that the award or gift is available and ready to be presented. When the moment arrives for you to transfer the award or gift to the donee, call him to the platform. If he is already there, address him by name so that he may rise in response. Then, in a few words properly chosen, present the gift by summarizing the reasons for the presentation. Mention the appropriateness of the award and offer the recipient good wishes for the future. After the recipient has accepted the object, permit him time to thank you or make other remarks to you or to the people gathered around. An acceptance speech will be in order.

A few technicalities to observe are these: Be sure you stand so that the audience can see and hear you. Do not stand in front of the gift. Let the audience see it. Near the conclusion of your speech, when you are ready to make the presentation, pick up the gift or award, being particular to hold it so that it is clearly visible to everyone. Stand at an angle with your side slightly toward the audience. Hand the gift to the recipient by using the hand nearest to him (the upstage hand). He will in turn accept it with his upstage hand. If it is a medal you wish to pin to his coat, stand with your side to the audience while pinning it on. Should the object be a picture, statue, or other material which cannot be transferred from hand to hand, it will of course be unveiled or shown at the moment of presentation.

Be sure you speak loudly enough to be heard by all, especially when you are turned partially away from the audience.

IMPROVE YOUR VOCABULARY

Summary – (sŭm'a-rĭ) a. Done at once without delay or formality, executed quickly. Example: The man was dealt a summary punishment. Use this word five times a day for the next week so that you can add to your verbal tools.

Interesting – Try omitting this word. You probably work it too much. Use a synonym. Examples are: amusing, entertaining, diverting, fascinating, unusual, curious, exceptional, unique, remarkable, fantastic, bizarre, exotic, unconventional, etc.

BIBLIOGRAPHY FOR PRESENTING A GIFT OR AWARD

Powell, J. Lewis, Executive Speaking: An Acquired Skill, Bureau of National Affairs, 1980.
Searle, J. R., Expression and Meaning, Cambridge Univ. Press, 1979.
Sproule, J. Michael, Language and Its Influence, McGraw, 1980.

★ ★ ★ ★ ★

SPEECH PRESENTING A GIFT OR AWARD

By Valerie Ritter

Fellow Parents and Athletes:

This awards banquet has been an annual event for several years. Some of you here tonight will look forward to many more banquets such as this, while others will reminisce of the banquets past. These are special nights for athletes and parents, for it is because of you that these banquets are held. As President of the Scholarship Selection Committee it is with great pleasure that I am able to present this award.

This evening there is a student present who has earned recognition by means of his outstanding performance as an athlete. This recognition presented by the University is an annual event arranged to provide financial assistance for students with athletic ability.

The recipient is a transfer student from the College of DuPage located in Glen Ellen, Illinois. He has been active as an athlete throughout his school years. Tonight I wish to present Mr. Rich Kielczewski with a scholarship recognizing his ability in the game of tennis.

Rich is honest and hard-working and is dedicated to the sport of tennis. He always seems to put forth more effort than is originally necessary. He is also a qualified and very competent tennis instructor.

Rich has entered many amateur tournaments. Among those in which he has captured the crown are the Chicago District Tournament and six consecutive conference titles. He has also received recognition of the people of Illinois by being ranked sixteenth in the state.

I have known Rich for a long time and have many times witnessed his stunning ability to overcome his opponent. I personally know of no other person more deserving of this tennis scholarship.

In view of these outstanding qualities and accomplishments, I am very pleased to present Rich Kielczewski with this scholarship in behalf of Northwest Missouri State University.

A GREAT SPEECH IN AMERICAN HISTORY

(The example below is for student appreciation and is not
intended for any particular assignment in this text.)

Benjamin Franklin

ON THE FEDERAL CONSTITUTION
(1787)

(The Constitution was adopted only after much debate. In the following speech one
well-known individual expresses his feelings about signing the document.)

I CONFESS that I do not entirely approve of this Constitution at present; but, sir, I am not sure I shall never approve of it, for, having lived long, I have experienced many instances of being obliged, by better information or fuller consideration, to change opinions even on important subjects, which I once thought right, but found to be otherwise. It is therefore that, the older I grow, the more apt I am to doubt my own judgment of others. Most men, indeed, as well as most sects in religion, think themselves in possession of all truth, and that wherever others differ from them, it is so far error. Steele, a Protestant, in a dedication, tells the pope that the only difference between our two churches in their opinions of the certainty of their doctrine is, the Romish Church is infallible, and the Church of England is never in the wrong. But, tho many private persons think almost as highly of their own infallibility as of that of their sect, few express it so naturally as a certain French lady, who, in a little dispute with her sister said: "But I meet with nobody but myself that is always in the right."

In these sentiments, sir, I agree to this Constitution with all its faults – if they are such – because I think a general government necessary for us, and there is no form of government but what may be a blessing to the people if well administered; and I believe, further, that this is likely to be well administered for a course of years, and can only end in despotism, as other forms have done before it, when the people shall become so corrupted as to need despotic government, being incapable of any other. I doubt, too, whether any other convention we can obtain may be able to make a better Constitution; for, when you assemble a number of men, to have the advantage of their joint wisdom, you inevitably assemble with those men all their prejudices, their passions, their errors of opinion, their local interests, and their selfish views. From such an assembly can a perfect production be expected?

It therefore astonishes me, sir, to find this system approaching so near to perfection as it does; and I think it will astonish our enemies, who are waiting with confidence to hear that our counsels are confounded like those of the builders of Babel, and that our States are on the point of separation, only to meet hereafter for the purpose of cutting one another's throats. Thus I consent, sir, to this Constitution, because I expect no better, and because I am not sure that it is not the best. The opinions I have had of its errors I sacrifice to the public good. I have never whispered a syllable of them abroad. Within these walls they were born, and here they shall die. If every one of us, in returning to our constituents, were to report the objections he has had to it, and endeavor to gain partizans in support of them, we might prevent its being generally received, and thereby lose all the salutary effects and great advantages resulting naturally in our favor among foreign nations, as well as among ourselves, from our real or apparent unanimity. Much of the strength and efficiency of any government, in procuring and securing happiness to the people, depends on opinion, on the general opinion of the goodness of that government, as well as of the wisdom and integrity of its governors. I hope, therefore, for our own sakes, as a part of the people, and for the sake of our posterity, that we shall act heartily and unanimously in recommending this Constitution wherever our influence may extend, and turn our future thoughts and endeavors to the means of having it well administered.

On the whole, sir, I can not help expressing a wish that every member of the convention who may still have objections to it, would, with me, on this occasion, doubt a little of his own infallibility, and, to make manifest our unanimity, put his name to this instrument.

From a speech in Philadelphia before the Constitutional Convention of 1787.

SPEECH OUTLINE

Construct a neat, complete sentence outline on this sheet, tear it out, and hand it to your instructor when you rise to speak. He may wish to write criticisms of the outline and speech in the margins.

Type of speech:_____ Name: _____

Number of words in outline: _____ Date: _____

Purpose of this speech: (What do you want your audience to learn, to think, to believe, to feel, or do because of this speech?) _____

_____

TITLE:

INTRODUCTION:

BODY:

CONCLUSION:

Instructor's comments may concern choice of topic, development of ideas, organization, language use, personal appearance, posture, physical activity, sources, and improvement.

(Write sources of information on back of sheet)

SOURCES FROM LITERATURE

Fill out source requirements completely.
Write "none listed" if an author's name or copyright date is not listed.

1. Author's name _____

   Title of book or magazine used _____

   Title of article in above book or magazine _____

   Chapter and/or pages read _____

   Date of above publication _____

2. Author's name _____

   Title of book or magazine used _____

   Title of article in above book or magazine _____

   Chapter and/or pages read _____

   Date of above publication _____

3. Author's name _____

   Title of book or magazine used _____

   Title of article in above book or magazine _____

   Chapter and/or pages read _____

   Date of above publication _____

INTERVIEW SOURCES

1. Person interviewed _____ Date of interview _____

   His position, occupation, and location _____

   Why is he a reliable source? Be specific _____

   _____

2. Person interviewed _____ Date of interview _____

   His position, occupation, and location _____

   Why is he a reliable source? Be specific _____

   _____

PERSONAL EXPERIENCE OF SPEAKER

1. Tell (1) when, (2) where, and (3) conditions under which you became an authority on subject matter in

   your speech _____

   _____

   _____

Chapter 20

ACCEPTING A GIFT OR AWARD

Question: *Should pitch vary much during a speech?*

Answer: *Yes. It will add variety.*

This speech is due:

Time limits: 1-2 minutes.

Speaking notes: None. Your remarks will be impromptu or, if not, then very brief.

Sources of information: None required. They may be real or fictitious.

Outline your speech: If this is not impromptu, prepare a 50-75 word complete sentence outline. Designate the exact number of words in your outline. Use the form at the end of this chapter.

PURPOSE OF THE SPEECH OF ACCEPTANCE OF A GIFT OR AWARD

Because untold numbers of presentation speeches for gifts and awards are made every year, we are justified in assuming that almost as many acceptance speeches are made by the persons who are honored with the awards. The custom is as old as the centuries. The recipient is not always told in advance that he will be honored by a gift or award; hence he can be embarrassed if he does not know how to accept the honor with simple sincerity. This speech experience will provide you a definite background for such an event; for this reason it is important.

To the teacher: It is a practical experience to assign this speech in conjunction with the one entitled "Presenting a Gift or Award." See the preceding chapter.

EXPLANATION OF THE ACCEPTANCE SPEECH

A speech made by the receiver of a gift or award is a sincere expression of his appreciation of the honor accorded him. It should establish him as a friendly, modest, and worthwhile individual to whom the people may rightfully pay tribute for merit and achievement. Its purpose should be to impress the donors with his worthiness and to make them happy in their choice. To do this will demand a gentility and nobleness that springs naturally from the heart of the receiver. There can be no artificial or hollow remarks uttered by a shallow mind.

It should be noted that in some instances no speech is necessary, the only essential propriety being a pleasant "thank you," accompanied by an appreciative smile. To do more than this when it is not appropriate to do so is awkward. However, when a speech is in order, it must be propitious. The recipient himself must decide on each occasion whether or not a speech is wanted or needed.

Occasions for acceptance speeches arise, potentially, every time an award or gift is presented. They occur in schools, clubs, societies, civic and religious organizations, business houses, government offices, . . . Any of these groups may wish to honor a member of their organization, another organization, or someone else for service, merit, achievement or winning a prize. Possibilities for presentations and their accompanying speeches are unlimited.

SUGGESTIONS FOR ACCEPTANCE SPEECHES

1. Accept a scholarship.
2. Accept a prize for writing poetry.
3. Accept a cup for winning a swimming contest.
4. Accept a prize for raising superior livestock.
5. Accept a prize for winning a golf match.
6. Accept a donation for a church.
7. Accept a donation of funds for the new ball park.
8. Accept a new cabin for the Boy Scouts or Girl Scouts.
9. Accept a cup for the debate team or some other team.
10. Accept a medal for saving a life.
11. Accept a medal for rescuing a drowning person.
12. Accept a medal for outstanding community service.
13. Accept a prize for a new invention.
14. Accept an award for long service on a particular job.
15. Accept an award for outstanding performance of duty.
16. Accept a prize for your school for winning a contest.
17. As captain of your basketball team accept a championship award.
18. Accept a birthday gift.
19. Accept a retirement award.
20. Speaker's choice.

HOW TO CHOOSE A TOPIC FOR AN ACCEPTANCE SPEECH

Study the above suggestions. Select the one you would like most to receive. Do not delay making a choice.

HOW TO PREPARE AN ACCEPTANCE SPEECH

This speech will necessarily be impromptu on some occasions; hence little preparation can be made other than by formulating a basic pattern of ideas about which you will speak. If you are warned or informed early that you will receive a gift or award, then, of course, you should certainly prepare a speech. In this case all the principles of good speech construction and organization should be followed. However, in either case, there are several important points to be noted: First, utilize simple language, without show or sham. Second, express in your initial remarks a true sense of gratitude and appreciation for the gift. If you are really surprised, you may say so; however, the surprise must be genuine. If you are not surprised, omit any reference to your feeling. No one will be moved by an attempt at naivete. Next, you should modestly disclaim total credit for winning the award. Give credit to those who assisted you in any way, for without them you could not have achieved your success. Praise their cooperation and support. Do not apologize for winning. Do not disclaim your worthiness. Inasmuch as you were selected to receive a tribute, be big enough to accept it modestly and graciously, but not grovelingly. Your next point may be the expression of appreciation for the beauty and significance of the gift. Its nature and kind will determine what you say. Do not overpraise it or over value it. Observe suitable restraint. In no manner should you express disappointment. Conclude your remarks by speaking of your plans or intentions for the future, especially as they may be connected with the award or gift or work associated with it. As a final word you may repeat your thanks for the object or recognition.

HOW TO PRESENT AN ACCEPTANCE SPEECH

Your attitude must be one of sincerity, friendliness, appreciation, modesty, and warm enthusiasm. Conceit and ego must be entirely lacking. You should be personal, if the award is for you. If you represent a group, use the pronoun "we" instead of "I."

When the donor speaks to you, either come to the platform or rise and step towards him if you are already there. Should you approach from the audience, move forward politely and alertly. Neither hurry nor loiter. Let your bearing be one of appreciation for what is to come. Arriving on the platform, stand near the donor but avoid viewing the award anxiously or reaching for it before it is extended to you. Do not stand in front of it. In accepting the award stand slightly sideways toward the audience, reach for and receive the object in the hand nearest the other person (this will be the upstage hand); in this way you avoid reaching in front of yourself or turning your body away from the audience. After receiving the object, hold it so it remains in full view of the audience. If it is too large to hold, place it in an appropriate spot on stage, step to one side and begin your speech; that is, if a speech is in accord with the proceedings and occasion. If you return to a seat in the audience, carry the gift in your hand, do not stuff it into a pocket if it is a small object.

Now as to the speech itself. Observe all the elements of acceptable stage presence. Be dressed appropriately, maintain an alert and polite posture, speak clearly and distinctly and loudly enough to be heard by all. If your speech is impromptu, you will not be expected to possess the fluency of one who was forewarned of the occasion. Insofar as is possible, let your manner express an undeniable friendliness and appreciation for the honor being accorded you. This sincerity is the most important part of your speech. It will have to be evident in your voice, your bodily actions, your gestures, the look on your face, everything about you. Be sure to express no shame. Do not be afraid of a little emotion; just control it so that you are not overcome by it. Make no apologies for your speaking. Avoid awkward positions that are indicative of too much self-consciousness. Do these things and your acceptance will be genuine and applauded by all who see and hear you.

IMPROVE YOUR VOCABULARY

Anomaly - (ȧ-nŏm'ȧ-lĭ) n. Deviation from the ordinary, irregularity, unnaturalness, abnormality. singularity, uniqueness, peculiarity, strangeness. Example: The sudden volcanic eruption was a great anomaly of nature. Use this word five times a day for the next week so that you may claim it for your own.

Mad - Let's use synonyms for this overworked language slave. Examples are: deluded, frustrated, insane, frenzied, annoyed, disappointed, chagrined, dismayed, irritated, disconcerted, confused, cross, peevish, ill-natured, touchy, crusty, testy, irascible, furious, enraged, etc.

BIBLIOGRAPHY FOR ACCEPTING A GIFT OR AWARD

Mudd, Charles S. and Sillars, M. O., Speech: Content and Communication, Harper & Row, 4th ed., 1979.
Taylor, Anita and Others, Communicating, Prentice-Hall, 1980.
Verderber, Rudolph F., Challenge of Effective Speaking, Wadsworth, 1979.

* * * * *

SPEECH ACCEPTING A GIFT OR AWARD

By Rich Kielczewski

I am very proud to be receiving this award. It was made possible by the recognition I earned when winning some amateur tournaments. Much of the credit, due to winning the award, must go to my high school coach, Steve Weiss, because he put in more time and effort than was required of a high school coach. I wish to thank my parents, for without their support and encouragement I never could have reached the point where I am today. My teammates also helped by contributing time to me, with their moral support and eagerness for me to excel. Finally, I wish to thank my instructors for their willingness to excuse me from their classes thus permitting me to travel. I plan to play for NMSU two more years and using that experience to venture out to the professional field.

Here at NMSU I shall contribute much time and effort to help my teammates supply the necessary requirements for a winning team. Thank you.

* * * * *

SPEECH ACCEPTING A GIFT OR AWARD

By Sherri Dunker

Three years ago if anyone had told I would someday join a sorority, I would have laughed in her face — there was just no way I was going to become a part of those, quote "cliquey snobs." But to this day I bless the friend who persuaded me to find out what sororities were really about. They weren't snobs at all but beautiful people with the same fears, frustrations, and hopes like many women.

Now I am very proud to say that I too am a sorority woman, and with honor I accept this "Most Spirited Kappa Delta Award." This sorority has taught me more than any text or instructor could have ever hoped to accomplish — it's given me my "people" degree in college.

Kappa Delta has shown me the importance of budgeting time wisely, accepting and utilizing criticism, respecting and listening to others' ideas, social etiquette, and especially leadership experience. Incalculable are KD's gifts, but I'll never forget the most precious of all — my vast circle of sisters who genuinely care. You accepted me for what I am and have helped me build my self-confidence. Thanks for standing by me through my moments of despair and making college a pleasant life.

I truly believe in you, Kappa Delta, and all for which you stand — the most "honorable, beautiful and highest!"* I shall treasure this award, and when I glance upon it long after I have graduated, I shall remember all the glorious memories and sisters of Kappa Delta. Thank you.

* Open Motto of Kappa Delta.

SPEECH OUTLINE

Construct a neat, complete sentence outline on this sheet, tear it out, and hand it to your instructor when you rise to speak. He may wish to write criticisms of the outline and speech in the margins.

Type of speech:_____ Name: _____

Number of words in outline: _____ Date: _____

Purpose of this speech: (What do you want your audience to learn, to think, to believe, to feel, or do because of this speech?) _____

_____

TITLE:

INTRODUCTION:

BODY:

CONCLUSION:

Instructor's comments may concern choice of topic, development of ideas, organization, language use, personal appearance, posture, physical activity, sources, and improvement.

(Write sources of information on back of sheet)

SOURCES FROM LITERATURE
Fill out source requirements completely.
Write "none listed" if an author's name or copyright date is not listed.

1. Author's name _____

   Title of book or magazine used _____

   Title of article in above book or magazine _____

   Chapter and/or pages read _____

   Date of above publication _____

2. Author's name _____

   Title of book or magazine used _____

   Title of article in above book or magazine _____

   Chapter and/or pages read _____

   Date of above publication _____

3. Author's name _____

   Title of book or magazine used _____

   Title of article in above book or magazine _____

   Chapter and/or pages read _____

   Date of above publication _____

INTERVIEW SOURCES

1. Person interviewed _____ Date of interview _____

   His position, occupation, and location _____

   Why is he a reliable source? Be specific _____

   _____

2. Person interviewed _____ Date of interview _____

   His position, occupation, and location _____

   Why is he a reliable source? Be specific _____

   _____

PERSONAL EXPERIENCE OF SPEAKER

1. Tell (1) when, (2) where, and (3) conditions under which you became an authority on subject matter in
   your speech _____

   _____

   _____

Chapter 21

THE FAREWELL SPEECH

Question: *How fast should you talk when giving a speech?*

Answer: *The rate varies with the ability to talk distinctly – 125 to 150 words per minute is about average, however, these figures vary considerably.*

This speech is due:
Time limits: 4–5 minutes.
Speaking notes: Do not use any for this speech.
Sources of information: None required. They may be real or fictitious.
Outline your speech: Prepare a 75–150 word complete sentence outline. Designate the exact number of words in your outline. Use the form at the end of this chapter.

PURPOSE OF THE FAREWELL SPEECH

Many times a person finds himself the guest of honor in which his business or social friends entertain him at a farewell party; or they may simply "call a group together" as a final gesture of their esteem and admiration for him. The guest of honor is invariably asked to say a few words as a last expression before he leaves. Too often, what he says may be only a mumbling of incoherent remarks, because he has never had a previous experience of this kind and does not know what is appropriate at such a time. This speech assignment will give you an experience that will point the way when you are called upon to make a farewell speech.

EXPLANATION OF THE FAREWELL SPEECH

A farewell speech is one in which a person publicly says goodbye to a group of acquaintances. It should express the speaker's appreciation for what his acquaintances have helped him accomplish and for the happiness they have brought him. It may be given at a formal or informal gathering, a luncheon or a dinner. Frequently, on this occasion, the guest of honor will receive a gift from the group. A common informal party occurs when "the boss," a superior, or some other leader calls an informal meeting following the day's work, at which time the person who is leaving will receive commendation, favorable testimonials, and possibly a gift. He will, too, be expected to "say something." The formal occasion is, of course, much more elaborate and is surrounded by formalities from start to finish.

Occasions for the farewell speech are of one general kind – leave taking. Situations may vary greatly; however, a few of the usual ones are the following: retirement after years of service in a certain employment; taking a new job; promotion to a different type of work that demands a change in location; concluding service in a civic or religious organization; leaving school; or moving to another community for any reason whatsoever.

The occasion, whatever its nature, should not be treated with too much sadness. It should be approached with true sincerity and honesty. Feelings of deep emotion may be present, and if so, they should be expressed in a manner in keeping with the occasion and all persons present.

SUGGESTED OCCASIONS FOR A FAREWELL SPEECH

1. Leaving school.
2. Going home from a foreign country.
3. Joining the Armed Services.
4. Moving to a new location - any reason.
5. Taking a new job elsewhere.
6. Retiring from employment after twenty years.
7. Retiring from a church position.
8. Retiring from a civic position.
9. Going back home after completing a year's job.
10. Leaving a community where you were "stationed" on a job.
11. Just married - moving away.
12. Going to Hollywood to try your hand at motion pictures.
13. Going on a two year's tour around the world.
14. Going to Africa to do research on tropical diseases.
15. Leaving for South America to hunt oil.
16. Leaving for the South Pole on a trip of exploration.
17. Going to New York to become an actor.
18. Going to Central America to survey jungle lands.

19. Leaving on a rocket for a distant planet.
20. Speaker's choice.

HOW TO CHOOSE A TOPIC

First of all, is there any one of these topics that really compels your interest? If so, select it. If not, choose the one that interests you most. Perhaps no suggestion suits you. In this event think of situations similar to some of those mentioned and then formulate your own topic. Do not postpone your selection because you cannot make up your mind. Get a topic now; begin thinking about its organization and development. Above all things, do not try to excuse yourself from making a selection now or in the very near future. This will only mean less time in which to prepare your speech.

HOW TO PREPARE A FAREWELL
SPEECH

Remember that this is a special occasion and that old friends are honoring you. Remember, too, that there may be an atmosphere of considerable sentiment and emotion, or there may be one merely of friendly gaiety. This means you must carefully analyze your audience, their probable mood, and the general atmosphere. If you are likely to be presented a gift, plan your remarks so that you may accept it graciously. Sincerity must dominate your utterances whatever they may be.

Farewell speeches usually follow a well-defined pattern with appropriate variations which the speaker deems necessary. It is advisable to begin your talk by referring to the past, the time when you first arrived and why you came to the community. A bit of humor of some interesting anecdotes may be in good taste. The way you were made welcome or to feel at home might be an excellent recollection. Continue your thoughts by pointing out how your ideals and those of the audience, though not completely attained, inspired you to do what you did, that work remains still to be done. Express appreciation for their support of your efforts which made your achievements possible. Commend the harmony and the coopera-

tion that prevailed. Tell them that you will always remember your associations with this group as one of the outstanding events in your life. Speak next of your future work briefly but sincerely. Explain why you are leaving, and what compelled you to go into a new field or location. Show that your work just completed will act as a background and inspiration to that which lies ahead. Continue by encouraging those who remain, predict greater achievements for them, praise your successor if you know who he is, and conclude with a genuine expression of your appreciation for them and a continued interest in their future. Remember, if you received a gift, to give a final word of thanks for it.

In your speech omit any and all references or illusions to unpleasantries or friction that may have existed. Do not make the occasion bitter or sad. Be happy and leave others with the same feeling. Smile. Make sure that a good impression will follow you.

Organize and practice this speech far enough in advance that you can conscientiously present it as representative of your best work.

HOW TO PRESENT A FAREWELL
SPEECH

In this speech fit your manner to the mood of the occasion and audience. Do not go overboard in solemnity, emotion, or gaiety. Be appropriate. Use a friendly and sincere approach throughout. Adjust your introductory remarks to the prevailing mood; then move into your speech. Speak loudly enough to be heard by all. Use bodily action suitable to the audience, the occasion, the speech, the environment, and yourself. Be sure that your language is appropriate to the five requirements just recited. Avoid ponderous phrases, over-emotionalized words and tones, redundancy, and flowery or florid attempts at oratory. Let everything you do and say, coupled with a good appearance and alert posture, be the evidence that you are genuinely and sincerely mindful of their appreciation of you at your departure.

IMPROVE YOUR VOCABULARY

Fatuity - (fȧ-tū'i̯-tĭ) n. Easily "taken in," stupidity, folly, self-complacency, dullness, imbecility. Example: A smart person seldom exhibits fatuity. Use this word in this speech and five times a day for the next week. Make it yours. You can.

Blue or down in the dumps - Omit these words. Too many people have overworked them. Give them a rest for at least a week. Use one of the following synonyms to add power to your vocabulary: melancholy, morose, dejected, distressed, pensive, despondent, disconsolate, doleful, gloomy, wretched, miserable, etc.

BIBLIOGRAPHY FOR THE FAREWELL SPEECH

Nelson, Paul E. and Pearson, J. C., <u>Confidence in Public Speaking</u>, Wm. C. Brown, 1981.
Peterson, Brent D. and Others, <u>Speak Easy: Introduction to Public Speaking</u>, West, 1980.
Rein, Irving J., <u>The Public Speaking Book</u>, Scott Foresman, 1981.

★ ★ ★ ★ ★

FAREWELL SPEECH

By Reed Adams

Fellow faculty members, students, parents, and guests. I am greatly honored by your presence tonight. I have always had a rule to live by when leaving a place to move on in the world, that is to just leave and try to forget the people left behind as soon as possible. However, that will not be possible for me to do with you. For the last eight years you have shared in my joys and my sorrows, we have shared in change but have learned that change just for change does not work. You people as the community have brought my family and myself from vagabonds of the educational system to actual professionals in that field. I am certain it is your ideals and your school that have made this change in me. Without this change I would not have the opportunity that has now availed itself to me.

I remember my first day at this school just like it was yesterday. I had such high hopes of how I was going to change the whole education system, but my first day at school changed that. The students entered the room and took their seats, but it seemed my techniques of teaching would not work. It seemed that the harder I tried the more the students seemed to resent me and what I was trying to teach them. Then one of the students came up to me at the end of the day and said that he really would have enjoyed my class if he had not had so much on his mind. I asked him if it was something I could help him with and he said he wished that I could, but I was a little bit too old to be on the football team. I had been so wrapped up in changing the system that I had forgotten to listen and learn what was happening in the school. The biggest game of the season was the first one with us playing Western High. The whole student body was more interested in that than what I was trying to teach, so that's how we got our ten minute rap sessions at the first of every class.

We have had good times, bad times, broken hearts, and romance, but the most important thing we have learned is that we are people and we all make mistakes. That is why we accept other people and their mistakes, as well as our imperfect selves. I am indebted to you all for the wonderful example you have set for me and my family in this area.

Next fall you will continue in your education. Some of you to become doctors and lawyers and others to find jobs out of high school, but whatever you do, I hope you will remember, as I will, the wonderful experiences and academic achievements as well as the sports of Highland High School.

The new house we have purchased in Mississippi has a large mantel in the center of the room and this plaque you have given me tonight will go there beautifully. We had been wondering what we were going to put there. Thank you very much and may whatever power you believe in bless and keep you happy.

A GREAT SPEECH IN AMERICAN HISTORY

Lincoln

HIS FAREWELL WORDS IN SPRINGFIELD
(1861)

My friends, no one, not in my situation, can appreciate my feeling of sadness at this parting. To this place and the kindness of this people I owe everything. Here I have lived a quarter of a century and have passed from a young to an old man. Here my children have been born and one is buried.

I now leave, not knowing when or whether ever I may return, with a task before me greater than that which rested upon Washington. Without the assistance of the Divine Being who ever attended him I can not succeed. With that assistance I cannot fail.

Trusting in Him who can go with me and remain with you and be everywhere for good, let us confidently hope that all will yet be well. To his care commending you, as I hope in your prayers you will commend me, I bid you an affectionate farewell.

★　★　★　★　★

Delivered on February 11, 1861, and here given as printed by Nicolay and Hay "from the original manuscript, having been written down immediately after the train started, partly by Mr. Lincoln's own hand and partly by that of his private secretary at his dictation."

"Early Monday morning (the 11th) found Mr. Lincoln, his family and suite at the rather dingy little railway station at Springfield, with a throng of at least one thousand of his neighbors who had come to bid him good-by. It was a stormy morning which served to add gloom and depression to their spirits. The leave-taking presented a scene of subdued anxiety, almost of solemnity. Mr. Lincoln took a position in the waiting-room where his friends filed past him, merely pressing his hand in silent emotion. The half-finished ceremony was broken in upon by the ringing bells and rushing train. The crowd closed about the railroad car into which the president-elect and his party made their way. Then came the central incident of the morning. The bell gave notice of starting, but as the conductor paused, with his hand lifted to the bell-rope, Mr. Lincoln appeared on the platform of the car and raised his hand to command attention. The bystanders bared their heads to snowflakes, and standing thus his neighbors heard his voice for the last time, in the city of his home, in a farewell address, so chaste and pathetic, that it reads as if he already felt the tragic shadow of forecasting fate."

SPEECH OUTLINE

Construct a neat, complete sentence outline on this sheet, tear it out, and hand it to your instructor when you rise to speak. He may wish to write criticisms of the outline and speech in the margins.

Type of speech: _____ Name: _____

Number of words in outline: _____ Date: _____

Purpose of this speech: (What do you want your audience to learn, to think, to believe, to feel, or do because of this speech?) _____

_____

TITLE:

INTRODUCTION:

BODY:

CONCLUSION:

Instructor's comments may concern choice of topic, development of ideas, organization, language use, personal appearance, posture, physical activity, sources, and improvement.

(Write sources of information on back of sheet)

SOURCES FROM LITERATURE

Fill out source requirements completely.
Write "none listed" if an author's name or copyright date is not listed.

1. Author's name _____

   Title of book or magazine used _____

   Title of article in above book or magazine _____

   Chapter and/or pages read _____

   Date of above publication _____

2. Author's name _____

   Title of book or magazine used _____

   Title of article in above book or magazine _____

   Chapter and/or pages read _____

   Date of above publication _____

3. Author's name _____

   Title of book or magazine used _____

   Title of article in above book or magazine _____

   Chapter and/or pages read _____

   Date of above publication _____

INTERVIEW SOURCES

1. Person interviewed _____ Date of interview _____

   His position, occupation, and location _____

   Why is he a reliable source? Be specific _____

   _____

2. Person interviewed _____ Date of interview _____

   His position, occupation, and location _____

   Why is he a reliable source? Be specific _____

   _____

PERSONAL EXPERIENCE OF SPEAKER

1. Tell (1) when, (2) where, and (3) conditions under which you became an authority on subject matter in
   your speech _____

   _____

   _____

   _____

NAME _____ DATE _____

(Ch. 15) 93. A speech to gain goodwill is usually presented to an audience that is:

(a) skeptical (b) hostile (c) indifferent (d) friendly

(Ch. 15) 94. A speech to gain goodwill is in reality:

(a) informative (b) to entertain (c) to stimulate (d) to get action

(Ch. 15) 95. A speech to gain goodwill should have: (mark correct answers)

(a) material familiar to the audience (b) new material

(c) out–of–the–ordinary subject matter (d) material that is unbelievable and exciting

(Ch. 15) 96. A goodwill speech should cause listeners to:

(a) want to buy your product (b) vote to meet again in your city or school

(c) to feel humorously entertained

(d) to see that their happiness and prosperity are tied in with your activities or those you represent

(Ch. 15) 97. Before concluding your goodwill speech you should: (one answer)

(a) offer your listeners a definite service (b) tell your listeners the cost of their luncheon

(c) be sure to demonstrate the product your company sells

(d) explain why the meeting began somewhat late

(Ch. 15) 98. (Blockbuster) "Laconic" is a word meaning: (mark correct answers)

(a) voluble (b) concise (c) garrulous (d) terse (e) lengthy (f) exciting

(g) powerful (h) elevated

(Ch. 15) 99. How many of the following words are synonyms of "funny"?

(a) ludicrous (b) waggish (c) droll (d) whimsical

(Ch. 15) 100. In the sentence, "He was an absurd, comical, freakish, and eccentric fellow" write the word from your text that is synonymous with the descriptive adjectives: Ans. _____

(Ch. 16) 101. An introduction speech should be:

(a) fairly long (b) short (c) quite descriptive

(d) sound something like an announcement

(Ch. 16) 102. An introduction speech should: (mark correct answers)

(a) make the audience and speaker feel comfortably acquainted

(b) interest the audience in the speaker and his subject

(c) make the speaker feel excited

(d) announce the speaker's subject and give his name

(Ch. 16) 103. (Blocked punt) When introducing a speaker you should: (mark correct answers)

    (a) be funny   (b) give the speaker a lot of praise, more than he deserves

    (c) be sure to call attention to yourself in a modest way

    (d) do not give the speaker much praise – just belittle him a bit so he can surprise the audience

(Ch. 16) 104. When preparing an introduction speech you draw on various sources. How many of the following are correct?

    (a) the occasion   (b) audience   (c) speaker's subject   (d) speaker

(Ch. 16) 105. Mark correct answers only as they refer to an introduction speech:

    (a) it is not important that all you say be pertinent and accurate

    (b) be sure you know the speaker's name

    (c) know the speaker's name but pronouncing it correctly is not necessary

    (d) find out about the speaker's education, travel experience, special honors, notable achievements, etc.

(Ch. 16) 106. When introducing a speaker you should: (mark correct answers)

    (a) introduce him briefly if he is quite well-known

    (b) introduce him more briefly if he is not at all well-known

    (c) know the correct title of the speaker's subject

    (d) be well acquainted with the occasion for the speech

(Ch. 16) 107. Before introducing a speaker you should consult with him and arrive at an understanding about what you plan to say.

    (a) true   (b) false

(Ch. 16) 108. (Blockbuster) If someone says, "This literature will be ephemeral", he means: (mark correct answers)

    (a) it will be long lasting, for years perhaps   (b) it will be transient

    (c) it will continue a short time only   (d) it will be outstanding in value

(Ch. 16) 109. Synonyms for ephemeral are: (mark correct answers)

    (a) enduring   (b) evanescent   (c) nonexistent   (d) momentary

(Ch. 16) 110. How many of the following words are synonymous with "good"?

    (a) beautiful   (b) exciting   (c) luscious   (d) meritorious   (e) superior

    (f) excellent   (g) marvelous

(Ch. 17) 111. (Long punt) The speech of welcome is characterized by four elements. Name them:

    (a) sentiment   (b) brevity   (c) vacuity   (d) sincerity   (e) simplicity

    (f) geniality

(Ch. 17) 112. A speech of welcome may be made to how many of the following?

    (a) one person   (b) two persons   (c) thirteen persons   (d) 250 persons

(Ch. 17) 113. Which one or more of the following may you include in a speech of welcome?

    (a) explain the organization you represent

    (b) briefly recount your organization's financial situation

    (c) mention the work your organization is doing including future plans

    (d) pay a tribute to your guests for their work

(Ch. 17) 114. When presenting a speech of welcome you should: (mark correct answers)

    (a) give your guests hospitality and warmth

    (b) be friendly   (c) be flippant   (d) be earnest

(Ch. 17) 115. (Blockbuster) Synonyms for "succinct" are: (mark correct answers)

    (a) laconic   (b) lengthy   (c) terse   (d) voluble   (e) volar   (f) summary

(Ch. 17) 116. (Short pass) How many of the following are synonyms for "hunch"?

    (a) chicanery   (b) cubature   (c) hallucination   (d) prevision   (e) premonition

    (f) cultrate

(Ch. 18) 117. A response to a speech of welcome is: (mark correct answers)

    (a) rather long (to impress your hosts)

    (b) short   (c) brief   (d) arbitrary   (e) friendly

(Ch. 18) 118. Your purpose in a response to a speech of welcome is: (one answer)

    (a) to make sure people like the product you represent

    (b) to advance your prestige in a subtle manner

    (c) to impress people with your honesty, integrity, etc.

    (d) to express appreciation of the hospitality extended to you

(Ch. 18) 119. Content in a response to a speech of welcome should be in part: (mark correct answers)

    (a) extend greetings from whomever you represent

    (b) show how your organization is superior to others like it

    (c) explain briefly what your organization is and what it stands for

    (d) predict future pleasant associations with the host organization

(Ch. 18) 120. When you know you may be called on without warning to respond to a welcome speech: (mark correct answers)

    (a) be prepared to speak impromptu   (b) have a few serious thoughts

    (c) be quite formal even though the occasion is informal

    (d) express appreciation to your hosts

(Ch. 18) 121. (Blockbuster) Synonyms for "invidious" are: (mark correct answers)

    (a) singularly   (b) preposterous   (c) disagreeable   (d) hateful   (e) heartfelt

    (f) sympathetic   (g) sad

(Ch. 18) 122. (Long bomb) Mark synonyms of "mighty" from the following:

    (a) inordinately   (b) enormously   (c) notably   (d) remarkably   (e) excessively

    (f) signally

(Ch. 19) 123. A presentation speech can be difficult because: (mark correct answers)

        (a) it is a long speech   (b) intense rivalry may have existed among contestants

        (c) feelings and emotions may have been high

        (d) the winner could easily be embarrassed by prior events surrounding the selection of winner

(Ch. 19) 124. When a contest winner is announced and a presentation speech is given the speaker should emphasize such ideas as: (two answers)

        (a) interest in the contest   (b) careful consideration of the judges

        (c) intense rivalry among contestants   (d) strong partisanship of supporters

(Ch. 19) 125. If an object is given to a school or church in a formal atmosphere and participants in the donation are known well in advance, the presentation speech will likely be organized: (one answer)

        (a) to emphasize the cost of the object

        (b) to emphasize the superiority of the school or church receiving the object

        (c) to emphasize the publicity the receiving church or school will get

        (d) to emphasize the symbolism or utility of the gift

(Ch. 19) 126. When a presentation speech awarding a medal or other recognition for service, with or without surprise, is made, the speaker should: (mark correct answers)

        (a) emphasize the award's value   (b) emphasize the deed which the recipient performed

        (c) pay tribute to the recipient   (d) say very little about the deed the recipient performed

(Ch. 19) 127. When a presentation is made in appreciation of service on an occasion such as retirement or moving from the community the speaker should emphasize: (mark correct answers)

        (a) the happy side of fellowship   (b) past rivalries   (c) regret for the person's departure

        (d) hope for the future of the recipient

(Ch. 19) 128. When giving a presentation speech you should: (mark correct answers)

        (a) overpraise the recipient so he will feel deserving

        (b) pay deserving tribute to the recipient while exercising wise restraint

        (c) overemphasize the gift's value just a little

        (d) stress the work or merit the award signifies

(Ch. 19) 129. (Short pass) A presentation speech may be organized to cover these points: (mark correct answers)

        (a) refer to the occasion   (b) relate a short history of the event

        (c) give reasons for the award

        (d) indicate the award is only a token of the real appreciation felt

        (e) recount personal worth of the recipient

        (f) explain purpose of the award or gift

(Ch. 19) 130. At the moment you present an award to the recipient: (mark all that is correct)

    (a) if person is in the audience ask him to stand

    (b) if person is sitting on platform address him by name so he may rise in response

    (c) be sure to stand in front of the gift if it is on a table

    (d) after taking the award from a table to present it, stand with your back to the audience

(Ch. 19) 131. In a presentation speech when you are ready to make the actual presentation of the award: (mark correct answers)

    (a) stand with your side slightly toward the audience

    (b) using your upstage hand present the award or gift

    (c) if you wish to pin a medal to his coat stand with your side to the audience while pinning it on

    (d) it's usually appropriate to shake recipient's hand or lightly kiss recipient, depending on sex, after presentation

(Ch. 19) 132. (Blockbuster) The word "summary" (adjective) means: (how many of the following?)

    (a) done with some delay   (b) executed with a long delay

    (c) done only after much contemplation   (d) done at once without delay

    (e) none of these answers

(Ch. 19) 133. Synonyms for "interesting" are: (mark correct answers)

    (a) curious   (b) unique   (c) fantastic   (d) bizarre   (e) exotic   (f) diverting

    (g) unusual   (h) unconventional

(Ch. 20) 134. An acceptance speech should: (mark correct answers)

    (a) establish recipient as friendly, modest, worthwhile

    (b) have as its purpose, to make donors happy with their choice of recipient

    (c) let audience know recipient is aware the entire event is artificial and shallow

    (d) may sometime be only "Thank you"

(Ch. 20) 135. In an acceptance speech: (mark correct answers)

    (a) you should act surprised even if you are not   (b) express gratitude and appreciation

    (c) give credit to all who helped you

    (d) apologize for winning even if you don't feel that way

    (e) overpraise your award or gift

    (f) conclude your remarks by speaking of future plans in whatever way they are associated with your award

(Ch. 20) 136. When accepting an award receive it as follows: (mark correct answers)

    (a) keep your eyes on the award and reach for it quickly so audience will know you are eager

    (b) stand slightly sideways to audience   (c) use your upstage hand to accept the award

    (d) if the award is large and heavy ask a friend in audience to come on stage to help you hold it while you make your acceptance speech

(Ch. 20) 137. (Blockbuster) Synonyms for "anomaly" are: (mark correct answers)

    (a) commonplace   (b) dull   (c) abnormality   (d) regal   (e) uniqueness

    (f) sameness   (g) hindrance   (h) velocity

(Ch. 20) 138. How many of the following are synonyms of "mad"?

    (a) ubiquitous   (b) crusty   (c) solemn   (d) frenzied   (e) annoyed   (f) spirited

    (g) deluded   (h) insane

(Ch. 21) 139. (Touchdown) Mark all correct answers regarding the farewell speech:

    (a) it may occur at a formal or informal gathering

    (b) the guest of honor may receive a gift

    (c) the occasion may be retirement, leave of absence or moving to a new location

    (d) the occasion should not be treated with too much sadness but with sincerity and honesty

(Ch. 21) 140. (Bad tackle) A farewell speech usually covers these points: (mark correct answers)

    (a) begin your remarks by recalling the worst events associated with the work you are leaving

    (b) after mentioning your worst experiences talk about how you overcame them

    (c) talk next about the people you disliked most

    (d) your fourth point will concern how you put up with the ones you disliked

    (e) conclude by saying you are glad to be leaving

(Ch. 21) 141. One way to present a farewell speech is as follows: (mark correct answers)

    (a) begin your remarks by talking about when you first arrived - add a bit of humor and interesting anecdotes   (b) tell how you were made to feel welcome

    (c) recall how your associates inspired you to do your best

    (d) state that much remains to be done in the work you are leaving

(Ch. 21) 142. The following ideas could be included in a farewell speech: (mark correct answers)

    (a) express appreciation to your fellow workers for their help

    (b) say you will always consider their cooperation and goodwill an outstanding event in your life   (c) speak of your future plans briefly but sincerely

    (d) tell why you are leaving and where you are going

    (e) thank everyone for the gift you received if you were given one

    (f) conclude by mentioning a few unpleasantnesses that occurred, then close your speech

(Ch. 21) 143. (Blockbuster) "Fatuity" means how many of the following:

    (a) intelligence   (b) imbecility   (c) dejection   (d) stupidity   (e) folly

    (f) greedy   (g) easily "taken in"

(Ch. 21) 144. This sentence uses "fatuity" correctly - "The brilliant lady exhibited no fatuity."

    (a) yes   (b) no

(Ch. 21) 145. Mark the synonyms for "blue" or "down in the dumps":

    (a) chicanery   (b) disconsolate   (c) doleful   (d) dauntless   (e) pensive

    (f) morose   (g) decisive

Chapter 22

THE EULOGY

Question: *What is a pleasant voice – high, low, medium?*

Answer: *A well-controlled voice of any pitch which is not extremely high or low may be "pleasant". It is not so much the pitch as how it is used.*

This speech is due:

Time limits: 5-6 minutes.

Speaking notes: 10-word maximum.

Sources of information: Two are required, preferably three. For each source give the specific magazine or book it was taken from, title of the article, author's full name, date of publication, and the chapter or pages telling where the material was found. If a source is a person, identify him completely by title, position, occupation, etc. List these on the outline form.

Outline your speech: Prepare a 75-150 word complete sentence outline. Designate the exact number of words in your outline. Use the form at the end of this chapter.

PURPOSE OF THE EULOGY

This speech is assigned so that you may learn by doing and thus become familiar with the speech of eulogy. Frequently a person is called upon to eulogize or praise someone. There are several ways to do this. Of course, the type of eulogy you may be asked to present will depend on different aspects of the speech situation. But whatever that requirement may be, you will be better prepared to do a creditable job if you have had previous experience. This assignment will provide that experience.

EXPLANATION OF THE EULOGY

The eulogy is a speech of praise that is delivered in honor or commemoration of someone living or dead. Sometimes eulogies are presented for animals, particularly dogs, horses, and others. A more fanciful and imaginative eulogy would be one to inanimate objects, such as the sea or the mountains. Some eulogies are written to trees and flowers, but these, too, are abstract and fanciful in nature.

The purpose of a eulogy is to praise and evaluate favorably that which is eulogized; it commends and lifts up the finer qualities and characteristics of the subject eulogized. It stresses the personality of the person (or thing) that it concerns; it tells of their greatness and achievements, their benefits to society, and their influence upon people. It is not merely a simple biographical sketch of someone. To illustrate the point, imagine a eulogy of a great oak, in which the speaker tells the date on which the acorn sprouted, and a later date when the tiny plant emerged from the soil; next the number in inches it grew each year thereafter; and finally the number of leaves it developed in forty years. Compare this with the eulogy of a person, and you can see why a biographical sketch is not a eulogy. Actually, it sounds like a scientific report on a man (or tree).

Occasions for eulogies are many. For persons who are living, the speech may be given on a birthday, at a dinner in honor of an individual, at the dedication of a project someone has created and/or donated. Eulogies often appear at the formal announcement of a political candidate or at an inauguration. For persons who are dead, not considering funeral tributes, eulogies are offered on birthday anniversaries or in connection with notable events or achievements in individuals' lives. Sometimes eulogies in the form of character studies are presented as evidences of good living. They become lessons of life.

SUGGESTIONS FOR EULOGIES

1. Eleanor Roosevelt	11. Marie Curie
2. Theodore Roosevelt	12. Louis Pasteur
3. Thomas A. Edison	13. Golda Mier
4. Nancy Reagan	14. A friend
5. Abraham Lincoln	15. A buddy
6. Robert E. Lee	16. A relative
7. Martin Luther King	17. Clara Barton
8. Jefferson Davis	18. Ernie Pyle
9. Susan B. Anthony	19. Helen Keller
10. Sam Houston	20. Speaker's choice

HOW TO SELECT A PERSON TO EULOGIZE

First, it is essential that you eulogize someone whom you greatly admire and who, in your opinion, is living or has lived a commendable life. This is necessary, because your eulogy must be completely sincere. Second, select someone about whom you can secure adequate information. Third, do not select a classmate or a town loafer, believing that your choice will be clever or smart. You will only embarrass your classmate or make yourself appear immature. Not only that, but what you might say would not likely be a true eulogy. Finally, think twice before deciding to eulogize a tree, the sea, or the mountains, a dog, horse or other animal, because these are probably more difficult to eulogize than persons. At least, for the sake of experience, you will be wiser to select a person as a subject to eulogize.

HOW TO PREPARE A EULOGY

The purpose of eulogy is a set objective, regardless of the time, place or occasion. Since eulogies are laudations intended to stimulate an audience favorably towards the subject and to inspire them to nobler heights by virtue of the examples set by the person being praised, the speaker is not required to determine a purpose in preparing a eulogy.

Having selected the person to be eulogized, you should decide upon the method which you will use in developing the eulogy. Your method and whether or not the individual is living will determine the material that is necessary. Let us examine several different methods of constructing a eulogy.

First, you may follow a chronological order, that is, you will take up events in the order of their development. This will permit a study of their growth and orderly evolution of character in the subject. As you touch upon these broad and influential events in the subject's life, you will point to them as evidences of (1) what he accomplished, (2) what he stood for, (3) the nature of his influence upon society, and (4) his probable place in history. In building your speech chronologically do not end by composing a simple biographical sketch. If you do, you will have an informative speech but not a eulogy. It is not enough to list the significant happenings in a man's life chronologically and consider that you have built a eulogy. You must state how he reacted to the events in his life and what happened as a result of them. For example, if you were eulogizing Franklin D. Roosevelt (chronologically), you would recount, as one event, how he was stricken with infantile paralysis when a grown man, but you would not merely make a statement regarding the tragedy that befell him and then pass on. Rather, you would show how his illness became a challenge to him, how he resolved to live a great life despite a pair of useless legs, how he did overcome his handicap. You would show that, as a result of his sickness, he became more resolute, more determined, more kindly, and that today the nation honors him on his birthday and contributes millions of dollars to the fund for the aid of children afflicted with infantile paralysis. Other incidents should be given similar treatment.

A second method of developing a eulogy might well be labeled the period method. It is the one which covers the growth of an individual by treating different periods in his life. It is very broad and makes no attempt to enumerate the many events of his life with their attached significance. Instead of this, using Franklin D. Roosevelt again as an example, you could speak of him as he grew through: (1) boyhood, (2) college life, (3) early political life, (4) late political life.

In following this method you would attempt to bring out the same basic points mentioned above – namely, (1) what he accomplished, (2) what he stood for, (3) his influence upon society, (4) his likely place in history. Although this treatment is broad, it is quite effective.

It should be emphasized at this point that, regardless of which method you use, there are certain necessary points to be observed. A discussion of these follows. First, omit the unimportant events, the small things, and the insignificant details. Second, in developing your speech, point up the struggles which he made in order to achieve his aims. Avoid overemphasis and exaggeration when you are doing this. Third, show the development of his ideas and ideals. Fourth, describe his relations and services to his fellow men and indicate their significance.

It is not necessary to cover up an individual but rather to admit the human element in him. In doing this, mentioning the human element is enough. It need not be dwelt on nor apologized for. It can be shown that despite weaknesses or shortcomings a man was great. It can be shown that a man lived above these frailties of human nature. But whatever the qualities of your subject, be honest in your treatment of him. It is only fair to assume that the good in him outweighed the bad by far, or you would not have elected to eulogize him.

In constructing your speech, be sure you pay careful attention to your introduction and conclusion. Aside from these, do not neglect the logical organization and arrangement of the remainder of your talk. Actually, a eulogy is a difficult speech to prepare. However, if you go about it knowing what you wish to put into it, you should have no particular trouble. When you have the eulogizing speech ready for rehearsal, it will be advisable to practice it aloud until you have thoroughly mastered the sequence of ideas. Do not memorize the speech word for word.

Materials for eulogies may be found in Who's Who, histories, biographies, autobiographies, encyclopedias, newspapers, magazines, and similar sources. Consult your librarian for assistance.

HOW TO PRESENT A EULOGY

Your overall attitude must be one of undoubted sincerity. You must be a true believer in the man about whom you speak. Aside from your attitude, you will, of course, observe all the requirements of good speech. There should be no showiness or gaudiness in your presentation that will call attention to you instead of your ideas about the subject of your speech.

You will need to be fully aware of the occasion and atmosphere into which you will step when you deliver the eulogy. It is your responsibility to know what will be required of you in the way of carrying out rituals or ceremonies if they are a part of the program. Since you will be in the limelight, you should fit easily into the situation without awkwardness. Naturally you must adjust your bodily actions and gestures to your environment - and your audience. Your voice should reach the ears of all present. If you are sincere, well prepared, and mean what you say, the eulogy which you present should be inspirational to all who hear it.

IMPROVE YOUR VOCABULARY

Placid - (plăs'ĭd) a. Undisturbed, quiet, peaceful, gentle, unruffled, calm. Example: The placid stream was beautiful in the twilight. Use this word in your everyday speech at least half a dozen times. It has many applications that will add variety to your language.

Old - There is too much work thrown on this word. Use one of the suggested synonyms instead. Examples are: aged, ancient, antiquated, decrepit, elderly, hoary, immemorial, senile, venerable, time-worn, etc.

BIBLIOGRAPHY FOR THE EULOGY

Mudd, Charles S. and Sillars, M. O., Speech: Content and Communication, Harper & Row, 4th ed., 1979.
Verderber, Rudolph F., Challenge of Effective Speaking, Wadsworth, 1979.

★ ★ ★ ★ ★

EULOGY TO THE LIVING

By Clark S. Carlile

THEY LABOR UNTIL TOMORROW

My parents are walking with slowed steps into the last sunset of a long evening. Together they have watched and waited sunsets more than half a century and now the sun hangs low. The night, when it comes, will be lighted by uncounted stars, each recalling days of doing, days of deeds, and love of life and living. The moon will shine through the mists of eternity as the glow of memory lingers after. It will be soft and warm and will light my way.

Our parents can give us life and they can love us. They can teach us truth and train us to be honest and humble. They can guide us to be self-sufficient and enterprising. They can imbue us with courage to do right, to abhor evil, and to so live that the life we leave behind will be exemplary. All this they did, and they were exemplary.

Courage and brave living were and are the moral fiber of my parents' lives. In the debacle of the great depression when financial failure, unemployment, sickness and the hand of death hovered over them they were never fugitives of fear. They knew it not. When land they lived on swirled in black clouds above them and when drought laid the land naked of crops and vegetation and cracked it open they did not flee from it nor did they abandon hope. When the years before them were bleak and barren and dry winds seemed interminable they looked each night to the west for the sign of rain.

I saw my father refuse money and aid when he was broken to disaster by blowing dust and the debts of others. I saw him in middle age assume an unbelievable burden helpless debtors placed on his shoulders to free their own. And in this same hour of horror death haunted his only daughter week after week from spring to summer. By his side in those days of doubt and torment my mother was his helpful, steady companion. Together they conquered uncertainty, calmly they waited, and with courage God gives only to kings and queens they saw life reappear in a wasted body and new hope whisper with each dawn.

Years passed as the family necessities were provided. Hands grew tired and calloused by labor, and unending work left its sign on their faces. In those times of distress there was never defeat. If it ever raised its voice my parents never let it show its form. The five children growing to adulthood knew no words touching despair nor did they hear them. "Things will be better next year," "We must work hard," "We'll wait a little while," "We'll do it later." These were the words. These were the courage. Never the admission that anything was wrong. And now since the years have hurried to yesterday I see their hope, I see their faith, and I know their sacrifice. I know their love and I shall never cease thanking God for them.

Man's religions teach him great principles of the ages and they teach him how to live with his fellowmen. My parents have never attended church often. They know well the charities of each day and not those on Sunday only. They live every day like Sunday and in their souls is peace of mind known only to those who live well. If God is righteousness, they are Godlike. If God is love, they are Godlike. If God is charity and hope, they are Godlike.

My parents have no wish for fame nor do they seek its fascination. They are not ostentatious. They are in their later years extremely busy. Almost a generation past the age when men retire, my parents are working each day giving to the world a new dignity to labor and hope eternal. And their children, impressed by the lifetime habit of work, attempt to emulate their example of more than a half century.

The sun is sinking low and soon twilight must mingle light and shadows into the darkness of eternity. My parents approach the horizon with uplifted faces and the light of a new day shines on them. They will pass into the setting sun leaving only their labors behind. Two people will have lived for their children and for the world. No parents could do more and no parents will have lived better.

★　★　★　★　★

EULOGY TO THE DEAD

By Sherri Dunker

PRAY TO BE A STRONG PERSON

The unexpected passing of our beloved Helen Wang has shaken us all. Our minds become smothered with confusion as we attempt to rationalize our loss. Why Helen? She has a young family and many friends who love and need her. Too soon was her time and too limited her life — she had too much to live for, to see, to do.

Helen was a sincere, unselfish and loving woman. When marriage to her Navy husband, James, required that she abandon her homeland, family, and friends, ne'er a sigh of grief nor complaint did her husband hear. No task surpassed the intense love and dedication she possessed for him. Willingly and repeatedly she pulled up roots in one land to start anew in another, but her radiant personality and enchanting smile beckoned new friends easily.

Always caring for the feelings and welfare of others was Helen's way, and those who were ever close to her never guessed she was stricken with terminal cancer. Her suffering she hid well; not a whimper nor tear did she ever exhibit in sorrow for herself. Her eyes constantly twinkled with cheer, her lips persistently curved toward the heavens, and her rapid weight loss she convincingly attributed to the success of her new diet.

And now Helen is gone, but the memory of her inner strength and concern for others shall be everlasting. Continuing life without her will be trying for us all, and her children will find it particularly difficult to develop without Helen's motherly help and wise guidance. But survive they will; they are the descendants of an optimistic and courageous woman who lived by one philosophy — "Do not pray for an easy life. Pray to be a strong person."

SPEECH OUTLINE

Construct a neat, complete sentence outline on this sheet, tear it out, and hand it to your instructor when you rise to speak. He may wish to write criticisms of the outline and speech in the margins.

Type of speech:_____ Name: _____

Number of words in outline: _____ Date: _____

Purpose of this speech: (What do you want your audience to learn, to think, to believe, to feel, or do because of this speech?) _____

_____

TITLE:

INTRODUCTION:

BODY:

CONCLUSION:

Instructor's comments may concern choice of topic, development of ideas, organization, language use, personal appearance, posture, physical activity, sources, and improvement.

(Write sources of information on back of sheet)

SOURCES FROM LITERATURE

Fill out source requirements completely.
Write "none listed" if an author's name or copyright date is not listed.

1. Author's name _____

   Title of book or magazine used _____

   Title of article in above book or magazine _____

   Chapter and/or pages read _____

   Date of above publication _____

2. Author's name _____

   Title of book or magazine used _____

   Title of article in above book or magazine _____

   Chapter and/or pages read _____

   Date of above publication _____

3. Author's name _____

   Title of book or magazine used _____

   Title of article in above book or magazine _____

   Chapter and/or pages read _____

   Date of above publication _____

INTERVIEW SOURCES

1. Person interviewed _____ Date of interview _____

   His position, occupation, and location _____

   Why is he a reliable source? Be specific _____

   _____

2. Person interviewed _____ Date of interview _____

   His position, occupation, and location _____

   Why is he a reliable source? Be specific _____

   _____

PERSONAL EXPERIENCE OF SPEAKER

1. Tell (1) when, (2) where, and (3) conditions under which you became an authority on subject matter in
   your speech _____

   _____

   _____

Chapter 23

THE DEDICATION SPEECH

Question: What is fluency?

Answer: It is the readiness and ease with which words are spoken.

This speech is due:

Time limits: 3-4 minutes.

Speaking notes: This is a short speech – you do not need any. "Prepare to meet thy audience."

Sources of information: Two are required, preferably three. For each source give the specific magazine or book it was taken from, title of the article, author's full name, date of publication, and the chapter or pages telling where the material was found. If a source is a person, identify him completely by title, position, occupation, etc. List these on the outline form.

Outline your speech: Prepare a 75-150 word complete sentence outline. Designate the exact number of words in your outline. Use the form at the end of this chapter.

PURPOSE OF THE DEDICATION SPEECH

You may not give a speech at dedication ceremonies for a long time, then again the occasion for a speech of this kind may arise sooner than you had thought possible. But regardless of when you are called on for this type of speech, one thing is sure, and that is that you must know its requirements. The dedication speech occurs on an occasion and in an atmosphere that requires very strict observance of certain aspects of speechmaking. This speech assignment is designed to give you an experience like the "real thing," so that you may do a creditable performance when the opportunity presents itself.

EXPLANATION OF THE DEDICATION SPEECH

The dedication speech is one presented on commemorative occasions. It is generally brief and carries a serious tone. It employs excellent language, demands careful construction, fine wording, and polished delivery. Its purpose should be to commemorate, to honor an occasion, and to praise the spirit of endeavor and progress that the dedication symbolizes. The speech should thrill the audience with pride regarding their community, ideals, and progress. Occasions for the dedication speech usually involve a group enterprise. Common among these are occasions such as: erecting monuments, completing buildings, stadiums, swimming pools, and baseball parks, or laying corner stones and opening institutions. Similar events considered as marks of progress are also occasions for dedication speeches. Lincoln's Gettysburg Address is one of the finest dedication speeches ever made.

SUGGESTED TOPICS FOR DEDICATION SPEECHES

A speech of dedication for any one of the following should be suitable:

1. A new college.
2. Laying the corner stone for a new Student Union building.
3. A new library.
4. A new stadium.
5. A new wilderness area.
6. A new courthouse.
7. A new recreation area.
8. A new high school building.
9. A new swimming pool.
10. Laying the corner stone for a new auditorium.
11. A new city hospital.
12. A new city park.
13. Laying a corner stone for a new "Lodge" building.
14. A monument to a local citizen.
15. A monument as a historical marker.
16. A monument to honor the war dead.
17. A monument to a great race horse.
18. A monument to a national hero.
19. Laying a corner stone for a new church.
20. Speaker's choice.

HOW TO CHOOSE A TOPIC

This will involve a bit of imagination on your part; however, choose an occasion that you wish were actually true, really being enacted. Be sure you could be thrilled at such an occasion. Look over the topics again, then make up your mind. Do not put it off. Choose, and start your preparation.

HOW TO PREPARE A DEDICATION SPEECH

First, know your purpose. It must dominate this speech the same as the purpose dominates every speech. This means that you are to compliment the ideals and achievements which the dedicated structure symbolizes, thus setting it apart for a certain use or purpose.

These are the points to cover in your speech. Give a brief history of events leading up to the present time. Mention the sacrifice, the work, the ideals, and the service that lie behind the project. Next, explain the future use or work, the influence or significance that will be associated with the structure being dedicated. Place the emphasis upon what the object dedicated stands for (ideals, progress, loyalty) rather than upon the object itself.

The above thoughts will constitute your material. Now, organize your speech carefully, very carefully. Pay particular attention to the introduction, the conclusion – yes, everything in your speech. It must have order. To accomplish the organization of the speech you will first outline it. Wording it follows. Do this meticulously. Do not be grandiose or grandiloquent, but be understandable and simple in language. The speech is serious, not frivolous. Leave your humor at home.

You are now ready to practice. Do this orally. Rehearse aloud until you have definitely fixed the order of the speech in your mind. Avoid complete word for word memorization. You may memorize certain words and phrases, but you should not memorize the entire speech. When you have mastered an effective presentation, you will be ready to speak, and not before. Remember to include appropriate bodily action, gesture, and voice in your practice.

HOW TO PRESENT A DEDICATION SPEECH

The attitude of the speaker should be one of appropriate dignity. Emotion and sentiment should be properly blended to fit the noble sentiments that will be present. The adequacy and poise of the speaker should be obvious from his appearance, his bearing, and his self-confidence.

Body language must be keyed to the tone of the speech. The environment surrounding the speaker may permit much action or limit it severely. If a public address system is used, the speaker cannot move from the microphone. He can and should utilize gestures.

Whether speaking with the aid of a microphone or not, the voice should be full and resonant and easily heard. If the crowd is large, a slower speaking rate should be used. Articulation must be carefully attended, yet not so much so that it becomes ponderous and labored. Voice and action must be in tune, neither one overbalancing the other. The speaker must be animated, alive to his purpose, desirous of communicating, and capable of presenting a polished speech.

IMPROVE YOUR VOCABULARY

Use the following word in your speech today and also five times each day for a week. Make it yours, a valuable asset.

Altruistic - (ăl'trōo-ĭs'tĭk) a. An attitude that causes a person to be helpful because of a regard for the welfare of others. Example: The building being dedicated was made possible only by the altruistic efforts of several local citizens.

Get - Omit this word. Do not use it for a week, it is tired and overworked. Use a synonym. Examples: obtain, induce, attain, procure, acquire, achieve, take, secure, win, contract, gain, etc.

BIBLIOGRAPHY FOR THE DEDICATION SPEECH

Modisett, Noah F. and Luter, J. G., Speaking Clearly: The Basics of Voice and Diction, Burgess, 1979.
Ross, Raymond S., Essentials of Speech Communication, Prentice-Hall, 1979.

DEDICATION SPEECH

By Philip Jones

DEDICATION OF THE MINI DOME

Faculty, students and guests. Some time ago an idea began in the heads of "Dubby" Holt, ISU's athletic director, and Ralph Clark, a construction engineer from Washington, D.C., whose son, Joe Clark, had been a football player at Idaho State University. The idea grew to include "Bud" Davis, ISU's president, who would be instrumental in carrying the idea to students, faculty, and the state board.

Four years ago, when ISU played the University of New Mexico at Albuquerque, Bud Davis, Dubby Holt, Ralph Clark, ISU's financial vice-president William Bartz, and Pocatello architect Cedric Allen went to see and inspect that university's basketball arena.

The arena was too small for ISU's football needs, but the trip strengthened the idea, and resolved that ISU could have its own indoor sports arena.

In December of that year the cost and program were submitted to the student body for approval. In January, by a popular vote the student body accepted the project and the necessary student revenue bonds.

From this point on we are indebted to the fine efforts of the design team who carried the project through. Many thanks and congratulations must go to those men who spent thousands of hours working on this project. The coordination, cooperation, and communication among the architect, engineers, contractors, sub-contractors, and university are commendable.

Special thanks must go to Cedric Allen - Architect, Ballif and Associates - Structural Engineers, Bridgers and Paxton - Consulting Engineers, Arthur Nelson, Jr. - Electrical Engineer, and John Korbis - ISU's Physical Plant Director for coordinating the design team's efforts.

The significance of the Mini Dome will be measured only by time. It is a structure with a multiplicity of uses. It brings to Idaho the first enclosed collegiate football stadium. This structure will be used for sports at ISU, football, basketball, and track, along with being used by the student body for intramurals and physical education.

The Mini Dome also provides for the community of Pocatello and to Southeast Idaho a large area for the presentation of cultural and civic events that would not otherwise be possible.

The Mini Dome stands for new ideas, vision, and progress. Progress we can be proud of in Pocatello, Idaho. And so by the authority vested in me by the Idaho State Board of Education, I hereby dedicate the Mini Dome to Idaho State University students — Past, Present, and Future.

A GREAT SPEECH IN AMERICAN HISTORY

Lincoln

THE SPEECH AT GETTYSBURG
(1863)

Four score and seven years ago our fathers brought forth upon this continent a new nation, conceived in liberty, and dedicated to the proposition that all men are created equal.

Now we are engaged in a great civil war, testing whether that nation, or any nation so conceived, and so dedicated, can long endure. We are met on a great battle-field of that war. We have come to dedicate a portion of that field as a final resting-place for those who here gave their lives that that nation might live. It is altogether fitting and proper that we should do this.

But in a larger sense, we can not dedicate - we can not consecrate - we can not hallow this ground. The brave men, living and dead, who struggled here, have consecrated it far above our poor power to add or detract. The world will little note, nor long remember, what we say here, but it can never forget what they did here. It is for us, the living, rather, to be dedicated here to the unfinished work which they who fought here have thus far so nobly advanced. It is rather for us to be here dedicated to the great task remaining before us - that from these honored dead we take increased devotion to that cause for which they gave the last full measure of devotion - that we here highly resolve that these dead shall not have died in vain - that this nation, under God, shall have a new birth of freedom and that government of the people, by the people, and for the people, shall not perish from the earth.

Delivered at the dedication of the cemetery in Gettysburg, November 19, 1863, after Edward Everett had made the formal speech of the day.

SPEECH OUTLINE

Construct a neat, complete sentence outline on this sheet, tear it out, and hand it to your instructor when you rise to speak. He may wish to write criticisms of the outline and speech in the margins.

Type of speech:_____ Name: _____

Number of words in outline: _____ Date: _____

Purpose of this speech: (What do you want your audience to learn, to think, to believe, to feel, or do because of this speech?) _____

_____

TITLE:

INTRODUCTION:

BODY:

CONCLUSION:

<u>Instructor's comments</u> may concern choice of topic, development of ideas, organization, language use, personal appearance, posture, physical activity, sources, and improvement.

(Write sources of information on back of sheet)

SOURCES FROM LITERATURE

Fill out source requirements completely.

Write "none listed" if an author's name or copyright date is not listed.

1. Author's name _____

   Title of book or magazine used _____

   Title of article in above book or magazine _____

   Chapter and/or pages read _____

   Date of above publication _____

2. Author's name _____

   Title of book or magazine used _____

   Title of article in above book or magazine _____

   Chapter and/or pages read _____

   Date of above publication _____

3. Author's name _____

   Title of book or magazine used _____

   Title of article in above book or magazine _____

   Chapter and/or pages read _____

   Date of above publication _____

INTERVIEW SOURCES

1. Person interviewed _____ Date of interview _____

   His position, occupation, and location _____

   Why is he a reliable source? Be specific _____

   _____

2. Person interviewed _____ Date of interview _____

   His position, occupation, and location _____

   Why is he a reliable source? Be specific _____

   _____

PERSONAL EXPERIENCE OF SPEAKER

1. Tell (1) when, (2) where, and (3) conditions under which you became an authority on subject matter in

   your speech _____

   _____

   _____

Chapter 24

THE ANNIVERSARY SPEECH

Question: *How do you speak fluently?*

Answer: *Fluency varies greatly. Whatever your fluency is you will be wise to accept it. Thorough preparation, much oral rehearsal, and experience will help.*

This speech is due:
Time limits: 5–6 minutes.
Speaking notes: It is advisable to use none. Try it.
Sources of information: Two are required, preferably three. For each source give the specific magazine or book it was taken from, title of the article, author's full name, date of publication, and the chapter or pages telling where the material was found. If a source is a person, identify him completely by title, position, occupation, etc. List these on the outline form.
Outline your speech: Prepare a 75-100 word complete sentence outline. Designate the exact number of words in your outline. Use the form at the end of this chapter.

PURPOSE OF THE ANNIVERSARY SPEECH

The experience of presenting an anniversary speech now will prove helpful to you at some later time when you meet the real situation requiring knowledge of its structure and presentation. A speaker is often disturbed, nervous, and ill at ease when speaking on an occasion that he has never previously experienced. His feelings of uncertainty probably spring from his lack of familiarity with the environment in which he finds himself. In your case, having known what it is to give an anniversary talk at least once, you should find future performances considerably easier and perhaps enjoyable. That is why you should do your best with this assignment.

EXPLANATION OF THE ANNIVERSARY SPEECH

The anniversary speech is one presented in commemoration of an event, a person, or occasion of the past. Its purpose is to recall and remember the past so that we may more adequately serve the present and courageously prepare for the future. It will weigh the past, observe the blessings of the present, and look to the future optimistically. Elements of loyalty and patriotism usually are contained in the remarks.

Because this talk is similar to the dedication speech, its requirements of the speaker do not vary noticeably from those for the dedication speech. The speaker should be a good man, both in character and ability. He should be fully acquainted with the history, the present status of the anniversary, and future plans as they pertain to it. You might think of the anniversary as a birthday celebration and incorporate all the ideals and ideas associated with such a day.

Occasions for anniversary speeches arise whenever the passing of time is marked by a pause in which people lay aside their work long enough to note what has been accomplished. The remembrance of Independence Day, landing of the Pilgrims, Armistice, Thanksgiving, Christmas, Labor Day, birthday of a national, state or local figure, are all examples of such occasions. Observance of the progress during a certain number of years of a business firm, a school, a church, a city, state or nation, or any organization, may form the basis of an anniversary speech. During recent years, state centennials marked by regional and state fairs have proved themselves worthwhile as anniversaries. Every day is the birthday of somebody or something; hence every day is a potential anniversary, whether it is observed or not.

SUGGESTED OCCASIONS FOR AN ANNIVERSARY SPEECH
1. Your school is a half century old.
2. The county was organized _____ years ago.
3. Today the state is _____ years old.
4. Your city observes a birthday.

5. It is Army Day.
6. The Navy has an anniversary.
7. Your church was established _____ years ago.
8. Your lodge is now twenty-five years old.
9. The fire department has been active _____ years.
10. It is Armed Forces Day.
11. It is Labor Day.
12. It is Thanksgiving.
13. Your business is fifty years old.
14. Your business produces its one-millionth car, watch, washing machine.
15. It is Lincoln's birthday (or anyone's).
16. This bridge was built _____ years ago.
17. Radium was discovered _____ years ago.
18. The first airplane flight occurred _____ years ago.
19. The radio, telephone, sewing machine, etc., were invented _____ years ago.
20. Speaker's choice.

HOW TO CHOOSE A TOPIC FOR AN ANNIVERSARY SPEECH

If you have a particular loyalty or devotion, it would be advisable to construct your speech around it at an imaginary or real anniversary. Otherwise, select one of the above suggestions in which you have an interest. Be sure you are interested in the topic you select for your speech. Make your choice soon. Do not wait until the day before your speech is due. The longer you delay choosing your topic the greater are your chances for a weak and insipid speech.

HOW TO PREPARE AN ANNIVERSARY SPEECH

Remember that your purpose is to commemorate. Keep this purpose in mind constantly. Your thoughts must be constructed to achieve this end.

Second, the organization of your speech is important. Here you must observe all the characteristics of adequate speech composition. You should include the following points: Tell why you are especially interested in this anniversary. Show historically that the people and their ideals are responsible for the organization's celebration. Trace the development of these ideals. Anecdotes, stories, incidents, and humor are appropriate and impressive if properly used. The past should vividly live again for your audience. Turn next to the present; compare it with the past. Avoid references to or implications of partisan or class views. Speak broadly for all the people by utilizing a spirit of friendliness and goodwill. Bend your energies toward unity and interest for the common good. Speak next of the future. By virtue of a splendid past and a significant present, the future holds promises of greater things to be. Speak confidently on this thesis. Indicate that the cooperation of all persons directed toward a determined effort for a greater service to mankind is the goal all are seeking. Show the relationship of this anniversary to the welfare of the state and nation.

After having constructed your speech, be sure to rehearse it aloud until you have fixed the order of points in your mind. Do not memorize it. Practice bodily action and gesture while rehearsing, but be sure to avoid mechanical movements.

HOW TO PRESENT AN ANNIVERSARY SPEECH

Speak sincerely. If you cannot and do not mean what you say, you should not speak. Your body language, your voice, your entire organism should evince sincerity. There should be no display either of voice or action. You should be easily heard by all and completely in their view. Your dress should be appropriate to the occasion. Observe your time limits.

IMPROVE YOUR VOCABULARY

Exigency - (ĕk'si-jĕn-si) n. Emergency, urgency: a situation which necessitates immediate action or remedy. Example: A resourceful person can meet a sudden exigency calmly. Use this word in this speech and five times a day for the next week. Make it yours.

Fine - Omit this word from your vocabulary for a week. It is tired to the point of insipidity. Give life to your conversation by using synonyms. Examples: excellent, tasteful, rare, enjoyable, superior, high-grade, pleasant, showy, subtle, refined, delicate, fashionable, etc.

BIBLIOGRAPHY FOR THE ANNIVERSARY SPEECH

Vasile, Albert J., Mintz, H. K., How to Speak With Confidence, Winthrop, 1980.
Weeks, Thelma E., Born to Talk, Newbury House, 1979.

ANNIVERSARY SPEECH

By Leo Cook

TIME TO REFLECT ON OUR PROGRESS

Fellow alumnae, ladies and gentlemen. Between twenty and thirty years ago, all of you hopped and skipped up the steps of the old former Oak Manor building while in Kindergarten, beginning an education that would take most of you through college. Those were euphoric days for us, with little to worry about. If I recall correctly, the spot I am standing on now was once the coat closet where I distinctly remember our teacher, Mrs. Hahn, hanging up Gary Weaver on a coat hook with his jacket on for disciplinary reasons. I'm sure such precautions helped Gary along the right road to where he became the fine principal of this school that he is today. I'm also sure no one is prouder of the tenth anniversary of Yokayo Elementary School than Gary, because these first ten years have been so successful under Gary's leadership and supervision.

Looking back on my schooling, I'm sure you would agree with me that we had an outstanding faculty, full of a superior variety of qualified people such as Mrs. Hahn, Mr. Bertch, Mrs. Weger and Miss Fitch. However, quality teachers need quality facilities to work from, and fortunately they have them now. Although sentimentally I'll always remember the old Oak Manor building, even if there were oddities to it like the bathrooms that flooded and filled the building with two feet of water back in fifty-one. We can be proud that progress isn't an alien word to Hopland, California, U.S.A. Believe me, folks, the reports from the excavation crew before the condemnation of the former building were no lies. There were crumbling inner walls throughout three-quarters of the building, and living on the earthquake fault that we do, we wouldn't want our children to be exposed to the dangers of enduring a tremor inside that crackerbox. You will be happy to note that Yokayo School, dedicated this day ten years ago, has endured with very minor damage three quakes whose power, according to all experts, would have left the former Oak Manor building in ruins.

For a small community like ours with limited funds to build such a beautiful school is a tribute to its citizens. I recall many of you out there being doubtful if we could do it, but we did and the results over the past ten years have been extraordinary. With Hopland's limited job opportunities, growth wouldn't be expected to be very much, but our natural beauty, honest hard-working people and attractiveness for bringing up a family have brought in more families over the last ten years than at any other time in the community's history. The census figures show our present population to be five thousand one hundred and thirty-seven, a ten percent growth over the past decade.

Certainly when a family arrives in a community, they are watchful over what kind of education their child gets. Well, Alice, Mable, Betty, Sue, Vera and Gretta, all of whom are new mothers, you won't have any worries over your young child's education in our fine community.

We all had doubts and all but gave up before our responsive state legislature granted us the bonds to build. I'm no exception. But through cooperation, diligent and sometimes showy pleadings in front of the State Board by Robert Tucker and James Frailey, then-governor Anderson secured us a generous bond for construction to begin. Our investment has been worthwhile as Hopland has had a fifteen percent increase in college bound students in the past decade. An education is a priceless commodity, and we owe it to see that our children aren't deprived of any less an education than a child from a larger or wealthier community. On this tenth anniversary of Yokayo Elementary School, we, the people of Hopland, can be proud in knowing that our children are getting a first-class education.

SPEECH OUTLINE

Construct a neat, complete sentence outline on this sheet, tear it out, and hand it to your instructor when you rise to speak. He may wish to write criticisms of the outline and speech in the margins.

Type of speech:_____ Name: _____

Number of words in outline: _____ Date: _____

Purpose of this speech: (What do you want your audience to learn, to think, to believe, to feel, or do because of this speech?) _____

_____

TITLE:

INTRODUCTION:

BODY:

CONCLUSION:

Instructor's comments may concern choice of topic, development of ideas, organization, language use, personal appearance, posture, physical activity, sources, and improvement.

(Write sources of information on back of sheet)

SOURCES FROM LITERATURE

Fill out source requirements completely.
Write "none listed" if an author's name or copyright date is not listed.

1. Author's name _____

   Title of book or magazine used _____

   Title of article in above book or magazine _____

   Chapter and/or pages read _____

   Date of above publication _____

2. Author's name _____

   Title of book or magazine used _____

   Title of article in above book or magazine _____

   Chapter and/or pages read _____

   Date of above publication _____

3. Author's name _____

   Title of book or magazine used _____

   Title of article in above book or magazine _____

   Chapter and/or pages read _____

   Date of above publication _____

INTERVIEW SOURCES

1. Person interviewed _____ Date of interview _____

   His position, occupation, and location _____

   Why is he a reliable source? Be specific _____

   _____

2. Person interviewed _____ Date of interview _____

   His position, occupation, and location _____

   Why is he a reliable source? Be specific _____

   _____

PERSONAL EXPERIENCE OF SPEAKER

1. Tell (1) when, (2) where, and (3) conditions under which you became an authority on subject matter in

   your speech _____

   _____

   _____

Chapter 25

THE NOMINATING SPEECH

Question: *If your remarks draw applause what should you do?*

Answer: *Be very happy, wait until it subsides, then go on.*

This speech is due:

Time limits: 2-4 minutes. Keep your speech within your allotted time.

Speaking notes: Nobody wants to watch you use notes so you will remember how good the candidate is. Do not use notes.

Sources of information: None required, however, you should be accurate in your statements regarding qualifications of your nominee and the office he will fill.

Outline your speech: Prepare a 75-150 word complete sentence outline. Designate the exact number of words in your outline. Use the form at the end of this chapter.

PURPOSE OF THE NOMINATING SPEECH

How many times have you heard the remark, "I wish I had nominated Henry Porter for president last night; I almost did. He's a lot better man than Bill Johnson." But, the sad fact remains that Henry Porter, well qualified and capable, was not nominated. Why? Probably because the person who wanted to nominate him lacked the courage to get on his feet and also lacked the knowledge of what to say in order to nominate him effectively. It is to be hoped that should you ever wish to nominate a capable leader, you will have the courage to rise and speak and the knowledge to utter appropriate thoughts. This experience should show you what to do and how to present an effective nominating speech should the occasion for one arise.

To the teacher: It is a practical experience to assign students in pairs to present this speech and the speech in which an office or nomination is accepted.

EXPLANATION OF THE NOMINATING SPEECH

A nominating speech is one in which a speaker places the name of another person before an assembly as a candidate for office. The speech is usually not long, most often lasting only a few minutes. There are exceptions, of course. In presenting the candidate to the audience, the speaker tells why his candidate is especially fitted for the office in question. All remarks made by the nominator should be expressed in such a way that they set forth, in an orderly manner, the reasons why the candidate should be elected.

Before a speaker can make a nomination, the chairman of the assembly must announce that nominations for the _____ office are in order. The speaker must be recognized by the chairman. This is accomplished when the speaker rises and addresses the chair by saying, "Mr. Chairman." At the time, the presiding officer will give the speaker permission to speak either by calling the man's name, by nodding, or by some other word or sign. Only then, will the nominating speech be in order.

Occasions for nominating speeches arise most often when officers for a society of any kind are elected by a group of people. Many common occasions occur at meetings of political delegates, church representatives, fraternity and sorority members, civic organizations, councils, charitable groups, business men, labor unions, school meetings, and many other assemblages or congregations.

SUGGESTED NOMINATING SPEECHES

Plan to nominate a candidate for one of the following positions:

1. Yell leader.
2. Class officer.
3. Student council president.
4. All-school representative.
5. Candidate for "outstanding student" award.
6. "Most popular student."
7. Who's Who.

8. Governor.
9. Mayor.
10. City council.
11. Representative.
12. Senator.
13. President of any civic organization.
14. Officer of a student legislature.
15. Most valuable athlete.
16. Boy Scout leader.
17. Candidate for "safety award."
18. Candidate for "good driving award."
19. Candidate for "good citizenship award."
20. Speaker's choice.

HOW TO CHOOSE A CANDIDATE FOR A NOMINATING SPEECH

First, you must have confidence in the ability of the person whom you nominate. Second, be sure that he will be acceptable as a candidate. Choose someone reasonably well-known with a good record. Make certain that if the candidate is elected he will do his work creditably.

HOW TO PREPARE THE NOMINATING SPEECH

The purpose of this speech is obvious. It is equally obvious that all of the elements of the speech should point in one direction: Elect This Candidate! A careful organization should be worked out in which you utilize an arrangement somewhat as follows: Name the office, set forth its specific requirements and indicate what its needs are. Once these points are established, show that your candidate has exceptional fitness to satisfy all the needs and demands of the office. Be specific. Mention his training, experience, abilities (especially those of leadership and cooperation with people), outstanding qualities of personality and character, and clinch your point with a statement to the effect that he is undoubtedly the person best fitted for the office. If your candidate is well-known, you may present his name at the conclusion of your speech. If he is not well-known, it will be advisable to offer his name earlier in your speech, mention it once or twice more at appropriate points; then conclude with it.

You should gather all your information, organize and arrange it as indicated above; then practice until you have it well enough in mind to make an effective extemporaneous delivery.

HOW TO PRESENT THE NOMINATING SPEECH

You must have confidence in yourself. The audience can and will sense this. The speaker may achieve the appearance of self-confidence by observing an alert, polite and erect (not stiff) posture. The use of appropriate body language and gesture will be evidence of poise and confidence. The words of the speech must be vivid, descriptive, and meaningful. They must be carried to your listeners in a voice that is heard clearly and distinctly without traces of straining. There must be a fluency and readiness of speech that fairly shout to your auditors that you know what you are talking about and that you want them to understand how important it is that the right man (your man) is elected for office. Your emphasis, spontaneity, and sincerity must be manifested by your entire organism. This will be shown by what you do, the way you look, and how you sound. You should avoid giving the appearance of being overconfident, overbearing, or conceited. Have a lively, energetic, unhesitant manner, as well as a pleasant, confident voice, an appropriate appearance, and a sincere desire to communicate; and then you will likely make a good speech.

IMPROVE YOUR VOCABULARY

Inexorable – (ĭn-ĕk'sŏ-rà-b'l) a. Not to be persuaded to change your mind or position; unyielding, relentless, inflexible, stubborn. Example: The student exhibited an inexorable tenacity and spirit in his efforts to overcome stage fright – and he was victorious. Use this word in this speech and five times a day for the next week. Make it yours. You can.

Cute – Omit this word. It occupies too much of your speaking time. There is nothing distinguishing about it except that you have probably used it too much. Here are a few synonyms. Try them: clever, shrewd, saucy, pert, impertinent, sprightly, etc.

BIBLIOGRAPHY FOR THE NOMINATING SPEECH

Richters, John Jr., Attacking the Myths of Public Speaking: Winning With Individuals and Groups, National Underwriter, 1979.
Snell, Frank, How to Win the Meeting, Dutton, 1979.

NOMINATING SPEECH

By John R. Knorr

(NOTE: The chairman recognized the speaker before he began his speech.)

In the past years, the Medical Practice Board of Missouri has made many innovative moves, a few of which have been nationwide firsts. These moves have often been spearheaded by a single person. Tonight I am proud to put before the Board such a person for nomination to the chairmanship of the Allied Health Advisory Committee, Neal Healy, R.N. Mr. Healy through his work as Head of Nursing at Washington University Hospital has seen the health care field from many sides. He not only has the foresight the chairmanship demands, but also the experience to convert the future into the present. Mr. Healy was at the head of the lobby for the Nurse Training Act that was adopted by the Missouri Legislature last month.

Mr. Healy has shown the Board that there is more to the health care field than patient care in understaffed hospitals. There are dedicated people today who would go into the nursing field if only given the chance. This is because the most vital programs of Nursing Education can't presently give them that chance.

As chairman of the Allied Health Advisory Committee, Mr. Healy will be an advisor to the Missouri Legislature on health care matters. He will be at the head of a branch of the Medical Practice Board that everyone will be proud to represent.

Mr. Healy has shown through his expressed views that the patient and the patient's health are our highest priorities. This post needs a chairman with this outlook. For these reasons I am proud to put before the Board Mr. Neal Healy for nomination to the chairmanship of the Allied Health Advisory Committee.

A GREAT SPEECH IN AMERICAN HISTORY

Robert G. Ingersoll

(A speech nominating James G. Blaine for President.
Delivered at the Republican National Convention, Cincinnati, Ohio, June 15, 1876.)

Massachusetts may be satisfied with the loyalty of Benjamin H. Bristow - so am I; but if any man nominated by this convention cannot carry the State of Massachusetts I am not satisfied with the loyalty of that State. If the nominee of this convention cannot carry the grand old Commonwealth of Massachusetts by seventy-five thousand majority, I would advise them to sell out Faneuil Hall as a Democratic headquarters. I would advise them to take from Bunker Hill that old monument of glory.

The Republicans of the United States demand as their leader in the great contest of 1876 a man of intellect, a man of integrity, a man of well-known and approved political opinion. They demand a politician in the highest and broadest and best sense of that word. They demand a man acquainted with public affairs - with the wants of the people - with not only the requirements of the hour, but with the demands of the future.

They demand a man broad enough to comprehend the relations of this government to the other nations of the earth. They demand a man well versed in the powers, duties, and prerogatives of each and every department of this government.

They demand a man who will sacredly preserve the financial honor of the United States - one who knows enough to know that the national debt must be paid through the prosperity of this people. One who knows enough to know that all the financial theories in the world cannot redeem a single dollar. One who knows enough to know that all the money must be made, not by law, but by labor. One who knows enough to know that the people of the United States have the industry to make the money and the honor to pay it over just as fast as they make it.

The Republicans of the United States demand a man who knows that prosperity and resumption, when they come, must come together. When they come they will come hand in hand through the golden harvest fields; hand in hand by the whirling spindle and the turning wheel; hand in hand past the open furnace doors; hand in hand by the flaming forges; hand in hand by the chimneys filled with eager fire by the hands of the countless sons of toil. This money has got to be dug out of the earth. You cannot make it by passing resolutions in a political meeting.

The Republicans of the United States want a man who knows that this government should protect every citizen at home and abroad; who knows that any government that will defend its defenders and will not protect its protectors is a disgrace to the map of the world. They demand a man who believes in the eternal separation and divorcement of church and school. They demand a man whose political reputation is spotless as a star; but they do not demand that their candidate shall have a certificate of moral character signed by a Confederate Congress. The man who has in full-heaped and rounded measure all of these splendid qualifications is the present grand and gallant leader of the Republican party - James G. Blaine.

Our country, crowned with the vast and marvelous achievements of its first century, asks for a man worthy of her past; prophetic of her future; asks for a man who has the audacity of genius; asks for a man who is the grandest combination of heart, conscience, and brains beneath the flag. That man is James G. Blaine.

For the Republican host led by that intrepid man there can be no such thing as defeat.

This is a grand year - a year filled with the recollections of the Revolution; filled with proud and tender memories of the sacred past; filled with the legends of liberty; a year in which the sons of freedom will drink from the fountain of enthusiasm; a year in which the people call for a man who has preserved in Congress what our soldiers won upon the field; a year in which we call for the man who has torn from the throat of treason the tongue of slander - a man that has snatched the mask of democracy from the hideous face of rebellion - a man who, like an intellectual athlete, stood in the arena of debate, challenged all comers, and who, up to the present moment, is a total stranger to defeat.

Like an armed warrior, like a plumed knight, James G. Blaine marched down the halls of the American Congress and threw his shining lances full and fair against the brazen foreheads of every defamer of his country and maligner of its honor.

For the Republican party to desert a gallant man now is worse than if an army would desert their general upon the field of battle.

James G. Blaine is now, and has been for years, the bearer of the sacred standard of the Republic. I call it sacred because no human being can stand beneath its folds without becoming, and without remaining, free.

Gentlemen of the Convention, in the name of the great Republic, the only republic that ever existed upon this earth; in the name of all her defenders and of all her supporters; in the name of all her soldiers living; in the name of all her soldiers who died upon the field of battle; and in the name of those who perished in the skeleton clutch of famine at Andersonville and Libby, whose sufferings he so eloquently remembers, Illinois nominates for the next president of this country that prince of parliamentarians, that leader of leaders - James C. Blaine.

SPEECH OUTLINE

Construct a neat, complete sentence outline on this sheet, tear it out, and hand it to your instructor when you rise to speak. He may wish to write criticisms of the outline and speech in the margins.

Type of speech: _____ Name: _____

Number of words in outline: _____ Date: _____

Purpose of this speech: (What do you want your audience to learn, to think, to believe, to feel, or do because of this speech?) _____

_____

TITLE:

INTRODUCTION:

BODY:

CONCLUSION:

Instructor's comments may concern choice of topic, development of ideas, organization, language use, personal appearance, posture, physical activity, sources, and improvement.

(Write sources of information on back of sheet)

SOURCES FROM LITERATURE

Fill out source requirements completely.
Write "none listed" if an author's name or copyright date is not listed.

1. Author's name _____

   Title of book or magazine used _____

   Title of article in above book or magazine _____

   Chapter and/or pages read _____

   Date of above publication _____

2. Author's name _____

   Title of book or magazine used _____

   Title of article in above book or magazine _____

   Chapter and/or pages read _____

   Date of above publication _____

3. Author's name _____

   Title of book or magazine used _____

   Title of article in above book or magazine _____

   Chapter and/or pages read _____

   Date of above publication _____

INTERVIEW SOURCES

1. Person interviewed _____ Date of interview _____

   His position, occupation, and location _____

   Why is he a reliable source? Be specific _____

   _____

2. Person interviewed _____ Date of interview _____

   His position, occupation, and location _____

   Why is he a reliable source? Be specific _____

   _____

PERSONAL EXPERIENCE OF SPEAKER

1. Tell (1) when, (2) where, and (3) conditions under which you became an authority on subject matter in

   your speech _____

   _____

   _____

Chapter 26

ACCEPTING A NOMINATION OR OFFICE

Question: Should a person try to speak like someone he admires?

Answer: No. Develop your own effective speaking style and personality.

This speech is due:
Time limits: 1-3 minutes.
Speaking notes: None.
Sources of information: Yourself.
Outline your speech: Prepare a 50-75 word complete sentence outline. Designate the exact number of words in your outline. Use the form at the end of this chapter.

PURPOSE OF THE SPEECH TO ACCEPT A NOMINATION OR AN OFFICE

Right now you may consider that you are the last person in the world who will ever be nominated for an office or elected to one. Because fate alters circumstances and changes men's minds, you may be among those to achieve the distinction of being asked to perform public service. On the other hand, you may openly seek nomination for public duty. Whatever the events that may place you on the rostrum at some future date, you should know beforehand something about accepting a nomination or an office. This speech experience will provide much useful information for you if you are ever to make a speech to accept a nomination or an office.

To the teacher: It is a practical experience to assign students in pairs to present the nominating speech after which this one is given.

EXPLANATION OF THE SPEECH TO ACCEPT A NOMINATION OR AN OFFICE

A speech in which you accept a nomination or an office is one in which you publicly recognize your own nomination or your election to an office. The speech is much the same for either occasion; hence it is unnecessary to make a distinction between the two as far as this discussion is concerned.

Your speech should firmly establish you as a man of ability, courage, and modesty. It should create confidence in you in the minds of the audience. Your purpose is to establish this confidence.

An occasion of this sort is potentially important. Anything you say may be used for you or against you. Hence it is essential to say the right thing. It is possible although a bit improbable that you could be nominated or elected and the situation be a total surprise to you. If this surprise should ever occur, you might be wise not to speak because of unpreparedness, for you could easily say the wrong thing. In such a situation, your own judgment will have to tell you what to do.

Occasions for accepting a nomination or an office may arise any time that candidates are selected or elections held. The selection of officers for private clubs, social and civic organizations, schools, churches, fraternal groups, and others offer occasions for the acceptance speech.

SUGGESTIONS FOR THE SPEECH ACCEPTING NOMINATION OR AN OFFICE

Accept nomination or office for one of the following:

1. Class president.
2. Student council president.
3. Student body president.
4. Official in a fraternity or sorority.
5. Official in a special organization.
6. Official in a farm organization.
7. Official in a church organization.
8. Official in a city government.
9. Official in a county government.
10. Official in a state government.
11. Official in a national government.
12. Official as a health executive.
13. Official in a corporation.
14. Official on a school board.
15. Official of a country club.
16. Official of a golf course.
17. Official of a charitable society.
18. Official of a taxpayers' league.
19. Official of a booster club.
20. Speaker's choice.

HOW TO CHOOSE A SUBJECT

Study the above list; then make a selection for your speech. Base your decision on your own interest in the topic and in the suitability to your audience. Make your choice without too much delay so that you will have adequate time to prepare your speech. There is no good reason why anyone should make a late and hasty choice of a subject for this speech.

HOW TO PREPARE A SPEECH ACCEPTING A NOMINATION OR AN OFFICE

First of all, be sure to adhere closely to the rules for preparing and constructing any speech. Assuming that you know these, the next point to consider is the purpose of your speech. Your purpose is to establish yourself as a leader and to impress upon people the fact that you are a capable leader. The next logical step is to discover how to accomplish this end. To do this, you will generally speak somewhat as follows: In appropriate and well-chosen words you will express your appreciation and thanks for the honor conferred upon you. (Do not talk about yourself.) Speak of the organization and its importance. Commend its history, its achievements, and its principles. Explain how these have made it grow and how they will continue to operate in the future. You may refer to the names of great men of past fame in the organization and pay them tribute. You should promise to uphold their ideals. Finally, pledge your loyalty and support to the principles of the organization. State frankly that you accept the nomination or office with a complete realization of its responsibilities and that you intend to carry them out. It will be appropriate as a last remark to express again your appreciation of the honor conferred upon you.

A few points to keep in mind are these: Do not belittle yourself or express doubt regarding your fitness. This would be a perfect opening for your opponent and it would not build confidence among your supporters. Do not express surprise at your nomination or election; this is an old trick, worn out long ago and it has little truth or sincerity in it anyway. In no way should you "let the people down" by causing them to feel that they have made a mistake. Finally, avoid grandiloquence by using a simple and sincere language.

Rehearse your speech aloud until you have the sequence of ideas well in mind. Give particular attention to the introduction and conclusion.

HOW TO PRESENT A SPEECH ACCEPTING A NOMINATION OR AN OFFICE

Your attitude should be one of dignity, friendliness, sincerity, and enthusiasm. Your manner, your voice, your non-verbal language should all reflect your attitude. Attention should be paid to your dress so that it is appropriate to the occasion, the audience, and yourself. It will be unwise to consider yourself a Lincoln by not being very careful about how your clothes fit.

When you rise to speak, it is likely that there will be applause. Wait until the applause subsides before you begin to speak. If the applause continues long, raise your hand to ask for silence and a chance to speak. Talk loudly enough to be heard by all, speak clearly and distinctly, and do not talk either too fast or too slowly. If your voice echoes, slow down. Try to make your ideas understandable, and you will be likely to present a good speech.

IMPROVE YOUR VOCABULARY

Graphic - (grăf'ĭk) a. A picturesque or vivid description is said to be graphic. Example: A good speaker will use graphic language to make his points clear. Use this word in this speech and five times a day for the next week. It is a good helper.

Dumb - Give this word a rest. Omit it. Try a synonym. Examples: uninteresting, stupid, uninspired, dull, asinine, irksome, monotonous, arid, inane, fatuous, maudlin, platitudinous, insipid, unimaginative, etc.

BIBLIOGRAPHY FOR ACCEPTING A NOMINATION OR OFFICE

Frank, Ted and Ray, David, Basic Business and Professional Speech Communication, Prentice-Hall, 1979.
Schiff, Roselyn L., Communication Strategy: A Guide to Speech Preparation, Scott Foresman, 1981.

ACCEPTING A NOMINATION

By Tom J. Mayer

(NOTE: The chairman recognized the speaker before he began his speech.)

Mr. President, officers, and fellow members of F.F.A., all of you are dedicated to a purpose which can be realized: The purpose of strengthening the agricultural backbone of our country and restoring the farmer to his rightful position. We have seen our parents and grandparents toil long hours to nurture life in once fallow tracts of land. The recognition they deserve still lies fallow, but the Future Farmers of America are seeing more than the vision of our parents — we are seeing the culmination of world events that must place the fruits of our labor in utmost demand.

The heritage of the farmer in this country is rich. Cities, towns, even countries have been fed, and they receive the fruit of our greatest office, that of provider. Each one of us stands in the gap as provider for the world. Let us stand boldly in recognition of the office handed us by our fathers, and make them as proud to be called our fathers as we are to be called their sons.

The nomination to the office of national president of Future Farmers of America is a special privilege, and one I accept with much pride and appreciation. The challenge demanded by this position is great, not only because of the decisions concerning future operation, but because of the standards realized by all of you. I accept this nomination with confidence in the foundation of our heritage and the progressive attitude of our membership.

SPEECH OUTLINE

Construct a neat, complete sentence outline on this sheet, tear it out, and hand it to your instructor when you rise to speak. He may wish to write criticisms of the outline and speech in the margins.

Type of speech: _____   Name: _____

Number of words in outline: _____   Date: _____

Purpose of this speech: (What do you want your audience to learn, to think, to believe, to feel, or do because of this speech?) _____

_____

TITLE:

INTRODUCTION:

BODY:

CONCLUSION:

Instructor's comments may concern choice of topic, development of ideas, organization, language use, personal appearance, posture, physical activity, sources, and improvement.

(Write sources of information on back of sheet)

SOURCES FROM LITERATURE

Fill out source requirements completely.
Write "none listed" if an author's name or copyright date is not listed.

1. Author's name _____

   Title of book or magazine used _____

   Title of article in above book or magazine _____

   Chapter and/or pages read _____

   Date of above publication _____

2. Author's name _____

   Title of book or magazine used _____

   Title of article in above book or magazine _____

   Chapter and/or pages read _____

   Date of above publication _____

3. Author's name _____

   Title of book or magazine used _____

   Title of article in above book or magazine _____

   Chapter and/or pages read _____

   Date of above publication _____

INTERVIEW SOURCES

1. Person interviewed _____ Date of interview _____

   His position, occupation, and location _____

   Why is he a reliable source? Be specific _____

   _____

2. Person interviewed _____ Date of interview _____

   His position, occupation, and location _____

   Why is he a reliable source? Be specific _____

   _____

PERSONAL EXPERIENCE OF SPEAKER

1. Tell (1) when, (2) where, and (3) conditions under which you became an authority on subject matter in
   your speech _____

   _____

   _____

   _____

QUIZ NO. 5 – COVERS CHAPTERS 22-26. <u>CIRCLE CORRECT ANSWERS.</u> THESE QUESTIONS MAY BE REPRODUCED FOR CLASSROOM USE.

NAME _____ DATE _____

(Ch. 22)   146.   The eulogy is said to be: (mark correct answers)
    (a) a speech of condemnation   (b) a speech of blame   (c) a speech of praise
    (d) a speech delivered in honor or commemoration of someone living or dead

(Ch. 22)   147.   (Blockbuster) A eulogy may be for: (mark correct answers)
    (a) trees   (b) persons   (c) fields   (d) dogs   (e) skunks   (f) anything living
    (g) anything dead   (h) dirt

(Ch. 22)   148.   A biographical sketch is a eulogy.
    (a) true   (b) false

(Ch. 22)   149.   A eulogy: (mark correct answers)
    (a) does not stress the finer qualities of whatever is eulogized since it is blame which the
        the speaker stresses   (b) tells of greatness and achievements
    (c) tells of benefits to society and influences upon people
    (d) may be given to a baby just born   (e) may be given to a person just deceased
    (f) may be given to a person dead for more than a hundred years

(Ch. 22)   150.   Eulogies are laudations which:
    (a) stimulate an audience favorably toward the subject
    (b) ask an audience to be careful about accepting the subject as an individual or object
        to be admired
    (c) inspire an audience to nobler heights by virtue of the examples set by the person
        being praised
    (d) none of the above answers

(Ch. 22)   151.   If your eulogy discusses events in the order of their development, you will be organized by what method? (one answer)
    (a) chronological order or method   (b) period method   (c) space method
    (d) special method

(Ch. 22)   152.   If you eulogized Franklin D. Roosevelt and developed your speech by talking about first his boyhood, second his college life, third his early political life, and fourth his late political life, you would be using what kind of speech development? (one answer)
    (a) chronological order or method   (b) period method   (c) space method
    (d) special method

(Ch. 22)   153.   (Recovered fumble) Regardless of what method you use to develop a eulogy you should: (mark correct answers)
    (a) omit the unimportant events   (b) point up the struggles he made to achieve his aims
    (c) show the development of his ideas and ideals
    (d) describe his relations and services to others and indicate their significance

(Ch. 22) 154. When preparing a eulogy: (mark correct answers)

(a) you should cover up your subject's faults

(b) you should show that despite weaknesses or short comings a person was great

(c) you should be honest in the treatment of your subject

(d) you should assume that the good in your subject outweighed the bad by far

(Ch. 22) 155. (Blockbuster) "Placid" is a word which means: (mark correct synonyms)

(a) aroused   (b) gentle   (c) excited   (d) peaceful   (e) angry   (f) undisturbed

(g) quiet   (h) unruffled   (i) stirred up

(Ch. 22) 156. Synonyms for "old" are: (mark correct answers)

(a) gentle   (b) mellow   (c) venerable   (d) senile   (e) decrepit   (f) antiquated

(g) worn   (h) ancient   (i) hoary

(Ch. 22) 157. (End run) Is this sentence correctly worded? "The hoary young man limped home."

(a) yes   (b) no

(Ch. 23) 158. The dedication speech is: (one answer)

(a) presented at funerals   (b) presented at school graduation exercises

(c) presented on national holidays   (d) presented on commemorative occasions

(Ch. 23) 159. In a dedication speech your purpose required that you should: (one answer)

(a) honor the men who constructed the dedicatory object

(b) request the community to support the project

(c) stress that no discrimination was evident in completing the dedicatory object

(d) compliment the ideals and achievements which the dedicated structure symbolizes

(Ch. 23) 160. The word "altruistic" means: (one answer)

(a) inclined to be stingy   (b) cautious   (c) an attitude of optimism

(d) an attitude of being helpful

(Ch. 23) 161. (Blockbuster) Mark all synonyms for the word "get":

(a) reduce   (b) induce   (c) contract   (d) procure   (e) obtain   (f) retain

(g) grasp   (h) secure   (i) lose   (j) win   (k) relieve   (l) achieve

(Ch. 24) 162. The anniversary speech is similar to what other speech? (one answer)

(a) the welcome   (b) the eulogy   (c) the farewell   (d) the dedication

(Ch. 24) 163. The anniversary speech is one presented: (mark correct answers)

(a) in commemoration of an event, a person, an occasion of the past

(b) on a birthday

(c) when a cornerstone is laid at a structure's completion

(d) to commemorate the day World War II ended

(Ch. 24) 164. Every day is the birthday of somebody or something, hence every day is a potential anniversary.

(a) true   (b) false

(Ch. 24) 165. (Pole vault) The content of an anniversary speech includes how many of the following points?

(a) historically the people and their ideals are responsible for their organization's anniversary celebration

(b) trace the development of the ideals of the people

(c) make the past live again for the audience

(d) compare the past with the present

(Ch. 24) 166. In an anniversary speech you should:

    (a) avoid references to, or implications of, partisan views

    (b) discuss unfriendly acts that occurred but tell how they were overcome

    (c) speak of the future and talk of great promises it holds

    (d) indicate that if more cooperation in the past had occurred things would be much better on the anniversary

(Ch. 24) 167. "Exigency" has numerous synonyms: (mark correct answers)

    (a) event   (b) insipidity   (c) emergency   (d) urgency

(Ch. 24) 168. (Blockbuster) Mark all correct synonyms for the word "fine":

    (a) shiny   (b) bright   (c) rare   (d) delicate   (e) lightly   (f) tasteful

    (g) refined   (h) superior   (i) showy   (j) beauty   (k) colorful   (l) pleasant

(Ch. 25) 169. A nominating speech: (mark correct answers)

    (a) is usually rather long   (b) usually lasts only a few minutes or less

    (c) the speaker tells why his candidate is especially fitted for the position

    (d) remarks made by the speaker need not set forth, in an orderly manner, why the candidate should be elected

(Ch. 25) 170. In a meeting using parliamentary procedure to conduct nominations: (mark correct answers)

    (a) the chair should announce that nominations are in order for _____ office

    (b) a person making a nomination merely calls out a candidate's name

    (c) a person should be recognized by the chair before making a nomination

    (d) if the chair has not announced that nominations for a particular office are in order, then no nominations should be made

(Ch. 25) 171. (Drop kick) To make a nomination a speaker should: (mark correct answers)

    (a) rise to his feet and nominate a candidate

    (b) when nominations are in order a speaker should call out, "Mr. Chairman" or "Madam Chairman" then wait for permission to nominate

    (c) only after the presiding officer gives permission may a person make his nomination

    (d) if a chairman is slow to recognize a person wanting to make a nomination the person should make his nomination regardless

(Ch. 25) 172. The basic purpose of a nominating speech is: (one answer)

    (a) to get your candidate chosen and elected

    (b) to show your candidate is a good moral individual who possesses strong character

    (c) to show your candidate is well-known

    (d) to show your candidate is honest.

(Ch. 25) 173. (Shotgun) The content of a nomination speech should contain how many of the following:

    (a) stress that your candidate is the best, however, he might not accept the office if elected

    (b) name the office and set forth its requirements

    (c) tell that although your candidate served time in prison for embezzlement he is reformed

    (d) stress your candidate's special training, experience, personality and character that qualify him for the position

(Ch. 25) 174. In a nomination speech: (mark correct answers)
    (a) regardless of who your candidate is you should withhold his name until the last
    (b) if your candidate is well-known you may present his name at the conclusion of your speech
    (c) if your candidate is not well-known offer his name early in your speech then once or twice again at appropriate points later

(Ch. 25) 175. (Blockbuster) Mark the correct synonyms of "inexorable":
    (a) strong   (b) relentless   (c) mighty   (d) unyielding   (e) inflexible
    (f) gigantic   (g) stubborn   (h) powerful

(Ch. 25) 176. Is this sentence correct in meaning? "The baby was inexorably beautiful."
    (a) yes   (b) no

(Ch. 25) 177. (Blockbuster) Mark all synonyms of the word "cute".
    (a) sweet   (b) sprightly   (c) sugary   (d) saucy   (e) pert   (f) honeyed
    (g) clever   (h) darling   (i) impertinent   (j) shrewd

(Ch. 26) 178. In a speech accepting a nomination or office you should establish yourself as:
(mark correct answers)
    (a) a person who has known much hard luck but who has worked hard to overcome it
    (b) a man of ability
    (c) a man who will compromise with no one because you do not make mistakes
    (d) a man of courage and modesty

(Ch. 26) 179. In a speech accepting a nomination or office you should: (mark correct answers)
    (a) create confidence in you from the audience
    (b) establish the fact that you believe your church is the best
    (c) tell your listeners what you dislike and what you will do about it
    (d) establish your own honesty and also that any person entering your office will have to demonstrate his honesty before you will listen to him

(Ch. 26) 180. (Home run) In a speech accepting a nomination or office: (mark correct answers)
    (a) you will thank people for the honor conferred upon you
    (b) you will talk much about yourself to establish your leadership
    (c) you will talk of the nomination or office and its importance
    (d) you will commend the history, achievements, and principles of the people who nominated and elected you
    (e) you will pledge your loyalty and support to the organization and people who nominated or elected you

(Ch. 26) 181. Synonyms for the word "graphic" are: (mark correct answers)
    (a) prosy   (b) picturesque   (c) flat   (d) vivid   (e) dull   (f) pictorial
    (g) uninteresting

(Ch. 26) 182. Is the following sentence correctly worded? "The dull and monotonous illustration was graphic in all details."
    (a) yes   (b) no

(Ch. 26) 183. (Blockbuster) Mark all synonyms for the word "dumb":
    (a) unimaginative   (b) insipid   (c) maudlin   (d) platitudinous   (e) fatuous
    (f) inane   (g) arid   (h) monotonous   (i) irksome   (j) dull   (k) asinine
    (l) uninspired   (m) stupid   (n) uninteresting

Chapter 27

THE INTERVIEW

Question: *Is loud and boisterous speech effective?*

Answer: *No. It may frighten little children but not adults.*

This speech is due:
Time limits: 4- 6 minutes for report of an interview.
⅓- 2 minutes for role-played telephone appointment.
5-10 minutes for a role-played interview.
Speaking notes: 25-50 words for interview report.
Sources of information: List the person interviewed.
Outline your speech: Prepare a 75-150 word complete sentence outline. Designate the exact number of words in your outline. Use the form at the end of this chapter.
To the teacher: All students should complete in class: (1) the role-played telephone appointments for an interview and (2) role-played class interviews for a job or for information to report. Only those students who are "ready" by virtue of maturity should be assigned to interview local business men - and they should be well trained.

PURPOSE OF THE INTERVIEW EXPERIENCE

Of all the probable events in your life you can bet the interview in some form or another will be one. Perhaps you have already interviewed for a job or you are planning to do so. Unless you are that one person in a million you will be interviewed (briefly or extensively) before you are employed and whether or not you get the job, or any other favorable response, will depend on how you conduct yourself under interview circumstances. And if you are interviewing for other reasons, to gain information, for a report, to prepare a newscast, to prepare a legal brief for a case in court, or to sell an article, the maturity, skill, and judgment you exercise will bring success or failure. This experience will add to your chances for success, help put money in your pocket, and give the confidence needed to do well.

EXPLANATION OF THE INTERVIEW

An interview is talking with another person or a group with a specific purpose. It is planned except for impromptu interviews among business people and others often observed on the street, in a store, even in a home. Unplanned interviews possess characteristics of conversation while more formal interviews tend to proceed in an orderly manner. It is the latter we wish to discuss here since they impose restrictions on the parties involved such as (1) making an appointment - you

don't walk into a place of business interrupting the manager from whatever he is doing; (2) there may be limited time for you to finish the interview; (3) you may have several separate meetings, all scheduled before you complete your interview purpose.

One common element in an interview is talk, thus if you can express yourself well things should go smoothly. If you cannot, you may have trouble. Another common element is your physical behavior, your appearance, your walk, your posture, subtle movements of your hands and feet, eye contact, facial expressions. Everything you say and do tells something about you and altogether it tells what you really are. It is your personality. Your thoughts and moods, attitudes and feelings, are all symbolized by your total behavior and you can't hide them. You are kidding yourself if you think you have secretly mastered an art of deceit and won't be discovered. Business executives or sales personnel are quick to detect a phony.

Since the interview situation often places the parties involved close together, perhaps in a small office, the interview permits many personal judgments and subconscious reactions. In effect the interview places all participants in positions of judgment with everyone revealing himself to other persons present. No one has yet invented a better way to formulate final evaluations of people whether it be a prospective employee or prospective boss.

Occasions for interviews occur in all kinds of employment, inquiries for information, sales situations, personnel work, special reports and surveys, and others.

Remember an interview may be conducted by a group such as when news reporters interview a governor or other official. In contrast to this a school board may interview a prospective teacher and the teacher may interview the board members. Or a single reporter might interview any executive or administrative group.

SUGGESTED INTERVIEW SITUATIONS
1. A school official.
2. A minister.
3. The mayer.
4. City official.
5. An internal revenue or state tax official.
6. An employment official.
7. A business man about his business.
8. A business man for a job.
9. A construction contractor for a progress report.
10. Conduct a survey by interviews. (Be sensible with survey.)
11. A school board for a job.
12. The city council about street improvement.
13. A board of directors about company policy.
14. A church board about church policies.
15. A religious group about their projects.
16. An insurance agent about insurance.
17. The city building inspector.
18. A fish and game official.
19. A chamber of commerce official.
20. A forest ranger.
21. Student's choice of a suitable interview.

HOW TO CHOOSE AN INTERVIEW SITUATION
Select an area that interests you and one you can complete. Avoid a person or group too distant to reach or who cannot grant the interview within a short time or at a time you can meet. Make your choice and arrangements within twenty-four hours. Why so soon? You may learn that the person you want to interview is on vacation or ill, thus you will be forced to start anew. Also supposing you wait until several days before your report of an interview is due and your appointment is cancelled. You then run to your instructor begging mercy saying you don't have time to do it. You are the dawdler and procrastinator, not your instructor, and you should expect no special consideration. Make your decision at once and do a superior interview.

HOW TO PREPARE FOR AN INTERVIEW
(THE INTERVIEWER)
1. Since you are the interviewer make an appoint and if it is made in person be prepared to conduct it on the spot should the interviewee suggest you do so. If your appointment is by telephone be pleasant and efficient by using a carefully prepared and rehearsed request constructed as follows: (a) make sure you are talking with the right person, (b) introduce yourself completely, (c) explain why you want the interview also suggesting the amount of time needed, the date, hour, and place. Do not apologize, (d) leave your name, telephone number, and ask to be called should it be necessary for the interviewee to change the appointment. Sometimes a secretary will take your appointment.

2. Regardless of whether you are interviewing for a job or to acquire information for a report you should acquaint yourself with background data about your interviewee. Examine biographical material in books of scholars, educators, renowned persons, scientific men, "Who's Who" compilations, and others or make inquiries about him.

Now comes the crux of your interview preparation. What is your purpose and what do you want to know? You will determine the purpose first; second you will prepare a list of about ten lead questions and twenty specific inquiries that will bring out the information you want. Do not read your list of questions verbatim while interviewing. Memorize selected questions from it to be used as needed. You will refer to your list occasionally and originate other questions as the interview proceeds.

3. Dress neatly, carefully and appropriately. Avoid being conspicuous by your appearance. Casual school clothes are not suitable. Dress for an adult's approval who is used to seeing secretaries and other employees attired to meet the business world. Gaudy hair styles or fads (men or women) should be avoided like a plague. You can fail an interview before opening your mouth to speak if your clothes

are shabby, dirty, outlandish, or your hair makes you look like a museum piece. Recently a personnel worker who interviewed job applicants for a large mercantile business told this writer that some applicants appeared for interviews without regard to their appearance seemingly with an attitude their appearance was a personal matter and none of the interviewer's business. They were not even considered and would have saved everyone's time by not applying.

4. Get the correct address and exact time for the interview. Be sure of this. Allow more time than needed to get there. You might have car trouble or traffic problems.

5. Study the background information and your list of questions. They should be partially memorized. Be sure you have your questions laid out with adequate space for writing responses to them or provide yourself with an additional notebook for recording the interviewer's answers. Also have a pencil or pen that writes.

6. Think of your approaching interview as enjoyable experience.

HOW TO CONDUCT AN INTERVIEW
(TO ACQUIRE INFORMATION)

Arrive ten minutes early at the office of the interviewee, not the parking lot which is several blocks away. Inquire where to locate Mr. _____, or tell the secretary, if one is present, who you are and that you are there to meet your appointment. When informed that Mr. _____ is ready, go into his office, introduce yourself if the secretary fails to do this, shake hands if you are a man (use a firm grip but don't pump for oil or hang on in a death struggle), politely wait to be seated when invited or seat yourself if your judgment tells you it is appropriate. The host may be busy at his desk and request you to wait a moment. You may stand or sit politely, or look over the office furnishings and arrangements casually, but don't fidget or pace nervously. You might glance over your list of questions to refresh your memory. When your host is ready you may sincerely comment on the office, the view, or something of general interest as an opening remark.

Start your interview by explaining why you are there. State your questions courteously, tactfully, and directly. Initial opening questions may concern

(1) history of the business, (2) the nature of the business such as products sold or services performed, (3) number of employees, labor practices, qualifications of employees, vacations, employee benefits, (4) advantages of this business, (5) etc. Do not press questions on any subject the interviewee obviously doesn't want to discuss. It's your obligation to direct the interview into the desired areas and bring the discussion back if it gets too far off the subject. Remember this is your interview. Bring the interview to a pleasant conclusion (perhaps by saying you have one more question), and do not overstay your time. Should the interviewee offer to show you his place of business, have a cup of coffee, or tour the grounds, accept graciously but don't forget that his time may be limited — don't overstay your invitation. Thank him when it seems appropriate and invite him to visit your school.

While the interview is underway take notes quickly and accurately. (Write clearly so you can read your notes later.) Listen attentively so you won't have to ask him to repeat, and should time run out request a later appointment to finish your interview. Thank the interviewee before leaving.

Be courteous at all times. Avoid random, nervous movements, any familiarities, excessive throat clearing, mumbling, and usually it's advisable not to smoke even if invited.

HOW TO INTERVIEW FOR A JOB

Let's suppose you must interview for a job. You will be the interviewee and the interviewer. Questions will be directed to you and you will ask questions about the work. Read again the preceding section on conducting an interview to refresh your thinking. Next, you should have a copy of your birth certificate with you, a complete transcript of your grades beginning with the ninth grade, also honors received, offices held, activities participated in, memberships, a record of your work experience, a list of at least three personal references with complete addresses and telephone numbers (a business man, minister, teacher or other influential person) and/or letters of recommendation. All of these may not be required but they should be available in neatly typed form and correct. A recent good small photograph is also advisable. Several extra copies of these records should be kept in your files. Before you are interviewed you may be required to fill out an application form and, if so, fill it out completely answering every question fully. Be neat and accurate. Omit nothing and don't assume that a stranger studying the form will be able to read your mind and fill in blank spaces.

When you go into the job interview conduct yourself as you would before any business or professional person. Greet the interviewer cordially, shake hands if appropriate, state your purpose and ask generally what positions are available unless you are applying for a particular one. So you will know what is expected of you ask about the qualifications, responsibilities, duties, and requirements of the offering. Most likely you will be asked questions about your experience, background, training and education. Answer these questions honestly and directly but don't belittle yourself. Suggest that the interviewer might like to examine summaries of your personal history, training, experience and recommendations you have with you. Sit politely while he reads them. Besides the job you are applying for he may be looking for someone to fill a special position he has not advertised and it's quite possible he would select you, especially if you conduct a superior interview showing alertness and intelligence. Or maybe he will try you out at something less important with the idea of moving you up if you are a superior worker. As the interview progresses you should be ready to talk and give answers or to wait with poise if anything unusual occurs. Sometimes interruptions are planned to test your reactions - the telephone rings, a secretary brings a message, an employee comes in. Or sometimes he asks a startling or unexpected question. Don't be surprised at anything - just respond intelligently and respectfully.

Before the interview ends, if you haven't been told, inquire about company policy concerning union membership, insurance, up-grading, salary or wages, vacations, sick leave, and other important matters. If it appears appropriate you might ask to be shown around the buildings or grounds where you would work. In all instances when you inquire avoid an attitude of distruct or suspicion - just be interested, courteous, alert.

Before the interview concludes ask when you will be notified about the job. If you receive a vague or indefinite answer ask if you may contact him or write him at a future date. It is only fair before you leave that you have his word you will be notified within a reasonable time. And if you do make a follow-up inquiry it is advisable to appear in person rather than telephoning unless you are asked to telephone.

When the interviewer indicates by words or rises from his chair indicating that the interview is ended bring your remarks to a close, thank him for his consideration, and leave. Sometimes it may be necessary for you to close the interview - you can stay too long.

Here's a hint: If you don't fill out an application form and you want the interviewer to remember you - instead of a dozen other applicants even though he writes your name on a pad - just as the interview ends hand him a three by five card, neatly typed, with your name, address, telephone number, age, sex, picture attached, education, work experience, and type of work you are interested in or qualified to do.

Assignment 1. (Appointment for job interview) The instructor may develop the Interview Assignment as follows:

Two persons at a time sitting back-to-back eight to ten feet apart carry out an imagined telephone conversation. One is a businessman, the other a student seeking an appointment for an interview. A third person, appointed by the instructor, or a fourth person, also appointed, in the audience, may occasionally answer the telephone instead of the businessman. The extra two persons may be secretary, janitor, partner, etc., who take calls for the businessman when he is out or busy. The student must make his appointment even if he has to call back twenty minutes later. Don't overdo the role-playing - and keep it realistic. The instructor may send the student outside the classroom while he sets up the appointment suitation. The person seeking the appointment then enters the room, seats himself, and indicates he is calling by saying "ding-a-ling" until the phone is answered.

Note: If time permits, students should participate in Assignment 1 before doing Assignments 2 or 3.

Assignment 2. (The job interview)

Two persons role-play the job interview from five to ten minutes. The interviewee should enter the classroom door after the instructor has set up any special circumstances the interviewer will confront. The businessman, a secretary, or someone else will admit the student who will take it from there. This should not be rehearsed by the participants since a real interview is not rehearsed; however, the participants should be well prepared to conduct their individual parts and try to make the entire affair true to life.

Assignment 3.

The appointment and interview aspects of this assignment should be role-played successfully before any student is permitted to actually complete the interview with a businessman. Here's the assignment.

1. By telephone make an appointment with a business or professional man whom you do not know personally.

2. Complete an interview to learn about the business, its general operations, policies (labor, products, organization, etc.), and future plans. Take notes. Prepare a five to six minute oral report of the interview and what you learned for the class.

The instructor should keep a list of all businessmen interviewed in order that future classes will not interview the same ones too often. A letter of appreciation from the instructor to the businessman expressing gratitude for his cooperation is a good practice.

Assignment 4.

Students wanting work should conduct actual job interviews, then prepare five to six minute oral reports of their experiences for the class.

IMPROVE YOUR VOCABULARY

Fallible - (făl'i-b'l) a. Subject to making errors or to being deceived. Subject to being erroneous. Subject to error. Example: Every man is fallible - also foolish if he thinks he is not.

Pay - Try using a synonym for this word. You will be surprised at the variety you can achieve. Here are a few examples: fee, hire, recompense, stipend, compensation, emolument, requital, remuneration, earnings, etc.

BIBLIOGRAPHY FOR THE INTERVIEW

Bradley, Patricia H. and Baird, J. E., Communication for Business and the Professions, Wm. C. Brown, 1980.

Frank, Ted and Ray, David, Basic Business and Professional Speech Communication, Prentice-Hall, 1979.

Mager, N. H. and Mager, S. K., eds., What to Say, How to Say It: Improving Your Image By Mail, On the Phone, In Person, Morrow, 1980.

A NOTABLE SPEECH IN AMERICAN HISTORY

(The example below is for student appreciation and is not
intended for any particular assignment in this text.)

Washington

ON HIS APPOINTMENT AS COMMANDER-IN-CHIEF
(1775)

(Washington had been chosen general and commander-in-chief by the Continental
Congress sitting in Philadelphia on June 15, 1775. On the following day the
president of Congress officially notified Washington of his appointment, requesting
his acceptance. In reply, Washington made the speech here given, as recorded in
the journals of Congress.)

Tho I am truly sensible of the high honor done me in
this appointment, yet I feel great distress from a conscious-
ness that my abilities and military experience may not be
equal to the extensive and important trust. However, as the
Congress desire it, I will enter upon the momentous duty,
and exert every power I possess in their service and for the
support of the glorious cause. I beg they will accept my
most cordial thanks for this distinguished testimony of their
approbation.

But lest some unlucky event should happen unfavor-
able to my reputation, I beg it may be remembered by every
gentleman in the room that I this day declare, with the utmost
sincerity, I do not think myself equal to the command I am
honored with.

As to pay, sir, I beg leave to assure the Congress that
as no pecuniary consideration could have tempted me to
accept this arduous employment at the expense of my domestic ease and happiness, I do not wish to make any profit
from it. I will keep an exact account of my expenses. Those,
I doubt not, they will discharge, and that is all I desire.

Washington kept such an account, and at the end of the war presented it to Congress as drawn up by his
own hand. A facsimile of it has been published by Franklin Knight.

SPEECH OUTLINE

Construct a neat, complete sentence outline on this sheet, tear it out, and hand it to your instructor when you rise to speak. He may wish to write criticisms of the outline and speech in the margins.

Type of speech: _____ Name: _____

Number of words in outline: _____ Date: _____

Purpose of this speech: (What do you want your audience to learn, to think, to believe, to feel, or do because of this speech?) _____

_____

TITLE:

INTRODUCTION:

BODY:

CONCLUSION:

Instructor's comments may concern choice of topic, development of ideas, organization, language use, personal appearance, posture, physical activity, sources, and improvement.

(Write sources of information on back of sheet)

SOURCES FROM LITERATURE
Fill out source requirements completely.
Write "none listed" if an author's name or copyright date is not listed.

1. Author's name _____

   Title of book or magazine used _____

   Title of article in above book or magazine _____

   Chapter and/or pages read _____

   Date of above publication _____

2. Author's name _____

   Title of book or magazine used _____

   Title of article in above book or magazine _____

   Chapter and/or pages read _____

   Date of above publication _____

3. Author's name _____

   Title of book or magazine used _____

   Title of article in above book or magazine _____

   Chapter and/or pages read _____

   Date of above publication _____

INTERVIEW SOURCES

1. Person interviewed _____ Date of interview _____

   His position, occupation, and location _____

   Why is he a reliable source? Be specific _____

   _____

2. Person interviewed _____ Date of interview _____

   His position, occupation, and location _____

   Why is he a reliable source? Be specific _____

   _____

PERSONAL EXPERIENCE OF SPEAKER

1. Tell (1) when, (2) where, and (3) conditions under which you became an authority on subject matter in

   your speech _____

   _____

   _____

Chapter 28

THE SALES TALK

Question: *Should a person vary his rate of speaking?*

Answer: *Yes, but be natural. Variety is a prerequisite of good speech.*

This speech is due:

Time limits: 5-6 minutes.

Speaking notes: Do not use notes when trying to sell something to an audience.

Sources of information: Two are required, preferably three. For each source give the specific magazine or book it was taken from, title of the article, author's full name, date of publication, and the chapter or page telling where the material was found. If a source is a person, identify him completely by title, position, occupation, etc. List these on the outline form.

Outline your speech: Prepare a 75-150 word complete sentence outline. Designate the exact number of words in your outline. Use the form at the end of this chapter.

PURPOSE OF THE SALES TALK

The sales talk is something you may be called upon to present much sooner than you now expect. It involves a situation in which you usually try to trade or sell a group of persons an article in exchange for their money. Sometimes this is a difficult task. Many persons have had little or no experience in this particular type of speaking and selling. This one experience is not intended to make a sales expert out of anyone, but certainly it will help the person who later finds it necessary to sell something to a group. That is why this assignment is made.

EXPLANATION OF THE SALES TALK

A sales talk is a speech in which you will attempt to persuade a group of persons to buy a product from you now or at a later date. In some instances, you will actually take orders at the conclusion of your remarks; in other cases, you will merely stimulate an interest in your goods so that prospective customers will buy from you later. But in either case, your purpose is to sell by stimulating the customer to want what you have and to be willing to part with his money to acquire the goods you have for sale.

The sales talk makes special demands on the speaker. He must be pleasing in appearance, pleasant to meet, congenial, and friendly. He must be thoroughly familiar with his product and be conversant with all matters pertaining to it, including many details. He should, by all means, be able and willing to answer questions regarding the production, the manufacturers (or the company sponsoring it, such as an insurance company), the cost, terms of selling, guarantees, repairs, cost of upkeep, and other such matters about his product.

The speaker should know how to meet objections, questions, or comparisons made relative to his product, as opposed to a competitive product.

Occasions for the sales talk are many. We might say that any time a speaker appears before one or more persons with the purpose of selling, he makes a sales talk. The groups, however, which compose the audience may be any one of these: a school board, a high school or college class, a gathering of church officials, a purchasing committee for a business house, a city council, a ladies' aid society, or a group of farmers who have met at a country schoolhouse to observe the demonstration of a new tractor hitch. The main idea is that prospective customers can be any kind of people and be met anywhere and at any time.

SUGGESTED TOPICS FOR A SALES TALK

Build your speech around one of the following suggestions which you attempt to sell:

1. Sporting equipment – golf clubs, tennis rackets, etc.
2. Hunting equipment – guns, ammunition, clothing, etc.
3. Fishing equipment.
4. Tractors.
5. Plows or drills, etc.
6. Horses.
7. A vacuum sweeper.
8. An electric razor.
9. A pen or pencil.
10. Stationery.
11. A watch.
12. A book or magazine.
13. An insurance policy.

14. A correspondence course.
15. Real estate.
16. A box of chocolates.
17. Clothing (any article).
18. Old coins or stamps.
19. Ticket to a movie.
20. Speaker's choice.

HOW TO CHOOSE A TOPIC FOR A SALES TALK

Choose a product for sale that you believe in; then build your talk around it. Be sure to select something your audience needs and can use. If none of the above suggestions is suitable, select something else. Do not put off a choice because you cannot make up your mind. You can choose a topic if you want to.

HOW TO PREPARE A SALES TALK

First of all, follow the regular steps of preparation used for any speech. You know these. Pay particular attention to diagnosing your audience. It would be fatal to misjudge your prospective buyers. You should know as much as possible about these items concerning their personal situations: probable incomes, credit ratings, occupations, religions, education, local beliefs, and anything else that concerns them. A wise salesman will find out what other salesmen have sold or tried to sell the group in the way of competitive products. He will also be familiar enough with these products that he can make comparisons favorable to his own.

It will be advisable in all cases to demonstrate whatever you are selling. This means that you must know how to show it to the best advantage. Be sure, very sure, that it is in good appearance and working order. Let your customers try it out. If it is candy, pass samples of it around. If it is a car, have them drive it - but demonstrate.

It is essential that you be ready to sign order contracts. This will necessitate your having pen and ink, order forms, credit information, checkbooks, and receipts for use. Do not make a buyer wait if he is ready to buy.

Another point is to be prepared to greet the audience promptly. Go to the designated meeting place early. Have everything in proper and neat arrangement before your audience arrives. After you think you have every display most advantageously placed, all sales forms in order, and everything in tip-top shape, go back for a final check. If you have omitted nothing, then you are ready, not before.

As for your speech, have it well in mind. Do not use notes. It would be foolish to attempt to sell something while referring to notes in order to discover the good points of your product.

The organization of your speech should be well thought out. One plan which can be recommended is the one that follows.

1. Give a friendly introduction, stating your pleasure in meeting the audience. Be sincere.

2. Present information about yourself and your product. Who are you? What position do you hold? How long have you been with this company? Why did you choose to work for your particular company? What is the name of the company? How old is it? Is it a nationwide organization? Is it financially sound? Is it reliable? Does it stand behind its products? Does it guarantee its products? Does it quibble over an adjustment if a customer asks for one? Does it have a large dealer organization? Can you get parts and repairs quickly if these are needed? Does the company plan to stay in business? Is it constantly improving its products? Does it test all of its products before placing them on the market? How large is its business? What special recommendations does the company have? Of course, it may not be necessary to answer all of these questions; however, many of them will have to be answered by giving information which establishes you as a reputable salesman and your company as a reputable firm.

Now that you have laid the groundwork, you are ready to show and explain the goods you have for sale. The nature of the article you are selling will demonstrate how you do this. Probably, the first thing you will do will be to explain the purpose of your product; that is, you will tell what it is for. Next you will explain and demonstrate how it operates. In doing this, be sure to play up its advantages, its special features, new improvements, economy of operation, dependability, beauty, ease of handling, and the like. Give enough details to be clear but not so much that you confuse your listeners.

At this point you have established yourself, your company, and you have explained and demonstrated your product. Your next step will require careful analysis of your audience. This is done to show how your product will benefit them: You must know their wants and needs and let them see vividly how your product satisfies these wants and needs. If the sales article is a tractor, the farmer will do his work more easily and economically by its use. If it is a box of chocolates, the housewife will delight her family and her friends by serving them. If the salesman is offering a correspondence school course, the buyer will make more money, gain prestige, secure advancements by buying the course. Whatever the sales item, you must show the advantages and benefits of the ownership of it. Sometimes it is helpful to mention the names of other persons who have bought the product from you and are now benefiting from ownership of it.

And now comes the last step. How may they buy it? Where? When? Who sells it, if you carry only samples? How much does it cost? Do you sell on the installment plan? What are the carrying charges? How much do you require as a down payment? How many months are allowed in paying for it? What is the amount of the monthly payments? Or is it cash? Is any discount allowed for cash? What special inducement is offered to those who buy now? How much can they save? Will future prices be higher? Do you take trade-ins? How much allowance is made on a trade-in? . . . Make it as easy and simple as possible to buy the goods you are selling. Be sure that your explanations are clear and exact. Do not use misleading terms or give wrong impressions. If your salesmanship will not withstand a full, complete, and candid examination, you will be wise to change your policies or change your vocation.

To be able to present the above information effectively, to demonstrate the product, to show the prospective customers how they will benefit from owning your goods, and how they may buy it, you will rehearse the demonstration and accompanying speech aloud many times. Do this until you have attained complete mastery of the entire speech. Avoid being trite, cocky, or insincere. Do your best, and all will be well.

HOW TO PRESENT A SALES TALK
Look good; be good. In other words have a neat and pleasing appearance, plus a friendly and polite attitude. These points are extremely important. Your own good judgment will tell you what is appropriate dress. Your common sense will provide the background for the right attitude. Generally, you should begin your speech directly, if this procedure is appropriate to the mood of your listeners. Avoid being smart or using questionable stories to impress your listeners. Put the group at ease and get on with your speech. Your manner should be conversational; your voice should be easily heard by all but not strained. Your bodily action should be suitable for holding attention, making transitions, and demonstrating what you are selling. Your language, of course, should be simple, descriptive, vivid, and devoid of technical terms. In using charts, pictures, diagrams, or the sales article itself, your familiarity with these should be so great that you can point out any information or refer to any part of the product while retaining a posture that permits focusing your attention on the audience. In answering questions you should be as clear as possible and sure that your questioner is satisfied with the information you give. Avoid embarrassing anyone. An alert and enthusiastic yet friendly attitude is most desirable.

SPECIAL HINTS
Do not knock your competitor or his product; it is better to praise him.

If you have any special inducements to encourage the buying of your products, be sure to present them at the appropriate time.

After concluding your talk allow your audience time to ask questions. It may be that some of them will wish to ask questions during your speech. If this is the case, be sure to answer them clearly; however, do not turn the meeting into a question and answer occasion before explaining your wares.

IMPROVE YOUR VOCABULARY

Trenchant - (trĕn'chănt) a. A trenchant remark is one that is cutting, sharp, keen or biting. Example: The speaker had a trenchant wit which worried his hecklers. Use this word in this speech and five times a day for the next week. Make it yours. You can.

Awful and terrible - Omit these words. Do not use them for a week at least. They are fatigued to the point of exhaustion. Give your vocabulary new life by using synonyms. Examples: frightful, monstrous, monotonous, ill-bred, plain, homely, unlovely, ugly, odious, serious, overpowering, disgusting, etc. Be careful that you do not use synonyms inappropriately. Save your more powerful words for situations that they accurately describe.

BIBLIOGRAPHY FOR THE SALES TALK

McGann, Mary, Coping with Language: Talk Your Way to Success, Rosen Press, 1980.
Minnick, Wayne C., Public Speaking, Houghton Mifflin, 1979.
Shaw, Harry, Better Jobs Through Better Speech, Littlefield, 1979.

SALES SPEECH

By Donald Rogers

What are your plans for next weekend? Are you planning to boat, hike, ski, fish, paint a room in your house, or participate in some other enjoyable form of relaxation? What was that? Painting — an enjoyable form of relaxation? I think it can be, and in a few moments I'll show you how you can make painting a pleasurable experience.

My name is Don Rogers, representing Montgomery Ward's hardwares division, and I'm here to demonstrate a remarkable product that has revolutionized home decorating, along with eliminating many of the headaches that are traditionally involved.

Here I have two samples of wallboard painted identically with dark green glossy enamel. Beneath each is a gallon of paint. (Speaker kneels beside first can.) This one is a very fine latex interior paint. (Speaker moves to second can.) This is LIFE, Montgomery Ward's new interior latex enamel. For years all paint, particularly rubber latex paints, were pretty much the same in that they all came in lovely colors, were washable, and offered easy clean-up. Now LIFE interior latex enamel offers all these advantages plus several important differences.

Let me show you exactly why I think LIFE is like no other paint you have ever used. (Speaker goes to first open can of paint.) First I will paint a sample with this paint. (Speaker starts to paint with roller.) Notice how this paint applies smoothly and quickly. It is a very fine paint. (Speaker finishes the sample and moves to the second.) Now I will paint this sample with Ward's LIFE. (Speaker begins to paint second sample.) Notice that it too rolls on smoothly, quickly and with absolutely no spattering and, as you can see, (Speaker holds up roller full of paint) LIFE is totally dripless. (Speaker picks up both sections of wallboard and brings them forward to his audience.) If you will, please look at this sample I just painted (pointing to first sample) and you will see that it will surely need another coat in order to cover. Up to now this has not been uncommon, but look at the sample painted with LIFE. It is completely covered. There is absolutely no green showing through the new white coating. This, ladies and gentlemen, is one of the most remarkable qualities of LIFE paint. Here is the Montgomery Ward's one-coat guarantee printed on each can of LIFE:

"THIS PAINT IS GUARANTEED TO COVER ANY PAINTED SURFACE WITH ONE COAT WHEN APPLIED ACCORDING TO LABEL DIRECTIONS AT A RATE NOT TO EXCEED 450 SQUARE FEET PER GALLON. IF THIS PAINT FAILS TO COVER AS STATED HERE, BRING THE LABEL OF THIS PAINT TO YOUR NEAREST WARD'S BRANCH AND WE WILL FURNISH ENOUGH PAINT TO INSURE COVERAGE, OR, TO YOUR OPTION, WILL REFUND THE COMPLETE PURCHASE PRICE."

In addition to being a one-coat paint, LIFE interior latex is extremely durable and washable and can be expected to last six years or more, retaining its velvet finish through frequent clean-ups with harsh solvents and powders. LIFE is as tough as enamel, and with the soft quality of latex.

Not only is LIFE a durable, long-lasting, beautiful coating to any wall surface, but it is safe to use. The aroma, lightly evident while painting, is non-toxic as well as pleasant; and of extreme importance when small children are in the house, LIFE is totally lead-free. This paint is also sanitized to help retard the growth of bacteria on the surface of the paint.

LIFE is truly a superb interior paint. It comes in over eight hundred beautiful colors allowing you to decorate your home in any combination of hues and tints. There is no need to pamper this improved paint. It satisfies the decorator's demands for a soft-look, flat-finish that can be washed repeatedly without losing its luxurious appearance. LIFE is dripless and spatterless, easy to clean up (with just soap and water) and is easy to apply (drying in thirty minutes). Again, LIFE paint is unconditionally guaranteed to cover any painted surface in one coat, which brings us to the best point of all. LIFE is inexpensive to use. You can paint a ten by twelve foot room with one gallon, at a cost of ten dollars and forty-nine cents, and do it in half the time.

Because Montgomery Ward is a nation-wide department store, LIFE interior latex is readily available almost anywhere. Since the one-coat guarantee is good at all Ward stores you can buy the paint in Chattanooga, Tennessee and Ward's will replace it, if desired, in beautiful downtown Burbank.

I urge you to try LIFE interior latex the next time you paint, and I'm sure you will find that for quality and convenience it cannot be duplicated. LIFE is as near as your Montgomery Ward store. Purchase a gallon. Get that job done . . . you know . . . the one you have been putting off, and you'll be enjoying your favorite sport sooner than you think.

SPEECH OUTLINE

Construct a neat, complete sentence outline on this sheet, tear it out, and hand it to your instructor when you rise to speak. He may wish to write criticisms of the outline and speech in the margins.

Type of speech: _____ Name: _____

Number of words in outline: _____ Date: _____

Purpose of this speech: (What do you want your audience to learn, to think, to believe, to feel, or do because of this speech?) _____

_____

TITLE:

INTRODUCTION:

BODY:

CONCLUSION:

Instructor's comments may concern choice of topic, development of ideas, organization, language use, personal appearance, posture, physical activity, sources, and improvement.

(Write sources of information on back of sheet)

SOURCES FROM LITERATURE

Fill out source requirements completely.
Write "none listed" if an author's name or copyright date is not listed.

1. Author's name _____

   Title of book or magazine used _____

   Title of article in above book or magazine _____

   Chapter and/or pages read _____

   Date of above publication _____

2. Author's name _____

   Title of book or magazine used _____

   Title of article in above book or magazine _____

   Chapter and/or pages read _____

   Date of above publication _____

3. Author's name _____

   Title of book or magazine used _____

   Title of article in above book or magazine _____

   Chapter and/or pages read _____

   Date of above publication _____

INTERVIEW SOURCES

1. Person interviewed _____ Date of interview _____

   His position, occupation, and location _____

   Why is he a reliable source? Be specific _____

   _____

2. Person interviewed _____ Date of interview _____

   His position, occupation, and location _____

   Why is he a reliable source? Be specific _____

   _____

PERSONAL EXPERIENCE OF SPEAKER

1. Tell (1) when, (2) where, and (3) conditions under which you became an authority on subject matter in

   your speech _____

   _____

   _____

Chapter 29

MAKING AN ANNOUNCEMENT

Question: *What can be done if your throat becomes
dry while speaking?*

Answer: *Not much when it happens. Don't panic.
Experience before an audience usually
causes this dryness to disappear.*

This speech is due:
Time limits: 2-4 minutes. (This means the total time to be used for all of your announcements combined.)
Speaking notes: Yes. Be sure you have exact information.
Special note to student: Prepare at least <u>two</u> or <u>three</u> announcements for this assignment.
Sources of information: If the announcements are real, state your sources of information on the outline
 form at the end of this chapter.
Outline your speech: Prepare a 20-40 word complete sentence outline for each announcement. Use the
 form at the end of this chapter.

PURPOSE OF MAKING AN ANNOUNCEMENT

Each year many millions of announcements are made. Each year many people who hear these announcements are left in a confused state of mind because the information presented was poorly organized, obscure, incomplete, or could not be heard. Often, as a result, attendance at clubs, schools, churches, and other organizations has been disappointing. It is true that you cannot force people to attend a gathering, but it is just as true that you can increase attendance by making absolutely certain that everyone within hearing distance of your voice is completely informed of and aware of the event that you are announcing. Because announcements are so very important, this speech experience is assigned to you.

EXPLANATION OF AN ANNOUNCEMENT

An announcement is a presentation of information. It is brief, concise, to the point, and pertinent. It tells specifically about something in the past (who won a prize), about immediate events to occur (the governor will appear in one minute, or, there will be an important business meeting following adjournment); it may concern a dance to be sponsored next month. An announcement should be crystal-clear in meaning, contain all necessary and helpful data, be stated in easily understandable terms, and be heard by everyone present. Occasions for its use arise at practically every kind of meeting where people convene.

SUGGESTED ANNOUNCEMENTS

Choose two or three of the following suggestions as bases for announcements:

1. A school dance.
2. A labor meeting.
3. A council meeting.
4. A skating party tomorrow night.
5. A picnic next week.
6. An all-school play next week.
7. Tickets for a barbecue supper.
8. A football game.
9. A basketball game.
10. A church meeting.
11. A convention.
12. A candy sale.
13. A contest with $1000 in prizes.
14. A class meeting.
15. A special Christmas sale.
16. A new train schedule.
17. A lecture.
18. A new schedule for classes.
19. A hunting expedition.
20. A ski meet.
21. A young people's convention.
22. The showing of a new car.
23. The demonstration of a new machine.
24. A typing contest.
25. New closing hours for library.
26. Sale of a new book.
27. A wrestling match.
28. A golf tournament.

29. Arrival of celebrities soon.
30. Speaker's choice.

HOW TO CHOOSE AN ANNOUNCEMENT

Study the above suggestions closely. Check the ones that attract you. From these select two or three that you think you would enjoy, as well as profit from, announcing. Remember that nothing will be gained by procrastination, insofar as choosing topics for practice announcements is concerned. If you make up your mind now, you will have much more time to prepare to present the information of the announcements you will make.

HOW TO PREPARE AN ANNOUNCEMENT

The chief purpose of an announcement is to inform. Keep this in mind as you prepare your material. Organize your information in the manner that you would organize any good speech. Have an interesting introduction and a strong conclusion, as well as good organization of the other necessary parts of a speech.

Your first job will be to gather information. Be sure you secure this from authentic and authoritative sources. Do not rely on hearsay. Be absolutely certain that your data are accurate and correct to the last detail. If there is any doubt at all, recheck the material before presenting your announcement. It is your responsibility to have in your possession any and all last minute information available. Ascertain whether any changes have occurred since you first received your information.

The organization of your announcement is important. You must determine the order in which you will present your information so that it will be in logical sequence. It is considered advisable according to some research to place your most important point first to achieve greatest effectiveness.

Generally, your announcement should follow an order of items for presentation similar to the following. Show that the event is timely and opportune. If there are known or probable objections, refute them impersonally; however, avoid going into defensive debate or offering a long list of excuses for the action your announcement proposes. (Show its value and happiness as related to the audience.) Second, name the exact place of meeting and its location. Tell how to get there, if this is advisable. If it is necessary, indicate the advantage of the place. State the time. Give the date, the day, and the exact hour. If there is an admission charge, give the price or prices. If desirable, tell about the reasonableness of the charges, and where the money will go, especially when the project is a worthy one. If there are tickets, tell where, when, and how they may be secured. If reserved seats are available, explain any special conditions concerning them. Finally, summarize by restating the occasion, the place, the time, and the admission. Omit "I thank you" when you finish.

Not all of the above points will have to be included in every announcement. Your own judgment will tell you what should be omitted or added, as the case may be.

Prepare notes to be used in making your announcements so that nothing essential is omitted. Use cards at least three inches by five inches in size. Make your notes brief, orderly, and legible. Rehearse them until you have everything well in mind.

HOW TO PRESENT AN ANNOUNCEMENT

Your attitude will be one of alertness and politeness. There will be no great need for bodily action other than that which naturally accompanies what you have to say. You must speak clearly and distinctly. All places, dates, days, and times must be articulated so that no misunderstanding prevails when the announcement is given.

Your place should be before the audience where all can see and hear you, not back in an obscure corner or elsewhere among the crowd. Go to the front and stand near the center of the platform. Observe good posture. Pause until you have gained the attention of the audience. Your first words should be heard by everyone. In some cases you may need to raise your hand or rap on a table to get attention. However, do not attempt to talk above crowd noises if the audience is slow to respond. When referring to your notes, hold them up so that you can keep your eyes on the assembly and avoid talking to the floor. When you finish, simply resume your former position in the house by going unostentatiously to your place. There should be no display in your entire performance. Pleasantness and a desire to be understood are enough.

IMPROVE YOUR VOCABULARY

Debacle - (dē-bä'kĕl, dē-bäk'ĕl) n. A sudden or unexpected break-up, a rout, a complete collapse, a stampede. Example: The failure of the giant corporation was the greatest debacle in the decade.

Lot – Here is a word that ordinarily receives too much attention. Try using synonyms in place of it. You will find it both enjoyable and enlightening. Examples: volume, multitude, mass, abundance, galaxy, horde, scores, numbers, profusion, host, wealth, etc.

BIBLIOGRAPHY FOR MAKING AN ANNOUNCEMENT

Vasile, Albert J. and Mintz, H. K., How to Speak With Confidence, Winthrop, 1980.
Zelko, Harold P. and Dance, F. E., Business and Professional Speech Communication, Holt, Rinehart & Winston, 2d ed., 1978.

★   ★   ★   ★   ★

ANNOUNCEMENT

By Kenneth Hartvigsen

Attention	Hear ye, hear ye, all is well for Pocatello's high school patriots.
Who	All high school students are invited to participate in a once-in-a-
What/When	life-time Bicentennial ceremony. On July 4, Pocatello will celebrate freedom by ringing its own exact replica of the Liberty Bell. This historic event accompanied by much pageantry will take
Where	place at the Pocatello Memorial Building, 776 Grant Street. High school students are especially invited to join in. All kinds of
Details	talent are needed, actors, writers, and musicians, to name just a few. Tryouts can be arranged by calling Mr. Adams at 233-0000
Benefits to Listeners	before June 30. All who participate will have their names engraved in bronze on the base of the Liberty Bell Monument.
Summary	Remember, to participate in this proud event simply call Mr. Adams, at 233-0000 before June 30.

SPEECH OUTLINE

Construct a neat, complete sentence outline on this sheet, tear it out, and hand it to your instructor when you rise to speak. He may wish to write criticisms of the outline and speech in the margins.

Type of speech:_____ Name: _____

Number of words in outline: _____ Date: _____

Purpose of this speech: (What do you want your audience to learn, to think, to believe, to feel, or do because of this speech?) _____

_____

TITLE:

INTRODUCTION:

BODY:

CONCLUSION:

Instructor's comments may concern choice of topic, development of ideas, organization, language use, personal appearance, posture, physical activity, sources, and improvement.

(Write sources of information on back of sheet)

SOURCES FROM LITERATURE
Fill out source requirements completely.
Write "none listed" if an author's name or copyright date is not listed.

1. Author's name _____

   Title of book or magazine used _____

   Title of article in above book or magazine _____

   Chapter and/or pages read _____

   Date of above publication _____

2. Author's name _____

   Title of book or magazine used _____

   Title of article in above book or magazine _____

   Chapter and/or pages read _____

   Date of above publication _____

3. Author's name _____

   Title of book or magazine used _____

   Title of article in above book or magazine _____

   Chapter and/or pages read _____

   Date of above publication _____

INTERVIEW SOURCES

1. Person interviewed _____ Date of interview _____

   His position, occupation, and location _____

   Why is he a reliable source? Be specific _____
   _____

2. Person interviewed _____ Date of interview _____

   His position, occupation, and location _____

   Why is he a reliable source? Be specific _____
   _____

PERSONAL EXPERIENCE OF SPEAKER

I. Tell (1) when, (2) where, and (3) conditions under which you became an authority on subject matter in

   your speech _____
   _____
   _____
   _____

Chapter 30
THE BOOK REVIEW

Question: *How do you enunciate correctly?*

Answer: *Sound the letters t, d, p, b, k, g, ch, s, sh, distinctly, especially those in the middle and at the end of words. Stress syllables properly.*

This speech is due:
Time limits: 15-16 minutes.
Speaking notes: Fifty word limit.
Outline your speech: Prepare a 75-150 word complete sentence outline. Designate the exact number of words in your outline. Use the form at the end of this chapter.

PURPOSE OF THE BOOK REVIEW

There are two reasons for this assignment of the book review. The first reason is that you should have the experience of preparing and presenting a book review so you will know first hand how it is done. While you are doing this, you will gain much valuable information and enjoyment from the book you are reviewing. The second reason is that as a class project you will, as one member of the group, add much to the knowledge of all of the members of the class. Because each member will review a separate book, many different authors' ideas will be presented. This in turn will provide a general fund of information that would otherwise be unattainable.

EXPLANATION OF THE BOOK REVIEW

An oral book review is orderly talk about a book and its author. This requires that you provide pertinent information about the author as well as what he wrote. Generally speaking, you should include an evaluation of his work relative to composition and ideas. The ends of your talk will be to inform, to stimulate, to entertain, and, possibly, to convince.

The book reviewer is expected to know his material well, to be informed regarding the methods of giving a review, and to be able to present his information in an organized and interesting manner. These requirements demand an unusually thorough preparation.

Occasions for the book review can occur almost anywhere. They arise in scholastic, civic, religious, and other organizations. In practically any kind of club or society, school or church, a book review often forms the basis of a program.

SUGGESTED TYPES OF BOOKS FOR A REVIEW

For this particular experience it is suggested that each student select a different speech book to review. The book should not be a brief copy, a military edition, or other short text unless the instructor specifically designates such a source. Whatever the book, it should be approved by the instructor before preparation of the speech is begun.

If the instructor prefers to do so, he may assign any type of book for review; however, reviews concerning speech will provide a wide coverage of speech and a wealth of information in a short time. Examine the bibliography near the end of this book.

HOW TO CHOOSE A BOOK FOR REVIEW

First of all, follow your instructor's assignment. If you are asked to review a speech text, go to the library, check out a number of books, examine their tables of contents carefully, and then make your selection upon the basis of their suitability, appeal, and interest to you and your audience. Be sure you do not choose a highly technical or scientific treatise on phonetics, rhetorical analysis, speech pathology, or similar subject unless you possess sufficient background to render a comprehensive and intelligible review. Now, should a book be approved that does not deal with speech, be sure that it is satisfactory for the occasion, audience, yourself, and the physical environment in which you will review it.

HOW TO PREPARE A BOOK REVIEW

Every speech must have a purpose. The book review is no exception; for this reason, you should determine your purpose whether it is to inform, to entertain, to convince, to stimulate.

Now you ask, "What should go into a book review and how should you go about organizing your material?" Succinctly, your procedure may follow this order if you consider it suitable.

Tell about the author. Who is he? What about his life? What anecdotes can you discover about him? Does he do more than write? What other books has he written? Where does he live? What is his environment? Has he written similar books? How old is he? Include other data of a similar kind.

Now, about the book. Why did you choose it? When was it written? Under what circumstances? Why was it written? Is it biographical, historical, fiction, what? What do the reviewers say about it? (Ask your librarian to show you lists of book reviews such as those in The New York Times, Christian Century, Saturday Review of Literature, New Republic, The Nation, and others.) What is your opinion? Formulate your own. Do not plagiarize someone else's evaluation of the book. Give examples and comments in answering the following questions: Are the plot and organization well constructed? Is the writer's style interesting? How are situations and characters portrayed? Do the characters seem real and alive? Does the story move forward to a climax? Is the information interesting and useful? Do you recommend the book? Why?

One of the best ways to master the above information is to read the book that you are preparing to review several times. First, read it through for enjoyment. The second and third times read for information you plan to use in your review. As for getting your material in mind, use your own method. It is advisable that you should either write the speech out in full or make a careful and detailed outline, after which you rehearse aloud until your sequence of thoughts has been firmly fixed in mind. If you use quotations, limit them to one hundred and fifty words each.

HOW TO PRESENT A BOOK REVIEW

First of all, have the review "in your head." Do not stand before your audience with the book in your hands so that you can use it as a crutch while you give your review by following previously marked pages, or occupy time by reading. This is not reviewing. Use the book only for your quotations and then for not more than one hundred and fifty words each. If you use notes, limit yourself to three words or less for each minute you speak.

Utilize all of the aspects of good speech – friendliness, animation, vigor, communicative attitude, bodily action, and gestures that are appropriate, a voice that is easily heard and well modulated, correct pronunciation, clear articulation, vivid and descriptive language, a neat appearance, poise and confidence. Utilize these and you cannot fail.

SPECIAL HINTS
1. Be sure you have an excellent introduction and conclusion.
2. Be sure your speech is logically organized all the way.
3. Do not fail to evaluate the book.

IMPROVE YOUR VOCABULARY

Enervate - (ĕn'ĕr-vāt') v. Weaken, make less vigorous, debilitate, unnerve, emasculate, unman, exhaust, jade, fatigue, tire, weary, enfeeble. Example: Hot weather enervates many persons but cold weather stimulates them. Use enervate in this speech and five times a day for a week. Next time you arise early and feel enervated, say so rather than using a commonplace term.

Wonderful - Omit this word. Give it a rest. Try a synonym for adding new life to your vocabulary. Examples: splendid, sublime, dazzling, superb, versatile, gifted, magnificent, amazing, astonishing, surprising, strange, admirable, rapturous, ecstatic, etc.

BIBLIOGRAPHY FOR THE BOOK REVIEW

Chen, Ching-Chih, Biomedical, Scientific & Technical Book Reviewing, Scarecrow Press, 1976.
Kamerman, Sylvia E., ed., Book Reviewing, Writer, Inc., 1978.

SPEECH OUTLINE

Construct a neat, complete sentence outline on this sheet, tear it out, and hand it to your instructor when you rise to speak. He may wish to write criticisms of the outline and speech in the margins.

Type of speech: _____ Name: _____

Number of words in outline: _____ Date: _____

Purpose of this speech: (What do you want your audience to learn, to think, to believe, to feel, or do because of this speech?) _____

_____

TITLE:

INTRODUCTION:

BODY:

CONCLUSION:

Instructor's comments may concern choice of topic, development of ideas, organization, language use, personal appearance, posture, physical activity, sources, and improvement.

(Write sources of information on back of sheet)

SOURCES FROM LITERATURE

Fill out source requirements completely.
Write "none listed" if an author's name or copyright date is not listed.

1. Author's name _____

   Title of book or magazine used _____

   Title of article in above book or magazine _____

   Chapter and/or pages read _____

   Date of above publication _____

2. Author's name _____

   Title of book or magazine used _____

   Title of article in above book or magazine _____

   Chapter and/or pages read _____

   Date of above publication _____

3. Author's name _____

   Title of book or magazine used _____

   Title of article in above book or magazine _____

   Chapter and/or pages read _____

   Date of above publication _____

INTERVIEW SOURCES

1. Person interviewed _____ Date of interview _____

   His position, occupation, and location _____

   Why is he a reliable source? Be specific _____

   _____

2. Person interviewed _____ Date of interview _____

   His position, occupation, and location _____

   Why is he a reliable source? Be specific _____

   _____

PERSONAL EXPERIENCE OF SPEAKER

1. Tell (1) when, (2) where, and (3) conditions under which you became an authority on subject matter in your speech _____

   _____

   _____

   _____

Chapter 31

READING ALOUD

Question: *How can one project his voice better?*

Answer: *Open your mouth wider and use more force. Articulate distinctly.*

This assignment is due:
Time limits: 4–5 minutes.
Sources for reading aloud: Study bibliography at end of this chapter. Consult school librarian.

PURPOSE OF READING ALOUD

Many persons find themselves in a quandary when confronted with a situation that demands oral reading. Too often they seemingly have no idea about the way oral reading should be done. As a result, excellent literary productions go unread or are so poorly read that much of their beauty and thought are lost. No one expects you to master the field of oral reading after concluding one appearance before your classmates, but certainly you should have a much clearer understanding of what is involved in reading aloud. This reading experience will help you improve your oral reading from the standpoint of personal enjoyment and ability to read for others.

EXPLANATION AND REQUIREMENTS OF ORAL READING

Oral reading, as we use the term here, is reading aloud from the printed page with the purpose of interpreting what is read so that its meaning is conveyed to those who are listening and watching. The purpose may be to inform, to entertain, to arouse, to convince, or to get action. Successful oral reading demands that the speaker must know his material well enough that he can interpret fully and accurately the ideas, meanings, and beauties placed in the composition by the author. To do this capably, a burden of careful, almost meticulous preparation is placed on the reader. Much attention must be given to understanding what the author is saying; the reader assumes the responsibility of discovering the author's meaning. When the reader starts to voice the author's ideas, he still faces the difficult problem of imparting accurate meanings and moods by properly using his voice and actions.

Occasions for oral reading are practically limitless. Any gathering at which it is appropriate to

read aloud is suitable. School, church, and civic gatherings are common scenes of oral reading. Clubs, societies, private groups, private parties, and even commercial organizations, such as the radio, utilize oral reading largely for entertainment. We are not considering the hundreds of news casts and other types of radio and television programs which are read daily in the category of oral reading.

HOW TO CHOOSE A SELECTION FOR ORAL READING

Choosing a selection is not easy; it is hard work. First of all, be sure to make your choice of a selection for reading early enough that you will have adequate time to prepare it. Your selection should be made on several important bases. Among these are the following: The selection should be suitable to you as its reader. In other words, choose something that you are capable of preparing and later interpreting. For this particular reading experience, it will probably be advisable that you do an interpretation that does not require characterization other than your own. If you select wisely, this matter need not concern you farther. Of course, if you have had sufficient experience so that you are qualified to portray different characters and make the necessary transitions involved in more difficult interpretations, then go ahead with such a choice of subject. Give close attention to your prospective audience and the occasion. Your choice of a selection must be applicable to both. This means that you need to analyze both your audience and the occasion carefully; otherwise you may read something entirely unappropriate. You must ascertain the kind of environment in which you will be required to read. The size of the building, the seating arrangement in relation to you, the reader, outside noises, building distractions, and other factors will definitely influence your selection. If you observe closely all these bases of choosing a topic, you have a good chance of presenting a creditable oral reading. On the other hand, if you are indifferent and lackadaisical and do not make a careful choice of a selection for reading, then you should expect nothing better than an apathetic response from your audience.

Sources of material are available in your school library. Check the Card Catalogue for poetry, prose readings, and interpretations. Your instructor and the librarian will gladly help you.

HOW TO PREPARE ORAL READING
Some important steps in preparation are these: Know the meaning of every word, as well as the use of all punctuation. The author wrote as he did for a reason. Learn all you can about the author so that you may understand why he used certain words, punctuations, and phrases. Try to understand his philosophy and point of view. Acquire a knowledge of the circumstances surrounding the writing of your particular selection. Do the same for the setting of the article so that you may enjoy its perspective more adequately. Try hard to capture its mood.

Adequate preparation may necessitate your paraphrasing and pantomiming the selection to better understand its meaning. This will assist you in obtaining a more complete comprehension of what the author meant and what he might have done had he read his own poetry or prose.

Practice reading aloud until you have the entire selection well enough in mind that you can give most of your attention (eighty to ninety percent) to your audience by maintaining eye contact. This will necessitate a form of memorization that will permit you to use the printed copy as a guide only.

HOW TO PRESENT ORAL READING
Do not forget that the audience is watching you at any time you are visible to it. This may be before and after you read. All this time, they are observing you and forming opinions. Thus it is imperative that you constantly maintain an alert, poised, and friendly appearance. When you rise to read, your confidence and poise should be evident. Do not hurry to your position, but rather take your place easily and politely without hesitation. Pause a few seconds to glance over your audience before beginning to read. Avoid being stiff and cold and unfriendly. Begin your presentation by telling why you made your particular selection; tell something

about the author so that the listeners may better understand him; provide information concerning the setting of the prose or poetry; and include anything else that will contribute to appreciation and enjoyment of your reading.

Your body should be appropriate to your selection both in posture and action. Any activity and gesture that will add to the interpretation of your reading should be included. Whatever will assist in imparting the mood, emotion, and meaning should be a part of your interpretation. Be careful that you do not make the reading an impersonation.

Naturally, your voice must tell and imply much. Its variety as to pause, rate, pitch, melody, and intensity should be in keeping with what you are interpreting. All of these qualities should have been determined during the periods of rehearsal. If you can feel the emotions and meanings, so much the better.

Your book, or your reading material, should be held in such a way that it does not hide your face nor block the flow of your voice. Your head should not move up and down, as you glance from book to audience. One hand placed palm down inside the book will permit you to mark your place with a forefinger. The other hand held conveniently under the book palm up will act as a support. You need not hold your book in exactly one position, especially while you are looking at your audience. The point to remember is to raise your book in preference to dropping your head in order to read. The audience wants to see your face to catch emotions and meanings portrayed by its changing expressions.

When concluding a reading, pause a second or two before politely returning to your chair. Avoid quickly closing your book and leaving the stage when you are three words from the end of the last line.

If you are reading several selections, treat each one separately. Allow sufficient time between numbers that the audience may applaud and relax slightly and otherwise express enjoyment of what you have done.

By keeping in mind your audience, the occasion, your material and its meanings, the environment in which you are reading, and your place in the entire picture, you can do an excellent interpretation.

IMPROVE YOUR VOCABULARY

Enigmatic - (ē'nĭg-măt'ĭk) a. Puzzling, hard to understand because of obscurity, like a riddle. Example: He possessed an enigmatic personality. Use this word in this speech and five times a day for the next week. Make it yours.

Fix - Omit this word. Do not use it for a week, then not more than once a day thereafter. People use it so often it has lost its potency. Use a synonym. Examples of fix in the sense of bribe are: bribe, influence, corrupt, induce, persuade, cajole - other synonyms in the sense of mend are: repair, adjust, arrange, renew, restore, replace, redeem - still other synonyms for fix as a noun are: predicament, condition, plight, dilemma, quandary, crisis, trial, imbroglio, muddle, etc.

BIBLIOGRAPHY FOR READING ALOUD

Ecroyd, Donald and Wagner, Hilda S., Communicate Through Oral Reading, McGraw, 1979.
Gottlieb, Marvin, Oral Interpretation, McGraw, 1980.
Ross, Raymond S., Speech Communication: Fundamentals and Practice, Prentice-Hall, 5th ed., 1980.
Tacey, William S., Business and Professional Speaking, Wm. C. Brown, 3d ed., 1980.
Tanner, Fran A., Basic Drama Projects, Clark Publishing, 4th ed., 1982.

★ ★ ★ ★ ★

ORAL READING SELECTIONS

*The following poems are suggested for oral reading. You will find most of these poems in the Pocket Book of Modern Verse, rev. ed., 1972, edited by Oscar Williams. These poems are suggested mainly because of the accessibility of this paperback in local and school book stores. (Or you may obtain it from the publishers: Pocket Books, 1230 Avenue of Americas, New York, NY 10020.) You may find equally good selections in other anthologies and in your own literature books.

W. H. Auden, "The Unknown Citizen," "Musee des Beaux Arts"
Rupert Brooke, "The Great Lover," "The Soldier"
E. E. Cummings, "Chanson Innocente," "Sweet Spring"
Walter de la Mare, "The Listeners"
Emily Dickinson, "Success is Counted Sweetest," "Because I Could Not Stop For Death"
Robert Frost, "The Mending Wall," "Birches"
A. E. Houseman, "When I Was One and Twenty," "Reveille"
Langston Hughes, "The Negro Speaks of Rivers," "Mother to Son"
Vachel Lindsay, "The Congo," "Abraham Lincoln Walks at Midnight"
Edgar Lee Masters, "Silence," "Lucinda Matlock"
Edna St. Vincent Millay, "Dirge Without Music," "To Jesus On His Birthday"
Ogden Nash, "Kindly Unhitch That Star, Buddy," "Bankers are Like Everybody Else, Except Richer"
Edward Arlington Robinson, "Richard Cory," "Mr. Flood's Party"
Christina Rosetti, "When I am Dead," "Remember"
Carl Sandburg, "Jazz Fantasia," "Cool Tombs"
Lew Sarett, "Four Little Foxes," "The World Has a Way With Eyes"
Karl Shapiro, "Auto Wreck," "Buick"
Dylan Thomas, "Poem in October," "Do Not Go Gentle Into That Goodnight"
William Butler Yeats, "Lake Isle of Innisfree," "The Second Coming"

---

*Reprinted from "Basic Drama Projects," 4th ed., 1982, by Fran Averett Tanner, Clark Publishing Company, c/o Caxton Printers, Ltd., Box 700, Caldwell, Idaho 83605.

A GREAT SPEECH IN AMERICAN HISTORY

(The example below is for student appreciation and is not
intended for any particular assignment in this text.)

Ingersoll

AT HIS BROTHER'S GRAVE
(1879)

MY FRIENDS: - I am going to do that which the dead oft promised he would do for me.

The loved and loving brother, husband, father, friend, died where manhood's morning almost touches noon, and while the shadows still were falling toward the west.

He had not passed on life's highway the stone that marks the highest point, but, being weary for a moment, lay down by the wayside, and, using his burden for a pillow, fell into that dreamless sleep that kisses down his eyelids still. While yet in love with life and raptured with the world, he passed to silence and pathetic dust.

Yet, after all, it may be best, just in the happiest, sunniest hour of all the voyage, while eager winds are kissing every sail, to dash against the unseen rock, and in an instant hear the billows roar above a sunken ship. For whether in midsea or 'mong the breakers of the farther shore, a wreck at last must mark the end of each and all. And every life, no matter if its every hour is rich with love and every moment jeweled with a joy, will, at its close, become a tragedy as sad and deep and dark as can be woven of the warp and woof of mystery and death.

This brave and tender man in every storm of life was oak and rock, but in the sunshine he was vine and flower. He was the friend of all heroic souls. He climbed the heights and left all superstitions far below, while on his forehead fell the golden dawning of the grander day.

He loved the beautiful, and was with color, form, and music touched to tears. He sided with the weak, and with a willing hand gave alms; with loyal heart and with purest hands he faithfully discharged all public trusts.

He was a worshiper of liberty, a friend of the oppressed. A thousand times I have heard him quote these words: "For justice all place a temple, and all seasons, summer." He believed that happiness was the only good, reason the only torch, justice the only worship, humanity the only religion, and love the only priest. He added to the sum of human joy; and were every one to whom he did some loving service to bring a blossom to his grave, he would sleep tonight beneath a wilderness of flowers.

Life is a narrow vale between the cold and barren peaks of two eternities. We strive in vain to look beyond the heights. We cry aloud, and the only answer is the echo of our wailing cry. From the voiceless lips of the unreplying dead there comes no word; but in the night of death hope sees a star, and listening love can hear the rustle of a wing.

He who sleeps here, when dying, mistaking the approach of death for the return of health, whispered with his last breath: "I am better now." Let us believe, in spite of doubts and dogmas, and tears and fears, that these dear words are true of all the countless dead.

And now to you who have been chosen, from among the many men he loved, to do the last sad office for the dead, we give this sacred dust. Speech can not contain our love. There was, there is, no greater, stronger, manlier man.

Delivered in Washington on June 3, 1879, at the funeral of Ebon C. Ingersoll.

Chapter 32

PARLIAMENTARY LAW AND
THE STUDENT CONGRESS

Question: *Can a person be sure his language is in good taste?*

Answer: *Yes. Simply avoid risque stories, words, and meanings. The same applies to your body language.*

This assignment will begin:

Time limits of speakers: Unless otherwise stated, in the organization's constitution, ten minutes is generally recognized as the maximum amount of time any person may occupy the floor to speak upon a proposal in one speech.

Student motions: Each student will be required to place at least three motions before the assembly and seek their adoption. He will report the motions which are adopted to his instructor.

PURPOSE OF THIS PARLIAMENTARY LAW EXPERIENCE

A great many persons attempt to lead an assembly in which group discussion is paramount, or they endeavor to participate in a group discussion when they are totally uninformed regarding orderly and proper parliamentary procedure. The results of haphazard procedures are notorious. Ill-will, ruffled feelings, rife confusion, impeded progress, and circuitous thinking are but a few of the by-products of such incidents.

By mastering the rules of parliamentary procedure, you will be enabled to take your place in any gathering whether you are chairman or audience participant. Furthermore, you will be qualified to assist in carrying on all matters of business pertaining to the group's needs.

These experiences are offered in order that you may learn through usage of parliamentary law, the proper procedure for conducting or participating in a deliberative assembly.

EXPLANATION OF PARLIAMENTARY LAW

Parliamentary law is a recognized procedure for conducting the business of a group of persons. Its purpose is to expedite the transaction of business in an orderly manner by observing definite procedures. These procedures may and do vary according to the constitutions and by-laws adopted by various groups. In the many state legislatures and the national congress, parliamentary procedures are basically the same, but differ in numerous interpre-

tations. The rules of each assembly determine the procedures which prevail for that assembly. There is no one set of rules which applies to all assemblies, despite the fact they may all adopt the same text on parliamentary procedure. The laws followed by a group are their own laws, adopted by themselves, interpreted and enforced by themselves. Kansas and Indiana legislatures might adopt Roberts Rules of Order as their rule book for conducting business, yet in actual practice differ widely. In fact, the House and Senate in the same state legislature normally operate under different regulations. This is true of the two houses in the national Congress. One of the obvious divergences here is the Unlimited Debate Ruling in the Senate (this is the reason for the Senate filibusters) and the Limited Debate allowed in the House. There are other dissimilarities which need not be discussed here. The fundamental point is that assemblies do operate under definite laws and regulations.

Occasions for using parliamentary law arise anytime a group meets to transact business. Whether the occasion is a meeting in a church, a schoolhouse, a pool hall, a corporation office, or any one of ten thousand other places, the opportunity for practicing parliamentary procedure arises. The formality which will govern the extent of the use of parliamentary procedure is dependent upon the group and their knowledge of its rules. Generally, the larger organized groups are more formal and observe their regulations more closely than do small informal gatherings.

CHART OF PRECEDENCE OF MOTIONS AND THEIR RULES

Key to Abbreviations of Their Rules:

No-S. — No second required
Und. — Undebatable
Int. — May interrupt a speaker
2/3 — Requires a 2/3 vote for adoption
Lim. — Limited debate

PRIVILEGED MOTIONS

1. To fix the time to which to adjourn.....................................Lim.
2. To adjourn (unqualified) ....Und.
3. To take a recess ....Lim.
4. To rise to a question of privilege ....Int., Und., No-S.
5. To call for orders of the day...............................Int., Und., No-S.

SUBSIDIARY MOTIONS

6. To lay on the table..Und.
7. To move the previous question (this stops debate)...................Und., 2/3
8. To limit or extend the limits of debate..........................Lim., 2/3
9. To postpone definitely..Lim.
10. To refer to committee ....Lim.
11. To amend..
12. To postpone indefinitely ....
13. A Main Motion -
      a. "To reconsider" is a specific main motion........................Int.

INCIDENTAL MOTIONS
(These Have No Precedence Of Order)

To suspend the rules ....Und., 2/3
To withdraw a motion...No-S., Und.
To object to a consideration ....Int., No-S., Und., 2/3
To rise to a point of order...Int., No-S., Und.
To rise to a point of information (parliamentary inquiry)...........Int., No-S., Und.
To appeal from the decision of the chair..............................Int., Lim.
To call for a division of the house..............................Int., No-S., Und.
To call for a division of a question ....Und.

HOW TO USE THE CHART OF PRECEDENCE OF MOTIONS AND THEIR RULES

The best, if not the only, way to prepare for participation in parliamentary law is to be familiar with the precedence of motions and their applications. This can be done with a reasonable amount of study through the use of any standard parliamentary law book. Without this knowledge, you will flounder in any assembly and slow down the entire proceedings. You will find the fundamentals discussed in the following paragraphs; however, it is necessary that you study a parliamentary text in considerable detail if you wish to master many of the technicalities.

Here are fundamentals you should know:

Precedence of motions - This term means that motions are debated in a certain order. To ascertain the meaning of this, study the chart entitled Chart of Precedence of Motions and Their Rules. You will notice that number 13 is a main motion. An example of a main motion would be a motion "That the Parliamentary Law Club have a party." This main motion is what the assembly must discuss. It is the only main motion that can be under discussion. It must be disposed of before any other main motion can legally be entertained by the assembly. If the group, after discussion, votes to have a party, the main motion is disposed of. If it votes not to have a party, the motion is disposed of. But supposing the Club does not want to adopt the motion as it stands. This raises another question.

Amendments - You see, as the motion stands, it simply states that the "Parliamentary Law Club have a party." It does not say when. It is obvious that a change will have to be made. Now look at number 11 on the Chart of Precedence of Motions. It is "To amend." It is in a position above the main motion of the chart. Hence, someone moves "to amend the main motion by adding the words 'Saturday night, June 16'." This is in order. It is discussed and voted on. If it carries, the group has decided to add the words "Saturday Night, June 16" to the motion. If it fails, the main motion stands as it was originally made and is open to discussion or ready to be voted on. Assuming for a moment that the amendment carried, the business before the house becomes that of disposing of the main motion as amended. It is debated and voted on.

If an assembly wishes to, it may amend an amendment in the same manner it amends the main motion. It then discusses and votes on the amendment to the amendment. If this does not carry, the amendment remains untouched. If it does carry, the amendment as amended is next discussed and voted on. If it, in turn, does not carry, then the main motion remains unchanged and the amendment plus the amendment to it is lost. If it does carry, the main motion as amended is debated and voted on.

It is illegal to change an amendment beyond adding one amendment to it.

Other motions - Supposing the group decided to amend the main motion by adding the words "Saturday night, June 16," but still is not ready to decide definitely about having a party. You will note that number 10, the motion directly above number 11, is "to refer to a committee." If someone wishes, he may move "to refer the motion to a committee"; all amendments automatically go with it. The motion "to refer" will be debated and voted on. If it carries, the main motion is disposed of and the house is ready for another main motion. If the motion "to refer to a committee" fails, then the main motion remains before the house as though the motion "to refer to a committee" had never been offered.

Now look at your Chart of Precedence of Motions again. You will note many more motions are listed above number 10. The higher you move up this list, the smaller the number of the motion is, but the more important it becomes, until you arrive at the very top of the list, at number 1. This is the most powerful motion of all. The motion on the chart may be placed before the assembly any time during debate on a main motion, provided you always put a motion on the floor that has precedence. In other words, John moves a main motion; Jim immediately moved number 9, to postpone the main motion definitely; George moves number 6, to lay the main motion on the table; Mary follows by moving number 3, to take a recess. This is all in order. However, when George moved number 6, Mary could not move number 8, since George's motion, number 6, had precedence.

Actually, the precedence of motions in its simplest form means that a person may place any of the motions on the floor at any time they are in order if he follows the rule of precedence. You have to understand that the numbers appearing before each motion are not put there to count them. Those numbers tell you exactly what motion has precedence over other motions. The most important motion, as far as having power over other motions is concerned, is number 1, to fix the time to which to adjourn. The second most important motion in order of precedence is number 2, to adjourn - unqualified; next is number 3; then number 4; and so on, clear down to number 13, the main motion itself.

Now let us look at the Chart of Precedence of Motions once more. You see the thirteen motions divided into three specific groups; namely, Privileged Motions from number 1 through number 5, Subsidiary Motions from number 6 through number 12, and last you see Main Motion, number 13, which can be a motion about anything from hanging Hitler to having a party. Here is the point you should get from studying these thirteen motions. After you have a main motion on the floor, there are seven actions you can take on it. These are the motions numbered 6, 7, 8, 9, 10, 11, 12. They are called subsidiary because they pertain to things you can do to a main motion. At a glance you can see that an assembly can do anything from postponing a motion indefinitely to laying it on the table and taking it off again. These motions do not conflict with the ruling that you can have only one main motion before the house at a time.

They are not main motions. They are the ways you change (amend) or dispose of a motion (postpone indefinitely, refer to a committee, lay on the table . . . .). Of course, you can dispose of a motion by adopting or rejecting it. It is obvious that once you have a main motion before the assembly, you have to do something with it and rules concerning precedence of motions tell you how to do it.

If you will now examine the privileged motions, 1 to 5, inclusive, you will see that they do not do anything to a main motion. They are the actions a group can take while it is disposing of a main motion. For example, if the club were discussing a main motion to have a party, someone could move number 3, to take a recess. If the group wanted to take a recess, they would vote to do so and then recess for five minutes, or whatever time the motion to recess called for. When the recess was over, they would convene again and once more start discussing the main motion where they left off when they voted to recess.

The section entitled Incidental Motions is largely self–explanatory. You will note that it concerns those things a person would normally do during debate on a motion. For example, if the assembly were debating the motion "to have a party," you might want to find out whether it was in order to offer an amendment to the main motion at that time, because you were not quite sure of the status of such a move. In this case you would "rise to a point of information," sometimes called "point of parliamentary inquiry." If you observed an infraction of the rules which the chair overlooked, you would immediately "rise to a point of order." You will notice that most incidental motions require "no second" and also permit you to interrupt a speaker. This is true because certain matters must be clarified while debate is in progress. Otherwise too many corrections would have to be made after a motion was adopted or defeated.

IMPORTANT INFORMATION YOU SHOULD KNOW
1. The chairman's duties: To call the meeting to order, to conduct the business of the assembly, to enforce rules, to appoint committees and their chairmen, to appoint a secretary for each meeting if one is not elected. He refrains from discussing any motion before the house.

2. The secretary's duties: To keep an accurate record of all business transacted by the house.

This includes all motions, whether carried or defeated, who seconded the motions and the votes upon them. Also a record of all committees appointed and any other actions of the assembly.

3. If the chairman wants to speak on a proposal, he appoints a member to take his place; then he assumes the position of a participant in the assembly. He gains recognition from the chairman he appointed, makes his remarks on an equal basis with other members of the group, and then resumes the chair at any time he desires.

4. To gain recognition from the chairman: Rise and address the chairman by saying "Mr. Chairman" or "Madame Chairman," depending on the sex of the chairman. The chair will then address you by name, Mr. _____, or he may nod to you, point towards you, or give some other sign of recognition. You are not allowed to speak until you get the chair's permission to do so, in other words, his recognition.

5. How to place a motion on the floor: Gain recognition from the chair; then state your motion by saying, "I move that_____."

6. How to dispose of a motion: Either adopt or reject it or apply subsidiary motions to it.

7. How to second a motion: Simply call out the word "second." You need not rise or have recognition from the chairman.

8. How to change (amend) a motion: Gain recognition; then say, "I move to amend the motion or amendment by adding the words _____ " or "by striking out the words _____ " or "by striking out the words _____ and inserting the words _____."

9. How to stop rambling or extended debate: Move the previous question, number 7, on all motions before the house. This will include the main motion and any subsidiary motions.

10. How to ask for information: Rise without gaining recognition, interrupt a speaker if necessary, and say, "Mr. Chairman, point of information" – or you may say, "Mr. Chairman, I rise to a point of parliamentary

inquiry." When the chair says, "State your point," you will ask your question.

11. <u>How to ask a member of the assembly a question:</u> Gain recognition; then say, "Will Mr._____ yield to a question?" The chairman then asks the person if he will yield. If the member says "yes," you may ask one question. If he says "no," you cannot ask your question.

12. <u>How to exercise personal privilege:</u> Rise without recognition, interrupt a speaker if necessary, and say, "Mr. Chairman, personal privilege!" The chair will say, "State your privilege." You may then ask to have a window closed because a draft is blowing on you, or you may ask whatever happens to be your privilege.

13. <u>How to call for "division of the house:"</u> Without rising to gain recognition, simply call out, "Division of the house." This means that you want the voting on a measure to be taken by a show of hands or by asking members to stand to indicate their vote. "Division of the house" is called for when a voice vote has been taken which was so close it was hard to determine what the vote actually was.

14. <u>What does "question" mean when called out?</u> This means the person who calls out "question" is ready to vote. It is not compulsory that the chairman put the motion to a vote. However, he generally does so if enough persons call out "question." This has nothing to do with the motion for the previous question.

15. <u>How do you reverse a ruling made by the chairman?</u> Just as soon as the chairman makes the ruling, the person who disagrees with it calls out without recognition, "Mr. Chairman, I appeal from the decision of the chair." A second is necessary to make the appeal valid. If it is forthcoming the chair asks the person who made the appeal to state his reasons for doing it. This done, discussion follows after which the chair asks for a vote from the assembly by saying, "All those in favor of sustaining the chair raise their hands," then after counting the votes he says, "those opposed, the same sign." He then announces the vote by saying, "The chair is sustained by a vote of seven to three" or "The chair stands corrected by a vote of six to four."

16. <u>How is a meeting adjourned?</u> Adjournment may be made by the chairman who declares the meeting adjourned, or it may be made after the motion to adjourn is placed on the floor, voted on and carried.

17. <u>How do you know what order of business to follow?</u> The assembly agrees upon an order of business. It is the chair's duty to see that it is followed unless rules are suspended by the group, which will permit a change temporarily.

18. <u>How do you suspend the rules?</u> A motion is put before the house "that the rules be suspended to consider" certain urgent business. If the motion carries by a two-thirds vote, the rules are suspended.

19. <u>How do you vote on a motion?</u> The chair asks for a vote. It may be by voice ("yes" and "no"), roll call, show of hands, by standing, or by ballot.

20. <u>How does a person object to the consideration of a motion?</u> Rise without recognition, interrupt a speaker if necessary, and say, "Mr. Chairman, I object to the consideration of the motion (or question)." No second is required. The chair immediately asks the assembly to vote "yes" or "no" as to whether they want to consider the question. If two-thirds vote against consideration of the question, it cannot be considered. The objection must be made immediately after the motion to which the member objects is placed before the assembly.

21. <u>How do you conduct nominations for office?</u> The chair opens the floor to nominations for a certain office. A member rises and says, "Mr. Chairman, I nominate_____." The secretary records nominations. After a reasonable time, the chairman rules that all nominations are closed, or someone moves that all nominations to be closed. This is a main motion. It is seconded, debated, and voted on. If it carries, nominations are closed. If not, they remain open. The chair may rule a quick "motion to close nominations" out of order if it is obviously an attempt to railroad a certain party into office before other nominations can be made.

22. <u>How does a chairman receive a motion and put it before the assembly?</u> If it requires a second he waits a short time to hear the second. If it does not come, he rules the motion dead for want of a second. If a second is made, he repeats the motion as follows: "It has been moved and seconded that the Parliamentary Law Club have a party Friday night. Is there any discussion?" This officially places the motion in the hands of the assembly.

HOW TO CONDUCT PARLIAMENTARY LAW SESSIONS

Your instructor will advise you in this matter. However, every class member should take his turn acting as chairman at one time and secretary another. It is advisable that the chairman be appointed by the instructor until the class learns how to nominate and elect a chairman. The following steps may then be carried out:

1. The chairman should appoint a committee to draw up a proposed constitution and by-laws. (The committee may be elected if the group wishes to do it this way.) If time is limited, the instructor may dispense with drawing up a constitution and by-laws.

2. An order of business should be set up. Normally, it will be something similar to the following:

   A. Call the meeting to order.

   B. Read the minutes from the preceding meeting. Make any necessary changes, then adopt them.

   C. Ask for old business. This may be unfinished business.

   D. Ask for committee reports.

   E. Ask for new business.

   F. Adjourn.

3. In carrying out practice parliamentary law sessions, it is necessary that motions be placed before the assembly. Each student is required to put at least three motions on the floor and seek their adoption. At the end of this chapter he should write out five prospective motions which he will submit to the assembly. These should be written on the chart labeled Motions To Be Placed Before the Assembly. Examples are:

   (a) A motion to petition teachers that all written examinations be limited to one hour.

   (b) A motion that tardy students should pay a twenty-five cent fine for each time tardy, the money to be contributed to a school social building fund.

- -

MOTIONS TO BE PLACED BEFORE THE ASSEMBLY

(Be prepared to hand this list to your instructor on request)

1. _____

2. _____

3. _____

4. _____

5. _____

Motions adopted were:

_____
(Signature)

A STUDENT CONGRESS

A student congress may be composed of a house and senate with different speech classes acting in each capacity or one group may form a unicameral legislature. In either instance the group purpose is to formulate bills, discuss them, and adopt or reject them by vote. To accomplish these activities the group must know parliamentary law and conduct its business in an orderly manner. This involves (1) determining the scope of legislation to come before the assembly, (2) organizing the legislature by electing officers, forming committees, and assigning seats, (3) holding committee meetings to consider and/or draft bills, and (4) debating and disposing of bills brought before the assembly.

THE FIRST MEETING OF THE GENERAL ASSEMBLY

At the first meeting of the general assembly a temporary chairman and a temporary secretary will be appointed or elected. Both will take office immediately. The instructor will act as parliamentarian unless one is elected or appointed. The temporary chairman will then open the meeting to nominations for a permanent chairman (speaker of the house or president of the senate) who will take office as soon as he is elected after which he will call for nominations for a permanent secretary who will be elected and take office at once. As next business the presiding officer will appoint standing committees and a chairman for each. The assembly may then discuss matters relative to its general objectives and procedures. Adjournment of the first meeting follows.

COMMITTEE MEETINGS

Committee meetings are next in order and, though informal, parliamentary procedure is advisable with an elected or appointed secretary to keep minutes for the group. A committee may originate its own bills and consider bills submitted by members of the assembly which the speaker of the house has referred to them. It will report bills out or "kill them" in committee, according to votes taken after discussion in the committee.

SAMPLE BILL

Keep bills short, not over 175 words. They must have a title, an enacting clause, and a body. A preamble is optional. The body is composed of sections and each line is numbered. Note the following example:

A BILL PROVIDING FOR LIMITING STUDENT DRIVERS AT BLANK HIGH SCHOOL

WHEREAS, Space is limited around Blank High School, and

WHEREAS, Parking on the street is limited to one hour, and

WHEREAS, Student enrollment is increasing each year, and

WHEREAS, Many students are within walking distance of Blank High School, therefore,

BE IT RESOLVED BY THE BLANK HIGH SCHOOL SPEECH CLASS, THAT:

1   SECTION I. The governing officials of Blank High School should prohibit all students
2   living within one mile of this school from operating a car to and from school as a means
3   of transportation.

This bill introduced by_____

If a bill originates in a committee a member of the committee should be selected to present it to the general assembly. Another member should agree to second the bill. Other members might well prepare to speak for the bill. In case there is a minority report against the bill, their presentation should be similarly organized, even to offering a substitute bill.

THE GENERAL ASSEMBLY IN DELIBERATION

Some student congresses follow the procedures and rules of their state legislatures. Others follow established rules of parliamentary procedure by designating a certain text as their guide. In either case, an agreed procedure must be used. To have a successful general assembly members should know parliamentary procedure and how to use it. Especially important to know are precedence of motions, how to apply the privileged and subsidiary motions. Incidental motions, which have no order of precedence, are of vital importance in the general conduct of the assembly's deliberations and should be thoroughly familiar to all participants.

Under a bicameral student congress the requirement is that each bill must pass the house in which it originates. It is then filed with the secretary of the other house after which the presiding officer of the house refers it to the proper committee. If reported out of this committee and passed by the second house it may be considered as "passed" unless there is a governor in which case he must act on it before it can be considered as "passed." When a governor is used, a lieutenant governor is ordinarily elected and serves as presiding officer in the senate. It thus becomes doubly important that all plans be laid before a student assembly convenes for the first time in order to know what officials to elect, what their duties are, what committees to set up, and what all procedures will be relative to activities of the congress.

A SUGGESTED ORDER OF BUSINESS

The following order of business meets most student congress needs:

1. The meeting is called to order.

2. Minutes of the last meeting are read and adopted as read or corrected.

3. The presiding officer announces the order in which committees will report and the group decides on (a) time limits for individual speakers and (b) the total time allowable on each bill.

4. The spokesman for the first committee reads the bill, moves its adoption, gives a copy to the secretary. Another member seconds. If the bill belongs to an individual, he presents it in a similar manner when granted permission by the chairman. A friend seconds. Whoever presents a bill then speaks for it. The bill is debated and disposed of according to the rules of the assembly.

5. Each succeeding committee reports and the process of discussing and disposing of each bill is continued until all bills have been acted upon.

6. The secretary announces the bills that were passed and those that were defeated.

7. The assembly conducts any business that is appropriate.

8. Adjournment is in order.

IMPROVE YOUR VOCABULARY

Obstreperous - (ŏb-strĕp'-ĕr-ŭs) a. Noisy, clamorous, vociferous, unruly, difficult to control, etc. Example: An obstreperous person in an assembly shouts loudly, but thinks little. Use this word three or four times daily until it becomes a natural part of your vocabulary.

Mix - Omit this word. Use synonyms for variety and new shades of meaning. Examples are: amalgamate, associate, blend, commingle, compound, fuse, merge, unite, confuse, intermingle, etc.

BIBLIOGRAPHY FOR PARLIAMENTARY LAW AND THE STUDENT CONGRESS

Bank, Dena C., How Things Get Done: The Nitty Gritty of Parliamentary Procedure, Univ. of South Carolina Press, 1979.

Farwell, Hermon W., The Majority Rules: A Manual of Procedure for MOST Groups, High Publishers, 1980.

Gondin, William R., Handbook Dictionary of Parliamentary Procedure, Littlefield, 1969.

Robert, H. M., Robert's Rules of Order, Revell, rev. ed., 1980.

NAME _____ DATE _____

(Ch. 27) 184. An interview may be described as: (mark only what is correct)

(a) talking with one or more persons about whatever comes to mind

(b) talking with a person or group in which there is little direction of conversation

(c) talking with a person or group with a specific purpose

(d) talking with a person or group in which only one person does the talking

(Ch. 27) 185. Mark all the following ideas that apply to an interview:

(a) an appointment is usually necessary

(b) you should expect to walk into a business and interview the manager without prior notice

(c) there may be limited time to conduct the interview

(d) you may have several meetings before completing an interview

(Ch. 27) 186. (Strike out) In an interview: (mark correct answers)

(a) your physical behavior will tell much about you

(b) you will be judged by your appearance

(c) your walk, your posture, subtle movements of your hands and feet, will give impressions about you

(d) everything you say and do will tell something about you

(e) business executives are usually good judges of people in interviews

(Ch. 27) 187. If you (the interviewer) make an appointment for an interview by telephone you should do how many of the following?

(a) make sure you are talking with the right person   (b) introduce yourself

(c) explain what you want and why, also how much time will be needed

(d) leave your name, telephone number, and address in case the other person needs to cancel or change the interview

(Ch. 27) 188. Before you (the interviewer) meet your interview appointment you will:

(mark correct answers)

(a) have a number of questions in mind you will use

(b) prepare a list of lead questions and numerous specific questions you may ask

(c) memorize certain selected questions to be used as needed

(d) dress neatly and appropriately

(e) be absolutely certain you have the correct address and exact time of the interview

(f) arrive two minutes early

(Ch. 27) 189. In an interview in which you are seeking employment you should: (mark correct answers)

(a) inquire about company policy, union membership, salary or wages, sick leave and other matters

(b) ask when you will be notified about the job

(c) be sure you chew your gum quietly

(d) leave a card (with the person interviewed) that contains all vital information about you

(Ch. 27) 190. The word "fallible" means: (mark correct answers)

(a) subject to unusual illness (b) subject to double vision and hallucinations

(c) subject to making errors (d) subject to being deceived

(Ch. 27) 191. (Blockbuster) Synonyms for the word "pay" are: (mark correct answers)

(a) recompense (b) requittal (c) labor (d) agreement (e) stipend

(f) emolument (g) hire (h) fee (i) compensation (j) remuneration

(Ch. 28) 192. In a sales talk you try: (mark correct answers)

(a) to make people change their minds

(b) to cause people to be interested in your product

(c) to persuade people to buy your product now

(d) to persuade people to buy your product later

(Ch. 28) 193. The sales speaker: (mark correct answers)

(a) need not pay attention to his appearance but rather his sales item

(b) must be thoroughly familiar with his product in all details

(c) need not (when selling his product) feel obligated to answer questions about its manufacturer

(d) should know about his product's cost of upkeep, repairs, and guarantee

(Ch. 28) 194. A sales speaker should know his prospective customers as follows: (mark correct answers)

(a) their occupations (b) how they get along with their relatives

(c) their credit ratings and religion (d) their education and local beliefs

(e) what products they have purchased from competitors

(Ch. 28) 195. A sales person should: (mark correct answers)

(a) politely tell any customer wanting a demonstration of the product to come to his office because he could do a better demonstration there

(b) refuse to let a customer try out the sales item unless the salesman could be with him at all times

(c) pass samples around if the product is candy, foods, etc.

(d) demonstrate his product at a customer's request or without request

(Ch. 28) 196. (Quarterback sneak) In preparing for a sales speech to a group you should:
(mark correct answers)

(a) arrive early enough that you can set up every display, etc., before the audience arrives

(b) be sure all order forms, receipts, etc., are ready for immediate use

(c) if you plan to show a film wait until the people arrive to set it up so they won't trip over electric cords

(d) as a final preparation check your speaking notes to be sure they are ready

(Ch. 28) 197. Organization of a sales speech follows these steps: (1) introduction; (2) present information about yourself and your product; (3) explain the purpose of your product, show how it is used or operates and demonstrate it; (4) show and/or tell how your product will benefit the group; (5) explain how your product may be purchased

    (a) the above organization is satisfactory

    (b) the above organization is not satisfactory

(Ch. 28) 198. In sales speaking when you are telling the customers how they may buy your product you will discuss how many of the following points?

    (a) you are not sure exactly what the guarantee covers

    (b) if cash is paid there is a discount in price

    (c) if credit is used the carrying charges are explained fully

    (d) you do not know how many months are allowed for payment if the customer buys on credit

    (e) you will downgrade your competitors because your product and service are better

(Ch. 28) 199. (Blockbuster) Mark all synonyms for the word "trenchant":

    (a) sharp   (b) jagged   (c) rough   (d) biting   (e) ripping   (f) heavy-handed
    (g) keen   (h) slashing   (i) tearing   (j) cutting   (k) gnashing   (l) gnawing

(Ch. 28) 200. Mark all synonyms for the words "awful" and "terrible":

    (a) monstrous   (b) big   (c) odious   (d) ill-bred   (e) terrific   (f) overpowering
    (g) ugly   (h) omnipotent

(Ch. 29) 201. An announcement is: (one answer)

    (a) to persuade   (b) to get action   (c) to entertain   (d) to interest   (e) to inform

(Ch. 29) 202. (Troublemarker) An announcement: (mark what is correct)

    (a) is generally loosely organized   (b) is pertinent and to the point

    (c) is indefinite concerning time and place

    (d) does not give location since this may be changed

(Ch. 29) 203. An announcement may concern: (mark correct answers)

    (a) a past event   (b) a future event   (c) something that will occur in one minute

    (d) something that happened thirty seconds ago

(Ch. 29) 204. (Bad fumble) An announcement: (mark what is correct)

    (a) must be authentic but may rely on hearsay   (b) must be hearsay only

    (c) must be authentic and authoritative   (d) must be correct except for details

(Ch. 29) 205. When presenting an announcement you should: (mark what is correct)

    (a) show that the event is timely   (b) name the exact place and location

    (c) tell how to get to the location if it seems advisable

    (d) if necessary indicate advantages of the place

(Ch. 29) 206. When presenting an announcement you should: (mark correct answers)

    (a) state the time

    (b) give the date, day, and exact time but state that it is not necessary to be on time since the event always starts late

    (c) state the admission

    (d) state where tickets may be purchased

    (e) explain about reserved seats

    (f) under no circumstances should you bore the audience by summarizing the event regarding occasion, place, time, and admission

(Ch. 29) 207. When you present an announcement you should: (mark what is correct)

    (a) rise from your seat regardless of where you are, then speak

    (b) stand at one side of the audience about halfway from front to back

    (c) stand at the back of the room so people can hear you

    (d) go to the front and stand near the center of the platform or room

(Ch. 29) 208. (Blockbuster) Mark all synonyms or meanings of the word "debacle":

    (a) a great storm   (b) an earthquake   (c) a stampede   (d) surprise

    (e) complete collapse   (f) unexpected event   (g) rout   (h) any flood

    (i) a loss   (j) an unexpected break-up   (k) a landslide

(Ch. 29) 209. Mark all synonyms for the word "lot":

    (a) host   (b) numbers   (c) profusion   (d) wealth   (e) horde   (f) scores

    (g) galaxy   (h) mass   (i) abundance   (j) multitude   (k) volume

(Ch. 29) 210. (Umpire's decision) In both these sentences is "debacle" correctly used? "It was a debacle when the child lost her only penny." "It was a debacle when the child's father lost his penny."

    (a) yes   (b) no

(Ch. 30) 211. A book review is: (one answer)

    (a) orderly talk about a book   (b) talk about a book and its author

    (c) talk about a book, its author, and publisher

    (d) orderly talk about a book and its author

(Ch. 30) 212. A book reviewer: (mark all correct answers)

    (a) should know his material well   (b) should know the methods of giving a review

    (c) should be able to present his information in an organized and interesting manner

    (d) all preceding answers are correct

(Ch. 30) 213. When presenting a book review you should include how many of the following?

    (a) the author's wife's name   (b) author's first child's name   (c) the author's name

    (d) tell about author's life

(Ch. 30) 214. A book review should include how many of the following? (mark correct answers)

    (a) activities other than writing that the author does

    (b) other books the author has written

    (c) where the author lives

    (d) how old the author is

(Ch. 30) 215. A reviewer should include how many of the following about the book?

    (mark correct answers)

    (a) why book was written   (b) what other reviewers say about it

    (c) reviewer's opinion about the plot

    (d) reviewer's evaluation of characters and how they are portrayed

(Ch. 30) 216. To prepare a book review a person should read the book as many as three times or more.

    (a) true   (b) false

(Ch. 30) 217. When presenting a book review you should: (mark correct answers)

    (a) read long passages so audience will understand it better

    (b) read quotes from the book - no more than about 150 words each

    (c) use limited notes - about three words for each minute you speak

    (d) use voluminous notes so you won't forget

(Ch. 30) 218. (Blockbuster) Mark all synonyms for the word "enervate":

    (a) wear   (b) debilitate   (c) use   (d) emasculate   (e) tire   (f) worry

    (g) unnerve   (h) exhaust   (i) work   (j) jade   (k) laborious   (l) arduous

    (m) enfeeble   (n) toilsome

(Ch. 30) 219. Synonyms for the word "wonderful" are:

    (a) great   (b) rapturous   (c) huge   (d) superb   (e) gigantic   (f) magnificent

    (g) dazzling   (h) beautiful   (i) sublime   (j) splendid   (k) gifted   (l) versatile

    (m) real

(Ch. 31) 220. Reading aloud effectively requires: (mark correct answers)

    (a) meticulous preparation   (b) understanding what the author is saying

    (c) much experience   (d) interpreting ideas and meanings accurately

(Ch. 31) 221. (Drop-kick) When selecting a reading to present to an audience you should:

    (mark correct answers)

    (a) select something suitable to you   (b) select something suitable to the audience

    (c) consider the size of the room and seating   (d) consider outside noises

(Ch. 31) 222. When preparing an oral reading you should: (mark correct answers)

    (a) disregard punctuation   (b) learn the meaning of all words

    (c) practice aloud until you can use 80 to 90 percent eye contact with the audience

    (d) plan to read at least 50 percent of the time looking at your material

(Ch. 31) 223. When beginning your oral reading presentation you should: (mark correct answers)

    (a) pause a few seconds before starting your performance

    (b) stand very much at attention and quite formally

    (c) tell why you chose your particular selection

    (d) speak briefly about the author and the setting of your selection

(Ch. 31) 224. Meanings and synonyms for the word "enigmatic" are: (mark everything that is correct)

    (a) foreign-like   (b) skillful   (c) puzzling   (d) scientific   (e) like a riddle

    (f) quandary   (g) hard to understand

(Ch. 31) 225. (Blockbuster) Mark all synonyms for the word "fix" while keeping in mind its many meanings:

    (a) imbroglio   (b) logistics   (c) restore   (d) crisis   (e) fair   (f) corrupt

    (g) mend   (h) arrange   (i) cajole   (j) condition   (k) redeem   (l) dilemma

    (m) adjust   (n) bribe

(Ch. 32) 226. (Bunt) Mark all correct statements:

(a) parliamentary law is a recognized procedure for conducting the business of groups

(b) parliamentary law's purpose is to expedite the transaction of business in an orderly manner

(c) parliamentary law is identical in all state legislatures

(d) the U.S. Senate and House of Representatives operate under the same rules

(Ch. 32) 227. The term "precedence of motions" means: (one answer)

(a) the chairman says which motion is most important

(b) the assembly decides which motion comes first

(c) that motions are debated in a certain order

(d) that the first motion placed on the floor is the only thing an assembly can discuss

(Ch. 32) 228. Under parliamentary procedure as generally practiced it is illegal to change an amendment beyond adding one amendment to it.

(a) true   (b) false

(Ch. 32) 229. Under parliamentary procedure: (mark correct answers)

(a) the chairman refrains from discussing any motion before the house

(b) if the chairman wants to speak on a proposal he appoints a member to take his place while he becomes a participant

(c) any member of an assembly must get the chair's permission to speak before he does so

(d) it is not necessary to get the chair's permission for a member to second a motion

(Ch. 32) 230. Under parliamentary procedure: (mark correct answers)

(a) to change a motion it must be voted down

(b) to change a motion it must be amended

(c) to stop rambling or extended debate you move "the previous question"

(d) "the previous question" (motion) is debatable and requires a majority vote to be adopted

(Ch. 32) 231. Under parliamentary procedure: (mark correct answers)

(a) you can ask another member of the assembly a question by getting the chair's permission to speak

(b) you may call for a division of the house without the chair's recognition

(c) division of the house means you want members to stand or raise their hands to indicate their vote

(d) rules may be suspended by a majority vote

(e) a nomination to an office is not required to be seconded

(Ch. 32) 232. (Blockbuster) Synonyms and meanings for the word "obstreperous" are:
(mark correct answers)

(a) uninhibited   (b) pathological   (c) difficult to control   (d) revengeful

(e) unruly   (f) vulgar   (g) vociferous   (h) maniacal   (i) clamorous

(j) hateful   (k) noisy

(Ch. 32) 233. Mark all synonyms for the word "mix":

(a) confuse   (b) commingle   (c) amalgamate   (d) adhere   (e) compound

(f) viscous   (g) blend   (h) unite   (i) characterize   (j) fuse   (k) associate

(l) submerge   (m) merge   (n) glutinous

Chapter 33

DISCUSSION - THE PANEL -
SMALL GROUP COMMUNICATION

Question: *Does a person who uses good grammar have much advantage?*

Answer: *Yes. A person is judged partially by his grammar.*

This discussion is due:
Participants: Three to six and a chairman.
Time limits: 30 minutes for most classroom performances. Others vary according to the amount of time available.
Speaking notes: Participants usually find it necessary and convenient to have notes which provide data such as figures, facts, sources, etc., concerning the points of view and information they present.
Sources of information: Three or more should be studied.
Outline of discussion: See "How To Prepare For a Panel Discussion" next page.

PURPOSE OF DISCUSSION - THE PANEL - SMALL GROUP COMMUNICATION

There is no better method for resolving the world's problems than by "talking them over." The panel discussion, when operating successfully, utilizes this method. It is democracy at work. Every citizen and, certainly, every student should have the experience of deliberately sitting down in the company of other persons to find the answers to problems of mutual concern. This assignment will give you this vital experience; hence you should study it carefully.

EXPLANATION OF THE PANEL DISCUSSION - SMALL GROUP COMMUNICATION

A panel discussion occurs when a group of persons sit down together to try to solve a problem or problems by pooling their knowledge and thus arriving at decisions satisfactory to the majority. If they reach these decisions, their purpose is fulfilled. This requires that the discussants enter the panel with open minds and a willingness and desire to hear other viewpoints, opinions, and evidence. Thus by gathering all possible information (facts) and by pooling it, the group can examine a problem bit by bit, point by point, and arrive at a logical solution. No one should consent to join a panel if he does so while harboring preconceived ideas, prejudices, and opinions, which he is unwilling to change in the light of evidence which he does not possess. An attitude of open mindedness is the most valuable asset a panel speaker or anyone else can possess. This does not mean he is vacillating but rather that he will easily and gladly change his mind when confronted by information which perhaps he did not know was in existence.

A panel may vary greatly in the number of members; however, if there are too many participants, progress tends to be slow and laborious. It is, therefore, advisable to limit membership to a maximum of five or six persons besides the chairman.

Occasions for a panel discussion are as numerous as the problems that face any group of people. Every club, every society or organization has recourse to the panel as a method of problem solving. Naturally, if an organization has a large membership, its problems will be submitted to committees which will in turn attack them through the discussion method, that is to say, the panel. Today the radio often features the panel as a public service. The student should not be led to believe that every panel must have an audience or that certain TV programs dominated by sarcasm, acrimony, and quibbling represent true discussion. Such discussions are not in any sense of the word good panel discussions because they often lack the quality of open mindedness and a sincere desire to solve a problem.

SUGGESTED PROBLEMS FOR PANEL DISCUSSION - SMALL GROUP COMMUNICATION

(Note that topics are phrased in the form of questions. This is considered desirable since the questions imply that their answers are to be found in the form of solutions.)

1. What is the most desirable method to control credit card abuse?
2. How may more people be encouraged to vote?

3. How may more efficient and capable persons be placed in public office?
4. How may white collar workers' salaries be raised?
5. How may political bosses be controlled?
6. How may more educational facilities be offered?
7. What should be done to decrease illiteracy in the U.S.?
8. What should be done to improve high school and college curriculums?
9. What should be done about cheating at school?
10. What should be the policy relative to paying athletes or granting them special privileges?
11. What should be the policy in regard to charging admission fees at school dances?
12. How should sororities and fraternities be improved?
13. What should be done to control the national debt?
14. What should be done to control illegal aliens in the U.S.A.?
15. Should required courses in marriage be taught in high schools?
16. Should teachers be retired automatically at a certain age?
17. Should all physically and mentally capable students be required to attend school until eighteen years of age, or until graduated from high school?
18. What should a young person's attitude be toward taking out life insurance?
19. Should the government assist young married couples by subsidizing their marriages?
20. Panel's choice of subject for discussion.

HOW TO CHOOSE A PROBLEM FOR PANEL DISCUSSION – SMALL GROUP COMMUNICATION

If the problem is not assigned, the panel should meet under the leadership of the chairman. At the meeting, various problems should be considered and a selection of a topic for discussion be made by majority vote. The selection should be based on interest to the discussants and the availability of material for research and study. If the discussion will be conducted before a group, then the audience should be considered when the choice is made. In either case the group should select a question they are capable of adequately discussing. In other words, a technical problem should be avoided, such as: How should the Federal Reserve System be organized?

HOW TO PREPARE FOR A PANEL DISCUSSION – SMALL GROUP COMMUNICATION

Participants should give careful thought to the purpose of a panel discussion, which is to <u>solve a problem</u>. They should prepare their material with this thought uppermost. Their attitude should be that of a farmer who sees a strange plant growing in his field. What should he do about it? Is it harmful? Is it valuable? Should he dig it out by the roots or cut it off? Who can tell him what kind of a plant it is? In other words, the student should not jump at conclusions immediately after selecting a problem, but, like the farmer, he should find out all he can about the question (plant) under discussion and then make up his mind regarding what opinions he should hold and what he should do sbout them.

Let us assume for a moment that the problem has been selected and that the discussants are ready to begin searching for possible solutions. Here are the steps each participant should follow in arriving at possible answers:

<u>The Problem:</u> What should be done to decrease the number of divorces?

<u>Procedure to follow in arriving at possible solutions:</u> (Keep detailed notes on the following data.)

1. Find out all the effects of divorce, both good and bad. Ask your teacher and librarian to help you locate sources of information.

2. Find out what caused these good and bad effects.

3. Now that you know the results of divorces and what causes them, you should decide that anything you suggest as solutions to the problem must meet certain standards. For example,

   (a) Any solution must be fair to both the man and woman.

   (b) Any solution must be fair to the children of divorced parents.

   (c) Any solution must be legal and constitutional.

   (d) Any solution must be acceptable to the church.

   (e) Etc.

4. State several tentative (possible) solutions to your problem of divorces. Be sure these answers meet the standards you set up. Under each suggested solution list both the advantages and disadvantages of

it. (Remember that you are not to be prejudiced for your solutions. You will soon say to the other discussants, "Here are my ideas with their good and bad points. This is what I believe on the basis of the information I could find. However, I'm willing to change my views if your information indicates I should.")

5. Now select the one solution which you think is the best from all those you have constructed.

6. Suggest ways and means to put your best solution into action. For example, newspaper publicity, beginning with your school paper.

Note: Outline all of your points, one through six, using complete sentences. State all your sources of information, giving dates, authors, names of books or magazines, pages, volumes, . . . Be sure to identify your authorities. Hand outline to your instructor as evidence of preparation.

Now that you have gathered all of the information on your problem, outlined it, and learned its contents sufficiently well, you are ready to meet with other members of the panel to see what they have discovered. Each one of them has done the same thing you did in trying to find out what should be done to decrease the divorce rate. You will all get together and pool your knowledge. Obviously you will not all have the same information, because you did not all read the same magazines and books and talk to the same people. This means you will not agree with each other because your information is different. Your possible solutions will be different too. Nevertheless, you will pool your knowledge and after thoroughly talking it over and examining all the data carefully, you will decide on possible solutions that are agreed on by a majority of the panel. These solutions will represent the co-operative effort of all of you, rather than only one person.

HOW TO PRESENT A PANEL DISCUSSION – SMALL GROUP COMMUNICATION

In presenting a panel you merely meet as a group and discuss the information and ideas each one has brought with him. To do this effectively, each discussant should approach the panel with an open mind. He must have a desire to find the answers to the mutual problem of the members, not a desire to propound and seek adoption of his personal ideas and solutions. This attitude of open mindedness is probably the most important aspect of discussion.

Now let us assume that the members of the panel have assembled. The chairman should have arrived first and previously placed the chairs in a semi-circle so that each person can easily see everyone else during the discussion. The chairman will sit near the middle of the group. If an audience attends to hear the panel, the chairman should be sure the discussants are all seated in such a manner that they are visible to the listeners. The speakers, in turn, should be just as sure that their remarks are easily heard by everyone present, and they should direct their voices toward the audience as well as the panel.

Before the actual participation begins, each speaker should remind himself that he is not to dominate the occasion, neither is he to withdraw and say little or nothing. Each one should remember further that he will not become angry, impolite, sarcastic, or acrimonious. He will be very earnest and sincere, however, and even persistent if necessary.

The chairman, in turn, will insist – gently, but firmly – on a policy of fairness. He will encourage the most timid to speak their minds. He will promote harmony and goodwill among the group. He will permit some digression from the main question but direct the discussion in such a way that the main problem is explored. He will note the passing of time and make certain that the discussion progresses rapidly enough to be completed within the allotted time.

Now we are ready to begin discussion. The chairman will make brief introductory remarks in which he will mention the occasion and reasons for discussing the topic at hand. He will introduce members of the panel (if there is an audience) and tell where each is from, his occupation, and anything else appropriate. If there is no audience, the chairman should be certain that all members of the panel are acquainted with each other.

The procedure for the actual discussion should be entirely informal throughout. It should be a spontaneous give-and-take affair with free and easy questions, answers, and contributions from everyone without promptings from the chairman. This does not mean the chairman may not call on a member if he thinks that it is necessary to do so.

The points to discuss should develop in the following order through informal talk.

1. Define the terms. Be sure you all agree on what you are talking about.

2. Limit your subject if it is too broad. Perhaps you should talk about decreasing divorces in the United States only or in one state, one city, or in one church.

   (Note: The statement of your question does not limit the discussion in this respect.)

3. Talk about the effects of the high divorce rate.

4. Discuss the causes of the effects of the high divorce rate.

5. Set up standards on which you will base any solutions to your problem.

6. Arrive at several tentative solutions or conclusions to your question. Be sure you discuss advantages and disadvantages of each one.

7. Select one tentative solution as the best one to put into action.

8. Decide on ways and means to go about putting your solution into action.

9. The chairman should summarize briefly what the panel has accomplished.

10. If it is desirable, the chairman will permit the audience (if there is one) to direct questions to the panel members. He will have to rule on questions that obviously have no bearing on the discussion or other questions that are out of order.

11. The chairman will conclude the meeting with a brief summary at the end of the allotted or appropriate time.

Note: To follow through all of these steps will necessitate a constant alertness on the part of all discussants and the chairman. Of course, if a number of meetings are scheduled, you may move gradually through the various stages of arriving at a solution. It is not wise, however, to prolong the sessions until the members become tired.

IMPROVE YOUR VOCABULARY

Versatile – (vŭr'sȧ-tĭl) a. Being able to do many things easily - easy to adjust to new situations. Example: A versatile secretary is a valuable person. Use this word in your conversation several times a day throughout the next week so that you can really call it your own.

Swell – Here is that word! Everybody owns it and works it to death. Why not omit it and use synonyms? Examples are: matchless, unequalled, priceless, gorgeous, costly, choice, rare, peerless, superlative, rich, capital, inimitable, ornate, etc.

BIBLIOGRAPHY FOR DISCUSSION - THE PANEL - SMALL GROUP COMMUNICATION

Bormann, Earnest G. and Bormann, Nancy C., Effective Small Group Communication, Burgess, 3d ed., 1980.

Crable, Richard E., One to Another: A Guidebook For Interpersonal Communication, Harper & Row, 1980.

Cragan, John F. and Wright, David W., Communications Small Group Discussions: A Case Study Approach, West, 1980.

Ferguson, Jeanne and Miller, Maria B., You're Speaking - Who's Listening?, Science Research Associates, 1980.

Chapter 34

DISCUSSION - THE SYMPOSIUM -
SMALL GROUP COMMUNICATION

Question: *Should a person use eloquent phrases
when appropriate?*

Answer: *Yes, if you remember eloquent phrases
are usually couched in simple language.*

This assignment is due:
Participants – Three to four speakers and a chairman.
Time limits for each speech: 5–6 minutes.
Speaking notes: None for the speakers. The chairman may use notes in order to be sure that the order of
speakers, topics for discussion, and other information do not become confused.
Sources of information: Three or more should be studied.
Outline of speech: None is required for instructor. Prepare your own to insure proper organization.

PURPOSE OF DISCUSSION - THE SYMPOSIUM - SMALL GROUP COMMUNICATION

The symposium, one type of discussion, is being used more and more as a means of informing and enlightening the public. Many persons are unaware of the different types of discussions and the advantages or disadvantages inherent in each of them. Because it will be to your advantage to understand the workings and the technique of the symposium, it is offered here as a new speech experience for you.

EXPLANATION OF THE SYMPOSIUM - SMALL GROUP COMMUNICATION

The symposium is a method of presenting representative aspects of a problem. Usually three or four speakers talk about one general question, with each speaker presenting his views on a particular aspect. A chairman acts as moderator and leader. He synchronizes the different speeches so that unification of ideas rather than a series of unrelated lectures is present. Each speaker is charged with the responsibility of fitting his remarks into the main question by making sure that he contributes to the proposition being explored. The time allotted each speaker is the same, except that the length of the speeches may vary from a few minutes to fifteen or twenty each if time allows. Following the conclusion of the speeches, the participants may form a panel, after which the audience is invited to ask questions of the speakers. Either one of the latter procedures may be omitted – the panel or questioning by the audience. The whole program may continue as long as an hour and a half or more if the audience is quite active and the discussants capable, and if time permits.

The purpose of a symposium is to inform and stimulate the listeners. This purpose is accomplished by virtue of the fact that each speaker may support a given point of view.

Occasions for the symposium may present themselves any time a group of persons meets. It may be the meeting of a club, a society, a religious, fraternal or business organization, an educational group, any civic gathering or other assemblage. Today radio and television utilize the symposium frequently on certain types of programs.

SUGGESTED TOPICS FOR A SYMPOSIUM - SMALL GROUP COMMUNICATION

1. How may world organizations for peace be improved?

2. What should be done to insure permanent peace in Europe?

3. What should be done to promote progress in China?

4. What should be done to conserve energy?

5. How should debts to the United States be settled?

6. What should be done to improve American–Russian relations?

7. What are the aspects of a federal world government?

8. Should the United States have compulsory military training?

9. Should the federal government subsidize high schools and colleges?

10. Should colleges be tuition free?

11. What should be done to stabilize marriage?

12. Should a national minimum age for marriage be established?

13. Should scholarships be given to all high school graduates with outstanding records?

14. Should the United States extablish new immigration laws?

15. What should be done to protect the environment?

16. What should be done to decrease juvenile delinquency?

17. How may moving pictures be improved?

18. What is a student's responsibility to his home?

19. What is a student's responsibility to his school?

20. Symposium's choice.

HOW TO CHOOSE A TOPIC

The members of the symposium should meet with their chairman and then by general agreement decide on a proposition. They should choose one that is interesting to everyone, if possible. However, if all of the members of the group do not agree, the one most suitable to the majority should be the choice. It is not to be expected that you can choose a topic on which everyone is well informed. Be sure that your selection is one about which you can secure information by interviews and reading. Make your decision soon.

HOW TO PREPARE A SYMPOSIUM – SMALL GROUP COMMUNICATION

First of all, it should be kept in mind that the individual speakers should prepare their speeches according to the suggestions laid down for any speech to inform or stimulate. All the steps of preparation should be included from audience analysis to rehearsal.

The mechanics of overall preparation may be as follows:

I. The members should meet with the chairman.

A. The topic to be discussed should then be divided by mutual agreement among the speakers so that each one presents a different aspect of it. For example, if the topic is "What should be done to improve the streets of our city?" the three speakers (if that is the number) could set up these questions:

(1) What should the city administration do to improve the streets?

(2) What should the citizens do to improve the streets?

(3) What should be done to improve the efficiency and use of present equipment?

II. Having agreed on the above divisions of the question, each speaker is next obligated to prepare his discussion making sure, of course, that he observes his time limits closely.

The chairman should be well prepared on the entire subject, because he will direct discussion on it. A routine responsibility of the chair is to set up the order of speakers. Having completed this, the chairman must prepare brief introductory remarks. These remarks will include these facts: (1) a history and statement of the proposition, (2) reasons for its discussion, (3) relationship and importance of the topic to the audience, (4) definitions of terms of the proposition, (5) names, topics, and order of the speakers, and (6) the manner in which the symposium will be conducted. The chairman should familiarize himself generally with the point of view each speaker will take. He should also be aware of the necessity for a brief summary at the conclusion of the performance by the speakers and after the questions are asked by the audience.

Let us assume now that everyone is ready for the symposium. A final check should provide answers to these questions: Does each speaker have sufficient authorities and accurate data to back up his information, ideas, and conclusions? Are these proofs in a form which he can use while he is being questioned by a member of the symposium or the audience? Does each member know how to answer questions from his own group or the audience, to meet objections, to restate arguments, to summarize his point of view? Will the speakers keep their heads, their sense of humor, and remain polite when under fire? Does the chairman know how to lead the symposium when they form a panel? Does the chairman know how to lead the audience and direct questions to the speakers? Does he know what types of questions to permit as legitimate and which to rule out of order? If the answers to these questions are not known to the participants, they are obligated to discover them by studying suggested references.

HOW TO PRESENT A SYMPOSIUM - SMALL GROUP COMMUNICATION

Throughout the entire symposium, good speech practices should be followed. Aside from keeping these in mind, the procedure may be as follows:

1. The members of the symposium may be seated side by side with the chairman at one end.

2. The chairman will make his introductory remarks, will introduce members of the symposium, and then will present the first speaker and his topic.

3. The first speaker will deliver his speech after which the chairman will present the other speakers in a similar manner.

4. At the conclusion of the speeches the chairman will briefly summarize the ideas of the speakers.

5. Following the chairman's summary, the symposium will be continued according to one of the alternatives listed below:

(a) The speakers will form a panel for a limited time and discuss the ideas that were presented after which the chairman will summarize briefly, then adjourn the meeting.

(b) The speakers will form a panel as indicated in a preceding, after which the audience will be permitted to question the speakers for a limited or unlimited time by directing questions through the chairman. The chairman will conclude the symposium with a brief summary followed by adjournment.

(c) Following the speeches and the chairman's brief summary, the audience will be permitted to question the speakers a definite or indefinite time by directing questions through the chairman. At the conclusion of audience participation, the chairman will summarize the matter of the individual speakers, and then adjourn the meeting. In this case there is no panel by the speakers.

IMPROVE YOUR VOCABULARY

Redolent – (rĕd'ō-lĕnt) a. Fragrant, odorous, aromatic, spicy, balmy, etc. Example: The odors of the redolent flowers filled the air. Use redolent in your vocabulary several times each day during the next week.

Sure – Sure is another slave. When used to mean certainly it is an error because it should be surely. Let us give it emancipation and enliven our vocabularies at the same time. Examples of synonyms are: certainly, unquestionably, gladly, undoubtedly, assuredly, unmistakably, decisively, decidedly, definitely, clearly, inevitably, undeniably, unavoidably, incontestably, conclusively, etc.

BIBLIOGRAPHY FOR DISCUSSION - THE SYMPOSIUM - SMALL GROUP COMMUNICATION

Hyman, Ronald, Improving Discussion Leadership, Teachers College Press, 1980.
Jensen, Vernon, Argumentation: Reasoning In Communication, Van Nostrand Reinhold, 1980.
Kell, Carl L. and Corts, Paul R., Fundamentals of Effective Group Communication, Macmillan, 1980.

Chapter 35

THE LECTURE FORUM COMMUNICATION

Question: *Do gestures make a speech better?*

Answer: *If they are appropriate to all elements of the speech situation, yes.*

This speech is due:
Time limits: 7–8 minute speech. Questioning period 5 minutes.
Speaking notes: 15 word maximum limit.
Sources of information: Three are required, preferably four. For each source give the specific magazine or book it was taken from, title of the article, author's full name, date of publication, and the chapter or pages telling where the material was found. If a source is a person, identify him completely by title, position, occupation, etc. List these on the outline form.
Outline your speech: Prepare a 75–150 word complete sentence outline. Designate the exact number of words in your outline. Use the form at the end of this chapter.

PURPOSE OF THE LECTURE FORUM COMMUNICATION

Persons who give speeches often do so without knowing how many unanswered questions they leave in the minds of their listeners. These questions are unanswered because the hearers have no chance to voice their questions. It is becoming evident daily that speakers can be more helpful to their listeners if the speakers remain on stage following their lectures to answer questions which have arisen in the minds of their audience.

Most students do not receive training in answering questions about the material they present in speeches; thus, when they are confronted with a forum (question period) following a speech they are in danger of awkwardly handling themselves and their audience. This lecture forum type of speech is designed to provide experience in speaking as well as answering questions. It should be both enlightening and challenging to student speakers. See what you can do with it.

EXPLANATION OF THE LECTURE FORUM COMMUNICATION

The lecture forum is a speech followed by a period in which members of the audience are permitted to direct questions to the speaker. The purpose of the lecturer generally is to inform his hearers on a worthwhile subject. He could present a speech intended to stimulate or one to convince; however, the speech to convince would probably not suit the lecture forum atmosphere so well as the speech to inform. We cannot preclude the speeches to stimulate and to convince, because they can well be followed by periods of questioning and often should be; but we <u>can</u> and <u>do</u> suggest that for most lecture forums the speaker should <u>utilize his time by discussing an informative subject</u>. The reason for this is that usually an expert or someone else equally informed is asked to speak for a group to analyze a subject. If, during his lecture the expert does arrive at a decision regarding a policy that he believes should be carried out, he does so scientifically, in the presence of his audience. Having reached a solution does not change his purpose to inform to that of attempting to convince the audience that they should adopt his solution. He <u>stops</u> when he reaches the solution, although he may <u>suggest</u> means for carrying it out. If the audience wants to follow his advice, that is their privilege. The speaker should not urge it on them.

The lecture forum demands that the speaker be well informed, better informed than any member of his audience. It demands further that he be capable of receiving and answering questions from an audience. In short, he should be something of an expert and an excellent speaker.

Occasions for the lecture forum occur whenever an informative speech is in order. These speeches may be given before committees, business groups, church organizations, civic audiences, educational meetings, fraternal orders, and the like. There is scarcely a limit to the occasions for lecture forums.

SUGGESTED TOPICS FOR A LECTURE
FORUM COMMUNICATION
1. How may our government be improved?
2. The problem of juvenile delinquency.
3. The influence of motion pictures.
4. Comic books and good reading.
5. Making the highways safe.
6. Radio or television programs.
7. Honesty in advertising.
8. Women in industry.
9. School assemblies.
10. The status of high school or college athletics.
11. The problem of an expanding population.
12. The problem of the feeble-minded.
13. How to live cheaply but well.
14. Proper clothes for the student.
15. Today's music.
16. The future of airplanes.
17. Beneath the ocean.
18. Difficulties of landing on the planets.
19. The problem of keeping peace.
20. Capital punishment.
21. New methods in selling.
22. Aliens in the United States.
23. New information about space.
24. New sources of water.
25. Oil supplies of the world.
26. The best vacation spots in the United States.
27. Choosing companions.
28. The right to die.
29. Industrial schools.
30. Speaker's choice.

HOW TO CHOOSE A TOPIC FOR A LECTURE
FORUM COMMUNICATION

You will be expected to know your subject unusually well, since you will appear before your audience to inform them and be present to open the meeting to questions centered around your remarks. Thus, it is advisable to choose a topic of interest to you and your listeners, as well as a subject about which you can secure plenty of information. Do not select a subject for which there are only limited sources. An apology to an audience for ignorance on your subject is not conducive to confidence in you as a speaker. Base your choice then, on interest, appropriateness, and the availability of source materials.

HOW TO PREPARE FOR A LECTURE
FORUM COMMUNICATION

Since this is an informative speech, you should read the chapter in this text entitled The Speech To Inform. Here you will find complete informa-

tion relative to preparing this type of speech. Follow it closely.

HOW TO PRESENT A LECTURE FORUM
COMMUNICATION

You should read the chapter in this text entitled The Speech To Inform. It will tell you how to present your speech but not how to conduct the period of questioning from your audience. A discussion of this point follows.

Immediately after the conclusion of your lecture the audience will be advised by the chairman or yourself that they may question you. In making this announcement several points should be explained politely but thoroughly, such as:

1. Tell the audience to please confine their questions to the material presented in the lecture, because you are not prepared to answer questions outside this scope.

2. Request your audience to ask questions only, unless you wish to permit short speeches on the subject. Whatever policy you intend to follow – that is, strictly a questioning period or a question and short speech period – must be specifically announced and understood, or you will run into trouble with those persons who want to make short speeches. If you allow short speeches, announce a definite time limit on them. For the classroom one minute is enough. In large public gatherings, three minutes is adequate.

3. If the audience is small and informal, permit the speakers to remain seated during the forum period; that is, do not ask them to stand while participating. If the gathering is large, require them to stand. Conduct yourself in a like manner, that is, by standing, or seating yourself.

4. Announce the exact amount of time which will be given to the period of questioning. Do not make this questioning period too long. You can always extend the time if the questions are coming briskly at the moment you are scheduled to close. On the other hand, do not continue to hold an audience for the announced time if it becomes obvious that they no longer care to ask questions. It is better to have them go away wanting more than having had too much.

5. Once your announcements are made, open the question and answer period by telling the audience to direct their questions to you. Also explain that you will answer the questions in the order in which they are asked. Thus, if two persons speak at once you will designate which one may ask his question first. The speaker should be urged to speak out rather than to raise his hand, and then wait to be called on.

Having made the above explanations to your audience, tell them you will be glad to answer their questions as best you can. Do not promise to answer all questions, since it is likely that no one could do that. (After all, you are human.) If a question is raised that you do not feel qualified to answer, tell your interrogator you do not have the information necessary to give him a reliable answer. However, if you do not know the answer because you are poorly prepared, you will quickly lose the confidence and respect of your audience - and you should.

If questions are asked which do not pertain to the subject under discussion, politely tell the interrogator that the question is beyond the scope of your talk and you are not prepared to answer it. Should you by chance possess information which will enable you to answer it, state briefly that the question is somewhat afield but you know that _____ ; then make a very brief reply. Do not let this take you off your subject more than a moment.

Should a heckler trouble you, handle him politely but firmly. Do nothing drastic. Read the chapter in this text dealing with heckling speeches if you want more information.

If some questions are obscure and long drawn out, it may be necessary for you to rephrase them. If you do this, inquire of the person who gave the question as to whether or not your rephrasing asks what he wants to know. At other times it may be necessary for you to ask for a restatement of an inquiry. Do this anytime that you do not hear or understand the question clearly.

Observe acceptable speaking practices throughout your lecture and the period following. Retain an alert and friendly attitude. Do not become ruffled when you meet obvious disagreement or criticism. Simply explain your position firmly but politely. Do not engage in a debate or an exchange of unfriendly remarks and accusations. Dismiss the matter and move on to the next question. If some of the questions are "hot" and they will be, keep your head, add a touch of humor to cool them off if it seems advisable; then reply as capably as you can.

If any person asks a question that cannot be heard by the entire audience, repeat it to the audience then give your answer.

When you are ready to turn the meeting back to the chairman, conclude with appropriate remarks in which you sincerely express your pleasure for having been with the audience. Also compliment them for their interest in the subject.

IMPROVE YOUR VOCABULARY

Criterion - (krī-tē'ri-ŭn) n. Standard - such as a standard for judging; a gage, a measure, proof, rule, test, yardstick, etc. Example: There was no criterion for the action he took. Use this word three times daily until it becomes a part of your speaking vocabulary.

Complain - Try using synonyms for this word. They will express many new shades of meaning. Here are examples: find fault, grunt, repine, murmur, remonstrate, croak, growl, grumble, grieve, etc.

BIBLIOGRAPHY FOR THE LECTURE FORUM COMMUNICATION

Johnson, Mary C., Discussion Dynamics: A Classroom Analysis, Newbury House, 1980.
Miles, Matthew B., Learning to Work in Groups, Teachers College Press, 2d ed., 1980.
Schmidt, Wallace V. and Graham, JoAnn, The Public Forum, Alfred Publishing, 1979.

A GREAT SPEECH IN AMERICAN HISTORY

(The example below is for student appreciation and is not
intended for any particular assignment in this text.)

Susan B. Anthony

ON WOMAN'S RIGHT TO VOTE
(1873)

Born in 1820, died in 1906; in early life a social reformer and advocate
of the suffrage and other civil rights for women, with which
she remained through life closely identified.

FRIENDS AND FELLOW CITIZENS: – I stand before you tonight under indictment for the alleged crime of having voted at the last presidential election, without having a lawful right to vote. It shall be my work this evening to prove to you that in thus voting, I not only committed no crime, but, instead, simply exercised my citizen's rights, guaranteed to me and all United States citizens by the National Constitution, beyond the power of any State to deny. * * * * * The preamble of the Federal Constitution says:

"We, the people of the United States, in order to form a more perfect union, establish justice,
insure domestic tranquillity, provide for the common defense, promote the general welfare,
and secure the blessings of liberty to ourselves and our posterity, do ordain and establish
this Constitution for the United States of America."

It was we, the people; not we, the white male citizens; nor yet we, the male citizens; but we, the whole people, who formed the Union. and we formed it, not to give the blessings of liberty, but to secure them; not to the half of ourselves and the half of our posterity, but to the whole people – women as well as men. And it is a downright mockery to talk to women of their enjoyment of the blessings of liberty while they are denied the use of the only means of securing them provided by this democratic-republican government – the ballot.

For any State to make sex a qualification that must ever result in the disfranchisement of one entire half of the people is to pass a bill of attainder, or an ex post facto law, and is therefore a violation of the supreme law of the land. By it the blessings of liberty are forever withheld from women and their female posterity. To them this government has no just powers derived from the consent of the governed. To them this government is not a democracy. It is not a republic. It is an odious aristocracy; a hateful oligarchy of sex; the most hateful aristocracy ever established on the face of the globe; an oligarchy of wealth, where the rich govern the poor. An oligarchy of learning, where the educated govern the ignorant, or even an oligarchy of race, where the Saxon rules the African might be endured; but this oligarchy of sex, which makes father, brothers, husband, sons, the oligarchs over the mother and sisters, the wife and daughters of every household – which ordains all men sovereigns, all women subjects, carries dissension, discord and rebellion into every home of the nation.

Webster, Worcester and Bouvier all define a citizen to be a person in the United States, entitled to vote and hold office.

The only question left to be settled now is: Are women persons? And I hardly believe any of our opponents will have the hardihood to say they are not. Being persons, then, women are citizens; and no State has a right to make any law, or to enforce any old law, that shall abridge their privileges or immunities. Hence, every discrimination against women in the constitutions and laws of the several States is today null and void, precisely as in every one against negroes.

Delivered in 1873 after she had been arrested, put on trial, and fined one hundred dollars for voting at the presidential election in 1872. She refused to pay the fine and never did pay it.

SPEECH OUTLINE

Construct a neat, complete sentence outline on this sheet, tear it out, and hand it to your instructor when you rise to speak. He may wish to write criticisms of the outline and speech in the margins.

Type of speech: _____ Name: _____

Number of words in outline: _____ Date: _____

Purpose of this speech: (What do you want your audience to learn, to think, to believe, to feel, or do because of this speech?) _____

_____

TITLE:

INTRODUCTION:

BODY:

CONCLUSION:

Instructor's comments may concern choice of topic, development of ideas, organization, language use, personal appearance, posture, physical activity, sources, and improvement.

(Write sources of information on back of sheet)

SOURCES FROM LITERATURE

Fill out source requirements completely.
Write "none listed" if an author's name or copyright date is not listed.

1. Author's name _____

    Title of book or magazine used _____

    Title of article in above book or magazine _____

    Chapter and/or pages read _____

    Date of above publication _____

2. Author's name _____

    Title of book or magazine used _____

    Title of article in above book or magazine _____

    Chapter and/or pages read _____

    Date of above publication _____

3. Author's name _____

    Title of book or magazine used _____

    Title of article in above book or magazine _____

    Chapter and/or pages read _____

    Date of above publication _____

INTERVIEW SOURCES

1. Person interviewed _____ Date of interview _____

    His position, occupation, and location _____

    Why is he a reliable source? Be specific _____

    _____

2. Person interviewed _____ Date of interview _____

    His position, occupation, and location _____

    Why is he a reliable source? Be specific _____

    _____

PERSONAL EXPERIENCE OF SPEAKER

1. Tell (1) when, (2) where, and (3) conditions under which you became an authority on subject matter in

    your speech _____

    _____

    _____

    _____

Chapter 36

DEBATE

Question: *Should a person slap or pound a speaker's stand?*

Answer: *Generally no, unless it is done lightly.*

This debate is due:

Time limits: 10 minutes on main speeches, 5 minutes for rebuttals. These time limits may be shortened proportionately for class debates if the instructor finds it necessary. Conventional debates require them, however.

Speaking notes: Use notes sparingly, but efficiently. They are necessary in good debating.

Sources of information: You will need many. In your debate you will be required to state your sources of information to prove the validity of your statements.

Outline of speech: Prepare a 75-150 word complete sentence outline to be handed to your instructor before the debate starts. Write the number of words in the upper left hand corner of the paper.

Number of speakers on a team: Two speakers on a team is the conventional number. A one-speaker team is not uncommon.

PURPOSE OF THE DEBATE

This assignment is proposed because many persons want the experience of debating. It is proposed also because debating can be done in speech classes without the long periods of training undergone by contest debaters. This does not mean that long periods of practice are not desirable. They are. Such training produces truly superior speakers. But debating can be done effectively and with good results in speech classes. It provides excellent experience in communicating, since it pits two or more speakers with opposing ideas against each other. It tests their ability to express these ideas and to defend them under direct challenge. This teaches tact, resourcefulness, ability to think on one's feet, and it teaches that ideas must be backed by evidence, not by mere, conjecture and opinion. Experience of this kind is beneficial and should be a part of every speech student's life.

EXPLANATION OF A DEBATE

A debate is a speaking situation in which two opposing ideas are presented and argued. The ideas represent solutions to a problem. The proponent of each solution attempts to convince his audience that his idea should be adopted in preference to all others. Actually, a debate, in the sense used here, consists of two opposing <u>speeches to convince</u>.

A debate team may be composed of one, two, or more persons. Today most teams have two speakers. One-speaker teams are not uncommon. Three speakers on a team may permit more exhaustive arguments, but they will take more time and unless they are skilled, much repetition and

haggling may be encountered, which will dull the debate.

Debates are divided into main speeches and rebuttals. In carrying out a debate, the usual order of speakers for main speeches is: (1) first affirmative, (2) first negative, (3) second affirmative, (4) second negative. For rebuttals the order is: (1) first negative, (2) first affirmative, (3) second negative, and (4) second affirmative. It is at once apparent when matching two-speaker teams, that the affirmative team leads off and closes the debate. Now should you have a one-speaker team, the affirmative will lead off with (for example) a ten-minute speech. The negative will reply for fifteen minutes, after which the affirmative will conclude with a five-minute rebuttal. This arrangement gives each debater an equal amount of time. Other arrangements are easy and add variety. For example, an arrangement for two-speaker teams can be worked out by permitting each of the speakers to present a ten-minute main speech in the usual order of speaking, but immediately following each speech an opponent rises to cross examine the speaker for five minutes before the speaker leaves the floor. To bring the debate to an end, after the speeches and cross examinations, one member of the negative team presents a final five-minute summary of the negative's position, after which one member of the affirmative concludes the debate with a like summary of his team's position.

It will be advisable to practice the conventional type of debating rather than the cross examination system. The cross examination method involves too many technicalities to be settled by a chairman or judge during the cross examining periods. Unless the rules are well-known to the participants and the judge, confusion instead of cross examination reigns.

Occasions for debates occur in practically all academic classes, although regularly organized debate groups and speech classes enjoy them most frequently. Inter-school debates among high schools are nation-wide, as are inter-college contests. Debates provide excellent program material in schools, over TV, radio, before civic organizations, churches, business groups, clubs, . . . Any group of persons willing to listen to a sound discussion of opposing ideas always welcomes good debate. For sheer enjoyment with, perhaps, some thought thrown in, humorous debates are a fine type of entertainment. Even though they are light in treatment of subject matter and their purpose is to entertain, they require the same skillful preparation that the regular debate does.

SUGGESTED TOPICS FOR DEBATE
1. Resolved that federal population controls should be established.
2. Resolved that the closed shop should be abolished by law.
3. Resolved that inter-racial marriages should be prohibited by law.
4. Resolved that national laws should be established for obtaining drivers' licenses.
5. Resolved that national uniform traffic signals should be established.
6. Resolved that all car owners should be compelled to carry liability insurance.
7. Resolved that hitchhiking should be made illegal.
8. Resolved that the national government should establish and maintain roadside parks at established intervals on all national highways.
9. Resolved that the federal government should establish permanent rent controls.
10. Resolved that the national government should be prohibited from spending more than it receives in taxes.
11. Resolved that inflation should be limited to three percent.
12. Resolved that minimum wages should be established for all teachers.
13. Resolved that students working their way through school should be required to carry lighter credit loads than unemployed students.
14. Resolved that fraternities and sororities should be established in all high schools.
15. Resolved that smoking should be prohibited by law.
16. Resolved that students should be permitted to choose all subjects they wish to take for academic credit.
17. Resolved that beer should be served in designated lounge rooms in colleges.
18. Resolved that all high schools should teach courses in sex education.
19. Resolved that students who have unexcused absences totaling ten percent or more of any class periods should automatically "flunk" those courses.
20. Resolved that persons convicted of killing wild game illegally should be prohibited from purchasing hunting licenses for at least one year from date of conviction.
21. Resolved that the federal government should own and operate all munitions industries.
22. Resolved that college athletes should be subsidized.
23. Resolves that wealth as well as men should be drafted in time of war.
24. Resolved that women as well as men should be drafted in time of war.
25. Resolved that a special tax should be levied to raise funds for the support of state hospitals.
26. Resolved that all cars must average 50 miles per gallon within ten years.
27. Resolves that women with children under the age of fourteen should be prohibited from working away from home.
28. Resolved that tipping should be abolished.
29. Resolved that students caught cheating should be expelled from school.
30. Resolved that liquor should be rationed, distributed and sold by the federal government.
31. Resolved that colleges should restrict enrollments to the higher intellectual students.
32. Resolved that inter-collegiate football should be abolished.
33. Resolved that every high school should require a course in speech for graduation.
34. Resolved that all retirement ages should be abolished.
35. Resolved that mercy killing should be legalized.
36. Resolved that capital punishment should be abolished.
37. Resolved that corporal punishment in schools should be abolished.
38. Speaker's choice.

HOW TO CHOOSE A TOPIC FOR DEBATE
Since two teams will be concerned with the choice of topic, it will be well to consult your opponents, at which time all of you will agree on a subject for debate. Remember that one team will uphold the proposition under debate, while the other will argue against it. So, in choosing a topic, it should also be decided which team will debate afirmative (for the topic) and which will debate negative (against it).

In arriving at an agreement on the subject, be sure that all of you have an interest in the subject and that you can find information about it. If you are in doubt about the availability of source materials, check with your school and city librarians before making a final decision.

If you decide to argue a proposition which is not listed in Suggested Topics For Debate, remember it must be phrased so that it proposes a specific proposition to be adopted or rejected. In other words, be sure that you have a debatable subject.

There should be no procrastination in deciding on a question for debate. An honest effort to select a subject should be made by the persons concerned. This does not imply that a hurried decision should be reached. It simply means that a logical approach to topic selection is necessary and that the inability of debaters to agree on a question for debate is no excuse for not having a subject.

One answer to the problem of what to debate is to ask your instructor to assign the subject and the side you will argue.

HOW TO PREPARE A DEBATE

As stated earlier in this chapter, a debate is really two or more opposing speeches to convince. Your purpose, then, is to convince your audience that you are correct in your point of view. To refresh your memory about the speech to convince, reread the chapter bearing this heading.

Because a debate is an activity in which two colleagues team against two other colleagues, it is necessary that preparation for the contest be made jointly by each pair of debaters. This can best be done if the following suggestions are carried out:

1. Decide who will be first speaker.

2. Make a mutual agreement that both colleagues will search for materials to prove your side of the question. Later these materials can be exchanged to help each of you to strengthen your cases.

3. Begin your hunt for information on your subject. Whenever you find something pertinent, take notes on it. Be sure to be able to give the exact reference for the information. Record the following items: The author's name and who he is, the name of the article, the name of the magazine, newspaper, or book in which you found the item, and the exact date of publication. Take your notes on four inch by six inch cards; then at the top of each card write briefly what the notes on that card concerned.

How to Organize a Debate Speech

After you have gathered your material, you will begin organizing your case. This part of your preparation will require some stiff head work; however, it is not particularly difficult. The following suggestions will tell you how to organize a debate case.

I. Divide your entire case into three parts. These parts are called stock issues. An affirmative must prove all three issues; a negative can win by disproving any one of the issues.

  A. Show a need for the specific proposal you are offering.

  B. Show that your proposal is practical. In other words, show that it will do what you say it will do.

  C. Show that your proposal is desirable. This means to show that the way in which it will work will be beneficial. If you are arguing that capital punishment should be abolished, the question arises as to whether or not it will be desirable for the nation to pay taxes to keep convicted murderers alive for thirty years.

II. Your finished case should be set up as follows:

  A. State your proposition.

  B. Define your terms. If you are arguing that compulsory military training should be established in the United States, you must tell what you mean by "compulsory." Will anyone be excepted? What does "military training" mean? Does it refer to the infantry, the air force, or a technical school for atomic specialists? In other words, state exactly what you are talking about.

  C. Show that your proposal is needed (stock issue).

    1. To prove the need give examples, illustrations, opinions of authorities, facts, and analogies which all point to the need for your proposition. Give enough of these proofs to establish your point.

D. Show that your proposition is practical (it will work). This is your second stock issue.

    1. Give proofs as you did to establish your need in point C, above.

E. Show that your proposal is desirable (its results will be beneficial). This is your third stock issue.

    1. Give proofs as you did in point C, above.

F. Summarize your speech, then close it by stating your belief in your proposal.

III. Colleagues should divide their case.

A. The first speaker often defines the terms and sets up the need. If time permits, he may establish the practicality and desirability of the proposal; however, the second speaker usually takes one or both of these points. This matter must be settled and agreed on by colleagues before cases are organized. A speaker should not spread himself so thin that he proves nothing. A second speaker should re-establish the need set up by his colleague if an opponent attacks it. After doing this, he goes into his points.

IV. Rebuttal is easy if you follow a plan.

A. Colleagues should agree ahead of time regarding which points each one will defend. This agreement should be adhered to, otherwise confusion results.

B. In refuting points, try to run the debate. Take the offensive. This is easy but you must follow a plan. The plan is to take your main speech point by point. Reiterate the first point you made, tell what the opposition did to disprove it; then give more evidence to re-establish it. Now take your second point, do exactly the same thing over again. Continue this strategy throughout your rebuttal and close with a summary, followed by a statement of your belief in the soundness of your proposal.

Do not talk about points brought up by your opponents, except as you refer to them while you re-emphasize your own points. You must carry out this plan of advancing your own case or you will be likely to confuse yourself and your audience. Refuse to be budged from the consideration of your plan for advancing your own case.

V. The points (stock issues) listed above apply to both affirmative and negative speakers. When each team tries to run the debate, that is, take the offensive, there is a real argument. Because each plays upon his own case, the two proposals and their arguments are easily followed.

It should be noted, too, that negative cases oppose affirmative cases by showing that any one of the stock issues does not hold, that is, the proposal is not needed, not practical, or not desirable. By disproving any one of these points, a negative causes an affirmative to fall, since the affirmative must prove all of them.

VI. Colleagues should plan their cases together and rehearse them together. They should have their material so well in mind that they need make little reference to their notes, except when bringing up objections raised by the opposition. Practice should be continued until a student feels complete mastery of his material. He should not memorize a debate speech word for word. He should know his sequence of points and his evidence to prove his point. Besides this, he needs a well-planned introduction and conclusion.

HOW TO PRESENT A DEBATE

A debater's attitude should be one of confidence but not "cockiness." He should be friendly, firm, polite and very eager to be understood. A sense of humor is helpful if well applied.

Bodily actions, gestures, and use of notes should be without awkwardness. Posture should be one of ease and alertness.

The voice should be conversational in quality, earnest, and sincere. Everyone should hear it easily. Shouting, "preaching," grandiloquence, "stage acting," and similar displays have no place in debate - or any good speaking. If a speaker is aroused and means what he says, generally, his voice will tell his story. He must, however, not permit his voice to slip from his control.

When a debater rises to speak, he should address the chairman, and then greet his audience and opponents by saying "Friends." No more is needed. Many debaters utter trite, stereotyped phrases which would be better left unsaid. The debater should make a few introductory remarks about the occasion, the audience, and pleasure of debating a timely question. He should move into the debate by defining his terms. This should all be done informally and sincerely in a truly communicative manner. There is no reason why a debate should be a formal, cold, stilted, unfriendly affair. The reason that some debates are conducted in this formal manner is probably a carry-over of last century's ideas concerning the formality of debating. Such practice, however, does not have a place in modern debating.

After a debate is concluded and the decision announced by the chairman, it is customary and advisable for the teams to rise, meet in mid-stage, and shake hands all around.

HOW A DEBATE IS CONDUCTED,

1. The two teams sit at tables on opposite sides of the platform. They face the audience. A chairman sits between the tables or in some other convenient place on stage.

2. A time-keeper sits on the front row in the audience. He signals the debaters by raising his fingers. If two fingers are up, he means that the speaker has two minutes left. When time is "up," he raises his hand palm out, or he stands. The speaker should stop speaking within ten seconds after the final signal.

3. One, three, or five judges may be used. They are provided with ballots which carry spaces in which to write their decisions. After a debate is concluded, the judges, without consultation, immediately write their decision, sign the ballots, and hand these to the chairman who acts as collector. The chairman may appoint someone to collect the ballots if he wishes. He then reads the decisions from the stage.

4. To start a debate, the chairman reads the debate question to the audience, introduces the speakers, the judges, and the time-keeper. He then announces the first speaker, who opens the debate. He announces each speaker thereafter in turn. If desirable, after once introducing the speakers, the chairman may refrain from further introductions of speakers. The debaters simply rise in their proper order and present their cases.

5. Debaters may refer to their teammates by name, such as "Mr. Jones," or "my colleague." Opponents may be referred to by name or as "my opponent" or "the first speaker for the opposition" or "the second speaker for the opposition" or "the negative" if that is their side of the debate. Debaters may refer to themselves as "we," "my colleague and I," "our position is _____," . . .

IMPROVE YOUR VOCABULARY

Propitious - (prō-pĭsh'ŭs) a. Favorable, fortunate, favorably disposed, opportune, promising, conducive to success, etc. Example: The senator's speech was so propitious for the occasion that he received the nomination. Use this word three or four times daily in your conversation until you completely master it. Use it propitiously at every opportunity.

Trip - Here is a word that can stand a few synonyms. Try omitting it for a while. Examples of synonyms are: journey, cruise, excursion, passage, voyage, tour, expedition, pilgrimage, mission, etc.

BIBLIOGRAPHY FOR THE DEBATE

Eisenberg, Abne M. and Llardo, Joseph A., A Guide to Formal and Informal Debate, Prentice-Hall, 2d ed., 1980.
Foster, William T., Argumentation and Debating, Arden Library, 1980.
Hensley, Dana and Prentice, Diana, Mastering Competitive Debate, Clark Publishing, 2d ed., 1982.
Sayer, James E., Argumentation and Debate, Alfred Publishing, 1980.

SPEECH OUTLINE

Construct a neat, complete sentence outline on this sheet, tear it out, and hand it to your instructor when you rise to speak. He may wish to write criticisms of the outline and speech in the margins.

Type of speech: _____ Name: _____

Number of words in outline: _____ Date: _____

Purpose of this speech: (What do you want your audience to learn, to think, to believe, to feel, or do because of this speech?) _____

_____

TITLE:

INTRODUCTION:

BODY:

CONCLUSION:

Instructor's comments may concern choice of topic, development of ideas, organization, language use, personal appearance, posture, physical activity, sources, and improvement.

(Write sources of information on back of sheet)

SOURCES FROM LITERATURE

Fill out source requirements completely.
Write "none listed" if an author's name or copyright date is not listed.

1. Author's name _____

    Title of book or magazine used _____

    Title of article in above book or magazine _____

    Chapter and/or pages read _____

    Date of above publication _____

2. Author's name _____

    Title of book or magazine used _____

    Title of article in above book or magazine _____

    Chapter and/or pages read _____

    Date of above publication _____

3. Author's name _____

    Title of book or magazine used _____

    Title of article in above book or magazine _____

    Chapter and/or pages read _____

    Date of above publication _____

INTERVIEW SOURCES

1. Person interviewed _____ Date of interview _____

    His position, occupation, and location _____

    Why is he a reliable source? Be specific _____

    _____

2. Person interviewed _____ Date of interview _____

    His position, occupation, and location _____

    Why is he a reliable source? Be specific _____

    _____

PERSONAL EXPERIENCE OF SPEAKER

1. Tell (1) when, (2) where, and (3) conditions under which you became an authority on subject matter in

    your speech _____

    _____

    _____

Chapter 37

RADIO AND TELEVISION SPEAKING

Question: *Should "beginners" use gestures?*

Answer: *Yes, from the start. Use what comes naturally and follow your instructor's advice.*

This speech is due:

Time limits: See your instructor for the exact time.

Speaking notes: Unless your instructor directs otherwise, you will write out your speech word for word. A copy of your speech should be in your instructor's hands at least one day before you are scheduled to speak.

Sources of information: Two or more. List them at end of your written speech.

Outline of speech: None is required for instructor.

PURPOSE OF RADIO AND TELEVISION SPEAKING

If one understands preparation and presentation of radio and television speech through first-hand knowledge and experience, he is much freer to evaluate and appreciate it as well as actually to participate in it. Real experience in studios provides at least an acquaintance. Such experience should enlighten and interest all speech students. It will pose real problems while answering many questions for all who take part.

Special note to the instructor:

The instructor may arrange with a local broadcasting company for time at their studios. He will reserve two rooms, one with a microphone from which to broadcast, the other in which to seat the class to receive the broadcasts and write criticisms on them at the conclusion of each speech. Even though the talks will not go on the air, this experience will be practical. Television studios may be arranged similarly. If real studios are not available, the school auditorium or other suitable rooms and loudspeaker systems may be substituted. By speaking behind a curtain or off-stage and using a microphone while seating the class in the auditorium or an adjoining room excellent results may be obtained.

EXPLANATION OF RADIO AND TELEVISION SPEAKING

Radio and television speech is that which is broadcast by means of radio or television. It may be dramatization, debate, discussion, or any of the many different types of speech. Its chief characteristics are its strict adherence to definite time limits and language usage suitable to an audience of average people. Generally such speeches

are read, which permits a person to meet these requisites of time and diction. The requirements of these mediums of public speaking are: a pleasing voice, proper speech construction, good English, correct pronunciation, clear enunciation, desirable appearance, stage presence, and cooperation of all who make the broadcast. Willingness to rehearse and promptness at the studio are of major importance. The person who is tardy or who arrives only five minutes before time to go on the air has no business near a studio.

SUGGESTED TOPICS FOR RADIO AND TELEVISION SPEAKING

1. Politics
2. Education
3. Schools
4. Hunting
5. Wild Life
6. Travel
7. Sports
8. Curricula
9. Aeronautics
10. Personality
11. Recreation
12. Marriage
13. Population
14. Government
15. Courtship
16. Automobiles
17. Atomic Power
18. Crime
19. Religion
20. Speaker's Choice

HOW TO CHOOSE A TOPIC FOR RADIO OR TELEVISION SPEAKING

Follow all of the principles set up for selecting any subject but keep in mind that a radio or television audience is the most diverse and varied in the world. Hence, unless you deliberately intend your speech for a limited group of persons, you will select a topic that can be presented to cross sections of listeners.

HOW TO PREPARE A RADIO OR TELEVISION SPEECH

All principles involving the preparation of the type of speech you intend to present apply here. It will be wise to do review work regarding your speech, whether it be informative, a eulogy, a goodwill speech, or any other kind of speech. After deciding what kind of speech you will present, prepare it by giving special attention to details and correctness. No excuses can be offered for errors when you have a written copy lying before you. It should be typed double-space for easy reading.

The final preparation should be the submission of your speech to the instructor for approval. After the preparation is completed, numerous rehearsals will be required before you are ready to step before the microphone. If possible you should practice with a microphone while a friend listens critically and offers suggestions for improvement. The use of a recording machine for practice will add greatly to the quality of your speech. If desirable, after several rehearsals, you may write time signals in the margins of your paper to tell you where you should be at the end of two, three, or four minutes, etc. These may be checked with the studio clock while you present your speech.

HOW TO PRESENT A RADIO OR TELEVISION SPEECH

Ordinarily, these speeches are presented with the thought that the audience will be scattered far and wide throughout the nation, possibly the world. They may be congregated in groups of two, three, four, or there may be only one person in a home. Your presentation should be so tempered that it meets all situations. If you ask yourself how you would speak were you to step before these small groups of people in person, your type of presentation becomes quite clear. It should be remembered that only your voice will be heard. This means that enough animation, clarity, force, and emphasis are needed to give interest. If you utilize television, then of course you are in full view for all to see and hear. This calls attention to posture, gestures, bodily action, and appearance.

In presenting your speech avoid rustling your paper in any way. Do not cough, sneeze, clear your throat, or shout into the mike. In radio speaking keep a uniform distance from the mike all the time. This will prevent fading or sudden increase in volume. If you feel like gesturing, go ahead. It will add life to your speech. Just be sure to talk into the microphone, with or without gestures. If you stand about ten inches from it you will be close enough provided the mechanism is sensitive. The best plan is to rehearse with a live microphone and thus be fully prepared. (If it is desirable each speaker may be assigned to another person who will introduce him. This will add realism to the project.)

In television speech various kinds of mechanical devices are used to give the impression the speaker is looking directly at the viewer although in reality he may be reading his speech. Microphones are kept out of camera range or may be in full view depending on the program. Should you be scheduled to speak on television, inquire ahead of time at the studio regarding the clothes that will look best, facial make-up, use of jewelry, what signals the manager will give, how to identify and respond to the "live" camera, and numerous other details, especially those concerning the stage crew. A visit to a television station will reveal many methods utilized to make speeches more effective when telecast. Become acquainted with them.

IMPROVE YOUR VOCABULARY

Insatiable – (ĭn-sā'shŭh-bl) a. Not satiable; not to be sated or satisfied; unappeasable; unsatisfied; not to be gratified; unquenchable, unslaked. Example: Her appetite was insatiable.

See – This verb has long called for a rest; let's oblige. How about a synonym. Examples are: observe, perceive, understand, comprehend, vision, envision, have a concept of, have insight, anticipate.

BIBLIOGRAPHY FOR RADIO AND TELEVISION SPEAKING

Chester, Giraud and Others, Television and Radio, Prentice-Hall, 5th ed., 1978.
Edmonds, I. G. and Gebhardt, W. H., Broadcasting for Beginners, Holt, Rinehart & Winston, 1980.
Evans, Elwyn, Radio - A Guide to Broadcasting Techniques, Transatlantic Arts, 1978.
McLeish, Robert, The Technique of Radio Production, Focal Press, 1978.
Orik, Peter B., Broadcast Copywriting, Allyn & Bacon, 1978.
Peigh, Terry D. and Others, The Use of Radio in Social Development, Community & Family Study Center, 1979.
Rider, John R., Your Future in Broadcasting, Rosin Press, 1978.
Smythe, Ted C. and Mastroianni, G. A., ed. Issues in Broadcasting Radio, TV, Cable, Mayfield Pub., 1975.
Stasheff, Edward and Others, The Television Program: Its Direction and Production, Hill & Wang, 5th ed., 1976.

Chapter 38

THE RADIO PLAY

Question: *What should you do if you run out of breath?*

Answer: *Pause and take a breath. Slow down and breathe deeper.*

This production is due:

Place of production is:

Time limits: See your instructor for exact time limits. Fifteen minutes should be adequate. Whatever it is, the variance should not be more than thirty seconds.

PURPOSE OF THE RADIO PLAY

A radio play will provide great enjoyment and add much to a person's background and experience. It will acquaint students with numerous problems relative to this type of production. It will build confidence in those who participate and give them improved stage poise. It offers an opportunity for self-expression not presented before. Sometimes students show a marked personality improvement after participation in dramatic productions. It is for these reasons that this experience is suggested.

EXPLANATION OF A RADIO PLAY

A radio play is a dramatic production for radio broadcast. It is characterized by musical backgrounds, involved sound effects, time limits, and lack of stage action by the players. The various parts are read, rather than memorized. An announcer is used to narrate or describe, according to the requirements of the drama. The purpose of radio drama is largely that of entertainment, although the purpose may be altered to suit any type of occasion and audience.

Requirements for a radio play are these: a cast, a director, a play, and an announcer, music and sound effects. The coordination of all these constitutes the play.

Occasions for radio plays are innumerable. Practically every station produces them in one form or another.

SUGGESTIONS FOR SELECTING RADIO PLAYS

Under your instructor's supervision, visit your school library and/or your dramatics department. Secure copies of different plays, read a number of them, and assist in selecting one or more for radio production.

It is probable that the selected play will have to be edited, cut considerably, or rewritten for radio adaptation. It might be helpful to ask your English or dramatics teachers for assistance. Further help can be secured by visiting a local radio station. The chances are that the staff at the radio station will supply you with some excellent scripts. If not, you should write to any of the large broadcasting companies for help. They are usually very willing to give free materials of good quality.

HOW TO PREPARE A RADIO PLAY

It should be kept in mind that you are not expected to be professional in this production. However, you are expected to do your best.

The following things must be done:

1. Be sure that radio studios or a loud speaking unit is available.

2. The instructor will appoint (or use some other method) a student director or chairman for each play.

3. Casts must be chosen. They should not be too large (four or five persons as a maximum) or difficulty in broadcasting may be encountered. In casting the players, it is desirable to select persons who have definite contrasts in voice so that listeners may identify them easily.

4. Narrators or announcers must be designated. They should prepare their own scripts in conjunction with those of the players.

5. Sound effects technicians must be designated and their equipment assembled. Considerable experimentation should be conducted until the desired effects are attained. Practice in timing sounds is extremely important. A door may slam too soon, or other sounds happen too late, if care is not exercised.

6. Scripts for the players may be secured by copying the various parts from the play books. This should be done only if a play is being produced for the class audience; otherwise, copyrights may be violated. If desirable, each group may write and produce its own play.

7. All players must follow the director's instructions willingly, regardless of any personal differences in interpretations.

8. Many rehearsals must be scheduled and held. For all practical purposes they should be conducted with a live microphone when possible.

HOW TO PRESENT A RADIO PLAY

The entire presentation must be a coordination of all the characters, sound effects, music, announcing, and timing so that they become a unit. Every detail should be so well-planned and worked out that there are no weak spots, breaks, or embarrassing silences.

Successful presentation demands close attention to scripts and cues, and absolute quiet from all players not engaged in speaking or producing sound effects. Special attention should be given to the mechanics of production, such as distance from the microphone and turning from it to create an illusion of distance. Rustling papers, careless whispers, clearing the throat, coughing, and incorrect reading must be avoided.

Players must read their parts in such a way that they impart the naturalness and ease of everyday, normal speaking individuals. Characters must be made to live each time a player reads, and the reading must seem to be a particular character caught on life's stage for a few moments.

The timing should be executed to the point of perfection. This can be done successfully by using scripts which are marked to show just how far the play should have progressed at the end of three, five, ten minutes, . . .

The director should use prearranged signals to indicate to the actors how the performance is progressing. These signals are well established among radio personnel and should be used. The more basic ones are listed in the following order:

1. Get ready or stand by – This is a warning signal which may be used to precede other cues. Its most general use is to warn the performers of the first cue which will place the program on the air. This stand-by cue consists of raising the arm vertically above the head.

2. Cue – The cue is the green light or go ahead signal which tells any member of the cast to execute whatever should be done at a particular moment. The actor will know what to do because the script will tell him. The cue consists of pointing to the actor who is to execute it. It should be made from the stand-by position by lowering the arm to horizontal and pointing to the person who is to execute the cue.

3. Speed up – If the director wishes the cast or any person in it to pick up the tempo, he indicates this by rotating an index finger clockwise. The speed of the rotating finger will indicate whether to speed up just a little or a great deal.

4. Slow down – The signal to stretch the time or slow the tempo is indicated by a movement which appears as though the director were stretching a rubber band between his two hands. The amount and manner of stretching will show how much slowing down is needed.

5. On the nose – When the director touches the tip of his nose with his index finger he means that the program is running on time.

6. To move closer to the microphone – To indicate this action the hand is placed in front of the face, palm inward.

7. To move away from the microphone – To incate this action the hand is placed before the face, palm outward.

8. To give more volume – The signal for more volume is made by extending the arm, palm upward, then raising the hand slowly or quickly to indicate how much volume is wanted.

9. To give less volume – The signal for less volume is made by extending the arm, palm down, and lowering the hand quickly or gently, depending on how much the volume should be decreased.

10. Everything is okay – This signal is a circle made with the index finger and thumb while extending the hand toward the performers.

Whenever given it means that as of that moment all is going well.

11. Cut – The cut signal is given by drawing the index finger across the throat. It means that the director wants somebody or something to stop. It may pertain to sound effects, crowd noises, or something else.

IMPROVE YOUR VOCABULARY

Assuage – (ă-swāj') v. To ease the feelings, to lessen or to allay, to soothe. Example: It is difficult to assuage the grief of a bereaved parent.

Do – This verb is called on for much, too much, work. Try using a synonym for greater effectiveness. Examples are: perform, perpetuate, affect, fulfill, finish, create, commit, consummate, achieve, actualize, accomplish, etc.

BIBLIOGRAPHY FOR THE RADIO PLAY

Brodkin, S. and Pearson, E., On The Air: A Collection of Radio and Television Plays, Scribner, 1976.
Hackett, Walter, Radio Plays for Young People, Plays, Inc., 1964.
Olfson, Lewy, Radio Plays of Famous Stories, Plays, Inc., 1969.
Olfson, Lewy, Radio Plays from Shakespeare, Plays, Inc., 1958.
Poteet, G. H., Comp., Published Radio, Television and Film Scripts: A Bibliography, Whitson Publishers, 1975.

NAME _____ DATE _____

(Ch. 33) 234. The purpose of a panel discussion is:

    (a) to change peoples' minds

    (b) to present unknown evidence to those present

    (c) to discuss issues without anger

    (d) to try to solve a problem

(Ch. 33) 235. A panel member's most valuable asset is:

    (a) much research

    (b) much reliable information to contribute

    (c) an insistence that various facts are most important

    (d) openmindedness and a willingness to consider other viewpoints

(Ch. 33) 236. (Double reverse) Members of a panel: (mark correct answers)

    (a) should gather much information

    (b) should consider all information submitted to the panel

    (c) should not give up their own ideas arrived at by research and study before meeting as a panel

    (d) should contact other panel members before they meet to get support for ideas they plan to submit

(Ch. 33) 237. It is advisable to limit the maximum number of panel members to how many persons besides the chairman?

    (a) 2-3   (b) 3-4   (c) 4-5   (d) 5-6

(Ch. 33) 238. When a panel meets, the members: (mark correct thinking only)

    (a) should withhold key information to be used only when it will support their ideas

    (b) should listen only to information that supports their point of view

    (c) should present special information they have researched only when forced to do so to defeat a bad point of another member

    (d) should pool their knowledge

(Ch. 33) 239. A good way to seat a panel is: (one answer)

    (a) in a semi-circle with the chairman in the middle

    (b) in a circle with the chairman joining the circle

    (c) in a straight line with the chairman at one end

(Ch. 33) 240. In a panel discussion the points under discussion develop in a certain order. The first thing to do is:

    (a) limit the subject if it is too broad

    (b) select one tentative solution

    (c) discuss the causes of the problem under discussion

    (d) define the terms of the problem you are going to discuss

(Ch. 33) 241. (Illegal motion) Since a panel discussion proceeds in a certain order which one of the following three steps will be considered before the other two? (these steps are not necessarily the first three in a discussion)

    (a) discuss the causes   (b) discuss the effects   (c) arrive at several tentative solutions

(Ch. 33) 242. The word "versatile" means: (mark correct answers)

    (a) being quite stubborn   (b) being able to do many things easily

    (c) being quite determined and not easily discouraged

    (d) easy to adjust to new situations

(Ch. 33) 243. (Blockbuster) Synonyms for the word "swell" are: (mark correct answers)

    (a) inimitable   (b) juicy   (c) sweet   (d) gorgeous   (e) costly   (f) beautiful
    (g) priceless   (h) matchless   (i) tremendous   (j) superlative   (k) peerless

(Ch. 33) 244. Is the word "versatile" correctly used in the following sentence? "A versatile person usually can do very little in strange circumstances."

    (a) yes   (b) no

(Ch. 34) 245. (Judgment call) When a symposium is used as a discussion method the members: (one answer)

    (a) all discuss completely different unrelated subjects

    (b) all discuss the same subject

    (c) all discuss different aspects of the same general subject

(Ch. 34) 246. In a symposium of three speakers each member could: (mark correct answers)

    (a) give an informative speech on different aspects of a general subject

    (b) choose to support his point of view of a general subject

    (c) give a different kind of speech such as to inform, to stimulate, to convince on a general subject

(Ch. 34) 247. After symposium speakers have all presented their individual speeches how many of the following procedures may be in order?

    (a) symposium members may form a panel and discuss the speeches they have just completed

    (b) symposium members, after forming a panel, may answer questions from the audience as in a forum

    (c) symposium members, after completing their individual speeches in the symposium, may immediately open the meeting to questions from the audience as in a forum

    (d) all procedures noted in answers (a), (b) and (c) are correct except (b)

(Ch. 34) 248. Synonyms for the word "redolent" are:

    (a) penetrating   (b) spicy   (c) exciting   (d) odorous   (e) rosy   (f) blooming

    (g) balmy   (h) aromatic   (i) fragrant

(Ch. 34) 249. (Blockbuster) Synonyms for the word "sure" are:

    (a) maybe   (b) clearly   (c) possibly   (d) decidedly   (e) certainly   (f) perhaps

    (g) gladly   (h) assuredly   (i) assume   (j) actually   (k) undeniably

    (l) conclusively   (m) unmistakably

(Ch. 35) 250. A lecture forum may be how many of the following?

    (a) to inform   (b) to stimulate   (c) to convince   (d) to entertain

(Ch. 35) 251. A lecture forum does not require the speaker to be quite as thoroughly informed as in a speech with no forum because he can clear up most points during the question period:

    (a) true   (b) false

(Ch. 35) 252. (Face mask) After a speaker in a lecture forum concludes his prepared speech he (or the chairman) should do how many of the following before beginning the forum period?

    (a) tell the audience they may ask questions about anything they wish

    (b) ask the audience to confine their questions to material presented in the lecture

    (c) tell the audience to ask questions but not make speeches

    (d) if short speeches are to be permitted advise the audience of this fact but also tell them they must limit their remarks to no more than three minutes or some other specified time

(Ch. 35) 253. In a lecture forum before the forum begins, the audience should be told the exact time the question period will last. (mark what is correct)

    (a) true   (b) false

    (c) however, when the question period time runs out the chairman may extend it if the audience wants more time

(Ch. 35) 254. Mark synonyms or meanings for the word "criterion":

(a) standard – a standard for judging   (b) a test   (c) a designation   (d) gauge

(e) a measure   (f) a proof   (g) a rule   (h) a yardstick

(Ch. 35) 255. (Blockbuster) Mark synonyms for the word "complain":

(a) grunt   (b) tense   (c) repine   (d) withdraw   (e) remonstrate

(f) grumble   (g) deny   (h) growl   (i) murmur   (j) retreat   (k) croak

(l) grieve

(Ch. 36) 256. A debate team may have how many speakers? (mark correct answers)

(a) one   (b) two   (c) three

(Ch. 36) 257. In conventional debating using two persons on a team: (mark correct answers)

(a) the affirmative team speaks first – opens the debate

(b) the affirmative team closes the debate – speaks last

(c) the negative team speaks first in rebuttal

(d) the negative team speaks third when main speeches are being presented

(Ch. 36) 258. (Short gain) The three stock issues in a debate are: (mark three answers)

(a) expense   (b) desirable   (c) enforcement   (d) practical   (e) need

(f) unconstitutional

(Ch. 36) 259. An affirmative team must "prove" all three stock issues to win; however, a negative team

can win by disproving only one stock issue.

(a) true   (b) false

(Ch. 36) 260. As a rule a certain speaker "defines the terms" in a debate. Which speaker does it?

(a) first affirmative   (b) first negative

(c) second affirmative   (d) second negative

(Ch. 36) 261. (Blockbuster) Mark synonyms for the word "propitious":

(a) desirable   (b) promising   (c) hindrance   (d) lofty   (e) opportune

(f) obstructing   (g) fortunate   (h) expeditious   (i) favorable   (j) companionable

(Ch. 36) 262. Mark all synonyms for the word "trip":

(a) going   (b) pilgrimage   (c) places   (d) expedition   (e) tour   (f) voyage

(g) ship   (h) passage   (i) excursion   (j) cruise   (k) ocean liner   (l) train

(m) airplane   (n) journey

(Ch. 37) 263. A radio or television speech is different from other speeches as follows: (mark correct answer)

(a) it has unspecified time limits

(b) it has definite and strict time limits

(c) radio or television speaking uses language adapted to well-educated people, not the average person

(d) radio or television speeches are usually read

(Ch. 37) 264. (Field goal attempt) Mark all correct statements that follow, regarding radio or television speaking:

(a) a pleasing voice is important

(b) correct grammar is not a basic requirement

(c) how you pronounce a word doesn't matter because speech patterns vary widely in a radio or television audience

(d) clear enunciation is desirable

(e) arriving five minutes before you go on the air or on camera is suitable

(f) rehearsal is not necessary or wanted for radio or television speaking because speeches are read

(Ch. 37) 265. Radio or television copy should be double-spaced and typed.

(a) true   (b) false

(Ch. 37) 266. It is often a good idea to write time signals in the margins of your paper to indicate where you should be at the end of one, two, three, four minutes, etc., if speaking on radio or television.

(a) partially true   (b) true   (c) partially false   (d) false

(Ch. 37) 267. (Blockbuster) Mark synonyms or meanings for the word "insatiable":

(a) over-indulge   (b) unslaked   (c) hungry   (d) unquenchable   (e) appetizing

(f) unappeasable   (g) not to be sated   (h) not to be satisfied   (i) devouring

(j) rapacious

(Ch. 37) 268. Mark synonyms or meanings for the word "see":

(a) eyes   (b) get   (c) anticipate   (d) have insight   (e) have a concept

(f) interrogate   (g) envision   (h) perceive   (i) observe   (j) understand

(k) comprehend   (l) vision

(Ch. 38) 269. A radio play is usually for entertainment although its purpose may be altered to suit any type of occasion and audience.

(a) true   (b) false

(Ch. 38) 270. (Roughing the kicker) Requirements for a radio play are: (mark correct answers)

    (a) a cast   (b) a director   (c) a play   (d) an announcer   (e) music

    (f) sound effects   (g) footlights   (h) a curtain   (i) an orchestra

(Ch. 38) 271. A radio play cast should normally not exceed how many characters? (one answer)

    (a) 2-3   (b) 3-4   (c) 4-5   (d) 5-6   (e) 6-7   (f) 7-8

(Ch. 38) 272. Mark the following statements that are true about a radio play:

    (a) characters should have definite voice contrasts

    (b) narrators and/or announcers should prepare their own scripts

    (c) sound effects technicians should assemble their own equipment

    (d) rehearsal for timing sounds is not necessary

(Ch. 38) 273. Scripts for radio-play characters may be secured by copying various parts from play books on two conditions: (mark two answers)

    (a) the play must be produced for a public audience

    (b) copyrights must not be violated

    (c) the number of characters must be equally divided as to sex

    (d) the play must be produced for a classroom audience only

(Ch. 38) 274. (Kickoff) When the director (radio play) raises his arm vertically above his head he means:

    (a) begin the play   (b) stop the sound effects   (c) get ready or stand by

(Ch. 38) 275. (Punt return) When the director (radio play) lowers his arm from vertical position and points to a certain character he means:

    (a) cease speaking at once   (b) execute the cue   (c) speak louder

(Ch. 38) 276. When the director (radio play) rotates his index finger clockwise he means:

    (a) move closer to microphone   (b) speak not so loud

    (c) speed up a little or a great deal according to how fast his finger rotates

(Ch. 38) 277. When the director (radio play) extends his arm, palm down, and lowers his hand quickly he means:

    (a) slow down your speech

    (b) lower your volume considerably

    (c) extend the play, you are going too fast

(Ch. 38) 278. Mark correct synonyms or meanings for the word "assuage":

    (a) to increase the amount of   (b) to decrease gradually   (c) to soothe

    (d) to ease the feelings   (e) to lessen or to allay

(Ch. 38) 279. (Blockbuster) Mark synonyms for the word "do":

    (a) perform   (b) jump   (c) achieve   (d) vault   (e) affect   (f) strain

    (g) create   (h) fulfill   (i) commit   (j) depend   (k) perpetuate   (l) linger

    (m) actualize   (n) accomplish

STUDENT SPEECH APPRAISALS

One part of a speech course is that which provides a student the opportunity to listen to a speech and to evaluate it. To appraise a speech is especially helpful because a student becomes a more careful listener, which enables him to better judge the worth of a speech.

The form shown below is a sample speech appraisal form which the instructor may duplicate for class use and which the student is to fill out at the instructor's direction. One-half to one-third of the class depending on its size, may be assigned to write criticisms for an individual speaker. At the conclusion of each speech, those persons who write criticisms will pass them to the instructor. (By doing this, the criticisms of each speaker will not have to be sorted later in order to place them in one group.) As soon as the appraisals have been examined by the instructor, he will give them to the speaker so that he may study them and thus learn just what his audience thought of him as a speaker.

From time to time throughout the course the instructor will assign certain speeches which will be appraised by the students.

- -

SPEECH APPRAISAL

The student listener should conscientiously complete this form and hand it to the instructor to study before he gives it to the speaker.

SPEAKER _____ DATE _____

SUBJECT _____

	Poor	Very Weak	Weak	Fair	Adequate	Good	Very Good	Excellent	Superior	Write Comments
	1	2	3	4	5	6	7	8	9	
1. Introduction										
2. Clarity of purpose										
3. Choice of words.										
4. Bodily action-gesture-posture . .										
5. Eye contact & facial expression .										
6. Vocal expression										
7. Desire to be understood.										
8. Poise & self-control										
9. Adapting material to audience . .										
10. Organization of material										
11. Conclusion. . . :										

J. Thomas Savage

THE

Text by J. Thomas Savage

CHARLESTON

Photography by N. Jane Iseley

INTERIOR

LEGACY PUBLICATIONS
A SUBSIDIARY OF PACE COMMUNICATIONS, INC.
GREENSBORO, NORTH CAROLINA

THIS BOOK WOULD NOT HAVE BEEN POSSIBLE
WITHOUT THE KINDNESS AND GENEROSITY
OF THE MANY OWNERS OF HOUSES,
BOTH PRIVATE AND PUBLIC, WHO GRACIOUSLY
ALLOWED US TO VISIT AND PHOTOGRAPH.
THE AUTHOR AND PHOTOGRAPHER ARE DEEPLY GRATEFUL
FOR THEIR COOPERATION AND HOSPITALITY.

TEXT © 1995 BY J. THOMAS SAVAGE
PHOTOGRAPHS © 1995 BY N. JANE ISELEY

DESIGN: JAIMEY EASLER
EDITOR: SHERYL KRIEGER MILLER
PROOFREADER: CAROL S. MEDFORD
PHOTOGRAPHY COORDINATOR & STYLIST:
ALICE TURNER MICHALAK

ISBN 0-933101-16-3
LIBRARY OF CONGRESS
CATALOG CARD NUMBER: 94-77721

PRINTED IN ALTONA, MANITOBA, CANADA
BY D.W. FRIESEN

Charlestonians use a delightful phrase to describe people whose lineage is not deeply rooted in their city. Such persons are quite simply "from off." And yet, visitors from off have left us some of the most detailed descriptions of the grandeur of Charleston, Colonial America's fourth largest seaport after Boston, New York, and Philadelphia, and the Colonial South's only urban center. Few visitors failed to be impressed. "The people of Charleston live rapidly, not willingly letting go untasted any of the pleasures of life. Few of them therefore reach a great age," noted a German visitor who further observed, "Luxury in Carolina has made the greatest advance and their manner of life, dress, equipages, furniture, everything denotes a higher degree of taste and love of show and less frugality than in the northern provinces."

Not all visitors were uncompromising in their praise. For 25 days in 1773, the young Boston lawyer Josiah Quincy enjoyed the hospitality of the city, but took keen notes on the shortcomings of its inhabitants. He noted:

> *The inhabitants may well be divided into opulent and lordly planters, poor and spiritless peasants, and vile slaves. State, magnificence and ostentation, the natural attendants of riches are conspicuous among this people. Cards, dice, the bottle and horses engross prodigious portions of time and attention.*

Despite his criticisms, when all was seen and done, Josiah Quincy was forced to conclude, "In grandeur, splendor of buildings, decorations, equipages, numbers, commerce, shipping and indeed in almost everything it far surpasses all I ever saw or ever expected to see in America."

What was it about Charleston and the Carolina Lowcountry that drew such lavish praise from one so well acquainted with the grandees of Boston? How did the buildings and their decorations differ from those he knew elsewhere? Quincy's visit coincided with Charleston's golden age. Enjoying the largest per capita wealth of any Colonial American center,

Charleston's consumers invested their fortunes from mercantile shipping, rice, and indigo to create some of the finest interiors known in early America. Despite early settlement by a variety of ethnic groups including the Dutch, Irish, Scots, Sephardic Jews, Germans, and French Huguenots, Charleston by the mid-18th century was closely aligned with British culture. By 1740, Eliza Lucas Pinckney could write an English friend that "Charles Town the principle one in this province is a polite agreeable place, the people live very Gentille and very much in the English Taste."

The Englishness of Charleston taste is attributable to several factors: the constant arrival of both foreign artisans and imported consumer goods, the availability of imported design books relating to both architecture and furniture, and the experiences of Charlestonians traveling abroad. The survival of an order for British furniture and silver dated April 2, 1771, from Charleston planter Peter Manigault to his factor Benjamin Stead in London is a very telling document regarding the importation of luxury goods. Manigault writes:

> *Sir, Having at last built myself a good House after having lived sixteen years in a very bad one, I stand in need of some Plate and Furniture of which I enclose you a list. I have fixed the Prices of the different articles, but shall not mind your being a little under or over the mark. I will be glad to have them out as soon as possible and the plainer the better so that they are fashionable. If a War send them not without convoy and have them insured war or peace. I think that I may have enough in your hands to defray the Expense. If not you will advance what is wanting and I suppose the next crop of Indigo will pay for it. I suppose you will think either my wife or myself very extravagant. I should almost think so myself. If I had not seen Brewton and Ln. Smith's Bills for furniture and Plate which I assure you, are twice as large as that of yours etc.* —P.M.

The impact of Peter Manigault's imports on both fellow consumers and local artisans was almost immediate. In 1772, Charleston cabinet-maker Richard McGrath offered a number of goods for sale "which he will engage to be as good as any imported from Europe." In particular, he noted that he made "carved chairs, of the newest Fashion, splat Backs, with hollow seats and commode fronts, of the same Pattern as those imported by Peter Manigault, Esq."

Like many sons of Charleston's ruling elite, Manigault had been educated in England. In fact, Carolinians represented the largest contingent of American students in England during the late Colonial period, and undoubtedly their taste was affected by that experience. The patronage of British portrait painters alone by traveling Charlestonians is exemplary. Manigault himself was painted by court artist Allan Ramsey. Ralph Izard posed for West, Copley, and Zoffany, and Mrs. Izard was painted by Gainsborough.

Figure 1: Peter Manigault and Friends *by George Roupell, c. 1760. Courtesy, Winterthur Museum.*

Mr. and Mrs. Arthur Middleton sat for their monumental portrait in Benjamin West's London studio, and Mary Rutledge Smith had 15 sittings in George Romney's fashionable painting room in 1786. Back on home turf, Jeremiah Theus had a virtual monopoly on limning from his arrival in Charleston about 1735 until his death in 1774. In the end, he succumbed to the same pressures that plagued his fellow craftsmen as modish imports arrived almost daily. In an effort to please and enhance the status of his clients, Theus turned to British mezzotints for poses and costumes of the latest vogue to imbue his sitters with fashion-conscious attributes.

We may never be able to fully reconstruct the interiors these portraits graced. The tangible remains of furniture, woodwork, silver, ceramics, and paintings are only part of the whole picture. Gone are the "elegant white and gold cabriole sophas and chairs, covered with blue and white silk, Window Curtains to Match; one other set of Sophas and Chairs, covered with black and yellow Figures in Nun's Work in Silk" sold in 1774 with the other elaborate effects of Sir Egerton Leigh, the profligate descendant of one of the colony's English proprietary founders who left Charleston before the revolution. Gone, too, are the "tapestry, damask, stuff, chints or paper hangings for rooms" advertised for sale by cabinetmaker Thomas Elfe in 1751 following his procurement of "a very good upholsterer from London."

Posterity has preserved only one depiction of an 18th-century Charleston interior, an ink-and-wash drawing by George Roupell of Peter Manigault and friends enjoying a convivial gathering at Manigault's Goose Creek plantation, Steepbrook *(figure 1)*. Now in the collection of the Winterthur Museum, the c. 1760 drawing illustrates the imported glassware, ceramics, and silver listed in Charleston probate inventories of the period, including those owned by Manigault. A comparison of the furnishings inventoried at Steepbrook and Manigault's Charleston townhouse after his death in 1773 suggests something of a dichotomy between plantation and city life. The Steepbrook inventory indicates that it was commodious but plain. There are no window curtains listed and only one Scotch carpet valued at 10 pounds.

Four sets of chairs are listed: one dozen Windsor chairs and two double Windsors, one dozen mahogany chairs, seven walnut tree chairs with leather bottoms, and one dozen straw bottom chairs and two arm chairs.

The townhouse, by comparison, had carpets in abundance and bed curtains of the most fashionable British textiles, including "one suit Blue and White Bed Furniture containing 4 window and 4 bed curtains, head cloth, teaster, valons and bags with cords and tassels" valued at 100 pounds. The extensive list of mahogany furniture included two large bookcases that undoubtedly housed the parcel of books and catalogs listed at 3,000 pounds, the most valuable library in Colonial Charleston.

By the third quarter of the 18th century, Charlestonians had acquired an urban affinity. Unlike Virginians, whose great country houses provided handsome and primary seats during the pre-Revolutionary period, it has been argued that South Carolinians looked on their country estates as sources of wealth to support city mansions. By 1750, it would seem that a shift occurred when the energies and funds expended on baronial seats like Drayton Hall of 1738–1742 began to lessen in favor of city houses like the lost mansion of Charles Pinckney on Colleton Square, built between 1746 and 1750 and splendidly fitted out with fully paneled interiors, the great stairs with rope twists and brackets, and a second-story dining room with a 14-foot cove ceiling.

The majority of Charleston's great and modest townhouses took one of two forms: the single house or the double house. The traditional Charleston single house was a typical single-pile Georgian house turned sideways to the street in response to narrow city lots and the climatic conditions of the area. Frequently combining a business function in the street-front, ground-floor room, living quarters for the occupants were located behind the shop and on the floors above. Piazzas were often incorporated or added later to provide outdoor living spaces as well as shade on the windowed facade. John Drayton described this characteristic housing unit in 1802: "The houses are, for the most part, of one or two stories. Piazzas are generally attached to their southern front, as well for the convenience of walking therein during the day as for preventing the sun's too great influence on the interior part of the house."

The double house was usually a five-bay house of a form well known in port cities on both sides of the Atlantic. Two rooms wide and deep with an intersecting passage on the first floor, the second-floor passage was truncated to allow communicating reception rooms on the street front of the second floor. Research on room nomenclature for the 18th century suggests that the larger of these rooms was most often called the dining room, while the smaller of the two served as principal drawing room. Bedchambers occupied the back, garden-front rooms on this floor, where the level of interior finish was more in keeping with nonceremonial private usage. Likewise, on the first floors, the front rooms tended to be more splendidly finished parlors, while the back, private spaces were often given over to use as libraries and butler's pantries or "steward's rooms."

These two basic house types persisted into the 19th century when they were joined by more complex Neoclassical variations incorporating projecting bays, elliptical rooms, and tri-part plans. The Nathaniel Russell and Joseph Manigault houses are both excellent examples of Charleston's Federal period mansions, designed for increasingly complex modes of entertainment and social interaction including balls and musicales. If Gabriel Manigault was Charleston's preeminent designer of such houses, his wife, Margaret Izard Manigault, was certainly the period's most delightful chronicler. Describing a party given by Mrs. Lucretia Radcliffe to honor Arthur Middleton and his new wife Alicia Russell, Mrs. Manigault wrote to her mother on March 12, 1809:

> *We have been very gay here lately. Many dances have been given—*
> *But none of the parties have been so pleasant as Mrs. Radcliffe's last.*
> *She had in the first place a musical party. That is the Miss Percys,*

Mrs. Smith Bee, & a Mrs. Hindeley, an English woman, (wife of an English merchant who is partner to Mr. Gregorie) who sings very well in a particular style, & accompanies herself delightfully on the Piano—were the chief performers. A little German sang two Italian songs accompanied by the Spanish guitar. He amused us with his affectation & conceit & said that he had determined to sing only one song, but that Mrs. Radcliffe was so anxious that he would oblige her with another. As soon as he had done, the fiddle, fife, & tambourine delighted the youthful crowd. After one dance, the elder part of the assembly had their time of pleasurable surprise— Gen'l Wilkinson's band charmed us with some well executed military pieces— during which we paced up & down the spacious Corridor which was brilliantly lighted.

When Lucretia Radcliffe died in 1821, her spectacular array of furnishings and ornaments was auctioned. Prior to the auction, a very thorough inventory of the house was taken, offering insight into its great beauty and expensive decoration. Valued at a staggering $600 in the drawing room were "1 sett curtains, hangings, drapery, cornices, pins compleat." Also inventoried with the town residence were over 35 slaves, many listed by skill and duties that enabled Mrs. Radcliffe's lavish hospitality. Thus we find among the house servants six carpenters, Jacob the coachman, Judy a cook, Rachael a pastry cook, Scipio a cook, Ned a hostler, Douglas a tailor, Peter a gardener, James the

Figure 2: Friends and Amateurs in Musick *by Thomas Middleton. Dated 1827. Courtesy, Gibbes Museum of Art.*

headwaiter, Sue a seamstress, Cooper a washerwoman, and sadly and lastly, Peter "infirm and nearly blind." It is impossible to understand the workings of these great sociable houses without knowledge of the slaves' contribution and the vast variety of skills needed to make them function.

The sociable nature of Arthur Middleton's household was captured by his brother Thomas in a delightful 1827 wash drawing called *Friends and Amateurs in Musick* (figure 2). A lengthy explanation on the back of the drawing in Thomas' hand explains that "a number of gentlemen friends and Amateurs in musick, frequently met at each others houses during the sultryness of a Summer afternoon to beguile away the time in listening to the soothing strains of their own music. I have to apologize for the representation of certain glasses both black and white on the table, but it was in vain to remonstrate." The effect of what Middleton called "respectable warmers of the blood" on the music was obvious: His friend on the far right plays not a cello but a guitar case! The picture is a valuable document for art historians as it depicts a sampling of Arthur Middleton's picture collection with a variety of painted subjects including religious, mythological, marine scenes, and landscapes. Above the sideboard hangs Benjamin West's portrait of the Middletons' father, Thomas. The depiction of rush-seated, painted "fancy" chairs is also noteworthy as few survive with documented Charleston histories despite appearing in inventories with great frequency.

Mid 19th-century eclecticism is represented in Charleston by numerous

Classical revival, Gothic revival, and Italianate structures. One of the best preserved examples is the Aiken-Rhett house, a veritable Pandora's box of the collecting interests of one accomplished family. Closed off room by room earlier this century, its comprehensive holdings were re-exposed for viewing only after 1975 when the property was acquired by The Charleston Museum. The Aikens were but one of many Charleston families who availed themselves of a European "grand tour" during the antebellum period. Such trips relieved the monotony of plantation life and exposed the travelers to the rich cultural resources of Europe unavailable even in the best American urban centers. South Carolinians were no doubt also fascinated by the complexity and sophistication of the Old World's social order. They returned home with mementos in the form of paintings and statuary with which to adorn their houses and elevate their neighbors. Recognizing the need for an art gallery to exist in a cultured community, the experiences of Charleston's grand tourists fostered a serious interest in art exhibitions that led to the founding of the Carolina Art Association in 1857.

The Civil War took a huge toll on Charleston architecture. Fires in both 1861 and 1865 leveled entire sections of the city. The loss of important interiors and furnishings cannot be quantified. Many of the city's residents took refuge during the assault on Charleston. In *Chronicles of Chicora Wood*, Elizabeth W. Allston Pringle records her family's removal from their townhouse that had been built by Nathaniel Russell in 1808:

It was a terrible undertaking to pack all that big, heavy furniture and get it away under stress. We found afterward that we had left many things of great value. At this moment, I remember especially two blue china Chinese vases, urn-shaped, which stood two feet high and were very heavy. It seemed impossible to get boxes and material to pack them and they were left. Daddy Moses remained alone to take charge of the house and garden.

Charleston's recovery from the war was slow, and many neighborhoods remained unrepaired well into the 1880s. In 1885, a cyclone hit the city, and in 1886 the great earthquake shook the Lowcountry destroying many buildings and damaging others. But Charleston persevered. With each disaster, the old houses were shored up and repaired.

The survival of Charleston's rich architectural legacy is usually attributed to poverty following the Civil War, and old sayings such as "too poor to paint and too proud to whitewash" lend credence to the statement. But that is only part of the story; poverty was accompanied by fierce pride and a protectionist attitude regarding family buildings and treasures. The Miles

Figure 3: *The second-floor drawing room of the 1769 Miles Brewton house photographed c. 1895. Used as the principal dining room in the 18th century, it had acquired the function of a drawing room in the 19th. Four of the suite of English upholstered "French" chairs c. 1770 are visible, each covered in a different textile. Edward Savage's 1792 full-length portrait of Mary Brewton Motte Alston hangs above the carved console bracket with pietra dura top. Courtesy, Historic Charleston Foundation.*

Brewton house *(figure 3)* had loving stewards in the Misses Frost, the three sisters who cherished the house and its contents, which they shared with "door guests" who received memorable tours from these ardent protectors of Charleston's heritage. When Standard Oil demolished the great house of Gabriel Manigault and others to provide space for two gasoline filling stations, there was considerable public outrage. Progress was threatening the very fabric of the city. Another threat came in the form of well-intentioned collectors and dealers who came south to buy antiques and entire rooms of Georgian paneling for installation in museum period rooms and private residences in the North and Midwest.

Such threats helped mobilize the preservation efforts of Charleston's citizenry. When the Joseph Manigault house was threatened by demolition in 1920, Susan Pringle Frost led the battle to save it, which spawned the founding of the Preservation Society of Charleston, then known as the Society for the Preservation of Old Dwellings. In 1929, the same organization assisted The Charleston Museum in the purchase of the Heyward-Washington house, which shortly thereafter became Charleston's first house museum. In 1947, the newly created Historic Charleston Foundation organized its first Festival of Houses, a spring tour of private houses that continues to raise preservation funds through the largess of homeowners. The great domestic interiors of the city were coming to be known by a wide audience who visited for the express purpose of viewing the architectural and artistic legacy preserved over generations.

In 1955, Historic Charleston Foundation under the leadership of Frances Ravenel Edmunds and Ben Scott Whaley acquired the Nathaniel Russell house. With very meager resources, it furnished the house to raise funds for preservation projects throughout the city. The decorating committee devoted countless hours as each carefully vetted object was thoughtfully placed. Lydia Bond Powell of the Metropolitan Museum of Art's American Wing was a frequent correspondent with the committee

Figure 4: The second-floor drawing room of the 1808 Nathaniel Russell House as furnished in the 1950s. Courtesy, Historic Charleston Foundation.

as they grappled with color schemes and scoured *Ackermann's Repository* for authentic curtain treatments. The rooms created in the 1950s are important milestones in the history of Colonial revival taste *(figure 4)*.

In *The Dwelling Houses of Charleston*, first published in 1917, Alice Ravenel Huger Smith wrote a passage that remains something of a credo for the preservationists and stewards of Charleston's built environment in the late 20th century:

Fortunately much remains in Charleston to mark a continuity in the character of its people as well as in its architecture. May it not therefore be hoped that what has accidentally been preserved may be long retained, and not marred by new and strange ideas, which, however suitable to places that have developed them, would be in Charleston merely imitation, and would perhaps destroy those very differences that make the place so interesting? It is not what is new, however but what is incongruous that should be avoided.

THE SOUTH PARLOR (*left*) ∼ The house built by merchant Miles Brewton is certainly among the finest surviving American townhouses of the Colonial period. The recent restoration has yielded considerable information about the transmission and emulation of British taste in the American colonies. The ceiling of the south parlor, for example, is now known to be imported papier-mâché, an easily exportable alternative to molded plasterwork. The door frieze carving is a veritable tour de force of the "Gothick" mode of Rococo design. It was executed by carver Ezra Waite whose bankruptcy notice appeared in the London *Gentleman's Magazine* for May 1764. He arrived in Charleston shortly thereafter to join the burgeoning community of British emigre craftsmen. The portrait over the 18th-century Dutch marquetry desk is by Thomas Sully (1783–1872) and depicts Mary Motte Alston Pringle (1803–1884), who inherited the house in 1839.

SOUTH PARLOR DETAIL (*below*) ∼ In the south parlor is a remarkable survival—the only known console table in a Colonial American house. During the recent restoration, ghost marks identifying its original location were found when the New England white pine woodwork was stripped of layers of paint. Under the paint is a layer of polished gesso, which calls to mind carver John Lord's advertisement for "gilding and all branches of house and furniture carving, in the Chinese, French, and Gothic tastes." The prints above the console table, which represent the story of the Prodigal Son, are in their original frames and may have been in the house in the 18th century.

The table is fitted with a pietra dura or hard stone top brought back by grand tour participants from Italy.

THE DINING ROOM (*right*) ~ This north parlor has a long history of use as a dining parlor. One of three imported marble chimneypieces in the house is found here. In 1767, while the house was under construction, John Ranier advertised, "A Parcel of Italian Marble Chimney Pieces of the newest fashion...." On the mantel and dining table are pieces from a large armorial service of Chinese export porcelain in a brown "Fitzhugh" pattern ordered by Charles Izard Manigault (1795–1874). The Manigault family arms on the porcelain were copied from a bookplate engraved by Samuel Clayton, an English engraver banished to Australia for counterfeiting. Having never seen a Native American, a feature of the Manigault arms, Clayton engraved a personage that resembles an Australian aboriginal. The painting in the overmantel depicts the ship *Mackinaw*, a square-rigged vessel owned by Ravenel & Company of Charleston.

THE LIBRARY (*below*) ~ The interior reflects the 18th-century use of architectural hierarchy in both room finish and use. Whereas the street-front rooms are fully paneled, those facing the garden have paneled chimney walls and plaster above the wainscot. In the library, a reproduction wallpaper with a contrasting border in a palmette design carefully replicates fragments of paper found during restoration. Above the mantel laden with miniatures of the Alston, Pringle, Horry, and Manigault families hangs a painting of the sloop *John Ravenel* in the Bay of Naples in the 1850s. Dutch delftware tiles lining the firebox were reproduced from fragments found when a later coal grate was removed.

In the stair passage is a mahogany linen press c.1810 attributed to Robert Walker, active in Charleston from 1795.

THE STAIRCASE (*left*) ⤳ Mahogany is used for virtually all elements of the Brewton house stair construction including the wainscoting and surround of the impressive Venetian window. As part of the processional route to the grand second-floor dining room, the landing is highly finished with Rococo papier-mâché wall appliques, gilded fillets in the coved ceiling, and a plaque representing the god Apollo with his lyre. An identical Apollo ceiling medallion survives in the entrance hall of Cottesbrooke in Northamptonshire, England, a Baroque country house of the early 18th century embellished with papier-mâché in the Rococo taste at mid-century. The pale blue finish of the cove ceiling is based on paint analysis of rag paper found attached to the papier-mâché fillets during conservation.

THE DRAWING ROOM (*following page*) ⤳ Used as a drawing room since the early 19th century, the second-floor long room of the Brewton house was originally intended as a setting for grand assemblies and dinners. On March 7, 1773, visiting New Englander Josiah Quincy Jr. dined here and recorded in his journal,

> *The grandest hall I ever beheld, azure blue satin window curtains, rich blue paper with gilt, machee borders, most elegant pictures, excessive grand and costly looking glasses etc.... At Mr. Brewton's side board was very magnificent plate: a very large exquisitely wrought Goblet, most excellent workmanship and singularly beautiful. A very fine bird kept familiarly playing over the room, under our chairs and the table, picking up the crumbs, etc. and perching on the window, side board and chairs: vastly pretty!*

An elegant imported chimneypiece in the Brewton house drawing room combines both Carrara and Siena marbles. The central plaque of a pastoral scene resembles the work of London carver Henry Cheere.

The suite of English upholstered "French" or "elbow" chairs dates to 1770 and may well be among the original furnishings of the room. Following a careful deupholstering process, they have been covered with azure blue silk damask based on tiny fibers found buried in the underupholstery. In 1771, Charleston upholsterer Richard Fowler offered "some very rich blue furniture damask for chairs." The gilded looking glass is a recent addition to the room commissioned by the present owners and carved by master craftsman John Bivins. ⤳ Above the marble mantel hangs a portrait of the builder, Miles Brewton (1731–1775), painted in London by Joshua Reynolds in 1756. As one of Charleston's mercantile elite, Brewton was part owner of eight commercial vessels and South Carolina's largest slave dealer. His 1759 marriage to Mary Izard brought him into the sphere of the leading planter families and aristocratic British officials. Lord William Campbell, South Carolina's last royal governor and the son of the fourth Duke of Argyll, married Mrs. Brewton's first cousin Sarah Izard in 1763. Lord and Lady Campbell were guests in Brewton's splendid townhouse while their leased house was readied for what proved to be a necessarily brief occupancy. Sadly, the Brewton family enjoyed the new house for a very brief period. In August 1775, Miles Brewton, his wife, and their children were lost at sea en route to Philadelphia to attend the second Provincial Congress. The portrait in

the center of the fireplace wall is of Dr. James Reid by Jeremiah Theus
(1716–1774). Dr. Reid's grandson, William Bull Pringle, occupied the
house from 1839 until his death in 1881.

THE CHANDELIER (*right*) ∾ The magnificent English cut-glass chandelier
is a rare survival of this 18th-century form and is arguably the earliest
glass chandelier to survive in an American domestic setting. It is possibly
the work of William Parker, London's pre-eminent chandelier manufacturer of the 1770s and 1780s. Parker supplied the Assembly Rooms at
Bath with glass chandeliers and enjoyed enormous patronage from the
English aristocracy. Bordering the cove ceiling is a gilt papier-mâché fillet,
the design of which was reconstructed from tiny fragments discovered in
an early rat's nest during architectural investigations. An identical fillet
was installed at the Wentworth house in Portsmouth, New Hampshire,
in the 18th century. Richard Fowler advertised, "rich double burnished
gold machee borders" in a 1771 Charleston newspaper.

THE LIBRARY *(right)* ⤳ Few houses enjoy the distinction of continuous ownership by the same family since the 18th century. Such is the case with the brick Neoclassical single house built by Daniel Ravenel about 1798 to replace an earlier structure on the city lot acquired by Mrs. Daniel Ravenel's ancestor, Isaac Mazyck, in 1710. Because of its unique chain of ownership, the Daniel Ravenel house represents the history and collecting interests of one Charleston family over almost three centuries. The library on the ground floor is a veritable museum of South Carolina history. Early books in the collection include several printed in 17th-century France and brought to South Carolina by early Huguenot settlers. Among the framed family documents are an 1838 letter from Joel R. Poinsett, Ambassador to Mexico, to Andrew Jackson recommending Daniel Ravenel for an appointment to the Naval Academy and one of the original copies of the South Carolina Ordinance of Secession.

THE DINING ROOM *(below)* ⤳ An American Empire sideboard c. 1840 from Houmas Plantation in Louisiana holds Ravenel family silver of the early to mid-19th century. The cupboard contains a variety of ceramics, all with family histories. On the second shelf from the bottom are pieces from the most extensive dinner service of Chinese export porcelain known to survive with a history of ownership in a Colonial American family. On the bottom shelf is a Wedgewood creamware plate from the service used by George Washington when he visited the Horry family at Hampton Plantation in 1791.

The dinner service, dating c. 1770, has a colorful, tobacco-leaf pattern and was owned by the Ravenel family.

THE DRAWING ROOM *(above)* ⤙ With fully paneled walls of painted cypress and an elaborate, composition decorated mantel, the second-floor drawing room upholds the urban tradition of having the principal reception room high above the street noise. A pair of English Neoclassical armchairs c. 1790–1800 may be part of the original furnishings of the room. Above an American Neoclassical card table with dolphin supports c. 1825 hangs John Beaufain Irving's 1857 painting *Sir Thomas More Taking Leave of His Daughter, Margaret Roper.* Irving (1825–1877) arrived in Germany in 1851 and was a student of Dusseldorf painter Emanuel Leutze. The Thomas More picture emphasizes the 19th-century liking for history pictures and was in the early collection of the Carolina Art Association.

DRAWING ROOM PAINTINGS *(left)* ⤙ Charles Fraser (1782–1860), best known as Charleston's most distinguished native miniature artist, had no training except that provided by Thomas Coram when Fraser was 13 years old. Fraser read law under John Julius Pringle for 11 years. In 1818, he pursued art as a career and enjoyed considerable patronage among Charlestonians as a miniature painter. In later life, perhaps due to failing eyesight, he devoted more time to oils of landscapes, still lifes, and literary themes.

SILVER SERVICE DETAIL *(above)* ⌐ A 19th-century American silver service once owned by Henry Ravenel is displayed in front of an unusual late Neoclassical sofa with eagle carving, probably made in New York c. 1825.

MANTEL DETAIL *(right)* ⌐ The composition ornament of the Ravenel house drawing room mantel would have been painted originally but has been cleaned to reveal the delicacy of this popular form of architectural embellishment.

THE DRAWING ROOMS *(preceding page)* ∼ Commanding a spectacular view of Charleston's historic harbor, the Robert William Roper house was completed by 1840 on two lots acquired by Roper, an enlightened planter and state legislator, in 1838. The vast double drawing rooms are characterized by floor length sash windows, providing access to the piazza and cast-iron balconies of the street front of the house. Furnished with a superlative collection of Neoclassical American furniture and decorative arts, noteworthy objects include a large set of curule or "Grecian cross" chairs attributed to the New York workshop of Duncan Phyfe (1768–1854). A reproduction carpet laid wall-to-wall in 19th-century fashion was copied from a document in the senate chamber of the old North Carolina State Capitol in Raleigh. Above the fireplace in the rear drawing room hangs Mather Brown's portrait of Charleston's great Revolutionary hero General William Moultrie (1730–1805).

THE DINING ROOM *(right)* ∼ Although no architect has been firmly credited with the design of the Roper house, circumstantial and stylistic evidence points to Charles F. Reichardt, who arrived in Charleston in 1836. A pupil of the great German proponent of the Greek revival, Karl Friedrich Schinkel, Reichardt designed such public buildings as the Charleston Hotel, Meeting Street Theater, and Guard House (all destroyed). ∼ The dining room chandelier and those in the other principal rooms were originally gas fixtures added after 1874 by the Rudolph Siegling family. A French porcelain centerpiece graces the Neoclassical dining table that, like the chairs around it, were made in Boston c. 1820.

THE STAIRCASE *(above)* ∾ The graceful curving staircase rises from a spacious entrance hall on the north side of the house, which allows connecting pairs of rooms on each of three floors. Decorative painter Robert Jackson created the trompe l'oeil parquetry patterns on the oak floor and re-created other popular 19th-century painted effects throughout the house.

THE CARD ROOM *(left)* ∾ The sabre leg chairs, pedestal breakfast table, and desk are all New York Federal-style pieces c. 1815. Framed documents in the card room relate to General William Moultrie (1730–1805) who commanded the palmetto fort on Sullivan's Island against the attack of British Admiral Sir Peter Parker in March 1776. The General Assembly named the fort in Moultrie's honor. A Brigadier General in the Continental Army, Moultrie served as governor of South Carolina from 1785 to 1787 and from 1792 to 1794.

MRS. WILLIAM HEYWARD HOUSE LIBRARY (*below*) ~ William Heyward's widow, Hannah Shubrick Heyward, is credited with the building of this substantial frame townhouse about 1789. A successful rice planter in her own right, Mrs. Heyward was the sister-in-law of Thomas Heyward, one of the South Carolina signers of the Declaration of Independence. There are architectural indications that the house may predate the Revolutionary War, and the apsidal south bay of the library is

MISS MARY SMITH HOUSE DRAWING ROOM (*below*) ~ In 1799, Josiah Smith built a three-story brick single house for his spinster daughter Mary, who lived here until her death in 1832. In the late 1960s, the house was purchased by Historic Charleston Foundation and moved 100 feet to the south of its original lot to protect it from demolition when a municipal auditorium was constructed. Unpretentious, original Federal woodwork provides a perfect foil for a collection of Continental objects.

an early 19th-century alteration intended as a Neoclassicizing feature. In 1870, the property was purchased by Augustine T. Smythe, a prominent lawyer in whose family the house remains today. In the 1920s, descendants of plantation owners met in the house for rehearsals of the Society for the Preservation of Spirituals, one of the premier efforts to preserve and record indigenous African-American songs of the Carolina Lowcountry. ~

French Directoire commodes flanking the fireplace support Italian marble obelisks. The 18th-century engravings of mythological subjects are Italian, and the ormolu mantel clock depicting a slave with a bale of cotton is late 18th-century Swedish. ~

PETER LEGER HOUSE LIBRARY (*below*) ~ One of the city's best preserved 18th-century single houses is that built by successful cooper Peter Leger c. 1759–1760 as a tenement. The level of interior finish and the fact that it was rented to Dr. Robert Wilson when completed confirms that Charleston's tenements or rental houses were quite often substantial and well finished. The hierarchy of room use in single houses usually designated the second-floor room overlooking the street as the best

THOMAS ROSE HOUSE DRAWING ROOM (*below*) ~ Having survived the great Charleston fire of 1740, the Thomas Rose house is one of the city's most important examples of early Georgian domestic architecture. Letters found in Belfast, Ireland, in 1988 indicate that Thomas Rose wrote his family in 1734 asking them to locate four workmen willing to immigrate to Charleston. The house was probably completed about 1735. The asymmetrical floor plan is typical of a merchant's house in both British and

parlor, whereas the room directly below functioned as a counting house, shop, or office. Today, the second-floor parlor of the Leger house is used as a comfortable library, its cypress woodwork stripped of centuries of paint to reveal the mellow grain of the wood, ironically a taste that would have been an anathema to the 18th-century occupants who did not regard cypress as a "show" wood.

American port cities. Occupying the entire front of the second floor, the magnificent drawing room would originally have been a dining parlor and is fully paneled in native cypress. The only architectural alteration since the second quarter of the 18th century is the diminutive mantel in the Neoclassical taste added about 1800. A handsome collection of English 18th-century furniture is arranged on a magnificent animal Tabriz carpet. The painting above the mantel is of the children of Willoughby Wood painted by John Berridge, a follower of Sir Joshua Reynolds.

The garden front of the house is entered through a classical temple-form lodge—"Summer House" on an 1852 plat.

THE STAIRCASE *(right)* ∾ Gabriel Manigault (1758–1809), the beneficiary of generations of rice planting and wholesale trading, was able to indulge his passion for architecture. Having studied in Geneva and London, Gabriel had firsthand exposure to European Neoclassicism and is generally credited with introducing it into Charleston. For his brother Joseph, he designed one of Charleston's grandest and most elegant residences completed in 1803. As Roger Kennedy wrote, "In Manigault's work one can see in fully developed form, the curved staircase, the gentle, almost frail style of Charleston's silver age." A semicircular projection on the north side of the house contains the spectacular stair, lighted by an elegant Venetian window. The Manigault house is open for tours daily by The Charleston Museum.

THE BEDROOM *(following page, far right)* ∾ Recent paint research documented the unusual spattered wall finish in the primary bedchamber. Framed by the post of a Charleston Neoclassical bedstead c. 1800 is an extraordinary desk and bookcase of similar date, one of only two examples of this form known from Charleston. Made in four sections—cornice, bookcase, tambour desk, and base—the mahogany piece is richly inlaid with zebra wood, bocote, and satinwood. The breakfast table was made in New York c. 1800.

THE DINING ROOM *(right, top)* ∽ The dining room incorporates an apsidal end or projecting curvilinear bay, a classical feature often found in rooms intended for dining. The dinner service is of English Derby soft paste porcelain dating c. 1800. The magnificent centerpiece of 1816 is by Paul Storr (1771–1844) and illustrates the work of the English master silversmith in its most sculptured Regency perfection. An unidentified Charleston cabinetmaker produced the veneered sideboard about 1810, and the chairs, of New York manufacture c. 1820, descended in the family of Governor George Mathews of South Carolina. Records suggest that, after dinner, ladies retired to the drawing room, leaving the men to their cigars, spirits, and political conversation. Visitors found the local populace overwhelmingly hospitable. In his 1806–1808 travel diary, John Lambert recorded, "The wine flows in abundance and nothing affords them greater satisfaction than to see their guests drop gradually under the table after dinner."

THE CARD ROOM *(right, bottom)* ∽ A small room located on the second floor of the Manigault house has been furnished as a card room. A tri-part jib window gives access to the shaded second-story piazza beyond. While in Charleston in 1796–1797, the Duc de La Rochefoucauld-Liancourt observed, "It is against the excessive heat of summer that all calculations of construction are made. One does not boast in Charleston of having the most beautiful house, but the coolest." Through the arched doorway into the bedroom is a clothes press labeled by Robert Walker (1771–1833), a Scottish cabinetmaker who settled in Charleston by 1795 after working briefly in New York.   ∽∜∽

THE LIBRARY *(above)* ∽ On a quiet, brick-paved street stands the tall single house probably built by William Holmes following his purchase of the site in 1795. James Ancrum is known to have occupied the property in 1809, having sold the Colonel William Rhett house, which he inherited from his mother, a great-granddaughter of Colonel Rhett. The second-floor library is a quiet haven adorned with a Federal mantel with elaborate applied composition decoration. In the foreground is a handsome silver-covered cup crafted in 1757 by London silversmith Thomas Whipham and originally owned by the Porcher family of Huguenot planters.

THE PIAZZA *(right)* ∽ The marble paving of the piazza floor is both decorative and functional, enhancing its role as a cool retreat. In the 19th century, many Charleston piazzas were fitted with Venetian blinds and lattices to regulate light and heat and deter insects.

FIREPLACE DETAIL *(above)* ～ Lining the fireplace of the dining room are tin-glazed earthenware tiles made in Liverpool, England, by John Sadler and Guy Green between 1761 and 1770. Transfer printed tiles by Sadler and Green survive in several Charleston houses. Merchant John Edwards advertised in the February 1765 *South Carolina Gazette*, "Just imported, in the FAIR AMERICAN, John Minshal, Master from Liverpool … A quantity of neat copper-plate chimney tiles both black and red."

THE LIBRARY *(left)* ～ Builder William Elliot purchased the lot on which this classic early single house stands in 1729 and began construction shortly thereafter. The house survives remarkably intact with early Georgian wood-work. In the first-floor library, 26 layers of paint were removed to reveal mellow cypress paneling and early vertical sheathing, an evocative back-drop for 17th- and 18th-century pewter, brass, and blown-glass bottles. On the mantel is Jackfield black lead-glazed pottery, named for the village on the Severn River in England where it was made in the 18th century. ～

*F*eatures added by Alston include the piazza third story, a roof balustrade, and a parapet with his coat of arms.

THE DRAWING ROOMS *(preceding page)* ~ Charles Alston, a member of the well-established rice planting dynasty, purchased his spacious townhouse in 1838 from its original builder, merchant Charles Edmondston. Enlarged and enhanced by Alston in the fashionable Greek revival taste, the house provided an urban base for the family's pursuit of both intellectual and social diversions. Designed to take full advantage of sea breezes, the second-floor drawing rooms are equipped with pocket doors to create more intimate spaces. Above the fireplace is a pastel portrait of Susan Pringle Alston painted in Paris by Constant-Joseph Brochart (1816–1899). Around an American Neoclassical card table c. 1820 are chairs of similar date probably made in Philadelphia for either the Pringle or Alston family. The chandeliers are recent additions to the drawing rooms and are the products of the Cornelius Company of Philadelphia c. 1850. Still in family ownership, the Edmondston-Alston house is a house museum of Middleton Place Foundation.

THE DINING ROOM *(right)* ~ The dining room houses family furniture and silver, representing the taste for Neoclassicism from 1800 to 1850. On the New York sideboard c. 1800 are knife boxes of the same date and an 1850 silver service engraved with the Alston crest by Bailey and Company of Philadelphia. A richly carved and gilded girandole mirror with candle branches is thought to be English c. 1825. London silversmith William Elliot crafted the silver épergne with cut-glass bowls. ~

TABLE DETAIL *(above)* ～ Enjoying a spectacular view of Charleston harbor, the front windows originally opened to a mammoth portico with columns copied from the ancient Tower of the Winds. The great Charleston earthquake of 1886 toppled the columns, which were never replaced. Flanked by New England shield-back chairs c. 1800 is a Charleston-made card table c. 1770, part of the early furnishings of Hampton Plantation.

THE DRAWING ROOM *(left)* ～ William Ravenel (1806–1888) was a partner in Ravenel Bros. & Company, one of Charleston's largest antebellum shipping and cotton brokerage firms. Completed about 1845, the house is one of Charleston's greatest Greek revival mansions. Occupying the entire width of the second floor is the vast drawing room with a fireplace at each end, possibly the largest domestic reception room in the city. The room is filled with an enviable collection of American and English furniture and Chinese export porcelain. The chest on chest, or double chest, is a fine Charleston piece of c. 1770. ～

THE DRAWING ROOM *(left)* ⁓ Patrick Duncan, a wealthy Scottish tallow chandler, began acquiring lots in the soon-to-be-fashionable suburb of Cannonsborough in 1798. The area provided opportunities for Charleston's planters and merchants to build substantial villas above the densely populated lower peninsula and was close enough to enjoy Charleston's social season. Mystery still surrounds the actual construction date and architect of Duncan's regency villa. The house has frequently been linked with English architect William Jay (1794–1837), but no documentary evidence has been found to support this. The principal drawing room on the second floor is indicative of the unusual spatial relationships in the floor plan and exhibits elaborate interior detailing that represents at least two periods of decoration. The column, window, and door pilasters are almost certainly Greek revival alterations carried out in the 1830s or 1840s. In 1909, Miss Mary Vardrine McBee established Ashley Hall School for Girls here, and the house remains the centerpiece of that educational complex.

THE BOARDROOM *(following page, left)* ⁓ A marble Rococo revival mantel, applied panel moldings, and richly embellished plaster cornice are alterations carried out by George Alfred Trenholm, shipping merchant, blockade runner, and secretary of the Confederate Treasury, after he acquired the house in 1845. The recent restoration of the room revealed the polychrome ceiling painting and stenciling, which has been meticulously restored and may represent further embellishments carried out by Charles O. Witte, German consul, who owned the house from 1870 to 1907.

THE STAIRCASE *(following page, right)* ⁓ A spectacular elliptical staircase, vaulted stair landing ceiling, and bowed walls with arches create a complex interplay of curves. The ornamental plaster medallion in high relief above the door was added during the Trenholm occupancy of 1845–1870. ⁓

PETIGRU LAW OFFICE DRAWING ROOM *(center)* ⌐ Born in Abbeville County, South Carolina, unallied with Charleston's established oligarchy, James Louis Petigru (1789–1863) was nonetheless a greatly respected citizen of antebellum Charleston. Despite his opposition to secession and nullification, he was admired by his followers and detractors alike. His simple tombstone includes the words, "In the great Civil War, He withstood his people for his country, But his People did homage to the man who held his conscience higher than their praise." For his law office, constructed in 1848–1849, Petigru turned to architect Edward Brickell White, the son of prominent Lowcountry artist John Blake White. Edward Brickell White was trained in engineering at West Point, and his architectural eclecticism produced buildings as diverse as Petigru's severely classical office and the flamboyantly Gothic French Huguenot church of 1844–1845. ⌐

T oday restored as a residence, the charming drawing room of the Petrigru Law Office is furnished with American decorative arts of the period 1820–1850. The portrait over the Empire sofa is thought to represent Petigru's wife and child.

JUDGE ROBERT PRINGLE HOUSE DRAWING ROOM *(right, top)* ⌐ A stone plaque inscribed "RP 1774" set into the wall of Judge Robert Pringle's house proclaims its construction date. Robert Pringle (1702–1776), a wealthy Scottish merchant and assistant judge of the Court of Common Pleas and General Sessions from 1761 to 1771, built one of Charleston's finest surviving single houses. The paneled drawing room is little altered, except for the projecting bay added late in the 19th century, and contains an excellent example of a carved Rococo chimneypiece with fully ornamented frieze. A mahogany desk and bookcase c. 1770 was made in Charleston and incorporates the figure-eight fret in its cornice frieze, a motif frequently encountered in Charleston case pieces of the 18th century. ⌐

GEORGE KINCAID TENEMENT DRAWING ROOM *(right, bottom)* ⌐ Built about 1777 by George Kincaid on reclaimed marshland, this tenement is one of two attached structures originally intended as rental property. The term tenement acquired a pejorative meaning only in the later 19th century. The second owner, merchant William Hopton, owned vast amounts of rental property throughout the city and left this building in his will to his daughter Sarah, who became Mrs. Nathaniel Russell in 1788. In the handsome second-floor drawing room is a magnificent American desk and bookcase c. 1760, probably made in Maryland. A French chair or elbow chair with blind fretwork carving was made in England at about the same time. ⌐

THE DRAWING ROOM *(left)* ∼ Constructed on lands originally acquired by Huguenot immigrant Isaac Mazyck in 1712, the two-story frame hip-roofed house built by Philip Porcher was described as "new" in a 1773 advertisement in the *South Carolina Gazette.* Porcher, a rich Huguenot planter, married Issac Mazyck's granddaughter Mary, who acquired this lot by family division in 1765. The handsome first-floor reception rooms retain their Georgian paneling of cypress, which were later embellished about 1835 with a wider classical door surround between the rooms and a doorway with a magnificent fanlight leading to the stair passage. The portrait in the withdrawing room was painted by Thomas Sully (1783–1872) in 1818 and depicts another Charleston planter, Ralph Izard (1741–1804). Izard's travels in Europe, diplomatic service, and patronage of artists make him among the most urbane of 18th-century Charlestonians. Sully copied the pose from Benjamin West's group portrait *The Cricketeers,* painted in at least two versions in 1763 and 1764 and depicting Izard while a student at Cambridge.

THE DINING ROOM *(below)* ∼ The inviting dining room is hung with a modern printing of the Zuber factory's wallpaper "L'Indoustan," first introduced in 1807. In his diary for 1826, Baltimorean Robert Gilmor recalled the Charleston dining room of his in-laws, James and Ann Ladson Gregorie, as having views of Switzerland. Gilmor's recollection refers to Zuber's first major landscape paper, "Les Vues de Suisse," developed between 1803 and 1805 and widely exported in Europe and America.

While French scenic wallpapers were known in early Charleston, no 19th-century installations survive.

Known in the 18th century as a compass head window, this example affords a view of the extensive garden.

THE STAIR LANDING *(left)* ∼ The compass head window lights a collection of early engravings collected by grand tourist and art patron Joseph Allen Smith (1769–1828), the son of leading Charleston merchant Benjamin Smith. Joseph Allen Smith went abroad in 1793, and for 14 years he traveled in Italy, Britain, Denmark, Holland, France, Russia, Turkey, and Greece.

Settling in Philadelphia upon his return, Smith married Charlotte Georgiana Izard, daughter of Ralph and Alice Delancey Izard, on May 1, 1809. Made an honorary member of the Pennsylvania Academy of Fine Arts in 1807, Smith presented the academy with gifts of paintings, printed works, and his collection of antique gems and medals.

THE BATHROOM *(right)* ∼ The creation of the present owners, the principal bath is stylishly conceived in the Regency revival taste of the early 20th century. Family heirlooms incorporated in the decoration include an intricately carved 19th-century chair from India. A bust of Eros after Praxiteles finds its niche in the arched recess above the tub. ∼

THE DRAWING ROOM *(left)* ∼
Few houses in the American
South provide a more complete
document of antebellum life than
the Aiken-Rhett house, a property
of the Charleston Museum.
Initially built by merchant John
Robinson after 1817, its acquisi-
tion by William Aiken Jr. in
1833 resulted in two phases of
remodeling in 1833–1836 and
1858, which created one of

*Aiken added a large Greek revival
window and remodeled the back northeast room as a grand entrance hall.*

Charleston's most palatial town mansions. A huge portrait of Harriet

Lowndes Aiken by George Whiting Flagg (1816–1897) surveys the

opulent surroundings. The French crystal and bronze doré chandelier,

one of a pair, was acquired by the Aikens in Europe in the 1830s.

THE ART GALLERY *(following page, left)* ∼ In 1858, William and Harriet

Aiken commenced the second remodeling of their house to include this art

gallery. The gallery is lit by four windows and a skylight and capped by an

elaborate plaster cornice in the Rococo revival style. Works of art owned by

the Aikens include E.S. Bartholomew's 1853 sculpture, *Shepherd Boy,* and

the painting of Paolo and Francesca by Luther Terry (1813–1869) of 1860.

THE DINING ROOM *(following page, right)* ∼ The original chandelier and

overmantel mirror still grace the dining room added by William Aiken Jr.

during the 1833–1836 alterations. Francis Kinloch Middleton described

a ball given in the house in February 1839: "Last night I was at the hand-

somest ball I have ever seen … the table was covered with a rich service of

silver—lights in profusion, & a handsomely dressed assembly." ∗

THE FIRST-FLOOR DRAWING ROOM *(above)* ⁓ A member of a distinguished Colonial New Jersey family, Timothy Ford was born in Morristown in 1762 and educated at Princeton. He came to South Carolina in 1785 after the marriage of his sister to Charlestonian Henry William DeSaussure and practiced law with his new brother-in-law. His substantial single house was built around 1800 for his second wife and witnessed considerable "Yankee" hospitality. In 1825, Ford was among those who entertained Lafayette during his memorable tour of Charleston.

THE SECOND-FLOOR DRAWING ROOM *(left)* ⁓ Despite the grandeur of its proportions, the second-floor drawing room makes an intimate gallery for an impressive collection of 20th-century art, some by Charleston artists. The original mantel in this room is an interesting combination of both applied composition ornament and carved gougework. Joseph King painted the portrait of the owner over the mantel, and the terra-cotta busts of the owners' children are by Lawrence Anthony.

THE DOORWAY *(left)* ⟶ The doorway between the two second-floor entertaining spaces illustrates the methods used to bring the 1772 Georgian interior in step with Neoclassical taste about 1800. To the original Georgian door surround with crossetted or "eared" moldings, an overdoor with composition ornament was added on top of the raised paneled woodwork. The central plaque represents the arts of painting, sculpture, architecture, and music.

THE DRAWING ROOM MANTEL *(center, top)* ⟶ William Gibbes' estate sold his town property to the widow Sarah Moore Smith in 1794, and Mrs. Smith or her son Peter introduced the lavish use of Neoclassical composition ornament found in the primary reception rooms. The great second-floor drawing room received in about 1800 an overlay of decoration to bring the bold earlier Georgian paneled interior in step with the vogue for classical taste and allusion. The central tablet of the room's chimney-piece is adorned with a depiction of Cupid and his mother Venus, a felicitous subject for a room that no doubt witnessed considerable merriment and jollity. Reflected in the overmantel mirror is the gilded metal and glass prism chandelier created for the drawing room during the 1928–1930 restoration.

THE STAIR LANDING *(center, bottom)* ⟶ When William Gibbes, one of Charleston's richest Colonial merchant-planters, completed his town mansion, it was intended to be viewed from the Ashley River as vessels approached his 300-foot wharf, which was complete with stores, ware-houses, a scale house for the weighing of rice, and a coffee house. The Venetian window (the term Palladian window was not used in 18th-century Charleston) on the land side of the house overlooked parterred gardens and an extensive work yard where the 22 slaves at Gibbes' town property lived and worked. A surviving original kitchen and wash house and an extensive stable block reflect the role of Charleston's elite town-houses as "urban plantations." The grounds were landscaped by Loutrel Briggs in the late 1920s, and today the garden is among the best preserved Colonial revival landscapes in Charleston. ⟶ The delicate wrought-iron stair balustrade is among the alterations made to the house by the Smith family c. 1800. Zuber's wallpaper "Eldorado," first introduced in 1848, was installed after 1928 when the house was purchased and restored by Cornelia Roebling of New York, a native of South Carolina. The present owners have done much to respect and preserve the features of each period of evolution and redecoration: Georgian, Neoclassical, and Colonial revival.

THE DINING ROOM *(above)* A charming portrait above the fireplace depicts the Marquis de Lafayette's niece and ward Elenore Marie Florimonde de Fay la Tour Maubourg, wife of Charles Lucas Pinckney Horry. The couple made their residence in France, where she was painted by the great female exponent of Neoclassicism, Madame Césarine Henriette Flore Davin-Mirvault (1773–1844).

THE SITTING ROOM *(left)* The stylish interior betrays its humbler origins as a dependency to a grand Rainbow Row townhouse. Built before 1788 when it appeared on Edmund Petrie's "Ichnography of Charleston," a fire insurance plat, the house was initially restored in the 1920s by Miss Susan Pringle Frost, an early champion for preservation in the city. Glimpsed through a garden-front window, the sitting room boasts many family heirlooms, including a portrait by Thomas Sully (1783–1872) of Harriott Pinckney Rutledge Holbrook painted in 1860 at a cost of $100. The green upholstered mahogany armchair in the foreground was made by Philadelphia Quaker cabinetmaker Thomas Affleck (1740–1795) between 1790 and 1793 for Congress Hall when it became the nation's capitol and descended in the Rutledge family.

OVERMANTEL DETAIL *(below)* ∽ The impact of British architectural design books on the Carolina Lowcountry is evident in the chimney-piece of the great hall. The overmantel design incorporates elements taken directly from plate 64 of William Kent's 1727 publication *Designs of Inigo Jones*. This design features a broken pediment with a fox head inset in a shell flanked by draped swags of fruit and flowers. Above, the cornice frieze is composed of triglyph and metope banding with

THE STAIRCASE *(below)* ∽ Built between 1738 and 1742, Drayton Hall has survived the centuries as an almost unblemished Lowcountry plantation house. Despite much research, the names of the master craftsmen responsible remain elusive. John Drayton, the builder, was a second generation Carolinian; his father, Thomas, immigrated to Carolina from Barbados in 1679. Thus began a chain of ownership in the family that lasted until 1974 when the property was acquired by the National Trust

alternating sunflower and dogwood medallions in the metope, executed in yellow poplar. ∽

for Historic Preservation, which still maintains and interprets the property. The elaborately carved brackets and turned balusters of the riverfront bifurcated staircase are original to the construction date. ∽

DRAWING ROOM CEILING DETAIL *(below)* ⁓ Of all the surviving original architectural elements at Drayton Hall, certainly one of the most miraculous is the plaster ceiling of the drawing room. A bit retarditaire stylistically when compared to the more up-to-date Palladian elements of the house, the ceiling documents the transmission of British craft traditions to the Carolina Lowcountry. The technique required carving the design into wet plaster. Native plants and flowers appear in the center

OVERMANTEL WITH COAT OF ARMS DETAIL *(below)* ⁓ Drayton Hall's second-floor reception room has as its focal point a marble chimneypiece with a carved overmantel that incorporates both Greek key and egg-and-dart moldings. The painting of the Drayton family's coat of arms is a 20th-century addition. Like most of the rooms in Drayton Hall, the woodwork was last painted during the fourth quarter of the 19th century when Charles Drayton (1847–1915) repaired the house with income

diamond moulding inset with two ears of corn, in each corner of the perimeter rectangle, and in the ceiling border featuring scrolls of flowers originating from vases in each of the four corners.

produced from the mining of phosphate on the property.

CHIMNEY DETAIL *(above)* ∽ Recently cleaned of centuries of paint, the lower volutes of the overmantel and the console brackets in the drawing room attest to the virtuosity of Charleston's pre-Revolutionary carvers, who produced some of Colonial America's most sophisticated architectural decoration.

THE DRAWING ROOM *(left)* ∽ In 1770, the year following his marriage to Elizabeth McLaughlin, Peter Bocquet received a city lot from his father, a Huguenot baker of considerable fortune, and began construction of a handsome townhouse. The spacious drawing room on the second floor contains one of Charleston's most spectacular Rococo carved chimney-pieces incorporating Neoclassical motifs such as round bosses, swags of husks, and an urn reflecting the taste for the "antique" style. The niches on either side of the chimney breast were created in the 19th century. A handsome collection of inherited and collected furniture mixed with reproductions produces a stylish urban setting for entertaining. ∽

THE BEDROOM *(right, top)* ∽ A handsome 19th-century American bed with heavily carved foot posts, originally from a New Orleans estate, is hung with a reproduction silk stripe. The fireplace, like most in the John Blake house, is faced with King of Prussia marble imported into Charleston from Pennsylvania.

THE LIBRARY *(right, bottom)* ∽ John Blake, president of the Bank of South Carolina, completed a handsome L-shaped frame house about 1800. The inventory of his property taken at the time of his death in 1810 indicates that this second-floor room was originally a formal drawing room expensively furnished with curtains, a carpet, piano, card table, and chairs. The early Charleston custom of having one or more second-floor reception rooms remains a part of Charleston living today. Now used as a library, the Federal woodwork has been faux painted in imitation of early 19th-century techniques. English ceramics on the mantel include a pair of Staffordshire dogs and 19th-century Spode plates in the Imari pattern.

THE KITCHEN *(far right)* ∽ Originally the dining room of the John Blake house, the kitchen preserves and incorporates the original woodwork of the room. The recently commissioned paintings in the over-mantel panels are by Charleston artist Karl Beckwith Smith. The view of Charleston is adapted from the C. Canot engraving of the city after the 1768 painting by T. Mellish.

WILLIAM PINCKNEY SHINGLER HOUSE

THE DINING ROOM *(right)* ⁓ The early 19th-century mantel in the dining room replaces the original marble mantel believed to have been shattered during the great earthquake of 1886. An intricate plaster cornice is enriched by light and shadow from the 19th-century chandelier salvaged from a demolished house that stood at the corner of Legare and Gibbes streets. A portrait of Hugh Hamilton Wilson is flanked by Chinese export porcelain chargers decorated with underglaze blue pineapples c. 1820. Japanese Imari porcelain of the 19th century is represented by the punch bowl and an heirloom charger on the Neoclassical sideboard made in New York c. 1800.

THE DRAWING ROOMS *(following page)* ⁓ Lighted chandeliers cast a warm light over the spectacular double drawing rooms. Shingler, a successful Charleston businessman and cotton factor, signed the Ordinance of Secession of December 20, 1860, and served as a colonel in the Confederate cavalry. One of the last great townhouses built in Charleston before the Civil War, the 1856 Shingler house has exuberant late Greek revival woodwork and elaborate plaster decoration. Over an original marble mantel hangs a portrait of Mrs. John Porter painted by Samuel F.B. Morse (1791–1872). The portrait over the desk is by Thomas Sully (1783–1872) and depicts Adèle Petigru Allston, wife of Governor R.F.W. Allston who owned Chicora Wood Plantation near Georgetown and the Nathaniel Russell house on Meeting Street. An English tall case clock imported into Charleston by local clock and watchmaker Joshua Lockwood before the American Revolution can be seen through the doorway to the dining room.

THE WITHDRAWING ROOM *(left)* ~ One of the most commanding case pieces ever produced in Colonial America is found in the Heyward-Washington house. Richly inlaid with marquetry floral decoration in the pediment and ivory fleurs-de-lis, the library bookcase was made about 1770 for Charleston merchant John Edwards, whose house survives on Meeting Street. It was listed in his

A *1792 description of the house listed a "carriage house and stables all of brick surrounded by brick walls."*

1781 inventory as "A Large Mahogany Book Case" valued at 100 pounds. This extraordinary object alludes to both British and German cabinet-making traditions, and it is tempting to link its manufacture to Charleston furniture maker Martin Pfeninger who advertised in the April 13, 1773, edition of the *South Carolina Gazette*, "Cabinet-making, in all its branches, Also, Inlaid-work in any Taste, by Martin Pfeninger."

The "Englishness" of mid-18th century Charleston furniture is exemplified by the dressing table of c. 1740 between the windows. Its tight cabriole legs and Baroque shaping of the skirt are typical of one identified school of Charleston tables. The Pembroke table c. 1790 also owes its inspiration to British models.

Joshua Lockwood retailed the English tall case clock in Charleston, having attached his name to the face.

THE BEDROOM *(left)* ~ Originally owned by the Heyward family, the Charleston inlaid bedstead c. 1790 contains both foliate and feather carving on its foot posts. The portrait above the fireplace depicts the second Mrs. Daniel Heyward (Jane Elizabeth Gignilliat) and is a copy by George Whiting Flagg (1816–1897) after the original portrait by Jeremiah Theus, which is now in the collection of The Albrecht Art Museum in St. Joseph, Missouri.

THE DRAWING ROOM *(right)* ~ Built in 1772 by rice planter Daniel Heyward and occupied by his son Thomas, the house was acquired by The Charleston Museum in 1929 and contains a superlative collection of Charleston furniture. The Charleston patron's fascination with fretwork is exemplified by the extensive use of sawn fret on the overmantel and mantel frieze. The pattern, incorporating a figure-eight and diamond motif, is found in both interior woodwork and furniture produced in Charleston during the third quarter of the 18th century, leading several early furniture historians to dub the design the "Elfe fret" for Charleston cabinetmaker Thomas Elfe (c. 1719–1775). Elfe's account book survives in the collection of The Charleston Library Society and is a pivotal document for the study of urban cabinetmaking practices in pre-Revolutionary Charleston. Ironically, to date, no piece of furniture may firmly be attributed to Elfe's shop. The table with chinoiserie latticework framed by carved scrollwork on the end rails retains its original leather castors. ~

THE DRAWING ROOM *(left)* Samuel Magwood built a handsome frame Charleston single house between 1825 and 1827 for his daughter Susan, who married a member of the Moreland family. Its survival during the earthquake of 1886 is attributed to the use of crisscrossed foundations of palmetto logs sunk in the mud, which enabled the house to sway with the tremors. The first-floor

The centerpiece is an epergne of old Sheffield plate c. 1840 that retains its original cut-glass bowls.

drawing room incorporates woodwork in the Regency taste, which bridged the delicacy of the Federal style and the bold austerity of the Greek revival period. An early 19th-century English convex mirror reflects period antiques, including a pair of French Empire fauteuils c. 1810, an English lyre-base card table c. 1800, and an English Regency rosewood library table c. 1815 behind the Hepplewhite sofa c. 1780.

THE DINING ROOM *(above)* A magnificent 19th-century Italian chandelier illuminates the dining room. An American inlaid sideboard c. 1790 and early 19th-century gilded looking glass complement the Neoclassical spirit of this inviting room.

THE FRONT DOOR FANLIGHT *(following page)* The arched transom of the Magwood house piazza door frames a view of the ubiquitous Charleston piazza.

LEGARE STREET DRAWING ROOM *(left, top)* ⁓ On property once owned by Robert William Roper before he built his massive East Battery mansion is found this drawing room with an assemblage of collected English furniture and family heirlooms. The portrait of Thomas Middleton of The Oaks (1753–1797) is a copy painted by his son Thomas Middleton (1797–1882) after Benjamin West's 1773 likeness now at the Gibbes Museum of Art. In the foreground is a pair of Rococo covered cups by English silversmith Richard Pargeter made in 1771. Known as the van Assendelft cups, they came to Charleston in 1799 when two sisters, Judith and Sarah Amelia van Assendelft, married John Lewis and George Annely, British-born partners in the Charleston mercantile firm of Annely and Lewis. ⛤

WILLIAM WASHINGTON HOUSE DRAWING ROOM *(left, bottom)* ⁓ Two famous suites of English Neoclassical seating furniture

Furnished with family pieces, noteworthy objects in the Jonathan Badger living room include a Federal caned settee of mahogany made about 1810 for the Pinckney family and attributed to the New York cabinetmaker Duncan Phyfe (1768–1854).

with Charleston histories grace the drawing room. Both sets descended in the Pinckney family and document Charleston's taste for fashionable imported British furniture well into the 19th century. The lacquered suite combines chinoiserie japanning with painted scenes of English cathedrals and ruined abbeys. Mistakenly identified as French for much of this century, the pieces were made and painted in England c. 1815. The rosewood Grecian "couches," as they were called in the period, are part of another extensive suite of drawing room furniture purchased by General

Charles Cotesworth Pinckney and stamped by Gillow and Company. In 1817, Isaac Coffin in England wrote to his former pupils, the Misses Pinckney in Charleston, that he regretted "more than ever your having rejected the Furniture imported by the General, for it is all the fashion in the Houses of the first Nobility & Gentry in England. True it is that it was made by Mr. Gillow at Lancaster, where many pieces of his Furniture are finish'd & sent to Town as the workmen are not so debauched as in the Capital, he is the first Upholsterer in the Kingdom." ⛤

JONATHAN BADGER TENEMENT LIVING ROOM *(center)* ⁓ Traditionally assigned the date 1746 when cabinetmaker Jonathan Badger purchased the lot, the interior finish of this pre-Revolutionary dwelling suggests a date in the 1760s or 1770s. The original street-front doorway indicated that the front room had a commercial use in the 18th century. The Charleston side chair features a splat design adapted from plate 10 of Thomas Chippendale's 1762 edition of *The Gentleman and Cabinet-Maker's Director.* It was originally owned by Ann Branford and her husband Thomas Horry. Also owned by Ann Branford and engraved with her name is the magnificent English hot water urn in the Rococo taste made in London in 1771 by Francis Butty and Nicholas Dumee. While several talented silversmiths worked in Charleston during the Colonial period, much of the finest silver was imported from England. ⛤

THE DRAWING ROOM *(left)* ∾ Merchant Benjamin Phillips built his Church Street residence in 1818, creating a variation on the Charleston single house known as the side-hall plan. Rather than being entered on the long facade, the house is entered directly from the street, and a long passage leads to living quarters behind and above the street-front office space. The light-filled drawing room is noteworthy for its gougework decoration in the rosettes of the window and door surrounds. Eighteenth-century English and American furniture and hand-painted wallpaper enhance the original architecture of this carefully conceived interior.

THE DINING ROOM *(following page, left)* ∾ The dining room features a hand-painted wallpaper in imitation of early 19th-century American wall paintings. Produced in modern Hong Kong, the paper is inspired by the stair hall of the 1820 Ezra Carroll house in East Springfield, New York, painted by William Price in 1831 and now installed at Delaware's Winterthur Museum.

THE GARDEN *(following page, right)* ∾ A recently created garden incorporating an extraordinary collection of old roses provides outdoor "rooms" at the Phillips house. The original dependency that housed the early kitchen and laundry is on the left. The rear piazza leads to the dining room on the garden facade of the house.

THE DINING ROOM *(left)* ∼ On the banks of the Ashley River is Middleton Place Plantation, the site of America's oldest landscaped garden, laid out about 1741. Home to one of the most distinguished families in South Carolina, owners have included Henry Middleton, president of the First Continental Congress; his son Arthur, a signer of the Declaration of Independence; and

Today, Middleton Place is the centerpiece for one of the Lowcountry's most evocative plantation properties.

his son Henry, a governor of South Carolina and America's first minister to Russia. The venerable plantation house and its flankers were burned beyond repair in 1865, victims of the Civil War. Williams Middleton rebuilt the south flanker, formerly a gentlemen's guest wing, and today it is the repository for surviving family furniture, paintings, silver, and books. The mahogany breakfront bookcase, which belonged to Henry Augustus Middleton (1793–1878), is attributed to Salem, Massachusetts, cabinetmaker Edmund Johnson. The magnificent epergne by Francis Butty and Nicholas Dumee and columnar candlesticks by John Carter were probably acquired in London by Arthur Middleton and his wife Mary Izard Middleton during the family's extended European tour of 1768–1771.

THE SUMMER BEDROOM *(following page)* ∼ Dressed for the summer months with a gauze "pavilion" that protected its occupants from flies and mosquitoes, this Charleston "rice" bed was crafted c. 1790. The hand-painted Chinese silk gown c. 1765–1775 was owned by Harriott Pinckney Horry, mistress of Hampton Plantation. French pastelist Constant-Joseph Brochart (1816–1899) painted the portrait of Elizabeth Mary Pringle Smith. ∼

THE DRAWING ROOM *(above)* Colonel William Rhett, perhaps best remembered for his capture of the pirate Stede Bonnet, built a substantial plantation house in 1712 on a 30-acre tract known as "The Point of Rhettsbury." The Rhettsbury lands were divided by Colonel Rhett's great-granddaughters in 1767. Redecorated during the third quarter of the 18th century and enlarged and extended about 1800, the house sits on a high foundation typical of early plantation structures. The elegant drawing room is furnished with a handsome assemblage of Continental, American, and English antiques. A suite of maple Neoclassical caned seating furniture was originally owned by South Carolina Governor Thomas Bennett and probably made in Philadelphia during the second decade of the 19th century.

DINING ROOM MANTEL DETAIL *(right)* The Rococo plasterwork decoration was added during the third quarter of the 18th century. One of the British-trained craftsmen who immigrated to Charleston during the Colonial period may have been responsible for this work. In 1774, Charles Robertson advertised, "Plaistering and carving in stucco in all its branches, either in the modern or Gothic taste, such as ornamental ceilings, Plain or Inriched cornices etc. executed by the subscriber who is just arrived here."

THE CHIMNEYPIECE *(above)* ∼ Scottish-born carpenter and contractor John Fullerton purchased a large tract of land from merchant William Gibbes in 1772 and began construction of this 3½-story frame single house shortly thereafter. The second-floor east parlor chimneypiece exhibits extensive use of sawn fretwork. In January 1773, Charleston cabinetmaker Thomas Elfe supplied Fullerton with "100 feet" and "2 ps frett," which may refer to the fret utilized here, although there is no conclusive documentation. An identical fret is found on the overmantel of the Heyward-Washington house. In the overmantel panel is a Dutch picture by Jan Vermeer of Haarlem (1628–1691). The Chinese plates are Qing Dynasty (1723–1735).

THE BEDROOM *(right)* ∼ In contrast to the fully paneled parlor directly below, this third-floor chamber is simply treated with a chair rail and plain chimney surround. The desk and bookcase is a fine English piece c. 1790.

THE LIBRARY *(left)* ⁓ A surviving contract between Miss Amarinthea Elliott, "plantress," and John Morrison and Hume Greenhill, Charleston house builders, dated August 13, 1789, documents the use of the term "single house" in 18th-century Charleston. Morrison and Greenhill agreed to build "a compleat well-finished dwelling house commonly called a single

Joseph Holt Ingraham noted that on piazzas South Carolinians "wash, lounge, sleep, and take their meals."

house, three stories high ... twenty-two feet wide or thereabouts and forty-six feet long or thereabouts, with two rooms on a floor and an entry leading to a stair case in or near the centre of the said house nine foot wide in the clear ... with two stacks of chimneys so as to allow one fire Place in each room." Furnished as an inviting and comfortable library, the second-floor, street-front room features a simple paneled chimney breast representing the transitional woodwork found in post-Revolutionary Charleston houses before the advent and widespread use of applied composition decoration.

ANDREW ALLEN TENEMENT LIVING ROOM *(below)* ∽ Situated on Tradd Street, one of America's earliest thoroughfares, is the Andrew Allen tenement, a building that originally combined the commercial and residential functions of many of the city's earliest structures. The site of the house was part of the lot on the Grand Modell, Charleston's earliest town plan, granted to Robert Tradd for whom Tradd Street is named. Probably damaged in the great fires of 1740 and 1778, little evidence of

GEORGE SOMMERS HOUSE DINING ROOM *(below)* ∽ Situated on lot number one of Charleston's Grand Modell plan, a tenement house was listed on this parcel when Adam Daniel sold the property to George Sommers in 1755. A handsome masonry single house restored in the 1930s, it retains much early woodwork, including a pair of architectural cupboards or "bowfats" in the dining parlor. The dining table and sideboard descended in the Chisolm family of Cherry Hill Plantation. On

the original interior survives. During 20th-century renovations, an early surviving corner mantelpiece was preserved in the second-floor living room. Now adapted for contemporary living, the room is furnished with both American and Continental antiques, including an unusual 19th-century painted leather commode.

the sideboard is an English Derby soft paste porcelain supper set with a Pinckney family history. The New York silver pitcher in the Neoclassical taste was presented by the South Carolina Agricultural Society to Thomas Pinckney for the best crop of flint corn in 1826.

JAMES LEGARE HOUSE DOUBLE DRAWING ROOMS *(below)* ⁓ A pair of magnificent double octagonal drawing rooms distinguishes the handsome frame Greek revival mansion built soon after 1832 by James Legare. In 1856, the house was acquired by Robert Barnwell Rhett, known as the "Father of Secession" due to his views on the rights of states and advocacy for an independent Southern Confederacy. From 1863 to 1866, the property was owned by wealthy shipping merchant and blockade runner

EDWIN L. KERRISON HOUSE DINING ROOM *(below)* ⁓ The splendid classical mansion built about 1838 by dry-goods baron Edwin L. Kerrison has been attributed to Rhode Island architect Russell Warren. When offered for rent in 1842, the property boasted "a kitchen with large accommodation for servants, a study, store house, bathing house, carriage house and stable, all newly built brick buildings, a very large cistern, and a well of water, the waters of which are conducted by means of pipes into

George Alfred Trenholm. By tradition, a wrought-iron gate to the property has remained shut since the fiancé of a young lady of the house was killed during the Civil War. She had promised that the gate would not open until he returned from war. Above the marble mantel in the east drawing room is a gilded Empire period convex mirror c. 1825. In recent years, the walls have been marbleized in imitation of ashlar blocks, a popular decorative technique of the 19th century.

various buildings where use and comfort may require them." In the boldly proportioned dining room is a sideboard c. 1790 and a late 18th-century inlaid mahogany chest, both of Charleston manufacture. The ancestral portrait was painted by Samuel Lovett Waldo.

THE ENTRANCE HALL *(left)* ✕ Visitors to Charleston are often surprised to learn that great wealth was occasionally present in the postbellum city. George W. Williams' life parallels the novels of Horatio Alger. Having joined an Augusta, Georgia, wholesale grocery establishment as a young man, Williams moved to Charleston in 1852 where his company began importing sugar and molasses from the West Indies and bagging from India. During the Civil War, the state legislature appointed Williams' commissary to procure provisions for the soldiers' families. Following the war, Williams retained substantial capital and built a baronial mansion designed by architect W.P. Russell. Constructed at a cost of $200,000, it was described by *The News and Courier* in 1876 as "probably the handsomest and most complete private residence in the South and one of the handsomest in the country." Through massive doors, guests enter the foyer paved with English Minton encaustic tiles and paneled in walnut with satinwood inlay. The property was acquired by Williams' daughter following his death. Her marriage to Patrick Calhoun, a grandson of John C. Calhoun, provides the simple name by which the grand house is known today, the Calhoun Mansion. It is open to the public by the

Over the mantel is an 1895 portrait of John Hargreaves Scott, mayor of Burnley, Lancashire, England, by Sydney Hodges. To the right of the 19th-century Sevres porcelain vase is an Italian desk made by Luigi Frullini of Florence in 1874.

present owner who continues the Herculean task of restoration and redecoration on a grand scale.

THE LIBRARY *(center)* ✕ The opulence of the 1870s is apparent in the library of the 35-room Calhoun Mansion. Gasoliers, now electrified, are original fixtures, and the leather-bound volumes of senate records belonged to John C. Calhoun. The mantel is faced with Minton tiles depicting the plays of Shakespeare.

THE BILLIARD ROOM *(following page, left)* ✕ The billiard room opens onto the spacious second-floor hall. A billiard table by the Brunswick-Balke-Callender Co. dates from the 1890s. During restoration work, the ceiling stenciling was revealed and renewed in the original colors. The chandeliers, originally piped for gas, are of nickel and brass. A stuffed alligator makes a whimsical doorstop.

THE BEDROOM *(following page, right)* ✕ The location of appropriately scaled furnishings is a daunting task when the entrance hall alone is 14 feet wide, 14 feet high, and 50 feet long. This guest room easily accommodates an early 17th-century English Jacobean bed with heavily carved posts and cornices and an inlaid and carved tester ceiling.

THE STAIRHALL *(left)* ◠ One of the city's most elaborately embellished Federal mansions, the Gaillard-Bennett house was completed in 1802 for Theodore Gaillard, a wealthy rice planter and factor who had previously lived in the more densely populated area of the Bay near his wharves. Sold in 1812 to General Jacob Read, a Revolutionary hero, and in 1819 to James Schoolbred,

The variety and quality of the Neoclassical plaster and applied composition decoration is unsurpassed in Charleston.

Charleston's first English Consul General, the house was purchased in 1851 by Washington Jefferson Bennett, son of South Carolina Governor Thomas Bennett. General Robert E. Lee was the guest of the Bennetts in April 1870. On the evening of April 27, a grand reception was given in honor of Lee's visit to the city. From the second-story balcony, the General addressed the crowd of well-wishers stating, "It is so grateful to see so much elasticity among your people; and I am astonished to see Charleston so wondrously recuperated after all her disasters." ◠ In the spacious central hall, a group portrait of children by Isaac Falconer Bird, an Exeter, England, artist, hangs over a George III painted and gilded side table c. 1775, originally made for the English country house Lytton Park. The extraordinary Masonic ceremonial chair under the stair is one of a pair made in England about 1800 as a commission for Charleston's Union Kilwinning Masonic Lodge #4. Its mate is now in the collection of Colonial Williamsburg.

MANTEL DETAIL *(right, top)* ∿ The richness and detail of the drawing room mantel's composition decoration was revealed in recent years when the decoration throughout the house was cleaned of successive layers of paint. Produced in molds from a mixture of resin, glue, whiting, and linseed oil, composition ornament was imported into Charleston from Philadelphia, New York, and Boston, as well as from England. This frieze, which depicts sea shells and the chase, is most likely of British manufacture. In 1796, Charleston architect Gabriel Manigault ordered from the firm of Bird, Savage and Bird in London "the following composition ornaments, vizt. 100 feet of composition for the Frieze of a room, of a simple pattern & such as will be easily put up, the Frieze is 7 1/2 inches wide.... You sent me some last spring wch was bought of John Jaques, & cost 2 1/2 per foot; 25 to of the best glue for fixing the composition. It frequently drops off here owing to bad glue."

THE DRAWING ROOM *(right, bottom)* ∿ The exuberance of the drawing room's Neoclassical decoration is a fitting background for a collection of important English furniture. Gilded armchairs in the French taste are from the workshop of Thomas Chippendale (1718–1779) and were made for Sir Robert Burdett of Foremark Hall, Derbyshire. A surviving account indicates that on February 17, 1766, Burdett paid Chippendale for "Chairs for the Country." The mahogany George II reading stand has been attributed to royal cabinetmaker William Vile (1700–1767), and the late 18th-century looking glass sconce, one of a pair, is distinctly Irish. A George I walnut upholstered armchair c. 1720 features an unusual carved and parcel gilt roundel. Above the fireplace, the painting *Joseph and Potifar's Wife* is by the Dutch artist Joachim Uytwael (1566–1638). Nodding Mandarin boy figures are products of the Meissen factory c. 1750. The superb engraved brass andirons c. 1785 were made in England for the Charleston market.

THE DINING ROOM *(above)* ⌇ From the central French window in the dining room can be seen the cast-iron railing of a decorative porch with pagoda roof added in 1852. Above the mantel with composition decoration depicting the birth of Zeus is the 1748 *View of Cassiobury Park and the Family of the Earl of Essex* by British painter John Wootton (1682–1764). A late 18th-century pedestal base dining table is surrounded by George III English mahogany oval-back chairs c. 1775. The 18th-century glass chandelier is Irish, and the pair of finely carved and gilded oval looking glasses were made in Boston, Massachusetts, c. 1790.

THE KITCHEN *(left)* ⌇ A functional and inviting kitchen has been created in the northwest room while carefully preserving its original woodwork. The blue and white tile panel above the mantel is late 17th-century Portuguese. Beneath a c. 1690 Dutch chandelier is a Charles II oak gateleg table c. 1670 and Regency yew wood chairs. The drawings and etchings of Charleston and Lowcountry scenes are by Alfred Hutty (1877–1954).

THE LIBRARY *(right)* ∼ The spacious library occupies the northeast corner of the principal floor, its hierarchy indicated by a wooden cornice rather than the more elaborate composition cornice of the front rooms. A superb pair of Louis XV fauteuils by Louis Cresson c. 1750 flank the mantel, above which is one of John Wootton's (1682–1764) most famous pictures depicting the second Earl of Oxford's monkey dancing with the fourth Duke of Leeds' poodle. The picture satirized the conflict between courtly affectation and nobler country virtues and may relate to the imagery depicted in Alexander Pope's poem *Bounce to Fop.* On a George II architect's table rests a rare 1835 edition of Captain Thomas Brown's *Birds of America* after Charles Lucien Bonaparte and Alexander Wilson printed in Edinburgh. The framed watercolors depicting birds of the southeast are by artist and naturalist John Abbot (1751–c. 1840) who arrived in Georgia from England in 1776 and spent nearly 65 years recording southern birds, insects, and butterflies. Between the windows, curtained with 17th-century crewel embroidery, is an important George I gilded wall bracket and an early 19th-century Masons ironstone potpourri urn decorated in Imari colors.

The satinwood writing desk and painted neo-Sheraton shield-back chair are both mid-19th century English.

THE BEDROOM *(left)* ∼ Gothic arches, Neoclassical urns, and plant forms in composition ornament embellish the principal bedroom's mantel. *La Fete, Place Pigalle* of 1896 by French academician Abel Truchet (1867–1918) hangs above four small pictures by Charles Jacques in their original frames. The posts of the English Neoclassical bed are formed from ivory tusks of the narwhal. ∼

THE STAIRCASE *(left)* ⸲ Glazed doors with decorative tracery divide the entrance vestibule from the inner sanctum of Nathaniel Russell's house, completed in 1808. The elliptical free-flying staircase ascends to the primary reception rooms on the second floor. Under the stair is George Romney's portrait of William Henry Lyttelton (1724–1820), royal governor of the colony of

The Nathaniel Russell house's garden facade features a projecting bay encasing an oval room on each of three floors.

South Carolina from 1755 to 1762. ⸲ Born in Bristol, Rhode Island, Nathaniel Russell (1738–1820) arrived in Charleston at age 27 and amassed a huge fortune through commerce. Russell was a leader of the merchant faction in the Federalist party that dominated post-Revolutionary Charleston. A philanthropist in later life, Russell served on the boards of the Charleston Orphan House and Charleston Dispensary, and in 1819 he founded and served as first president of the New England Society.

THE DRAWING ROOM *(following page, left)* ⸲ The richly finished drawing room occupies the entire street front of the second floor. South Carolina Governor Robert F.W. Allston (1801–1864) purchased the house in 1857 and used the English painted and gilded armchairs c. 1800 as dining chairs. On the English Pembroke table c. 1790 with a history of ownership in the city is a London silver hot-water urn by John Robbins of 1790/91 with the engraved crest of the Kinloch family. Through the doorway is the magnificent portrait of Charlestonian Mary Rutledge Smith (1747–1837) painted in London by George Romney (1734–1802) during 15 sittings in 1786.

THE BEDROOM *(right)* ∼ An imposing Charleston-made Neo-classical bedstead with its original inlaid cornice c. 1800 dominates the second-floor chamber. The hangings reproduce an English glazed chinoiserie chintz first made in 1808. The recent restoration of the room replicates the original color scheme of pale wheat yellow walls and white woodwork. Above the Charleston

A *Brussels carpet laid wall-to-wall copies an original point paper design of the early 19th-century.*

Neoclassical chair c. 1800 with a history of ownership in the Vanderhorst family hangs a silk embroidered needlework picture representing Shakespeare's Timon of Athens. Copied from a print of a painting by Nathaniel Dance now at Hampton Court Palace, the backing panel is inscribed, "Dorothy Johnston of Charlestown, South Carolina, Fecit Anno 1775." Charleston merchant James Gregorie (1740–1807) who married Mrs. Nathaniel Russell's sister, Mary Christiana Hopton, is known to have imported British brass andirons and serpentine fenders of the type displayed here for retail sale in post-Revolutionary Charleston.

THE MUSIC ROOM *(following page)* ∼ Reflected in the mirrored panels is a charming portrait of the Russell's elder daughter, Alicia Russell Middleton (1789–1840). Mirrored panels with surrounds in imitation of window openings are known in America's most ambitious Federal mansions, including those of William Bingham in Philadelphia (1790) and Elias Hasket Derby in Salem, Massachusetts (1796), both now demolished. The grain painted and gilded chair is English c. 1815. ∼